Sustainable Cities

Concepts and Strategies
for Eco-City Development

Sustainable Cities

Concepts and Strategies
for Eco-City Development

Edited by

Bob Walter • Lois Arkin • Richard Crenshaw

EHM
Eco-Home Media

4344 Russell Avenue
Los Angeles, CA 90027
(213) 662-5207

First Printing 1992

Published in the United States by:

Eco-Home Media
4344 Russell Avenue
Los Angeles, CA 90027

Discounts for bulk orders are available from the publisher.
Call: (213) 662-5207

Publisher's Cataloging in Publication Data

Walter, Bob; Arkin, Lois; Crenshaw, Richard

Sustainable Cities: Concepts and Strategies for Eco-City Development

1, City planning — environmental aspects.
2, Urban ecology.
3, Environmental Engineering.

NA 9108.S87 1992   307.12   92-090568

ISBN 0-9633511-0-9

Dedication

To Julia Scofield Russell
who conceived of the First Los Angeles Ecological Cities Conference
and the Los Angeles Eco-Cities Council
to start bringing environmentally and economically compatible
community building into the mainstream.

To everyone living in the city
who dreams that cities can bloom not just survive.
To everyone who wants to know how real this dream can be.

PRODUCTION STAFF

DESIGN
Bob Walter
David Spellman
Sharon Dvora

LAYOUT
David Spellman
Daniel Donnelly
Bob Walter
Sharon Dvora
Carolyn Plumley
Rick Ripley

COVER ART
David Spellman

ART DIRECTION
Bob Walter
William Warren

RESOURCE GUIDE
Lois Arkin
Esfandiar Abbassi
James Bailey
Shiva Bailey

EDITORIAL ASSISTANCE
Julia Russell
Dianne Herring
Jeannie Trizzino
Leonard Lickerman
Marga Walter
Joel Lorimer
Matthew Miller
Mary Proteau
Brad Mowers

AUTHOR/CONFERENCE PHOTOGRAPHY
William James Warren

TRANSCRIBERS
James Bailey
Darlene Boord
Bob Brytan
Gretchen Holmblad
James McCormick
Karen Merickel
Ian McIlvaine
Daena Saunders
Trish Strouse

PRINTER
Optima Graphics

PRODUCTION FUNDING BY
Walter and Lorenz Foundation
and
David Zucker
E^2 Environmental Consultants
Maguire Thomas Partners
Southern California Edison
Garden of Eatin' Foundation

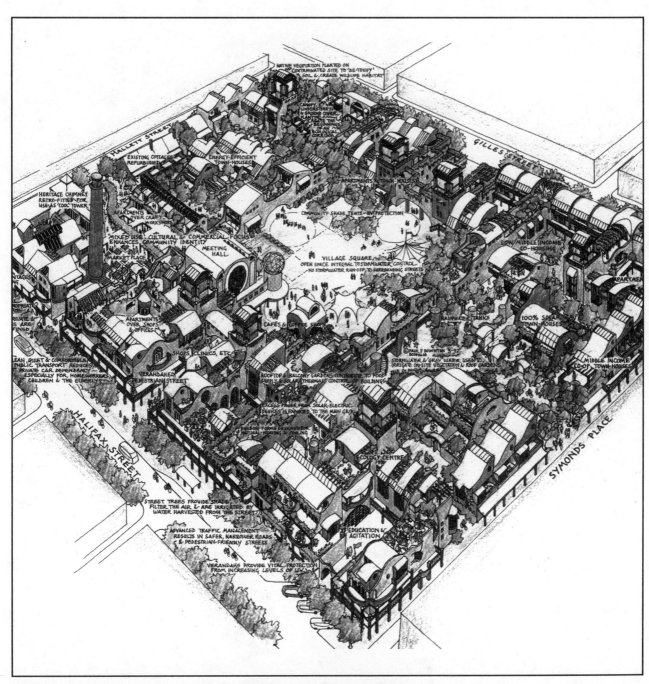

Eco village proposal for a central city neighborhood in Adelaide, South Australia.
Architect and urban ecologist Paul Downton's "ecopolitan" design is based on
principles of ecological sustainability, bioregional integrity and social equity.

CONTENTS

THE HUMAN COMPONENT — CITIZEN PLANNER INTERFACE

CONTEXT

It's widely agreed that this is the decade in which our ecological fate will be determined, and that cities must be a central focus of strategies for a sustainable future. Over 74% of the U.S. population lives in cities. In California the percentage is even higher and growing every year. Pressure on our economic, social and ecological systems is intensifying as our populations swell. Growing awareness of our deteriorating environment, air and water pollution, ozone depletion, toxic waste, and traffic congestion is forcing us to confront the reality that sound economic development must be directly tied to environmental sustainability.

— **Julia Scofield Russell**
Director, Eco-Home Network

INTRODUCTION

Michael Woo

At first glance, it seems that the expression "ecological cities" is an oxymoron. It is difficult to imagine how a city can be ecological. A lot of the conditions that we associate with cities are unecological, unhealthy, and perhaps even unnatural.

Los Angeles is an embodiment of this contradiction, because our growth has been seemingly based upon a limitless supply of undeveloped land and a limitless supply of water coming from elsewhere. We also assumed there was a limitless supply of clean air and a continuing supply of cheap gasoline. And now in the 1990s we are finding that none of those premises are true.

While those of us here in Los Angeles are coming to the realization that we are running out of land, air and space on our streets and freeways, and that gasoline is becoming more expensive, it is alarming to realize that other cities around the world are increasingly looking to us as an example of what they want to be. I noticed this myself when I was visiting Jakarta and some of the other islands of Indonesia. It amazed me to see that there was very little vernacular development that told you that you were in Jakarta. Instead, there were a lot of office buildings that could easily have been found in Century City. The Los Angeles model of success has been adopted by trendsetters or people with money, who think that what it takes to achieve "first world" status is to become another Los Angeles.

So consider that we have a dual mission. We have a mission to serve our own needs here trying to deal with the growing population, and the whole conflict between growth and the need to preserve our environment. Also, we have a responsibility to be a leader for the world, because the eyes of the world are on our city.

I think the central issue facing Los Angeles in the 1990s is how we can avoid becoming a city of only the rich and the poor. That means finding ways of meeting the needs of the poor, whether people of color, immigrants, or those with special needs; while not pushing out the middle class who have the economic choice to leave, thus depriving our city of the economic and tax base which provides for stability. We must try, in this respect, to facilitate economic niches for the poor, such as street vendor opportunities, so that they too can work in meaningful ways without being dependent.

I do recognize there will have to be sharp limitations on certain types of economic activities which have negative environmental effects. I also recognize that it will be necessary to redistribute density resulting from population growth. I think we can use our common sense and ingenuity to build coalitions that address environmental change in this area, in a way which can be a complement to economic health.

Michael Woo is one of only two trained urban planners to serve on the Los Angeles City Council. Since his 1985 election to the Council, his environmentally conscious agenda has included preventing hillside overdevelopment, preserving scenic Fryman Canyon, reforming urban forest policy, crusading on behalf of pedestrian rights, and his ongoing effort to redevelop Hollywood's blighted areas on a more sustainable basis.

Councilman Michael Woo
City Hall, Room 239
200 North Spring Street
Los Angeles, CA 90012
(213) 485-3353

Environmental issues such as air quality, traffic and the availability of parks and open space cut across economic lines. We can address many of these issues simultaneously by promoting a pedestrian-friendly environment and decreasing auto dependency. I believe we are capable of implementing equitable solutions to these problems.

I encourage you to think about a variety of ways that Los Angeles and other dense urban centers in this country can provide world leadership in putting together coalitions that cut across economic and ethnic lines, to address both the need for environmental quality and the economic needs of our growing population. This is a way we can take care of ourselves, and become a beacon for the rest of the world.

THE NEW PARTNERSHIP

June 21st, 1991 — 5:00 AM

Bob Walter

In the cool and cloudy pre-dawn of an overcast morning, an assortment of hardy souls began to gather on the windswept patio outside UCLA's Dickson Auditorium. Walkie-talkies fired up, parking fiascoes were being ironed out, enrollment tables were being arranged. The caterers arrived and commenced setting out breakfast and brewing coffee, its welcome aroma warming the workers. Last minute signs were lettered and hung. The nondescript auditorium started to bloom as landscapers rolled in trees and flowers. Teams of volunteers, loosely formed several weeks before, started to mesh, and a bubble of energy began to grow on campus.

Out in the city, some four hundred attendees were wending their way toward the campus, secure in the knowledge that a conference was about to take place. We, on the other hand, were rushing last minute adjustments into place like a theater company on opening night. All the right parts and pieces were there. The question was: could we assemble them before the curtain went up?

But the components did mesh, and what followed as the hall filled to the point of standing-room-only, was a growing vortex of excitement and good feeling that some called "a turning point for the City of Los Angeles", and others "an historic gathering". To those of us who had been planning The First Los Angeles Ecological Cities Conference for over a year, it was the pay-off on our gamble that the theme, "Urban Growth and the Environment: Forging a Partnership for Our Future" was ready to be received. As it turned out, this message was being delivered in the right place at the right time.

Bob Walter is the President of the Los Angeles-based Eco-Home Network, and was one of the three principal planners of the **First Los Angeles Ecological Cities Conference**. *He is an environmental writer and consultant who co-edits the* **Ecolution** *magazine/newsletter and writes the "New City Living" column for* **The City Planet**.

Eco-Home Network
4344 Russell Avenue
Los Angeles, CA 90027
(213) 664-7706

During the next forty-eight hours, a vision was imparted of a city filled with bustling, tree-lined, pedestrian-oriented urban centers, clean skies, economic vitality and social cohesion, all working in concert with the environment. The Conference laid out the foundations for actualizing such a transformation, including the principles of eco-city design, structure and infrastructure, planning, politics and economics.

As the conference unfolded, consultant relationships were forming, mini-follow-up conferences were born, and seeds were sown for the incorporation of sustainable city criteria into the General Plans of Los Angeles and surrounding municipalities.

The enthusiasm these ideas generated is based in part on the premise that some far-reaching goals seem clearly accessible. These concepts and strategies are not counting on future technology, nor are they based on some utopian, unfinanceable vision, but rather they are founded on techniques and theories being put into practice right now, all around the country in major projects.

This book continues the work begun at the conference. It brings the same breadth of overview and the same sense of achievable potential, but it adds a depth and detail to the ideas presented, which were not

The New Partnership

possible within a two-day conference. In addition to the chapters with their individual reference sources, there is an extensive Resource Guide of books, periodicals, businesses and individuals listed at the back of the book, to help you dig even more deeply into any specific area you are researching. Our goal is to put as rich an array of material at your fingertips as we can, and to make it as easy as possible to access the information or consultancy sources you need.

We also present this book as a tangible example of the new kind of partnership that can be formed among citizens, government and business. As you examine *Sustainable Cities*, you will see it has been written by a team made up of architects, educators, planners, government representatives, developers, builders, environmental leaders and citizen planners.

Here is proof that we can work together to reinvent our cities, and to establish a new standard that brings economically and environmentally compatible community building into the mainstream. The partnerships begun at this conference and similar events in other cities, have an unprecedented opportunity. All the tools to redefine and redesign according to nature are so very close at hand. Now is the time to pick them up with common purpose and become facile in their use.

William James Warren is a photographer of international reputation. This photo essay and the authors' portraits that appear throughout the book were taken during the two-day span of the **First Los Angeles Ecological Cities Conference**. *His photo journalism, elaborate photo-illustrations and nature photography have appeared in magazines, annual reports and books over the last 25 years.*

*William James Warren
& Associates
509 S. Gramercy Place
Suite 1
Los Angeles, CA 90020*

THE FATE OF OUR CITIES IS THE FATE OF THE EARTH

Ernest Callenbach

Ernest Callenbach's novel
Ecotopia *has sold over half a million copies and has been described by* **Time Magazine** *as an environmental classic. He writes and lectures on ecological topics all over the globe. A founding council member of the Elmwood Institute, he is editor-in-chief of its Global File Project which transfers successful innovations across national boundaries.*

1963 El Dorado Ave.
Berkeley, CA 94707
(415) 642-6333

We Americans still think of ourselves as rural folks. Our housing ideal, the suburban detached house, may be only a shrunken version of the mythical frontier farmhouse, inhabited by Mom and plentifully supplied with apple pie; but it's still our way of "hitting out for the Territory," as Huck Finn put it, in other words: getting away from other Americans. After World War II, we of course urbanized on a colossal scale, all the while trying to define ourselves as not urban. Today, what is sometimes called decentralization into smaller outlying cities, goes on creating urban areas.

There is a dreadful and immensely costly paradox here. Our apparently "modern" technological instrument for organizing our cities, the private automobile, in fact is a kind of mechanical horse, symbolically a cowboy mode of travel. It was well adapted only to a population spread thinly on the land, the way our grandparents lived. But now we are living out the tragic consequences of allowing a mechanical horse to dominate the design of our cities. We have turned our fate over to traffic engineers, who have rebuilt America, except for a few remaining city centers, in a way that leaves us in the oil-dependent grip of that outdated rural 19th-century technology.

The challenge we face is to start rebuilding America yet again, in a way that is habitable by human beings instead of just cars, and that is vastly less ecologically destructive. It is crucial to realize that using an automobile is the single most environmentally harmful thing we do, aside from the indirect effects of having children who will grow up and become relatively rich, chronic consumers of the earth's resources.

In being overwhelmingly urban, or at least "metropolitan", we are like most of the earth's people today. But we are different because of two conflicting desires. On the one hand, we have inherited the idea that the best way to live is in the manner of English country gentry, and on the other, we insist on doing this through the use of a transportation system that makes country ease impossible. The car, in economic terminology, is called a "positional good". It's something that can be wonderful to have, but only so long as you're one of the very few persons in a position to have one.

So in recent decades, we have had unique difficulty in creating anything that could live up to the name of "town", much less "city". What we have created instead is sprawl, both suburban and urban, and it is through this metropolitan sprawl that our primary impacts on the earth take place. It is to city sprawl that, as the saying goes, the water flows, uphill, towards money — dewatering rivers and destroying species. It is to the cities that the power lines, the gas pipelines and the ships run, sucking in the treasures of the Third World. It is there that the trucks carry the produce derived from pumping groundwater that can not be replenished for centuries, if ever, and from applying stupendous quantities of pesticides, herbicides, and fertilizers in attempts to counter the slowly decreasing fertility of the soil.

We are a very rich people, consuming a vast proportion of the world's wealth, and consequently doing a vast proportion of the damage caused by producing that wealth. The poet John Donne might today say: "Ask not for whom the rainforest burns; it burns for thee"; so your hamburgers can be produced. If we are to lessen that impact, both the political ideas of a more decently modest lifestyle and the design impetus for ecologically responsible building are going to have to come from the cities. Cities are where change comes from.

I happen to be a country boy by origin; I grew up in a rural village in central Pennsylvania, and never really saw a city until I went away to college in Chicago, an environment about as opposite as you can find. But I have lived in a city all my adult life and have no plans to live anywhere else. I have learned that cities are not only capable of being absolutely delightful places to live, but they are also the engines of human creation, as well as the engines of a lot of destruction. Cities are where almost all new ideas come from. Ecological organizations have their headquarters there. Cities are where most important universities are located. They are the seats of art, politics, and commerce. They are where symphony orchestras, and public-interest and civil-liberties lawyers live. They are where human interactions are dense and accidental enough to be very productive. When they are well-designed they are immensely appealing to almost everybody.

> *. . . cities are not only capable of being absolutely delightful places to live but they are also the engines of human creation.*

Andres Duany, the great new-town planner of Seaside in Florida, likes to make nasty fun of the standard Planned Unit Development (PUD), our ordinary suburban land-use pattern. I'm sure there are some decent PUDs out there, but Duany focuses on what he calls their worm-shaped cul-de-sacs and collector streets that automatically create gridlock, and sidewalks where nobody sets foot once the construction crew leaves, and the general atmosphere of terminal boredom. Then he shows a slide of an old-fashioned American street in Disney World. There are no cars in sight, just Disney gingerbread, but there are pleasant, walkable spaces. Now this is, as Duany says, a place that people will fly all the way across the country to visit, spending a hundred bucks for a hotel and $27 more to get in. Once they are there, they spend only 7% of their visiting time waiting for rides or on the rides. Mostly they are just walking around and enjoying the urban ambiance; even though it is, of course, entirely fake. Imagine then, Duany says, how attractive real towns with real stores and real cafes and real small businesses and squares can be!

Duany and Elizabeth Plater-Zyberk argue that it is well-known how to design towns that will work. They have in fact codified and computerized the design rules. They will come into a development project, do a 6-day crash charette, consulting with all local interested parties including planners and environmental groups, and at the end of it, the developer has a plan, complete with detailed codes, that can probably be approved and will certainly produce a livable town, rather than another ghastly suburban wasteland. I have never met Duany and Plater-Zyberk, and I'm certainly not on their payroll, but I would venture that anybody who designs a new development these days without being familiar with their ideas is being really stupid with his or her money. There are, of course, related approaches that show great promise too. Peter Calthorpe's "Pedestrian Pockets" projects are beautiful and imaginative windows into a workable urban pattern rather like what I imagined Ecotopian "mini-cities" to be. Mike and Judy Corbett produced in the Village Homes development in Davis, a solar community of immense charm and stupefyingly low energy consumption. Half the people in Davis would like to live there, in modest, sensible homes with bike-paths and tiny, narrow streets.

But I'm an ecology-oriented person, not a profit-oriented person, and what is striking about these towns from my perspective is how they diminish automobile dependence, and thus ecological impacts. Detached houses still make up what seems to be a majority of Duany's total floor space but Duany locates a good many apartments over stores around the core of their towns. This has often proved to be a good lesson that we have learned from history. The core, by the way, is defined by the presence of things that people will actually frequent: a branch post office, a convenience store, a cafe and newsstand next to the bus stop, maybe a church or a dry cleaner or a photo shop. Duany dedicates land for these items in his original plans.

In ecological terms, detached houses are atrocities, because they consume so much energy and materials. According to one calculation, they can use up to five times as much energy to build and live in as an apartment of comparable area. They lose heat, or take in heat in hot climates, much faster because of more exposed wall and roof and floor surfaces; their internal piping and wiring is much less efficient; they cannot share energy-intensive services like space and water heating.

But most of all, living in detached houses generally requires people to use several cars, and to drive them a lot. So the impacts ripple out: air pollution from exhausts and refineries, destruction to the earth through mining, high-energy ore smelting, steel-stamping, paint-fume emissions, and all the rest of it; not to mention the sheer coverage of the earth with asphalt. Duany thinks his town designs cut people's car use by half, mostly because of great decrease in chauffeured trips that suburban parents, usually mothers, have to make. Kids can walk to playmates' houses nearby, or to playgrounds nearby, or to the corner store to pick up bread or milk. It also makes towns livable for seniors, who often can't drive, but who can live perfectly decent uninstitutionalized lives for many years, if they can get to the essentials they need on foot.

> *... detached houses according to one calculation, can use up to five times as much energy to build and live in as an apartment of comparable area.*

Reducing driving by half may not sound like enough, and in my *Ecotopia* I envisage truly car-free mini-cities. But we're talking real world here, and if even a quarter of Americans lived in a Duany-style town, that would go a long way toward stopping the global greenhouse effect, not to mention giving cleaner air. We could go back to not caring where Iraq was. It would be more effective than mandating efficiency standards, tailpipe regulations, catalytic converters, or any other technofixes whatsoever. And it would be a permanent solution.

And this, I submit, is a quite general conclusion: the solution to our transportation problems is too often thought of as: How can we devise a better machine to get us from point A to point B? We turn to more gas-efficient cars, to less polluting cars, even to electric cars. But no matter how we twist and turn, no matter how technically ingenious we get, in the end we cannot escape the fact that we have formulated the problem wrong. The problem really is: how do we get the most-frequented points A and points B closer together, so people can comfortably and happily walk or bicycle between them? Until we realize that, and learn how to do it, and learn how to make money doing it, we are living under the shadow of a curse, which I formulate thus: "Those who live by the car will die by the car."

Those may seem like strong words. They are not. Indeed, the fate of American civilization hangs on whether we can recover from our addiction to the private car. In our impact on the environment, the physical habitability of our public spaces, our children's future safety, and our economic sustainability depend on changing our ideas about cities and towns to escape the baleful influence of automobile-driven sprawl. And we can do it. It means giving up a set of old ideas, and getting used to a new perception, a new paradigm.

> *. . . the fate of American civilization hangs on whether we can recover from our addiction to the private car.*

Amory Lovins taught us how to think differently about electrical energy, and as a result the intelligently managed utilities of our state, and many elsewhere, are awash with electricity from conservation and alternate, renewable sources. We have limited water in California, as well as almost everywhere else these days. Fine: cities are much less water-intensive than suburbs, and re-using waste water there is much more feasible. We are losing tens of billions of dollars from the corrosive and health effects of smog? Fine: don't extend sprawl and the smog it creates ever further out into the valley and deserts, but in-fill, densify, and rebuild urban environments so that not only yuppies but ordinary working citizens can walk or bike, or at least bus quickly to work and back. Are we worried about crumbling infrastructure? Fine: city infrastructure is substantially more economically efficient than infrastructure out in the country. Almost everything is: street lighting, water piping, postal delivery, medical emergency service, and UPS. In fact, by living in car-dependent suburbia, America gives itself, I would guess, something like a 5% economic handicap in our competition with the Germans and Japanese, who move around quicker and cheaper by train and bus and tend to live in compact, largely self-sufficient neighborhoods.

Most of these arguments for the advantages of cities have been around for many centuries, of course, and they are why the great cities of the world are the way they are: dense, varied, exciting, economically resilient, and often strikingly beautiful places. The only pity is that we don't have them in America any more, and have to take petroleum-burning airplanes to go visit them.

The reasons why we don't have them are not, I think, because we Americans are stupider than other, older and perhaps wiser peoples, but because after World War II, our governments, federal and state both, deliberately abandoned the cities. The political reasons for this are not yet clearly known to historians, though racism is surely a big part of it. After World War II we gave subsidies to masses of GI homebuyers; we subsidized suburban infrastructure, particularly through highways and roads, but also in other institutional ways. On a national level, we allowed the highway-car-oil lobby to hold sway and triumph over the railroad-streetcar-lobby while being distracted, I suspect, by the military-industrial lobby.

Now all these 747-sized chickens have come home to roost, leaving us with an economy hyper-competent in building smart bombs and hopelessly incompetent in almost everything else, including building sensible and ecologically sustainable towns and cities. But peoples go through periods like this; we learn slowly, maybe, but in the end we have to learn. The alternative, after all, is chaos; it's Ecotopia or bust.

So I have a proposal for you. The greatest single national need today is a new type of train, a gravy train. As you know, this is not a country where altruism gets much done; perhaps no country is. When we want lots of bombs, or planes, or whatever, in a hurry, we get Congress to bribe rich people to build them for us, and they do. It's the American Way, time-tested and true. So at this crucial juncture in our history, if salvation has to come through greed, and it probably does, let's work on Congress to replace its subsidies to military contractors with subsidies to city-rebuilders. Let's end protectionism of American gas-guzzlers, and start protecting streetcar builders for a change, so we don't have to buy German trolleys. Let's turn Bechtel around from building airports and nuclear plants, to building inexpensive but delightful dense mixed-use structures for dwellings, stores, and offices, such as great cities have always relied on. Let's put Boeing to work building a decent long-distance train network, so we can recapture some of the land wasted in vast airports, and get people from center-city to center-city, the way every other advanced country does. We need a new America that will work ecologically and economically, and it's within our grasp. If we can continue working to dramatize the vision, the legislators will come around. As the old saying says: If the people will lead, the leaders will follow. It's time.

OVERALL DESIGN PARAMETERS: A FOUNDATION TO BUILD ON

THE THREE-STAGE EVOLUTION OF ECO-CITIES — REDUCE, REUSE, RECYCLE

Tony Dominski, Ph.D

T ransforming today's cities, which are based on destructive consumption and the production of waste is, to say the least, awkward. It is like the punch line of the joke about the Maine farmer who is asked for directions to Boston: "You can't get there from here."

There are hundreds of billions of dollars and over a century of effort invested in today's urban infrastructure, the buildings sheltering homes, stores, offices and factories; the connecting freeways and road grids; the utility networks carrying electricity, gas and water, and finally in the landscapes in which everything else is embedded. Parallel to the physical infrastructure is a legal and financial infrastructure in which there is a huge emotional investment.

Just as the ocean luxury liner cannot be turned on a dime, thousands of square miles of buildings, roads and landscapes cannot be changed overnight. Its complete renovation will take a century or more.

THE FIRST STAGE: REDUCE

Nevertheless, the first stage of the transformation has already begun. This first stage may be termed the reduction or quick fix stage. In Los Angeles and other California cities, people are trying to reduce the impact of their over-consuming lifestyles by changing light bulbs, insulating their homes, recycling trash, buying non-toxic cleaners, using graywater, compost and mulch in their backyards and carpooling.

This reduction stage is valuable ecologically and educationally. It is an introduction to a new ethic, and encourages the more far-reaching measures of the reuse and recycling stages of evolution.

THE SECOND STAGE: REUSE

In the reuse stage, existing buildings, roads, landscape and utility networks are employed in novel ways. For example, commercial and office buildings can be partially converted to residential units to relieve housing shortages. Roofs now used only for weather protection become gardens or energy collectors with skylights and solar panels. Existing roadways can become rights-of-way for electric trains and bicycles. Existing downtown streets can become pedestrian malls, and residential streets can become slow streets. Ornamental landscapes can be converted to fruit orchards. The electric grid of rooftop panels can be used to recharge small in-town electric vehicles, and the corner gas station becomes a battery exchange shop.

The reuse stage is much more far-reaching than the reduction stage in reducing consumption and improving quality of life. It also sets into motion the forces which will allow the modified building, road and utility elements to be repatterned together within the ultimate recycling stage.

Tony Dominski is the former Education Director of the Community Environmental Council in Santa Barbara, a research center and community resource on issues of water conservation, waste management and urban sustainablity. He has taught at Pratt Institute School of Architecture, worked in Environmmental Planning in Connecticut and New York, and is author of "The Bottom Line: Restructuring for Sustainabilty."

Community Environmental Council
930 Miramonte Drive
Santa Barbara, CA 93109
805 963-0583

Tony Dominsky
2505 Schley Street
Tallahasse, FL 32304
(904) 576-2411

THE THIRD STAGE: RECYCLE

The recycling stage is the stage where the previously-transformed urban elements are reinforced within a new urban pattern. This is the stage where the urban village reigns supreme. The urban villages condense around nuclei consisting of the denser suburban and inner city areas. Adjacent, less dense areas might be reconverted to farms, meadows and forests.

The local electric train systems are linked regionally, as are local sections of bike paths and footpaths. Similarly, sections of stream rescued from culverts are linked in linear parks and forests.

In this urban evolutionary succession, each stage prepares necessary conditions for the next step. This parallels the process by which a forest develops and regenerates itself. The three stages — reduce, reuse, recycle — will be going on simultaneously in a patchwork fashion, much as regeneration occurs in a large forest. As forest patches are always changing in response to episodes of wind, fire, and disease, urban patches evolve in response to social, ecological and demographic conditions.

SHAPING THE CONDITIONS FOR ECO-CITY EVOLUTION

Human beings are constantly influencing the conditions upon which their survival and evolution depend. The successful evolution of an eco-city will depend on the extent to which we are conscious and can shape the forces propelling its evolution.

> *Social justice is the gateway to sustainability.*

Three imperatives will form the basis for eco-city evolution: the need for social justice, prosperity, and a healthy ecology. These are sometimes viewed as separate and even contradictory, but are merging in the overarching vision of sustainability.

Social justice is the gateway to sustainability. Good social conditions are the political foundation upon which eco-cities must rest. A widening gap between the "haves" and "have nots" will retard the change.

Secondly, an eco-city is economically driven by a coalition of businesses capable of serving and generating new enlightened consumers, retrofitting the urban fabric along ecological lines, and planning and building the new urban infrastructures. These businesses will be reinforced by changing consumer preferences and new government policies.

Extraction taxes for oil, coal and uranium will favor energy conservation firms and suppliers of solar energy. Similarly, pollution taxes and high fees for landfills will encourage the manufacture of non-toxic and recyclable products. To ensure fairness, these government policies will have to ensure that lower income groups are protected from carrying the major share of any extra financial burdens.

These businesses will be synergistic. For example, a graywater plumbing retrofit business needs another business to generate a non-toxic detergent. When drought-stricken Santa Barbara legalized graywater, Oasis, an ecological design firm in that city, produced a soap for graywater systems that biodegrades into a plant fertilizer. An electric car manufacturer will want to purchase efficient non-toxic batteries. Energy conservation firms need non-toxic insulation and excellent roof-top solar panels. Organic farmers and gardeners will want to purchase mulch and compost products produced from recycling firms.

The third major evolutionary force is the knowledge of the links between health, lifestyle, ecological destruction and human survival. Environmental destruction is inevitably accompanied by a decline in health, quality of life, and ultimately, of the economy. In this regard our current media have done a good job in showing the problems, but a poor job in showing their origins and solutions.

CONCLUSION

The evolution of an eco-city will be a long process, and will take over a century to complete. It is encouraging that the first stage of awareness and application of conservation techniques is already here. The second phase, the creative reuse of what is already built, is a logical extension of the first stage. The recycling of existing roads and buildings and landscapes into qualitatively new forms will mark the eco-city's mature stage.

There is a lot of interesting work to do. An evolutionary perspective can illuminate the way, forging a new eco-social ethic, synthesizing the heretofore conflicting elements of fairness, prosperity and ecological survival.

ECOLOGICAL PLANNING PRINCIPLES FOR SUSTAINABLE DEVELOPMENT

n Earth Day 1991, Ian McHarg, author of *Design with Nature*, said: "The fine art of the 21st century will be that of restoration of the natural environment. We need not only a better view of humans and nature, but a working method by which the least of us can ensure that the product of our works is not more despoliation." Redirecting our energy and intelligence towards this task will become increasingly important to our quality of life and our survival.

We must act on our growing awareness that a healthy ecosystem and natural environment be the foundation for all that we do. The natural environment, our life support system, is the basis for a healthy world, healthy economy, healthy society, and a healthy quality of life.

Pivotal to this principle is letting go of the idea that good business and a sound ecology are at odds. Ecological design that restores and preserves natural environment can result in a more attractive product with greater sales appeal. The stumbling block we face is not an economic issue, but the resistance we have toward taking the time to learn a new way of doing business.

SAMPLE DESIGN & POLICY CRITERIA

1. Create an inventory of natural and human-made aspects of your bioregion.
2. Define study areas in the context of local and regional watersheds, maintaining integrity of streambelts.
3. Maintain a continuous system of greenbelts and wildlife corridors to be determined by natural conditions, and maintain large contiguous pieces of natural habitat as wildlife sanctuaries.
4. Protect and restore cyclical processes, biological diversity, and natural beauty.
5. Develop equitable land preservation and restoration agreements through fair market acquisition and development rights transfer. If a privately-owned property is marked for preservation as open space, the property owner would be paid for the land at fair market rate by selling his development rights, which can be transferred to another more suitable site.
6. Initiate formal agreements with surrounding cities or counties to share inventory information and call for regional action to protect area ecosystems.

SAMPLE QUESTIONS

1. How should local, county and region-wide inventories of current natural and human-made features and conditions be funded?
2. How much undisturbed land is required, and in what configuration must it be, to sustain native plant and animal life?
3. Can new coastal wetlands be created to sustain the diversity of life that once flourished in such natural areas?
4. Can equitable land transfer agreements be worked out to protect both land owners and the public interests?
5. How do we work with surrounding counties and local communities that share common watersheds, wildlife habitats and corridors?
6. How can functional migratory routes be re-established and paid for in light of current human-made barriers, such as freeways and fences?

PRINCIPLE 1

Protect, Preserve and Restore the Natural Environment

*These **Eight Principles** were created by the **Citizens Planners Project of Ventura County** coordinated by Joseph Smyth, to help guide development in that Southern California county. Initial input came from a team of concerned Ventura citizens and a consultancy group, which included the principal planners of the **First Los Angeles Ecological Cities Conference** and a number of speakers and participants from the conference. These principles are offered as sustainable building blocks whose specifics can be customized to fit any community or county. In this version, the original wording of the principles is retained and the text modified.*

PRINCIPLE 2

Establish True-Cost Pricing as the Basis of Economic Viability

B y utilizing true-cost pricing to evaluate a course of action, we move toward long-term economic viability and sustainability without compromising our quality of life. In true-cost pricing, long-term economic gains and preservation of the quality of life are valued above short-term profits. In order to evaluate true short-term financial profit and long-term economic gains, the "eco-nomic" (ecological + economic) sustainability of the natural environment and society as a whole must be included in the balance sheet.

The specific types of expenses to factor into our new economic equations incorporate payment for the total negative impacts that current business practices cause. We need to include pollution mitigation costs, related medical expenses, loss of pay due to related illness, repairs required for buildings, and loss of forest revenues due to forest depletion from acid rain. In addition to these more quantifiable factors, we should also consider accounting for related intangibles such as pain and suffering, bereavement, and loss of scenery.

True-cost accounting also factors in the use of non-renewable materials. We need to shift from the current situation that favors use of virgin resources over recycled materials. A more appropriate state of affairs would be economic inducements to utilize recycled raw materials and penalties for using non-renewable resources where sustainable alternatives are possible.

The goals are: sustainable economic prosperity to meet human needs and wants, building efficient infrastructure, and at the same time protecting the life-giving abundance and beauty of nature, for ourselves and for all future generations.

SAMPLE DESIGN & POLICY CRITERIA
1. Economic analysis must be based on cyclic patterns and a whole-systems approach to planning.
2. Long-term impacts on environmental and social issues must be considered as part of an economic analysis.
3. Give developers project preference points and tax breaks for planning clustered, mixed-use, public transit/pedestrian-oriented projects which reduce infrastructure and maintenance costs.
4. Provide incentives for industries to clean up their operations by charging them for the pollution they emit, and also to tax non-reusable and non-recyclable products to discourage their production and sale.
5. Redefine the rules of the market place so that the most beneficial environmental opportunities are also those which make the most economic sense at the individual level.

SAMPLE QUESTIONS
1. How can we keep ecological and economic wealth circulating within our local communities?
2. How can we work with neighboring jurisdictions to coordinate positive economic incentives for sustainable practices in business and development in our region, creating a level playing field?
3. How do we measure long-term impacts of proposed actions on our economic, environmental and social well-being?

L ocal production of food, goods, and services creates jobs in local businesses, and is a key aspect of a healthy community. Local production of necessities also reduces dependency on imports, allows economic wealth to be recycled, provides security in case of an emergency, and turns our communities into self-sufficient garden-cities. For example, locally grown food supports local farmers, is fresher, and can be brought to market with less travel time and expense.

While some communities throw their front door open to recruit new businesses, The *Rocky Mountain Institute* reports that in Lane County, Oregon, the locals recognized that their most important and stable economic opportunities were with their existing local businesses. Lane County created Oregon Marketplace, which helps local firms thrive by linking buyers and sellers. In Great Barrington, Massachusetts, and dozens of other communities around the country, including Los Angeles, residents are encouraging new local enterprise by helping hometown entrepreneurs gain access to capital. Through a Community Loan Fund account at the local bank, they can collateralize loans that the bank might not otherwise grant to local businesses.

Mixed-use cluster-development helps to support local businesses by making it easier and more attractive to shop locally by foot and by bike, which helps guarantee a built-in clientele for local businesses. This increases the opportunity for more personalized business/customer relations that also makes shopping locally more appealing. This mutual support which has been by and large lost in our depersonalized, automobile-based urban world, is a key aspect of a sustainable city, which improves the overall quality of life.

SAMPLE DESIGN & POLICY CRITERIA
1. Develop business strategies for recycling wealth within the community, e.g., local exchange trading systems and local currencies.
2. Link producers and consumers in a variety of community and cooperative associations.
3. Encourage small, local organic farming operations wherever possible. Organic farming eliminates the need for toxic pesticides, and can minimize dust by reducing the extent of plowing required to grow crops.
4. Include food production in community open spaces, parks, community gardens, rooftop gardens, private homes and multi-family buildings, so that our cities increasingly have edible landscapes.
5. Promote rooftop gardens by changing building codes to stipulate sufficient structural integrity, railings, drainage, access to water and designated planting areas.

SAMPLE QUESTIONS
1. How can the community protect its agricultural lands from development and at the same time provide equitable arrangements with land owners?
2. What kind of incentive would be required to ensure adequate food production within the local jurisdiction of a community?
3. What kind of business products and services would provide a basis for community self-sufficiency?
4. Given the specialized nature of our current economy, is it possible to accomplish these objectives?
5. How can people be encouraged to change their eating habits to be in greater alignment with what is most ecologically healthy and appropriate for the region?

PRINCIPLE 3

Support Local Agriculture and Local Business, Products and Services

PRINCIPLE 4

**Develop
Clustered,
Mixed-Use,
Pedestrian-
Oriented
Ecological
Communities**

 lustering communities preserves open space in rural areas and can restore open space within existing communities. Clustering also encourages living within a safe, pleasant walk to work, schools, shopping, services, parks, recreation, and public transit. We are also learning that appropriate density enhances security, and can be a positive force for creating community and a sense of place.

While the social and environmental benefits of clustering communities are becoming clearer, the major economic benefits still remain hidden, according to architect/planner Joseph Smyth. He adds: "The truth is, the economic benefits of clustered communities are so massive and so comprehensive they seem too good to be true. The tip-off clue in this treasure hunt is the following: 40% of the cost of development is automobile-related. In other words, when a town or city is built, 40% of the initial costs go to pay for freeways, streets, stop lights, parking lots, driveways, garages, parking structures, and the land they cover. In my opinion, automobile dependency, with all of its side effects, is the root cause of local, state and national insolvency. It's time the true-cost of living in automobile-dependent communities is known. Most importantly, it's time for the economic power of sustainable development to be discovered!"

Richard Register states in his book, *Ecocity Berkeley*, "The Garden is the paradise of nature, and the City is the paradise of culture. Or at least they could be... Today, both are out of balance. If we build the eco-city, we will regain the Garden and finally aspire to the full ideal of the City — the City built with, not against, nature. Then, when we hold in reverence that which we cannot build, which is given to us by the Earth herself, we will create not just a home for ourselves but a future for all who follow."

SAMPLE DESIGN & POLICY CRITERIA
1. Establish integrated, ecological, whole-systems thinking as the planning and developing norm in communities, and redesign the zoning patterns accordingly.
2. Create town centers composed of public buildings and spaces for governance and the arts that will generate civic pride and a sense of place. Create architectural forms and spaces that promote cultural diversity and positive social interaction. Create neighborhoods that encourage walking and biking. Create a variety of housing types and sizes, suited to different income levels, life-styles, cultures, and age groups. Define clusters by creating permanent greenbelts. Create green spaces within the community to support visual and sound privacy.
3. Adjust building codes to require a much higher level of sound-proofing that will permit privacy amidst higher density.

SAMPLE QUESTIONS
1. How large can a community be, in acres and in height, and still maintain a human scale and sense of place?
2. When does a community get too large for a person to feel that their participation makes a difference?
3. What is the maximum size of a neighborhood that is large enough to provide a basic range of goods and services, and still is personal enough for the individual to feel at home?
4. What new cultural norms can be created to support low-impact, high-quality lifestyles within denser neighborhoods?

ommunities that gear up to move information instead of people and materials, and which encourage the use of advanced production systems are on their way to long-term sustainability. Transportation, communication, food and production, water and material reclamation, and the delivery of human services, all play a part in that scenario. A Japanese panel convened in early 1990 to advise the U.S. on strengthening its economy. They counseled us to build high-speed rail systems and "get Americans out of their cars," reports Francesca Lyman in *E Magazine* (September/October, 1990).

Americans lose more than 2 billion hours a year to traffic delays. According to the Federal Highway Administration, by the year 2005 at current growth rates, that number will increase to 7 billion hours! This does not count commuting time, just the delays, reports *Nation's Business* (September, 1991).

Clean and quiet transit will be commonplace in the years to come, and the sooner communities make the change, the faster things will improve. Advantages will include major reductions in air and noise pollution, less lost time due to long commutes and traffic jams, less travel expense, and fewer accidents. Homes in clustered communities can be typically located within a short walk, bike or trolley ride of the train station.

Advanced communication systems (e.g., fiber optic cable, satellite, computer data bases, FAX, CD-ROM) are already commonplace. When built into the community as standard components and coupled with advanced, efficient, non-polluting production technologies, such systems will permit large businesses to decentralize into small, local branch offices that easily fit into mixed-use-cluster patterns. Providing the home workplace with a direct-link access to global information and transactions will also be a major benefit.

As industry, through new levels of efficiency in the consumption of materials and energy, advances to the point where it is able to guarantee no measurable impact on air and water, it can begin to be integrated into the fabric of sustainable neighborhoods. This will mean a large additional supply of jobs which can be reached without the need for a long commute.

SAMPLE DESIGN & POLICY CRITERIA

1. Develop a quality-of-life index to support an ecologically balanced carrying capacity.
2. Locate walkways and bikeways through park and greenbelt settings separate from automobile streets.
3. Wire new and existing communities with fiber-optic cable to serve the needs of large and small business, the home-based workplace, educational and entertainment facilities.
4. Require all public and private transportation to convert to clean power sources, such as natural gas, hydrogen or electricity from renewable sources, and locate transit stops within a short walk or bike ride of destinations.

SAMPLE QUESTIONS

1. Can the savings in infrastructure cost made by clustering development pay the total installation cost of advanced transportation systems? And can adequate convenient private transportation systems be accommodated?
2. How long will it take before clustered communities that utilize advanced architectural, transportation, communication and production technologies can run on local renewable sources of energy?

PRINCIPLE 5

Utilize Advanced Transportation, Communication and Production Systems

PRINCIPLE 6

**Maximize
Conservation
and Develop
Renewable
Resources**

T he use of conservation technology and practices to reduce consumption of energy, water and materials is an area which has a vast potential we are only starting to tap. Not only are the physical resources saved available for future use, but the funds saved equal more local wealth that stays within the community. Conservation also reduces pollution and minimizes the cost of waste management (e.g., water reclamation, materials recovery and recycling, toxic waste disposal and landfills).

"The United States wastes some $300 billion a year due to lack of insulation, inefficient refrigerators, drafty doors, and other energy leaks in buildings, industry and transportation," say researchers at the Rocky Mountain Institute. That's why the Rocky Mountain Institute's Economic Renewal Program is helping towns like Osage, Iowa (population 3,800). Osage has created the equivalent of 60 new jobs by implementing a variety of energy efficiency programs. $1.2 million dollars that leaked out of the community to pay energy bills each year now stays in the town, generating more local wealth.

An energy-conserving, longer-lasting refrigerator has a higher purchase price than a conventional refrigerator. However, the savings in electricity over the life of the refrigerator will more than justify the increased purchase price, including interest on the difference. Historically, utilities have been reluctant to promote "Negawatts" conservation programs, because to do so lowered their profits. Today, however, growing numbers of states are changing their regulations to allow utilities to keep part of the money that their efficiency programs save. According to John Rowe, New England Electric System's (NEES) chief executive, "Under the old rates, there was no way we could make money on conservation, but now it's the most profitable investment we make."

Converting from dependence on non-renewable resources from distant sources to local renewable resources moves the community closer to self-sufficiency. The conversion should include measures such as using local ground water and developing water catchments to reduce dependence on imported water, and utilizing solar technologies to reduce fossil fuel use.

SAMPLE DESIGN & POLICY CRITERIA
1. Provide economic incentives for water, energy and materials conservation, for installing water-saving and catchment devices, for solar panels that produce electricity and hot water, for driving more efficient small cars and using alternative fuels, for working within the home and/or neighborhood where walking or biking replaces most auto uses.
2. Set strict water quality standards and take steps to eliminate pollution of ground water basins, and purify wastewater to safe levels for use in community landscaping, industry and recharging ground water supplies.

SAMPLE QUESTIONS
1. What fiscal incentives are needed to support community self-reliance and sustainability? Will these incentives be supported by the residents?
2. How much extra wealth can be retained in a community due to conservation measures such as water and energy conservation and materials recycling? Are the community economic benefits sufficient to motivate residents to support vigorous conservation programs?
3. Will citizens support the investment in infrastructure required to develop local renewable energy, water and material resources?

ommunity programs for recycling and composting along with changed packaging and purchasing patterns, and community composting of yard waste, can lower landfill levels by 50-90%. However, recycling is only complete if the end product is reused by industries such as paper mills, steel mills, bottling plants, etc.

According to international business and government consultant Karl-Henrik Robert, humans have been disrupting the cyclical processes of nature at an accelerating pace for roughly the past 100 years. All human societies, in varying degrees, now process natural resources in a linear direction, rapidly transforming them into useless garbage. A small part of this garbage is seen in dumps and as other visible waste. But the larger portion, which escapes our awareness, is "molecular garbage" — vast quantities of tiny particles that are daily spewed out into the earth's air, water and soil.

With few exceptions, none of this garbage finds its way back into the cycles of society or nature; it is not taken up for repeated use by industry, nor put back into the soil. As a result of poor or non-existent planning, the volume of garbage is too large for nature to reassimilate, and some of it — toxic metals and stable unnatural compounds — cannot be processed by the cells at all.

The earth was once clean, healthy and nurturing, and can be again if we will make the choice to clean up our mess. First, we must stop dumping and start recycling, reusing everything. Second, we must support development of industries using recycled materials, change our farming, manufacturing, packaging, waste disposal, transportation and energy systems to non-polluting technologies reducing and eventually eliminating pollution of all kinds. Long-life toxic substances, such as nuclear waste and chemical pesticides, must stop being produced; they must be closely monitored above ground for what may be human eternity in some cases. Third, we must start the clean-up now.

PRINCIPLE 7

Establish Recycling Programs and Recycled Materials Industries

SAMPLE DESIGN & POLICY CRITERIA

1. Establish community recycling facilities and programs such as curbside pickup of recyclables, backyard composting bins, community drop-off and buy-back centers, and toxic substance collection stations.
2. Create economic and policy incentives that encourage the use of non-toxic biodegradable materials.
3. Set landfill tipping fees at levels that encourage reduction in the amount of wastes generated.
4. Establish policy and economic incentives that help create strong markets for recycled materials and facilitate siting of local recycling industries. Support the establishment of regional facilities to recycle bulk materials such as construction debris, thus diverting them from landfills. These facilities could be supported by fees from the waste generators and the sale of the recyclable materials recovered, e.g., wood chips, metal, concrete and asphalt.

SAMPLE QUESTIONS

1. In what volume and proportion are recyclable materials found in the average community wastestream?
2. How effective are existing community recycling programs?
3. Can relatively small local industries utilize recyclables generated in the local community?
4. What kinds of market and voluntary incentives can be created to prevent illegal dumping?

PRINCIPLE 8

Support Broad-Based Education for Participatory Governance

The original twenty-five page booklet, Ecological Planning Principles for Sustainable Living in Ventura County, is available from:

Citizen Planners of Ventura County
509 Marin Street
Suite 131
Thousand Oaks, CA 91360
(805) 495-1025

T he implementation of ecological planning principles is strengthened by public education and the building of consensus through citizen participation in the planning and policy-making process. By participating in public forums, citizens can better understand the issues, discover common ground, develop a common vision and support positive action. Consensus is based on the belief that each person has a part of the truth.

It has been said that the greatest number of individual perspectives reveals the larger truth. If this idea is applied to discover common ground among the citizens of your area, the democratic ideal of a government "of the people, by the people, and for the people", takes on a new meaning. Through effective citizen participation, the present adversarial, win-lose model of conflict and deadlock can be replaced with agreement and action from a posture of cooperation and stewardship.

"Stewardship is an attitude which when held by a large number of people makes participatory governance happen efficiently. Stewardship is at the other end of the spectrum from narrow self-interest. The posture of stewardship comes from seeing that as individuals, we will always necessarily see only a piece of the puzzle and that to be the best stewards we can be, we must learn from others, particularly those who see differently from us. The people we have the most disagreement with are probably the people from whom we can learn the most and with whom we can be the most productive stewards, when we can find that common ground. The common ground is always there, it already exists, the challenge is to uncover it together." (J. W. "John" Ballard.) A great tragedy of our low density, automobile-dependent, single-use life style is the resulting isolation, separation and alienation that overcomes so many people. As a society, many are losing the skills of cordial neighborly association and cooperation.

SAMPLE DESIGN & POLICY CRITERIA

1. Establish a meeting place within each community and utilize advanced communication technologies to form a network within and between communities, including electronic participation from home.
2. Establish consensus building processes with a clear commitment to discover common ground and to reach an understanding that with veto power comes responsibility.
3. Encourage elected officials and government staff, along with the business community, to take part fully as citizens in the participatory planning process.
4. Establish effective education and training programs for lay people in planning and citizen participation.

SAMPLE QUESTIONS

1. What incentives can be established to encourage participation in community meetings and/or electronic participation from home?
2. Can special-interest groups from all sides help fund participatory processes and still keep the processes objective?
3. What is the potential for regional education, coordination and cooperation in planning, policy and decision-making?
4. Can citizen-based networking groups be formed in all cities to play integral, active roles in all phases of the planning process?

THE PEDESTRIAN POCKET: NEW STRATEGIES FOR SUBURBAN GROWTH

Peter Calthorpe, AIA

The current round of suburban growth is generating a crisis of many dimensions: mounting traffic congestion, diminishing affordable housing, receding open space, and stressful social patterns. The truth is, we are using planning strategies which are forty years old and no longer relevant to today's needs. Our household makeup has changed dramatically, the workplace and work force have been transformed, real wealth is shrinking, and serious environmental concerns have surfaced. But we are still building World War II suburbs as if families were large and had only one breadwinner, as if the jobs were all downtown, as if land and energy were endless, and as if another lane on the freeway would end traffic congestion.

This proposal is for an alternative suburban pattern of growth, the Pedestrian Pocket. The Pedestrian Pocket is a simple cluster of housing, retail space, and offices within a quarter-mile walking radius of a light rail system. The convenience of the car and the opportunity to walk would be blended in an environment in which the economic engine of new growth, jobs in the service and information industry, would be balanced with affordable housing and local stores. It is a planning strategy which would preserve open space, and reduce auto traffic without increasing density in existing neighborhoods. By its clustering, the Pedestrian Pocket would allow people a choice of walking, driving or the convenient use of mass transit. These pockets would reconnect an existing suburban fabric and its towns by the creation of new light rail lines and a corresponding upzoning at each of its stations. The increments of growth are small, but the whole system would accommodate regional growth with minimal environmental impact: less land consumed, less traffic generated, less pollution produced.

The Pedestrian Pocket is a concept for some new growth; it is not intended to displace urban-renewal efforts, and it will certainly not totally eclipse typical suburban sprawl. It will, however, extend the range of choices available to the home buyer, the business seeking relocation, the environmentalist seeking to preserve open space, and the existing communities attempting to balance the benefits of growth with liabilities.

THE NEW SUBURBAN CONDITION

There is a profound mismatch between the old suburban patterns of settlement we have evolved since World War II and the post-industrial culture we now find ourselves in. This mismatch is generating traffic congestion, a dearth of affordable and appropriate housing forms, environmental stress, loss of irreplaceable open space, and lifestyles that burden working families as well as isolate elderly people and single households. This mismatch has two primary sources: a dramatic shift in the nature and location of our workplace and a fundamental change in the character of our increasingly diverse households.

Peter Calthorpe was named by **Newsweek Magazine** *as an "innovator on the cutting edge" for his work redefining the models of urban and suburban growth in America. Since 1983, this award-winning architect/planner's firm has planned projects for over 40,000 acres. His special emphasis is on creating mixed-use communities which are environmentally sound, economically feasible and socially progressive.*

Calthorpe & Associates
246 First Street #400
San Francisco, CA 94105
(415) 777-0181

Mixed-use / village green. South Brentwood Village, Brentwood, California.

Traffic congestion in the suburbs is the signal of a deep shift in the structure of our culture. The computer and the service industry have led to the decentralization of the workplace, causing new traffic patterns and "suburban gridlock". Where downtown employment once dominated, suburb-to-suburb traffic patterns now produce greater commute distances and driving time. Over 40% of all commute trips are now from suburb to suburb. These new patterns have seriously eroded the quality of life in formerly quiet suburban towns. In the San Francisco Bay area, for example, 212 miles of the region's 812 miles of suburban freeway are regularly backed up during rush hours. That figure is projected to double within the next 12 years. As a result, recent polls have traffic continually heading the list as the primary regional problem followed only by the difficulty of finding good affordable housing.

Home ownership has become a troublesome — if not unattainable — goal, even with our double-income families. Affordable housing is growing ever more elusive and families have to move to cheaper but distant peripheral sites, consuming irreplaceable agricultural land and overloading the roads. In 1970 about half of all families could afford a median-priced single-family home; today less than a quarter can. And the basic criteria for housing have changed dramatically as single occupants, single parents, the elderly, and small double-income families redefine the traditional home.

> *Our old suburbs are designed around a stereotypical household which is no longer so prevalent.*

Our old suburbs are designed around a stereotypical household which is no longer so prevalent. Of the approximate 17 million new households to be formed in the 80s, 51% will be occupied by single people and unrelated individuals, 22% by single-parent families, and only 27% by married couples with or without children. Of the percentage with children, the family now typically has two workers. Close to half of the single households will be elderly people over 65 and will make up 23% of the total of new homeowners. Certainly the traditional three-bedroom, single-family residence is relevant to a decreasing segment of the population. Add to this the problem of affordability, and the suburban dream becomes even more complicated.

In addition to these dominant problems of housing and traffic, longer-range problems of pollution, open-space preservation, prime agricultural land conversion, and growing infrastructure costs add to the crisis of our post-industrial sprawl. Along with this is a growing sense of frustration and placelessness, a fractured quality in our suburban mega-centers, which overlays the unique qualities of each place with chainstore architecture, scaleless office parks, and monotonous subdivisions.

THE SERVICE ECONOMY: DRIVING TO DECENTRALIZATION

As new jobs have shifted from blue collar to white and grey, the computer has allowed the decentralization of the new service industries into mammoth low-rise office parks on cheap and sometimes remote sites. The shift is dramatic from 1973 to 1985, when five million blue-collar jobs were lost nationwide, while the service and knowledge fields gained from 82 to 110 million jobs. This translated directly into new office complexes, with 1.1 billion square feet of new office space constructed. Nationwide, these complexes have moved outside the central cities with the percentage of total office space in the suburbs shifting from 25% in 1970 to 57% in 1984.

Central to this shift is a phenomenon called the "back-office," the new sweat-shop of the post-industrial economy. The typical back-office is large, often with a single floor area of one to two acres. On an average, about 80% of its employees are clerical, 12% supervisory, and only 8% management. In a survey of criteria for back-office locations, 47 major Manhattan corporations ranked cost of space first, followed by the quality of the labor pool and site safety. These criteria led directly to the suburbs, where the land is cheap, parking easy, and where, most importantly, the workforce is supplemented by housewives: college-educated, poorly paid, non-unionized, and dependable.

> *The Pedestrian Pocket is defined as a balanced, mixed-use area within a 1/4-mile walking radius of a light rail station.*

This back-office explosion has rejuvenated suburban growth just as urban "gentrification" seems to have run its course. The young urban professional has recently become a family person and the draw of the suburbs is being felt. Therefore, most of the growth areas in the U.S. are suburban in character: built from freeways, office parks, shopping malls, and single-family-dwelling subdivisions. Although such growth continually seems to reach its limits with auto congestion and building moratoriums, there are no readily available alternatives to enrich the dialogue between growth and no-growth factions, between the public benefit and private gain, between environmentalists and businesspersons.

THE PEDESTRIAN POCKET: A POST-INDUSTRIAL SUBURB

Single-function land-use zoning at a scale and density which eliminate the pedestrian has been the norm for so long that Americans have forgotten that walking could be part of their daily lives. Certainly, the present suburban environment is unwalkable, much to the detriment of children, their chauffeur parents, the elderly, and the general health of the population and its environment. Urban redevelopment is a strong and compelling alternative to the suburban world, but doesn't seem to fit the character or aspirations of major parts of our population or of many businesses. Mixed-use new towns are not an alternative at this time, because the political consensus needed to back the massive infrastructure investments is lacking. By default, growth is directed mainly by the locations of new freeway systems, the economic strength of the region, and standard single-use zoning practices. Environmental and local opposition to growth only seems to spread the problem, either transferring the congestion to the next county or creating lower and more auto-dependent densities.

Much smaller than a new town, the Pedestrian Pocket is defined as a balanced, mixed-use area within a 1/4-mile walking radius of a light rail station. The uses within this zone of approximately 50 to 120 acres would include housing, back-offices, retail, daycare, recreation and open space. Up to 2,000 units of housing and 1,000,000 sq. ft. of office space can be located within three blocks of the light rail station, using typical condominium densities and four-story office configurations.

The Pedestrian Pockets would act in concert with new transit lines, reinforcing ridership along a line which connects existing employment centers, towns and neighborhoods. Light rail lines are currently under construction in many suburban environments in Sacramento, San Jose, San Diego, Long Beach and Orange County in California alone. They emphasize the economies of using existing rights-of-way and a simpler, more cost-effective technology than heavy rail. In creating a line of Pedestrian Pockets, the public sector's role is merely to organize the transit system and set new zoning guidelines, leaving development to the private sector. Much of the cost of the transit line could be covered by assessing the property owner who benefits from the windfall increased densities. Diversity and architectural interest would be the product of individual developers and homeowners building small sections of the Pockets independently.

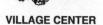

VILLAGE CENTER

The lightrail station area would be bordered by ground floor retail and neighborhood services. The office courtyard and the "main street" would intersect in a public plaza.

The commercial center of the Pedestrian Pocket would mix large back-office jobs with ground floor stores, restaurants and smaller businesses. All employees would be within walking distance of the station. Cars would circulate on the shopping street, and parking structures would provide for those who choose to drive.

The Pedestrian Pocket would accommodate the car as well as public transit. Parking would be provided for all housing and commercial space. The housing types would be standard low-rise, high-density forms such as three-story walk-up apartments and two-story townhouses. Only the interrelationships and adjacent land use would change. People would have a choice: walk to work or walk to a store within the Pedestrian Pocket; take the light rail to work or shop at another station; drive on crowded freeways. Within a small Pedestrian Pocket, 1,000 homes are within walking distance of a typical neighborhood shopping center, several three-acre parks, daycare, various services, and 2,000 jobs. Within four stops of the light rail in either direction (ten minutes) is employment for 16,000, or the equivalent back-office growth of Contra Costa County, California, one of the nation's high-growth suburbs during the last five years.

The light rails in current use provide primarily a park-and-ride system to link low-density sprawl with downtown commercial areas. In contrast, the Pedestrian Pocket system would be decentralized, linking many nodes of higher-density housing with many commercial destinations. Peak-hour traffic would be multi-directional, reducing congestion and making the system more efficient. The office would be right at the station, avoiding the need for secondary mass transit or large parking areas. Additionally, locating retail and services near the offices would make arriving without a car more practical, since mid-day errands could be handled on foot.

Express bus systems could not substitute for light rail, because their peak capacity is lower and they couldn't sustain the land values needed for mixed-use development. However, existing bus systems could tie into the light rail along with car-pool systems. Several of the Pockets on a line would have large parking facilities for park-and-ride access, allowing the existing suburban development to enjoy the services and opportunities of the Pedestrian Pockets.

The importance of the Pedestrian Pocket is that it would provide balanced growth in jobs, housing and services, while creating a healthy mass-transit alternative for the existing community. But the key lies in the form and mix of the Pocket. The pedestrian path system must be carefully designed and form a primary order for the place. If this is configured to allow the pedestrian comfortable and safe access, up to 50% of a household's typical auto trips could be replaced by walking, and light rail journeys. Not only does it make for a better living environment within the pocket, but the reduction of traffic in the region would be significant.

HOUSING: DIVERSITY IN NEEDS AND MEANS

Housing in the Pedestrian Pocket is planned to meet the needs of each of the primary household types with affordable homes. For families with children, single parents or couples, an environment in which kids could move safely, in which daycare is integrated into the neighborhood, and in which commute time is reduced, would be very desirable. The townhouses and duplexes proposed for the Pedestrian Pocket would allow such families to have this with an attached garage, land ownership, and a small private yard. These building types are more affordable to build and maintain than their detached counterparts, while still offering simple ownership and a private identity. And the common open space, recreation, daycare and convenient shopping would make these houses even more desirable. Common play areas are located off the townhouses' private yards, and are connected to the central park and the commercial section by paths. One-third of the housing in the Pockets would be this type.

For singles and "empty-nesters", traditional two- and three-story apartment buildings or condominiums are even more affordable, while sharing in the civic, retail, and recreational amenities of the extended community. This segment of the population is traditionally more mobile and would have an option of rental or ownership housing. Elderly housing could be located close to the parks, light rail, and service retail. This would eliminate some of the distance and alienation of their current housing facilities. The housing would be formed into courtyard clusters of two-story buildings, to provide a private retreat area and the capacity for common facilities for dining and social activities. Living in a pedestrian community would allow the elderly to become a part of our everyday culture again, and to enjoy the parks, stores, and restaurants close at hand.

Several parks would double as paths to the station area, a route which is pleasant and free of auto crossings. The housing overlooking the park would provide security surveillance and 24-hour activity. Within each park would be daycare buildings and general recreation facilities that could vary from Pocket to Pocket. Although the housing would be formed into small clusters, the central park and facilities would tend to unify the neighborhood, giving it an identity and sense of community missing in most of our suburban tracts. The centers would be used and maintained by an organization, much like a condominium homeowners association, which includes landlords, townhouse owners, tenants, office managers, and worker representatives.

AFFORDABLE HOUSING

Family housing would cluster around a large common open space connected to the central green, daycare and store. Each townhouse would have a private yard area and an attached garage. Children would have free access to common open space, daycare and central facilities.

The goal of this tight mix of housing and open space is not just to provide more appropriate homes for the different users or to offer the convenience of walking, but hopefully to reintegrate the currently separated age and social types of our diverse culture. The shared common spaces and local stores may create a rebirth of our often lost sense of community and place.

COMMERCE AND COMMUNITY

Jobs are the fuel of new growth, of which the service and high-tech fields are the spearhead. For example, the San Francisco Bay area has currently about 63% of all its jobs in these areas, with that proportion expected to increase in the next 20 years, adding about 200,000 new jobs in the high-tech area and 370,000 new jobs in the service areas. Retail activity and housing growth always follow in proportion to these primary income generators. The Pedestrian Pocket provides a framework for these jobs, and housing to grow in tandem.

> *The Pedestrian Pocket provides a framework for jobs and housing to grow in tandem.*

The commercial buildings in the Pocket provide retail opportunities at their ground floor with offices above. The retail would enjoy the local walk-in trade from offices and housing, as well as exposure to the light rail and drive-in customers. All the stores would face a "main street" on which the light rail line, station, and convenient parking for cars would be mixed. This multiple exposure and access, along with the office workers, would create a strong market for roughly 100,000 sq. ft. of retail business.

The offices above the retail stores would provide space for smaller entrepreneurial businesses, start-up firms, and local services for the community. Behind all this would be parking structures capable of providing space for one-half the workers in all the commercial space. It is assumed that the other half would walk, carpool, or arrive by light rail.

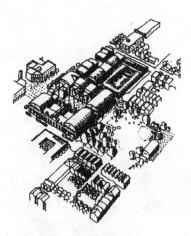

INCREMENTAL GROWTH

Architectural diversity and interest in the Pedestrian Pocket would be insured by having different developers for each section of the site. Townhouse lots would be built by individuals, and clusters by housing co-ops. Different commercial parcels would be developed incrementally in balance with housing and demand.

The large back-offices would share facilities and open space with the neighborhood, and would have both auto and light rail access. At 500,000 to 1,000,000 sq. ft. potential in two to four buildings per Pedestrian Pocket, these four-story buildings with 60,000 sq. ft. floors would fit the size and cost criteria of most large back-office employers. The building would be formed around courtyards that opened to the station on one side, and the park on the other. The workers would enjoy the opportunity to shop nearby, use the park, visit their children at the daycare, or visit any number of restaurants in the Pocket. Space for theaters, library, post office, food stores, and other daily needs would all be developed in the nearly 100,000 sq. ft. of ground-floor commercial space.

The goal of the commercial mix would be to balance the housing with a desirable job market, stores, entertainment, and services. The commercial facilities and the offices would not be financially dependent only on the local housing; drive-access from the existing neighborhoods and people passing on the light rail would be an important segment of the support. Similarly, it is important to recognize that workers will travel from a large "employee shed" of up to twenty miles, connected by the light rail and other transit modes.

REGIONAL PLANNING AND THE PEDESTRIAN POCKET

Pedestrian Pockets are not meant to be stand-alone developments, but are intended to form a long-range growth network within a region. They will vary considerably, given the complexities of place and their varying internal makeup. The quarter-mile walking radius actually encloses 120 acres, although some Pockets may be as small as 60 acres. Some may have a different focus: one providing a regional shopping center, one a cultural center, a third simply housing and recreation. Some may be used to provide economic incentives in a depressed area as a redevelopment tool, others may rejuvenate aging shopping areas, others may be located in new areas currently zoned for low-density sprawl over a large area and serve to save much of the land from development.

But it is also important to use the Pockets and their rail line as a connector of the existing assets of an area. Certainly the major towns, office parks, shopping areas, and government facilities should be linked by the system. And several of the Pockets should offer an opportunity for park-and-ride, so that existing housing in the region could take advantage of the rail line. Many new light rail systems which are built only to connect existing low-density development, are experiencing some resistance from people who do not want to leave their cars. The importance of re-zoning for a comfortable walking distance from house to station is to ease people out of their cars, to give them an alternative that is convenient and pleasing.

LEXINGTON PARK. Polk County, Florida

As an example of this regional planning, I have taken an area north of San Francisco, combining Marin and Sonoma counties. This area is considered by many as prime turf for new post-industrial sprawl. Sonoma is projected to have a 61% growth in employment in the next 20 years, the highest in the Bay region. Combined, these areas are to grow by about 88,000 jobs in the next 15 years and by about 63,000 households. Of the new jobs, about 60,000 will be in the service, high-tech, and knowledge fields, the equivalent of 20 million sq. ft. of office and light industrial space. With standard planning techniques, this growth will consume massive quantities of open space, and will necessitate a major expansion of the freeway system. The result would still involve frustrating traffic jams.

By contrast, 20 Pedestrian Pockets along a new light rail line could accommodate this office growth with matching retail, support business and about 30,000 new houses. With several additional pockets dedicated primarily to housing, two-thirds of the area's home demand will be met while linking the counties' main cities with a viable mass-transit system. A recently acquired Northwestern Pacific Railroad abandoned right-of-way connecting a San Francisco ferry terminal to the northernmost county seat will form the spine for such a new pattern of growth.

SOCIAL AND ENVIRONMENTAL FORM

It is easy to talk quantitatively about the physical and environmental consequences of urban sprawl, but very difficult to postulate their social implications. Many argue that there is no longer a causal relationship between the structure of our physical environment and human well-being or social health. We are adaptable, they claim, and our communities are formed around interest groups and work, rather than by any sense of place or group of individuals. Our center seems to be more abstract, less grounded in place, and our social forms are more disconnected from home and neighborhood. Simultaneously, planning ideology has been polarized between urban and suburban forms. Some have advocated a rigorous return to traditional city forms and an almost pre-industrial culture, while others have praised the evolution of the suburban megalopolis as the inevitable and desirable expression of our new technologies and hyper-individualized culture. However rationalized, these new forms seem to have a restless and hollow feel, reinforcing our mobile state and perhaps the instability of our families. Moving at a speed that allows generic symbols to be recognized, we cannot wonder that the humanmade environment seems trite and overstated.

In proposing the Pedestrian Pocket, the practical comes first: that land, energy, and resources would be saved, that traffic would be reduced, that homes would be more affordable, that children and elderly would have more access, that working people would not be burdened with long commutes. The social consequences are less quantitative, but perhaps equally compelling. They have to do with the quality of our shared world, our commons.

The traditional commons, which once centered our communities with convivial gathering and meeting places, is increasingly displaced by corridors of mobility and the private domain. Our shared public space is given over to the car and its accommodation, while our private world becomes bloated and isolated. As the private world grows in breadth, the public world becomes more remote

GROWTH AND PRESERVATION

Balancing and clustering jobs, housing, shopping, recreation and childcare, the Pedestrian Pocket uses 1/16 the land area of typical suburban development. Open space and precious agricultural land could be preserved, along with a region's growth.

A lightrail line within a comfortable walking distance of all development connects several Pockets with local towns and cities to provide an alternative to freeway congestion.

Diverse open space would be provided in the Pedestrian Pocket; private yards for the families; open space for a group of houses; central parks to be used by all; courtyards and a "main street" shopping area around the station at the center. Walking paths connect the whole site without crossing any streets.

and impersonal. As a result, our public space lacks identity, and is largely anonymous, while our private space lacks identity, is also largely anonymous, and strains toward a narcissistic autonomy. Our communities are zoned black and white, private or public, my space or nobody's. The auto destroys the joys of urban streets, the shopping center destroys neighborhood stores, and depersonalization of public space grows with the scale of government. Inversely, private space is strained by the physical need to provide for many activities that were once shared, and is further burdened by the need to create some identity in a surrounding sea of monotony. Although the connection between such social issues and development is elusive and complex, it must be addressed by any serious theory of growth.

In a way, Pedestrian Pockets are utopian — they involve the conscious choice of an ideal rather than laissez-faire planning, and they make certain assumptions about social well-being. But they are not utopian in that they do not assume a transformation of our society or its people. They represent, instead, a response to a transformation that has already expressed itself, the transformation from the industrial forms of segregation and centralization to the decentralized and integrated forms of the post-industrial era. And, perhaps, Pedestrian Pockets can express the positive environmental and social results of a culture adjusting itself to this new reality.

A SENSE OF PLACE: RETROFITTING OLDER NEIGHBORHOODS

Adapted from a presentation given at the First Los Angeles Ecological Cities Conference

Sam Hall Kaplan

After 12 years as the architecture and design critic for the **L.A. Times**, *Sam Hall Kaplan is now putting his ideas into practice as principal in the West Coast office of Ehrenkrantz, Eckstut & Whitlaw. Working from the premise that urban design is recognizing your responsibility to your user, neighbor, community and city, his special focus is creating a viable urban design out of existing communities.*

Ehrenkrantz, Eckstut &
*   Whitlaw*
823 20th Street
Santa Monica, CA 90403

No slides today! I'm trying something different, because I have gotten quite prejudiced against slides. Especially for what I want to talk about this afternoon.

Slides and pictures tend to be fanciful. We've gotten so used to packaging things based on how they look, not how they work. We're getting used to looking at images of other communities that may bear no relationship to us at all, and these pictures tend to generate false expectations. I want to move away from that.

The wonderful thing about L.A., which we all keep on trashing, is that there are hundreds of different communities. There are many varied worlds off those freeways, just waiting to be discovered. When I had this great travel/study grant for the *L.A. Times* (which they called being a critic), it allowed me access into lots of these communities. And each expressed itself in unique ways. So what works for Santa Monica, what works for Beverly Hills, doesn't work for East L.A., doesn't work for North Central, or doesn't work for South Pasadena, which has landmark oak trees in the middle of its streets.

So, sort of close your eyes and say what works in Laguna may not work in Brentwood, may not work someplace else. Because, thank goodness, every place is different.

What I want us to think about, and what I think is so exciting about this conference, is that we're talking about cultural context. That's what we're designing around. Too many of us still act like we're in a throw-away city: "Hey, this ain't working anymore, let's move to Irvine, or Laguna South." You name it, everybody's on the move. "Hey, Santa Barbara! I heard it's pretty good!" And we keep on abandoning our neighborhoods where we live.

I think the real challenge is not in the suburbs, as pretty as they may be. It is not starting to plow over our vanishing farmland, creating false lakes. The real challenge is in our existing communities and on our streets. We just can't afford to throw away communities ever again. It's time we start looking around, not at models elsewhere, but at what can be done where we live right now.

I'm convinced it's not design (I'm saying this as a designer) that people are searching for. It's not about that pretty idealized picture, but rather about a sense of place. A community where they feel secure and happy, where they can let go of their children's hands and let them walk without always worrying. That's why I think Disneyland is the biggest pedestrian experience in the world. What do we learn from it? We learn questions of visual scale, comfort, and security. People are happy to get out of their cars, and happy to get on a tram, albeit, they pay for it. The question is can we create environments where you don't have to pay an admission fee?

And this gets into the whole issue of retrofitting. You don't want to take away flavor and blend it. I've always figured you find out what's different about your community, and you celebrate it. And there's a need now for what I call "microplanning". Now, it's odd for me to say that. The name of the firm I work for is Ehrenkrantz and Eckstut. We did Chicago's Central Station. We did Battery Park City. We did Inner Harbor, Baltimore. Talk about big! We're doing the Alameda Plan for downtown. And what marks these projects is that we're thinking small. Places are the goal, not projects. You're talking about small rather than large. You're talking about maximizing what exists. No demolition. The familiar should be relied on whenever possible.

We want to deal with public spaces, the nature of our streets. You know, dozens of businesses haven't made any impact in terms of striving to widen the sidewalks and narrow the streets. But that's where I'm absolutely convinced community happens, where communities are formed, and that the streets and our public places are the focus. How can we recapture that? By fronting houses with porches on them? By widening sidewalks? Yes, but also just by looking at the nature of people's use patterns. For example: alleys are great places. I live on an alley, and everybody knows everyone on the alley, because that's where you take out the garbage. That's where you meet the neighbors, that's where the cars are illegally parked. God forbid you should park illegally on the street. And that's where the social fabric is. I wrote a couple of columns on how we could save these alleys and make them into mews.

So what do you do, and how do you do it? We talk about implementation and building a consensus. How do you build a consensus? It's something that has always meant to me: no secrets, none of these developer meetings behind closed doors. It has to be an open process.

In Santa Fe we turned to the community and asked: what do you really like about Santa Fe? What really makes you feel good about it? You could ask that about wherever you live. And what we ultimately came up with was really interesting. We found that people there liked the streets being confused; they liked dead ends. They didn't like the parks, they liked the walkways, and the little paseos. And so you create that which they feel comfortable with.

> *... you find out what's different about your community and you celebrate it.*

It's the same thing that we're looking at in Long Beach. What do they really like about it? And how can we emphasize that? Here's an older city, the coast of Iowa. Take the Pike: how do we start infilling that? Using vacant land to create housing, to create commercial opportunities that add a vibrancy to the place. And I think we just have to stop looking at our suburban models going further out, and start looking at ourselves in our own communities. Because we're just going to keep chasing our tail if we don't.

So the emphasis is on consensus building, with no secrets. The emphasis is on public places. Everybody likes to design a house, a second floor. But if we build public places, if we treat our streets correctly, if we create our parks where housing can surround it, if we do care about the nature of street life, the private sector will take care of itself. I'm convinced that we must concentrate on the nature of our public sector. That is what creates community. And that's why, instead of having a lake that everybody looks at, I'd rather have a community garden. And we must concentrate on having flexibility. And the most important thing and perhaps the most frustrating, is making no grand plans. This must be done on a block by block basis. We're talking incremental. I think the bigger the plan, the bigger chance for failure. It's an excuse not to do something.

And the idea of how do we enjoy the city? If we create a safe, secure environment, where people feel comfortable, we will have an ecologically pure environment. People will care about themselves, care about their neighbors, and care about maintaining their neighborhood, not just as some sort of ideological model up on a wall or handout, but as some place where they can live. How do we deal with South Central in terms of creating block associations and building up better civic identity? Those are the sorts of little things that count. And once you have one small success, once you close a street in Carthay Circle like Darrow did, or close a street off Fairfax, you will find that the kids are playing out there again. And once the kids come out, the neighbors come out. And all of a sudden people are looking out for each other and crime goes down. This is a little bit of success that can be repeated and repeated and repeated. Just as the cancers of the city are repeated.

> *If we create a safe, secure environment, we'll have an ecologically pure environment.*

When people ask if I'm a futurist, I answer: no. Futurism, I always thought, was an excuse not to do anything now. But if we start looking, indeed, at what our own communities are saying, and stop building a sort of utopian community elsewhere, we can come to see that utopia basically exists in our backyard. Utopia exists in us. And we build out from that: The question of a common walkway with a neighbor, the question of a block association getting together and saying "Hey, let's neck the street. Let's create a place where we close one end of the alley so the kids can play. I don't care if the garbage truck can't get in once a week. We'll change something around." It's those little incremental steps that we can build upon. And that's how we infill, that's how we retrofit, and that's how we make a livable place.

There is a wonderful consciousness surrounding this conference. I can feel that energy coming out of the audience. Now if we only can take that energy and turn to ourselves, to our own blocks and our own communities, we'll have that environment we're all searching for.

ECOLOGICAL COMMUNITY DESIGN

Adapted from a presentation given at the First Los Angeles Ecological Cities Conference

Richard Register

I 'm an activist in urban ecology. The first organization I founded, Urban Ecology, is essentially a grassroots organization. We are very involved in local politics and actually trying to build what we think of as an ecologically healthy city.

I'd like to start from a very broad perspective. Right now, we are leaving the Cenozoic geological era and entering into a new era which people like the philosopher Thomas Berry are calling the Ecozoic Era, the era of ecology and life. I hope he's right and believe we have almost no choice but to do that. It's not going to be an easy transition. There are many, many major problems out there. All this brings us to the question: what is it we are really doing on planet Earth? We are appreciating things. We are exploring things through science and art and through trying to understand each other psychologically as human beings. We are discovering things around us. We are creating. We are very creative entities on this planet, like nothing that has ever existed before. Where are we going? Maybe we've lost track, or maybe we've never really explored it properly, because somehow we're destroying at an absolutely enormous rate in the way that we build and in what we are doing on the planet. Let me briefly review some of the issues:

POPULATION — We are now entering the double-baby-boom era. As the baby boomers are now having many babies themselves, the population explosion is actually beginning to speed up. This is a very wealthy country. Runaway population growth is not supposed to happen in very wealthy countries but mostly poor countries.

POLLUTION/SPECIES EXTINCTION — In the air, on the land and in the sea. You've seen slides about it. You know about it from the newspapers and your everyday experience: The ozone holes over the Antarctic and the Arctic, the ongoing destruction of the ozone layer, climate change, extinctions that have not been so serious since the extinction of the dinosaurs 65 million years ago. This is all happening very rapidly, and there is absolutely no going back on this situation. When a species is extinct, it is gone forever.

RESOURCE EXHAUSTION — It took 100 million years of geologic time to put down most of the oil, and we're using it up at about one million years worth every year.

DEFORESTATION — We lose an area of forest the size of Nebraska every year.

LOSS OF AGRICULTURAL LAND — This speaks directly to the subject of ecological cities. Sprawl is overcoming agricultural land at the rate of about three million acres a year, according to the American Farmland Trust. I might mention also that 30% of the agricultural product by value in the United States comes from the 12% of the land that is closest to the cities. So you can see the impact of sprawl on agriculture.

Richard Register is the founding president of Urban Ecology, an organization focused on ecological city design since 1975. He is the convener of the **First International Ecocity Conference** *held in 1990 in Berkeley, has written for numerous magazines on environmental planning and alternative technology, and has authored the book,* **Ecocity Berkeley**, *which has had an impact on many cities. Most recently, he has founded* **Ecocity Builders** *to focus on the creation of built projects.*

Urban Ecology
P.O. Box 10144
Berkeley, CA
(415) 549-1724

Ecocity Builders
5427 Telegraph Avenue W2
Oakland, CA 94609

Since it seems that all this might be building into some sort of mass planetary crescendo and a crash, I wonder about the times we live in, and whether we can summon enough imagination and commitment to actually do something about it. Meantime, we notice that about half the people in the world will be living in cities by the turn of the century. Certainly, three-quarters now live in cities in the developed parts of the world. Cities are at the very heart of the ecological crisis because they are so big. It is as simple as that. The largest things that people create are the cities that we live in. The buildings, the infrastructure, the transportation systems, the cars, trains, and so on.

I could go on in some detail on this, but there are some specifics that are kind of interesting to notice: some strange little items to contemplate that are happening right now. Geo automobiles, for example, is offering to plant one tree for every car that you buy from them. I have calculated it out and discovered that between 600 and 900 trees would have to be planted to make up for the CO_2 produced by one Geo alone. So we have to think more in terms of the overall systems, the whole system, the whole city, not just the vehicle, not just the

> *. . . about half the people in the world will be living in cities by the turn of the century.*

single item. If you put a solar collector on your house, then use 10-12 times as much energy to move about in your automobile as you could possibly collect in your solar collector, what has been the gain? So we have to think deeper than just solar energy or planting trees.

There's the paradox of the efficient automobile. The more efficient the automobile becomes, the more you can travel in it at no apparent increase in cost. There are people in my Berkeley neighborhood who are now moving out to Tracy, 60 miles from San Francisco, and commuting because they think they can do it inexpensively. So obviously, we are going to have to think a lot deeper than we've been doing in a lot of areas. What if we had the perfect solar automobile? Then we're still dealing with massive amounts of asphalt and the loss of agricultural lands. Asphalt is also an oil product, by the way. Cars are riding on tires that are made from an oil product. More and more plastics that are in the cars are made from oil.

So what is the solution to this debacle anyway? It seems to me that when we think about ecologically healthy cities, there are two major approaches we can think about: the mythology and the methodology. With respect to the mythology, we might begin by asking: what is the city? What does it do for us? How is the ecological city part of our nature? In a very real way, as we define the world we live in, we actually are making that world possible. What we define largely determines the results we get. It follows that the way we design ends up being what we get. So there's the mythology. Are we going to commit to building a creative, healthy place for humans to live in, or are we just randomly wandering into the future?

The methodology is another thing. Here we need an insight. The insight is that the way we build very largely determines the way we live. Now most people don't quite grasp this insight because if they did, they would be thinking along very different lines when they think about the way cities are built. For example, I have gone to conference after conference among environmentalists where the word "sprawl" doesn't even come up, or where the way to fix the situation of the automobile is to make the automobile more efficient. So we need the insight that what we build very much determines what it is that can happen, and whether or not it's going to be happy or not, or whether or not it's going to be healthy or advance human evolution in whatever directions we think might be important.

And then there's the unifying term "Ecological City" or "Eco City" which is all right, but beyond that, we need to have tools and strategies for getting there. We need to somehow come up with an overall program as governments and large institutions and businesses do to accomplish particular goals. We need this just as we had to have a program to get out of the depression, or to run a major war or to get to the moon. We have to start thinking about programs to rebuild our cities because the present ones are such a disaster, and because the ones we could be building could be quite exciting.

Here is an image gallery to help illustrate some of my points:

Phoenix, Arizona-style sprawl takes an enormous amount of energy to get around. Basically, what's going on here is almost entirely composed of single-use areas of land at enormous distances from one another. Of course, the city is multi-use but the distances between particular land use functions are enormous, very wasteful and, of course, automobile-dependent. We're all very familiar with that here in Los Angeles.

Another way of building uniform uses is to do it three dimensionally in gigantic boxes. At the World Trade Center in New York City, each tower contains 15,000 people doing work only and only one kind of work—office work—consuming tremendous amounts of energy. There's one zip code for each of these particular structures.

A more diverse way of living, on a more human scale, is exhibited by a town in the south of France, which was created before the automobile, in around 800AD. There, people's work, their friends, their homes, their public life, their shops are all a very short walk within the city.

Turrette-sur-Loup, France

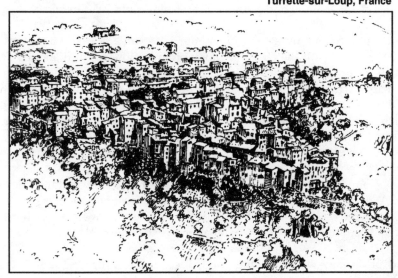

Working with the natural environment was second nature to many of our ancestors. The American Indians in Mesa Verde built under the edge of a cliff. They were protected from a lot of the precipitation and the snow. In the winter, the sun poured in under the cliff warming the dwellings, and, in the summer, the sun was high overhead and the shadows cooled the dwellings. Very simple and very elegant.

Another example are the windscoops commonly used in East Pakistan and other parts of the world. Instead of having electric power plants to cool these places, they simply tap into the natural flow of the wind over that particular part of the world.

The Permaculture people are interested in an agriculture that is more permanent and a culture that can be sustained. They integrate aspects of structure design with natural flows of energy and natural principles. A typical Permaculture residence in Australia will have its solar greenhouse facing north because that continent's orientation to the path of the sun is opposite to ours. An artificial pond may also be created so fish can be raised. The solar greenhouse becomes a nursery for the food that they grow and the building can be protected from cooling winds by a berm of earth on the end opposite the greenhouse. Nuts and berries grow wild in the forest, as a lot of the food in a Permacultural system is produced simply by being planted with very minimal maintenance.

In Arizona, Paolo Soleri is building an experimental town called Arcosanti. Students from around the world go there to theorize about and study Paolo's work and think about ecologically healthy cities of the future.

Arcosanti, Arizona, 1986

More and more buildings around the world are being tuned to the environment. There is a building in Copenhagen which has a solar greenhouse on the south side which works very well. Floyd Stein, the architect/artist, paints on the sides of some of the buildings he has designed and lives in one of them.

Urban Ecology has built a solar greenhouse. It is on a house that several of us bought together with the Urban Ecology organization in San Francisco. On the day that we put the glass in, we got a tremendous surprise. We were expecting it to help warm the house and to start our garden plants. It did those things well. But on the day we put the glass in, we were absolutely amazed because, suddenly, the noisy street outside went silent. This illustrates that there is an opposite to the vicious cycle, what you might call a "virtuous cycle," meaning that when you start doing good things, you start getting pleasant surprises.

Some of our large buildings are even being inhabited by automobiles these days. And, of course one of the largest rooms in most houses these days is the garage. So the fact that the automobile is very much a member of the family pops up in strange ways that may be offensive to some ecologists.

In Urban Ecology we take some of our ideas to the street in funny ways. We turned a car into a planter box. It is a monument to the first automobile fatality, which took place in New York in 1899. A fellow named H.H. Bliss was run over by an electric taxi, probably the best of all possible cars. Once somebody who had seen our planter box said, "Well this is terrible. What if everyone did that to their car?" And I thought that was a very good fantasy to think about.

All around the world now, especially in northern Europe, there are efforts to do what's called "street calming." The people themselves, the planners, and everyone who cares about this, gets out there and slows down cars in various ways. In one instance, the neighbors took it into their own hands to do something and simply wrote "Kids on the Street" on the pavement in the middle of the street, and it worked pretty admirably to slow traffic down on that hill.

Another idea is to either leave trees when you build streets or if it's too late to do that in an already existing city, you can simply replace them. That might sound like it's a difficult thing to accomplish when one has to work with City Hall, but it's worth trying. In some places it actually happens.

Another notion that I thought of as a joke when I wrote the book, *Ecocity Berkeley: Building Cities for a Healthy Future*, was putting freeways underground, because I thought that's where people should be if they're despoiling the atmosphere, so they actually live with what they are creating. But the idea struck me

A good place for freeways.

as a little crazy until I discovered that some places have actually done it. In Seattle they have designed Freeway Park. The freeway goes under the park for two blocks, and they've made this nice waterfall where people on their lunch breaks like to sit and listen to the sound of the water. It's a very interesting and lovely environment.

Another way to calm the streets is to make them narrower. Engineers are constantly making streets wider. You can simply turn it around and make them narrower.

One of my fantasy illustrations depicts food gardens appearing on the north side of the street as well as south facing greenhouses and so on. In Berkeley, Urban Ecology got together with some of its neighbors and redesigned one of the streets. We call it a slow street. Parking moves from one side of the street to the other as you go from the first half of the block to the second, creating a weave in the street, and we've put bumps in the street, so that the cars have to go slower. These are very gentle bumps. You basically don't feel them very much at 15 mph; at 20 mph you start to feel them, and at 25 mph it's pretty bad.

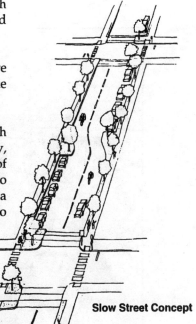

Slow Street Concept

In Europe, the residential street is becoming very popular as a place where cars mostly park. In Oslo, they will take a street, turn it into a parking lot and make the automobile driver almost feel like a guest in somebody's living room. One of the ways to do this is to take the curbs away. It has a very interesting psychological effect. Another way is to simply block off the streets that you want to have quiet and get people to use transit more.

In San Francisco, they have done the same thing for certain hours. At eleven o'clock in the morning, a street closes and becomes a café called Maiden Lane in downtown San Francisco. At three o'clock in the afternoon, the café folds up its chairs and the traffic comes back to the street.

Then there are many different kinds of bicycle streets and paths all around the world, and they are getting much more popular. The bicycle is an incredibly elegant energy-saving device. You can ride about eight times as far on a bicycle for the same breakfast as you can walk — Very, very efficient means of transportation.

In Europe, of course, a lot of people simply hop on their bicycles, no matter what the weather is. You just have to have good rainy weather gear.

In a suburb just outside of Copenhagen, they have another trick. They cover their bicycles with little plastic shields, so when it's raining you have a dry seat to sit on instead of a wet one. Very simple, yet it makes a difference for a lot of people.

If we're talking about the foot mode of transport, transportation alternatives can include bridges between buildings. In San Francisco, there are nine bridges connecting the new towers of the California Center. Bridges between some other buildings can be on a more intimate scale and quite wonderful.

In Berkeley, people have taken sails to skateboards and zip around on flat surfaces.

The French have a luxury cruise ship called the Windstar which gets 60% of its energy from the wind. It travels the South Pacific where it takes tourists between the islands. More and more commerce might end up being accomplished with ships like this.

Rooftop gardens bring ecology into the city — right onto the tops of the buildings. In Oakland there is a garden that looks like any public park, but if you get up in the building and look back down, you'll notice it's on the top of a six-story garage. The secret is to put the trees on the pillars instead of the spans.

Bridges between buildings.

You can tear up your own sidewalk, as we did in front of our building, provided you leave enough to walk on. Sidewalks are often paved all the way to the curb, but they really don't have to be. Now we have an apricot and an apple tree in front of our house, which produce a lot of food for our neighbors as well as ourselves.

One of the most exciting things about the ecological cities idea is to bring back to the cities the really rich environments like the marshes and the creeks. In Berkeley, we made some stencils and went around identifying all the creeks. We got the City Council to give us permission to do this. Now everywhere that there is a creek running under a street, we have marked the curbs with the name of the creek. Last year at the First International Ecocity Conference, we celebrated the creeks by flying banners downtown celebrating the twelve creeks of Berkeley, which are about 80% underground.

One of my favorite projects that brings many pieces together started with a parking garage in Berlin, where the neighbors got together and politically managed to change the usage. It was a four-level parking garage, and now it's a daycare center and a nursery school instead. They simply took a masonry saw and cut through the slab, opened up an atrium on the inside to bring air and light into the interior, and built trellises for plants.

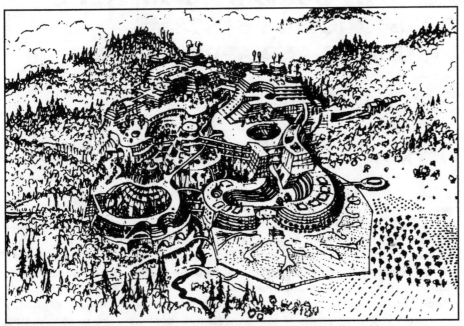

Compact city of canyons and bridges in a canyon with access by train and foot. Greenhouses and agriculture on one quarter, forest surrounding.

Included here is one of my future images. It is a fantasy of layers of artificial land, one built on another. The notion of platforms is used so that the architect becomes a kind of interior decorator for building exteriors. You get from one layer to the next by bridges. Here you see agriculture on the downhill side, facing south in this case; greenhouses collecting warmth for the buildings; a slight climate change in the interior canyons; people buzzing overhead on bicycle or on foot between the buildings; a different kind of climate in the buildings but still open to the air that blows through; windmills on the tops of some of the buildings; train connection to the outside world; and so on. An Ecological City designed from scratch.

No one will ever agree on when we will have an ecocity because ecocities are a direction, not a destination. No city stands still. Each is a dynamic dance of stone, wood, flesh, and shimmering energy flows, an interplay of the ancient forces of nature and history upon the volatile spirit of humanity.

In Berkeley, we are rethinking the city in terms of centers of walkable distances. If you examine these distances over a period of time, the city begins to withdraw into more

> *The principles by which nature designs its living creatures can be adopted by us human beings in our own designs.*

compact areas in certain parts of town, opening up in others, and eventually looking like a series of smaller cities with open space in between.

It all comes down to this: Design is the process by which form comes into being through time. Nature is always doing it. People do it too, but sometimes unconsciously or badly. The principles by which nature designs its living creatures, and the environments they inhabit and help create, can be adopted by us human beings in our own designs.

All illustrations reprinted from **Ecocity Berkeley** *by Richard Register.*

HEALTHY BUILDING: LOW TOXIC CONSTRUCTION SYSTEMS, PRODUCTS AND APPROACHES

Paul Bierman-Lytle, AIA

Paul Bierman-Lytle is President of The Masters Corporation and Environmental Outfitters and a member of the AIA Steering Committee on the Environment. In addition to having built over 50 custom homes, he is co-author of Home Safe Home *and has appeared on a worldwide basis as one of this country's leading advocates for non-toxic building.*

Masters Corporation
P.O. Box 514
New Canaan, CT 06840
(203) 966-3541

T he subject of indoor air quality in buildings is important for one very simple reason: People are getting sick from occupying buildings, whether offices, schools, or homes. In order to understand the problem, indoor air quality is being studied on many fronts by NASA, the Navy, the Department of Energy, E.P.A., A.I.A., regional utility companies, universities, and private consumer agencies. Also, indoor air quality is now included in most building conference agendas. In Europe, particularly Scandinavia and West Germany, the subject is so important that it has its own dedicated international conferences. However, understanding indoor air quality in buildings and its effects on human health is still in its infant stage. In fact, if there is one thing that all the various indoor air quality professionals can agree on, it is that we need more data, more studies and more information.

With the advent of modern efficient construction, indoor health symptoms known as the "sick building syndrome" have become a familiar topic. Energy efficiency techniques in building, though not entirely responsible for these health reactions, do contribute by requiring tighter outdoor and indoor air management, more insulation, and a variety of active and passive solar systems. Conventional, everyday building components, products, and techniques are also responsible, posing serious health hazards not only to the occupants, but to the installer or builder as well.

Part of the problem in understanding indoor air quality issues is that a building is a very complex object. Like the human body, it has a skeleton, skin, air exchange apparatus, plumbing, and electricity. It also requires upkeep and maintenance to prevent it from performing poorly, cracking, peeling, and getting sick. In some instances, sickness can be the result of an isolated product, system, or natural phenomenon. Examples would be high levels of radon, mold, decay, fungus growth, or formaldehyde released from a newly installed carpet or newly urethane-coated wood floor. A more serious problem is the gradual, long-term exposure to low levels of off-gassing contaminants from more than 60,000 building and decorating products. Children and the elderly are particularly at risk.

In addition to poorly designed or installed "systems" (such as air, heating and cooling), poor building design (such as locating the garage under bedrooms), natural health hazards (such as radon), the quality of domestic water supplies (polluted with lead and pesticides), there is mold, fungus, dust-mites, indoor pollen, and dust. A building is, indeed, a complicated "animal." It may take many years of research to sort through the multitude of scenarios of how we, as individuals who react differently, specifically get sick from our buildings. In the meantime, however, there is much we can do to improve our buildings' health, which should, in turn, protect our health.

These improvements can be considered using the following simple outline and frequently have simple, common-sense solutions:

1) Design Approaches
2) Building Systems
3) Building Products
4) Maintenance

DESIGN APPROACHES

Designing a "healthy" building, fortunately, is not limited to any one architectural style. It can be modern, post-modern, classical, rustic, underground, an apartment, a townhouse, a mobile home. All have the opportunity to become healthier buildings. Designing a healthier indoor environment primarily requires the adjustment of one's thinking about indoor spaces and how the activities which will take place there may affect the health of the occupant. The place to begin is the site, whether it be a new building or an existing one. If the site is unhealthy (for example, in proximity to auto exhaust, high-tension power lines, radon, pesticide spraying, or waste dump sites), then the task of creating a healthy indoor environment is made that much more difficult.

> *Designing a "healthy" building, fortunately, is not limited to any one architectural style.*

As part of building design one should include considerations for protecting occupants from noise pollution both within and outside the building. Bedrooms, for example, should provide an environment where one can safely sleep, since usually one-third of a day is spent there. They also should not be located over combustion-producing spaces, such as garages, or mechanical rooms. Building designs should also accommodate an easy flow of fresh air, providing not only for the circulation of stagnant air, but also for the drying of moist and damp areas. Lighting designs should provide appropriate access to natural light and insure proper locations and amounts of artificial lighting. More attention during the design process needs to be given to the integration of the building's mechanical systems into the lives of the occupants in order to improve the quality of the air management system, for heating, cooling, ventilation and purification. Too often these important systems get left out of the design, leaving contractors to "wing it" as they install them.

BUILDING SYSTEMS

Familiarly known as the "mechanicals" in a building, these systems include heating, air cooling, ventilation, air purification, plumbing, water purification, electricity, electromagnetic shielding, security and safety systems, entertainment/ media/intercom, maintenance systems like central vacuums, and computer monitoring of the building's operation and performance. These systems represent the vital organs of the building, and as such, are vital to the health of the occupants.

In the future, our buildings probably won't tolerate the combustion of fossil fuels with its resulting contaminants. Already chimneys are becoming artifacts of the past, except for the "decorative" token fireplace. Modern heating systems already in existence include ground-water source heat pumps, photovoltaics, and passive and active solar systems. Most occupants prefer hot water radiant heat delivery systems, since these neither dry the air nor carry pollutants into the air stream. However, to provide mechanical humidification control (better known as air conditioning), air ducts are normally required and since air travels long distances in these systems and can pick up pollutants along the way, air cleaners and purifiers are required. As a separate function, interior air should be exchanged with fresher air, at different locations, in different quantities, and at different times. To be most effective, this system should be separate from other air systems and monitored carefully. It acts as the "lungs" of the building.

Since our water quality is diminishing as rapidly as the air we breathe, the building's plumbing and water management systems need more attention. A healthy design might see the plumbing system separated into two parts: a potable water network of filtered, and treated water for bathing and drinking; and a "working" water (or graywater) network for waste removal, drip irrigation, and mechanical systems. Alternative sewage treatments could also be used to reclaim over 90% of what we call waste water.

MAINTENANCE

Buildings should incorporate a communication and monitoring system to help the occupant "manage" the building's performance. Many owners feel this duty is a low priority job. The car (which was a smaller investment) gets serviced and pampered more often than the home. Home management systems are available today to assist us in doing what we are not inclined to do for ourselves. Most are designs to manage lighting, music, security, or telephones; but one should incorporate those which manage the air, monitor pollutants, and provide maintenance schedules and records as well. And finally, once the investment of building a healthy structure is made and carried out, one should, of course, not pollute it by spraying pesticides around or by mopping up with toxic cleaners and aerosols.

> *. . . once the investment of building a healthy structure is made, one should not pollute it by mopping up with toxic cleaners and aerosols.*

BUILDING PRODUCTS

A building can only be healthy if the products specified in the design and maintenance systems are in themselves low toxic or hazard-free. This is an area where all current professional studies and research fall short. What alternative products are available for use and which need to be developed? The general response by scientific and governmental bodies is to cope with the current products by restricting the amounts of suspected health hazard ingredients in the product to an "acceptable risk level." There are many reasons for taking this approach, but the most common is that few organizations spend research funds or time in looking for products that might be safer. This may be because these communities see no reward in doing so. Perhaps this role is more suited to the architectural and building professionals who specify and use these products. Recently, the AIA has established a special Committee on the Environment, whose focus is producing an environmental resource guide. This guidebook for professionals will investigate building materials in a cradle-to-grave environmental study. It will consider, among other things, issues related to the rainforest, energy, environmental site planning, waste disposal, recycling, and policy making.

The Masters Corporation, which is an architectural design and general contracting business, has tried to fill this void in its small way. In its quest for building to the highest standard of quality, it searches for manufacturers around the globe who either claim to offer safer and healthier products, or who market a product which appears to meet the cradle-to-grave standards set by The Masters Corporation. Then these manufacturers are asked to submit a sample of their product for review. Once the product sample is received and accessible product information is reviewed, the product is evaluated by outside testing companies, by the occupant who will be using it, and by The Masters Corporation team for its quality and integrity after functioning in its intended use. These products are then modified if necessary, and incorporated into the design and construction of a building, where they are monitored for their installation performance. Afterward the manufacturer is given feedback on the product's use, installation, performance and cost.

Products investigated by The Masters Corporation include radon prevention and mitigation systems, moisture and foundation seals and barriers, drainage techniques, alternative pesticides, pressure-treated wood alternatives, plywood alternatives, exterior paints and wood stains, caulks, glues and adhesives, doors and windows, insulation, vapor barriers, "breathing" wall systems, flooring finishes, carpets, wallpapers, kitchen cabinets and appliances, furniture, interior paints, drywall alternatives, lighting, electromagnetic shielding, mechanical systems for heating/cooling/ventilation, air and water purification systems, computer management systems, and maintenance products. The Masters Corporation has also assisted in the formation of a new company, Environmental Outfitters, which is intended to serve as a wholesale/retail outlet for making these products more accessible to contractors and builders. A catalog of the products sold through this company is going to be made available. It should be noted however, that incorporating this wide variety of products and systems into a new or existing building usually increases the costs from 25% to 30%.

New products and systems are becoming more and more available all the time. Clearly, we in the architectural and building industry must begin setting higher building standards than we currently do. Today standards are established based on "minimum" criteria, and after installation they usually fall short of meeting even those "minimums." Future generations deserve better than that. We deserve better than that. Perhaps the 1990s will be the beginning of a decade which associates health with quality.

ENERGY CONSERVATION BENEFITS OF HIGH-DENSITY MIXED-USE LAND DEVELOPMENT

Douglas Simms Stenhouse, AIA, AICP

Douglas Simms Stenhouse is the President of Energy Management Consultants, Inc., a multi-disciplinary firm providing energy conservation consulting services to federal, state and local government agencies, school boards, architects, engineers, developers, building contractors, owners and professional design associations.

Energy Management Consultants
20329 Roslin Avenue
Torrance, CA 90503-2515
(213) 370-0076

I t has been observed that energy use, with the exception of regional differentiations, can be conveniently divided into three basic categories: buildings, industry, and transportation, each representing more or less a third of the total energy used in our country. The pie chart shown below illustrates this distribution of energy use and various subcategories within individual sectors.

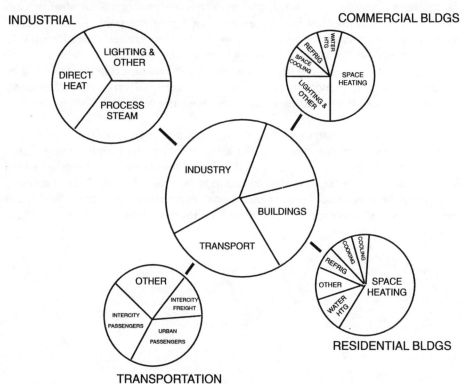

DISTRIBUTION OF ENERGY USE

It also suggests the basic premise of this discussion: the linkages between various sectors or project elements and their subcategories, which may be exploited as a strategy for energy conservation. For example, if spaces for living and working, places for shopping, and entertainment and recreation facilities can be located within easy access of one another, the transportation sector energy use for getting to and from them would be less. If by mixing residential, commercial, and retail and recreational land uses, we can show that less energy would be required for each, then energy use for the whole project would be less, and the size of the whole "pie" would shrink.

Making the right decisions in the planning of high-density mixed-use land developments can achieve an additional 10-15% savings in energy and other operational costs above the considerable savings attainable by using passive solar architecture, superior insulation and energy conserving technology. Mixed-use development can also help achieve economic and social diversity, a method for organizing metropolitan growth, and a potential tool for treating blight and decay. Such projects can make a city come alive! What distinguishes mixed-use land developments from most other single purpose development projects is their dynamic quality derived from the concentration and diversity of activities and the proper design of their physical configuration, internal circulation, and external access. These factors enhance the opportunity to conserve energy and reduce its cost.

The concept of mixed-uses and more intense development of land goes as far back in history as the ancient Greek agora, medieval market squares, and the mixture of commercial and residential occupancies found in many nineteenth century European cities. Rockefeller Center, built during the Depression, is a noteworthy predecessor to developments during the 1950s which embraced multiple functions. The observed need for revitalizing our cities, innovations in zoning, increased capital expenditures for infrastructure improvements, and special tax incentives led to development of such substantial projects as the Penn Center in Philadelphia and Charles Center in Baltimore, MD.[1]

Many other such projects have been built across the U.S. since that time. Each involved significant physical and functional integration of at least three major, different, but complementary activities: gross built-up areas ranging from 500,000 to 30 million square foot megastructures, land areas of 5 to 50 acres, and densities from 3 to 10 FAR (ratio of floor to land area). All are pedestrian-oriented, with direct access from more than one transportation mode (See below).

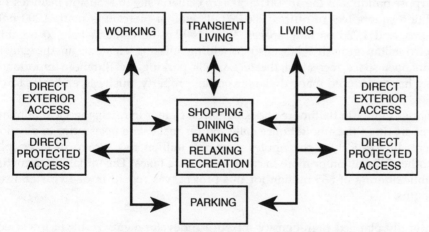

**SCHEMATIC DESIGN OF PHYSICAL AND FUNCTIONAL INTEGRATION
FOUND IN THE TYPICAL MIXED-USE DEVELOPMENT**

In the case of the San Francisco Embarcadero Center and Washington, DC, Watergate projects, blight and decay were reversed by introducing residential, hotel and related activities to areas which had been virtually dead during non-working hours of the day. The 51-acre Embarcadero Center has 2.6 million square feet of offices, 275,000 of retail, an 860 room hotel, and 2,000 parking spaces. The 10 acre Watergate site has 461,000 square feet of offices, 100,000 of retail, a 330-room hotel, 643 residential units, a health club, and 2,000 parking spaces. These and other projects stabilized or increased land values for surrounding neighborhoods.

The 33-acre Charles Center site includes 1.7 million square feet of offices, 335,000 sq. ft. of retail, a 650-room hotel, 400 residential units, a 1000-seat legitimate theater, another 600-seat movie theater, and 3700 parking spaces. This project

California State Energy-Efficient Office Building—South Building Atrium

had a far greater effect on revitalizing development than any other large single purpose building in the area. The 50-acre Galleria site in Houston includes 1.09 million square feet of offices, 300,000 of retail, a mercantile mart, 2,200 hotel rooms, and 1,780 parking spaces. Projects like the Galleria help to organize metropolitan growth while also providing missing elements in the general plan: open space, recreation, theaters, hotels, parking, etc. But more importantly, they have produced many dollars in added property, business, and sales taxes.

Charles Center in Baltimore and Kalamazoo Center in Michigan yield annually over six times the amount once collected for real estate taxes prior to development. Illinois Center contributes over $56 million to Chicago in taxes, plus another $62 million or more in county and state taxes. The initial infrastructure public offering of $65 million for this project was repaid in one year and two months.

Carefully planned high-density mixed-use developments result in lower economic and environmental costs, less consumption of natural resources, and a reduction in personal costs compared to lower density, single purpose projects. In terms of total public and private costs to occupants, other taxpayers, and municipal governments, costs for high-density mixed-use developments are typically 44 percent less than for low-density sprawl community developments, and they generate 45% less air pollution.[2]

The substitution of more efficient vertical and horizontal people movers within a mixed-use project and between various components eliminates much of the real need for automobile transportation. Therefore, requirements for parking can be less. Transportation energy savings and reductions in air pollution are maximized by placing high-density mixed-use developments in close proximity to primary transportation modes. Mixed-use developments make mass transit work by generating tens of thousands of relatively short trips and by spreading travel demand throughout the day, rather than at peak morning or evening rush hours.

Coordinating public and private-sector investments can have exponential benefits by creating better value and a larger tax base. Major components of Baltimore's Charles Center are a 460,000 square foot Federal Office Building and a Federal Courthouse and Office Building in the adjacent Inner Harbor West project. Public sector participation can be in the form of land assembly through powers of eminent domain, allowance for write-downs and/or tax abatements on construction and additional energy conservation investments in cogeneration equipment such as "saved energy" storage or distribution components. Public utilities can help form neighborhood utility districts to utilize excess thermal energy produced by cogeneration plants.

Government infrastucture investments can include provisions for public parking, civic center and convention facilities, utility relocations, street closures, overhead pedestrian walkways and people-movers, as well as technical assistance for developers in coordinating improvements or new facilities. But there is a recognized need for institutional arrangements that will insure the fulfillment of public as well as private developer commitments over time, commitments that are essential vis-à-vis the capital-intensive and high risk nature of such long-range development projects.

Correctly designed mixed-use developments justify a greater level of financial exposure, because they generally provide the investor a higher rate of return than single-purpose projects. The proper integration of design elements results in operational savings in energy, maintenance, security, management, communications, utility access, parking, and water supply. By virtue of project size and mix of uses, all investments, including those in energy conservation, are more stable and will more likely appreciate over the long term.

Mixed-uses, which have the characteristic of requiring energy at different times of the day or seasons of the year, make it possible to spread out electrical power requirements, other utility usages and project services. Because these areas don't have the same high peak demands of single-use areas, high-density mixed-use projects generally command lower utility rates. Energy efficiency can also be enhanced, and initial investment reduced, by on-site energy generation. In the typical off-site power generation scenario, a much greater peak capacity is generated than what the normal peak demand ever calls for, in order to insure that demand will never exceed emergency peak needs. When generating power on-site, energy use and cost will be less, because peak loading can be managed more cost-effectively through central computerized monitoring and control systems. This means that peak capacity need not be much greater than peak demand.

> *The underlying assumption that different land uses or building occupancies should be segregated has become highly questionable. . .*

The underlying assumption that different land uses or building occupancies should be segregated has become highly questionable, from an energy planning and environmental quality point of view, and because of economic and social considerations. Some time ago, Jane Jacobs attacked the conventional zoning of "incompatible" uses by arguing that cities needed instead "a most intricate and close-grained diversity of uses that give each other constant mutual support, both economically and socially."[3] Today, most high-density mixed-use land developments respond to these concerns. More recent accommodations in zoning practice provide opportunities for beneficial integration of different land uses, emphasizing incentives for improved design, additional amenities, and shared public goals.

The special purpose district, planned unit development (PUD), or planned development area ordinance is most often used to accommodate mixed-use developments. These allow for freer placement of buildings than normal lot-by-lot or street-by-street zoning techniques. The floor plans and the massing of individual buildings can be designed to minimize difficult-to-shade east and west exposures. And they can be oriented so as to protect one another from unwanted solar heat gain. Densities are calculated on an overall project basis, allowing for the clustering of buildings and the creation of open spaces at various levels to preserve natural, desirable site features. Increased flexibility is obtained in the arrangement of housing, office structures, retail space, people mover systems, open spaces, and utilities.

For these reasons, local jurisdictions should develop three-dimensional ordinances and avoid language that limits the amount of commercial, retail, or other uses; or that attempts to tie these into some specific ratio of, for example, a proposed or required housing component. Greater flexibility is needed to insure the success of a viable, planned, high-density, mixed-use land development.

Zoning regulations should also provide incentives, such as increased FARs, to encourage higher density land use in exchange for energy conservation measures proposed by the developer that are in addition to those required by law. For example, a project energy budget that is less than required might warrant a higher FAR than otherwise permitted. Developers could be encouraged through such tradeoffs to invest X amount of dollars in energy conservation items that have at least some agreed-upon minimum rate of return. Projects must still demonstrate proper orientation and massing of buildings to achieve effective daylighting and shading and solar access for passive solar heating of housing units, swimming pools, and proper growing within landscaped open areas.

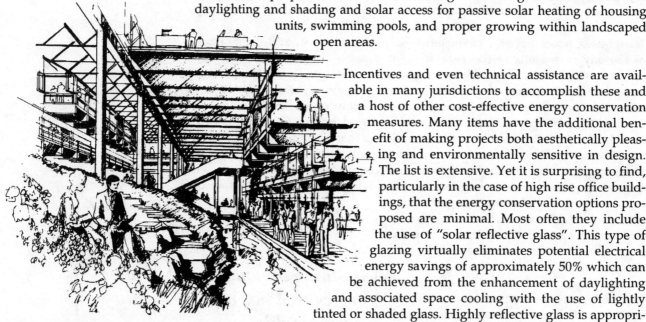

California State Energy-Efficient Office Building—Atrium from lower level

Incentives and even technical assistance are available in many jurisdictions to accomplish these and a host of other cost-effective energy conservation measures. Many items have the additional benefit of making projects both aesthetically pleasing and environmentally sensitive in design. The list is extensive. Yet it is surprising to find, particularly in the case of high rise office buildings, that the energy conservation options proposed are minimal. Most often they include the use of "solar reflective glass". This type of glazing virtually eliminates potential electrical energy savings of approximately 50% which can be achieved from the enhancement of daylighting and associated space cooling with the use of lightly tinted or shaded glass. Highly reflective glass is appropriate for buildings that are used primarily at night or interior spaces where natural lighting is undesirable. But it just doesn't make sense for most places where people work during the day!

Great care must be taken in the selection of glass type, its location, and the percentage of the facade which is to be clad with reflective glass, since the pattern and path of reflections may result in objectionable glare, unwanted additional cooling loads for neighboring buildings, traffic safety hazards, and landscape burnout. Many cities, like Long Beach, require detailed glare studies indicating there will be no such problems before they permit the use of reflective glass.

ENERGY CRITIQUE OF THE PROPOSED FARMER'S MARKET MALL

The design and analysis of large scale urban development projects offers a number of opportunities, particularly with respect to energy conservation, that may be impractical for smaller, single purpose projects. Structures that cover a large area or that extend far up into the sky, and which invariably include multiple subterranean levels are of such scope and size that they demand our

California State Energy-Efficient Office Building—View from upper gallery

undivided attention. And they get it. Such developments are by their very nature controversial. A case in point is the Third Street and Fairfax Avenue Farmer's Market Mall development proposal by the JMB/Urban Development of Chicago and A. F. Gilmore Co., a family-run company that has owned the 31-acre property since 1880. The original proposal included a million-square-foot shopping mall anchored by two or three major department stores. Also planned are a 600-room hotel, a multi-story 250,000 square foot office structure, theaters, restaurants, and a 150-unit residential complex.

The historic Gilmore Adobe, built on the site in 1852, and its gardens would be preserved and enhanced with an open plaza and new retailing to house a number of the merchants that would be displaced by new construction.[4&5] The proposal offers a number of opportunities for energy conservation, but the development unfortunately falls short of doing anything other than meeting the minimal energy regulations. There are also other problems that have been exposed in public reviews.

The land area is known for ground fires that result from methane gas leaking through the pavement. Like the La Brea Tar Pits to the east, the site was once covered with oil derricks. It seems appalling that the developer didn't consider the possibility of harnessing this methane gas, as is being done in a number of abandoned landfills, to offset conventional demands for natural gas or to generate on-site electrical power. A project of this scope could justify a 4-5 megawatt cogeneration plant.

There are several advantages to generating electricity on site. First is the fact that the thermodynamic efficiency of cogeneration is three times greater than the method by which DWP can deliver equivalent capacity to the proposed site. Secondly, this improved efficiency will result in a 67% reduction in combustion of hydrocarbons to the atmosphere. Third, by generating electricity on site, one is able to make use of free waste heat from the generating process. Waste heat can be used as a source of thermal energy for space heating in the winter or hot water heating year round.

If the project were to produce its own power, as most high-density mixed-use developments can, this would free up DWP capacity for other future demand; enough capacity, in this case, to meet the average demand of about 10,000 homes! Freeing up demand is the main objective of the State Energy Plan and the State Building Energy Conservation Regulations. Freeing up demand means that we don't have to go through the hassle of finding sites and increasing rates to repay the huge investment needed to build new power plants.

CALIFORNIA STATE ENERGY EFFICIENT OFFICE BUILDING

Sim Van der Ryn, who once served as the State Architect, was almost single handedly responsible for initiating and encouraging energy efficient design of state-owned buildings. We, in a joint venture with the architectural firm of Gluth & Quigley, San Diego, were one of six finalists in a national competition which Van der Ryn sponsored for the design of one of the first of these buildings to be located in Sacramento.

Many of the energy conservation concepts we proposed were later incorporated into other building designs for which we served as energy consultants. Discussion of the California State Energy Efficient Office Building Competition is appropriate because the program included a number of different, but complementary, uses: housing, office space, a public auditorium, retail areas, and open landscaped areas. We proposed over 40 specific passive techniques to conserve and collect energy. They included daylighting, evaporative/radiative cooling, night-time ventilation, passive solar heating and sun control, proper building geometry or massing, orientation and envelope design, and good interior task area layout. (A complete list is shown on page 57.)

California State Energy-Efficient Office Building—Typical executive office.

Daylighting was found to be the most significant strategy for conserving energy in the larger office portion of the project, displacing over half of the annual kilowatt-hour load. Rooftop spray ponds provided precooling through night sky radiation and evaporation. The exposed concrete structural system in the office portion was precooled by summer night-time ventilation. Water reuse was proposed as well as conversion of on-site agricultural and paper wastes into methane gas. Efficient mechanical and electrical systems and equipment, waste heat recovery, improved methods of irrigation, and even careful selection of plant materials were included.

A greenhouse was provided for the propagation of potted plants for office interiors and public spaces. Interior office spaces were submetered by department so that each could subsequently be held accountable for their own energy use. Air distribution systems were intentionally oversized to reduce friction losses in ducts and therefore, the necessary fan horsepower to push air around. We recommended variable pitch axial vane fans for individual air handling units to reduce electrical loads because they can more efficiently match the ever-changing air distribution load.

LIST OF ENERGY CONSERVATION TECHNIQUES PROPOSED FOR OFFICES IN STATE OFFICE BUILDING COMPETITION

DESCRIPTION	ENERGY-USING FUNCTION
1. Daylighting	Space Lighting
2. Nighttime Radiation and Evaporation	Space Cooling
3. Nighttime Cool-Down	Space Cooling
4. Reduction of Space Lighting Needs	Space Lighting/Cooling
5. Natural Ventilation	Space Cooling
6. Passive Solar Energy	Space Heating
7. Medium Temperature Active Solar Energy System	Space Heating
8. Collection/Filtration of "Grey" Water	Water Use
9. Collection/Filtration of "Brown" Water	Water Use
10. Community Farming in Greenhouse	Food Production
11. Controls for Daylighting	Space Heating
12. Submetering of Interior Spaces	Electrical Power for Fans
13. Oversized Air Distribution System	Electrical Power For Fans
14. Variable Pitch Axial Fans	Electrical Power For Fans
15. Split Face Heating System	Space Heating/Cooling
16. Economizer Cycle	Space Cooling
17. Pre-cooling of Conditioned Air	Space Cooling
18. Additional Insulation	Space Cooling/Heating
19. Reflective/Light Colored Roof Surfaces	Space Cooling
20. Off-Peak Storage of Chilled Water	Space Cooling
21. Exterior/Interior Landscaping	Space Cooling
22. Buffering at Perimeter of Building	Space Cooling
23. Low Infiltration Windows	Space Cooling/Heating
24. Exterior Shading Devices	Space Cooling
25. Movable Insulation	Space Heating
26. Increased Surface Area of Heat Exchangers	Space Heating
27. Hot Heat Exchangers	Space Heating
27. Hot Water Waste Heat Recovery	Service Hot Water Heating
28. Hot Water Flow Control Devices	Space Heating
29. Proportional Hot Water Control	Space Heating
30. Increased Convector Enclosure Height Stack Effect	Space Cooling
31. Locate Main Air Returns at Bottom of Buildings	Space Heating
32. Steam Condensate Waste Heat Recovery	Space Heating
33. Improved Landscape Irrigation Methods	Water Use
34. Careful Selection of Plant Materials	Water Use
35. Use of Counter-Balanced Traction Elevators	Electrical Power

LIST OF ENERGY CONSERVATION TECHNIQUES PROPOSED FOR HOUSING IN STATE OFFICE BUILDING COMPETITION

DESCRIPTION	ENERGY USING FUNCTION
1. Submetering of Each Living Unit	Electrical Power
2. Location and Size of Exterior Openings	Electrical Power for Fans
3. Light Colored Roof and Walls	Space Cooling
4. Calculated Overhangs	Space Cooling/Heating
5. Movable Insulation	Space Heating/Cooling
6. Increased Building Mass	Space Heating/Cooling
7. Exterior Landscaping	Space Cooling/Heating
8. Hot Water Flow Control Devices	Domestic Hot Water Heating
9. Swimming Pool Cover	Hot Water Heating
10. Collection/Filtration of "Black" Water	Water Use
11. Methane Digester	Hot Water Heating/Fertilizer

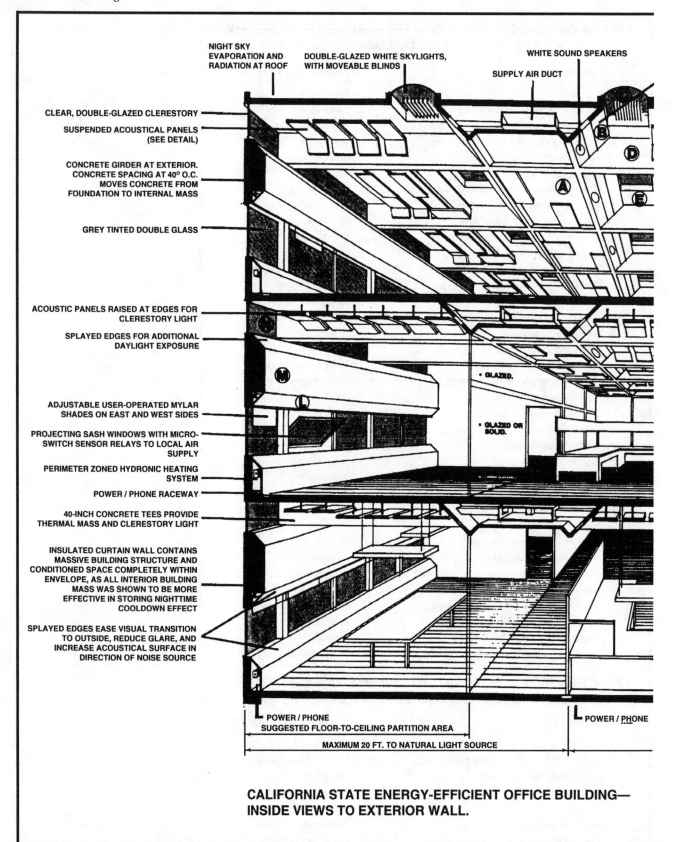

NIGHT SKY EVAPORATION AND RADIATION AT ROOF

DOUBLE-GLAZED WHITE SKYLIGHTS, WITH MOVEABLE BLINDS

WHITE SOUND SPEAKERS

SUPPLY AIR DUCT

CLEAR, DOUBLE-GLAZED CLERESTORY

SUSPENDED ACOUSTICAL PANELS (SEE DETAIL)

CONCRETE GIRDER AT EXTERIOR. CONCRETE SPACING AT 40° O.C. MOVES CONCRETE FROM FOUNDATION TO INTERNAL MASS

GREY TINTED DOUBLE GLASS

ACOUSTIC PANELS RAISED AT EDGES FOR CLERESTORY LIGHT

SPLAYED EDGES FOR ADDITIONAL DAYLIGHT EXPOSURE

ADJUSTABLE USER-OPERATED MYLAR SHADES ON EAST AND WEST SIDES

PROJECTING SASH WINDOWS WITH MICRO-SWITCH SENSOR RELAYS TO LOCAL AIR SUPPLY

PERIMETER ZONED HYDRONIC HEATING SYSTEM

POWER / PHONE RACEWAY

40-INCH CONCRETE TEES PROVIDE THERMAL MASS AND CLERESTORY LIGHT

INSULATED CURTAIN WALL CONTAINS MASSIVE BUILDING STRUCTURE AND CONDITIONED SPACE COMPLETELY WITHIN ENVELOPE, AS ALL INTERIOR BUILDING MASS WAS SHOWN TO BE MORE EFFECTIVE IN STORING NIGHTTIME COOLDOWN EFFECT

SPLAYED EDGES EASE VISUAL TRANSITION TO OUTSIDE, REDUCE GLARE, AND INCREASE ACOUSTICAL SURFACE IN DIRECTION OF NOISE SOURCE

GLAZED.

GLAZED OR SOLID.

POWER / PHONE SUGGESTED FLOOR-TO-CEILING PARTITION AREA

POWER / PHONE

MAXIMUM 20 FT. TO NATURAL LIGHT SOURCE

CALIFORNIA STATE ENERGY-EFFICIENT OFFICE BUILDING— INSIDE VIEWS TO EXTERIOR WALL.

More energy-efficient counter-balanced traction elevators were proposed. Reflective, light-colored roof and wall surfaces were employed to reduce space cooling loads. Large underground water storage tanks for fire protection

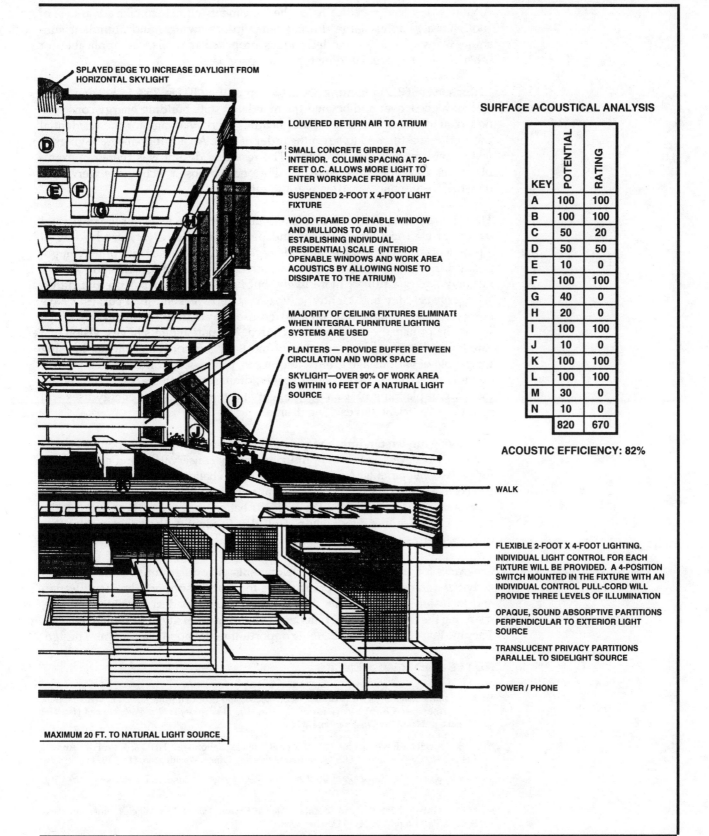

SPLAYED EDGE TO INCREASE DAYLIGHT FROM HORIZONTAL SKYLIGHT

LOUVERED RETURN AIR TO ATRIUM

SMALL CONCRETE GIRDER AT INTERIOR. COLUMN SPACING AT 20-FEET O.C. ALLOWS MORE LIGHT TO ENTER WORKSPACE FROM ATRIUM

SUSPENDED 2-FOOT X 4-FOOT LIGHT FIXTURE

WOOD FRAMED OPENABLE WINDOW AND MULLIONS TO AID IN ESTABLISHING INDIVIDUAL (RESIDENTIAL) SCALE (INTERIOR OPENABLE WINDOWS AND WORK AREA ACOUSTICS BY ALLOWING NOISE TO DISSIPATE TO THE ATRIUM)

MAJORITY OF CEILING FIXTURES ELIMINATE WHEN INTEGRAL FURNITURE LIGHTING SYSTEMS ARE USED

PLANTERS — PROVIDE BUFFER BETWEEN CIRCULATION AND WORK SPACE

SKYLIGHT—OVER 90% OF WORK AREA IS WITHIN 10 FEET OF A NATURAL LIGHT SOURCE

WALK

FLEXIBLE 2-FOOT X 4-FOOT LIGHTING. INDIVIDUAL LIGHT CONTROL FOR EACH FIXTURE WILL BE PROVIDED. A 4-POSITION SWITCH MOUNTED IN THE FIXTURE WITH AN INDIVIDUAL CONTROL PULL-CORD WILL PROVIDE THREE LEVELS OF ILLUMINATION

OPAQUE, SOUND ABSORPTIVE PARTITIONS PERPENDICULAR TO EXTERIOR LIGHT SOURCE

TRANSLUCENT PRIVACY PARTITIONS PARALLEL TO SIDELIGHT SOURCE

POWER / PHONE

MAXIMUM 20 FT. TO NATURAL LIGHT SOURCE

SURFACE ACOUSTICAL ANALYSIS

KEY	POTENTIAL	RATING
A	100	100
B	100	100
C	50	20
D	50	50
E	10	0
F	100	100
G	40	0
H	20	0
I	100	100
J	10	0
K	100	100
L	100	100
M	30	0
N	10	0
	820	670

ACOUSTIC EFFICIENCY: 82%

doubled-up as chilled water storage "cool sinks". Waste heat recovery from various project elements was used to preheat make-up air/water. "Black" water was to be processed for use with "grey" water for irrigation.

Although designed specifically for the Sacramento climate to take advantage of cool summer nights, large diurnal temperature swings, and abundant sunshine, many of the passive techniques proposed may also be applicable for other climate regions, building types, or space uses.

Reductions of 60% in lighting Kwh, 85% in cooling BTUs, 75% in heating BTUs were achieved, over and beyond the mandated state building energy conservation regulations. Space cooling and heating energy savings for the residential portion were estimated to be on the order of 95%. An additional 85% savings in water consumption was projected. The resulting design was therefore exemplary, yet also an existing and pleasing one. Proposed techniques were "off-the-shelf", economically attractive, and interactive.

The diverse nature of mixed-use developments tends to level out the peaks and valleys of electrical load patterns and permits more efficient base loading of equipment. Evening residential loads replace daytime office and other component loads. The addition of theaters, health clubs, restaurants, and sport arenas, not only makes a project more lively, but helps to further balance out differences between day and nighttime, weekday and weekend load curves. I have been working for some time on a mixed-use project in downtown Long Beach where the principal component is a church. The parishioners have a vision of a safe haven that includes a number of mutually supportive elements: housing for people of various age groups and needs, professional offices, retail areas, a day school, parking, shared open spaces, dining, and other areas. I am certain that careful planning of each component and their respective energy uses will result in an efficient and exciting design.

Identifying, understanding, and acting upon various defined component energy needs is, I believe, the key to optimizing energy conservation and energy costs for such developments. And it is also the key to balancing the components of a project to achieve other objectives such as minimum vacancy rates, maintenance costs and management fees. We need to better understand how we use the places where we live, work, shop, and play to identify the key variables that must be addressed to bring us closer to achieving project synergy.

Programs for mixed-use land developments encourage interactions between activities and energy uses, opportunities for mutual support, the identification and inclusion of components that respond to the broadest possible audience, spanning the widest time intervals, and providing diversity in a preplanned way. They are marvelous and challenging opportunities for good planning and design.

NOTES AND REFERENCES

1. Much of the material in the preamble of this discussion is drawn from Robert E. Witherspoon, Jon P. Abbett, and Robert M. Gladstone's *Mixed-Use Developments: New Ways of Land Use*; The Urban Land Institute; Washington, D.C.; 1976.

2. U..S. Council on Environmental Quality (CEQ) in association with HUD & EPA; Fifth Annual Report: *The Costs of Sprawl*; U.S. Government Printing Office, Washington, D.C.; 1974.

3. Jane Jacobs; *The Death and Life of Great American Cities*; page 14; Random House, New York City, 1961.

4. Martha Groves; *2 Big Retailers To Anchor Mall at Farmers Market*; Los Angeles Times, Business Section, Part IV, pp 1 & 24; 10 October 1989.

5. Mathis Chazanov; *Bradley Hails Report on Plan for Farmers Market*; Los Angeles Times, p B9; 8 June 1990.

SUSTAINABILITY

BUILDING A SUSTAINABLE FUTURE

Sim Van der Ryn, AIA

THE WORLD PROBLEM

Sim Van der Ryn is an award-winning architect and co-author of Sustainable Communities. *His firm has designed a range of projects from new communities to public buildings to mixed-use facilities and custom homes. As California State Architect, he initiated a landmark program in energy efficient building. He teaches at U.C. Berkeley, and is President of the Farallones Institute, which has been a leading center for research in environmentally sustainable design.*

Sim Van der Ryn & Associates
55 Gate 5 Road
Sausilito, CA 94965
(415) 332-5806

"Reality is the Leading Cause of Stress"
The major issue facing humanity today is how to transform technology and values that threaten planetary life. Cities and megacities like Los Angeles, Tokyo, Mexico City, and London are the dominant form of habitation on the planet. It is in the redesign of our cities and in the change in consciousness of urban dwellers that a new way of living and a new way of relating to both nature and technology must emerge. How we deal with these issues in the coming decade may determine whether life has a future here on earth. What we do in the next several decades will establish the conditions that our children, grandchildren, and their children will be living with.

Everyone is familiar with the worldwide environmental crisis resulting from waste and over-consumption, over-population, obsolete values and political structures, and what I call, "dumb design," that is, design which ignores ecological reality in both its social and physical dimensions.

The two major biomes, oceans and tropical rain forests, which are responsible for maintaining planetary health are under deadly assault. Earth's climate is undergoing change due to a binge of fossil fuel burning, forest clearing, and too many cattle. The protective layer of atmospheric ozone is being destroyed by chemical pollution. Our life support systems—air, soil and water—are growing more fragile each day.

Our planet's human inhabitants are faring no better than the other forms of life we are destroying. Ignorance, disease, violence, and starvation are part of daily life for many. Cities that once offered the poor and dispossessed opportunities to better their lives, are becoming dead-ends of permanent despair. Ancient cultures and traditions, along with thousands of living species, are disappearing yearly. We are losing the genetic and learned intelligence and adaptability that are the true harvest of evolution.

We are here to scan this grim background for signs of hope, for visions of a better way, for concrete examples of more ecologically sane, more sustainable ways of designing and living in our cities. We are here to explore how ecological principles applied to the design and construction of our built environment can reduce the damage that current practices are doing to the environment. Let's not kid ourselves. I say " reduce" rather than "solve," because more intelligent, ecologically-sound design alone cannot solve the mess that industrial technology, driven by an outmoded world view, has produced. However, in creating examples and new models, ecological design can point the way towards values compatible with our long term habitation on this planet.

THE ROLE OF ECOLOGICAL DESIGN, THE MEANINGS AND FUNCTIONS OF SUSTAINABILITY

Nowadays, we hear the words, "ecology," "ecological," "sustainable," and "sustainability" a lot. What do they mean? What do they tell us about how we might redesign our cities and our built environment? Sustainability is rooted primarily in the ecology of natural systems. If you look at the processes that caused great societies in the past to collapse, you discover that the stressing of basic environmental systems such as soil, water and vegetative cover to be primary causes that ended those civilizations. At a certain point, these systems could no longer support the populations that depended on them for basic sustenance. Sustainability implies that the needs of a population and the flow of resources needed to support them are in dynamic balance. If they are not, stress and exhaustion set in. Either a balance is struck, or the whole system collapses and finds a new balance point. In the last hundred years, the tremendous leverage provided by fossil fuel technologies has obscured fundamental relationships, but it has not changed underlying structure.

As an architect and urban designer, the connection between agriculture, architecture, and cities is obvious and fundamental. Agriculture and architecture are intimately connected. People don't invest in permanent settlements until they can create agricultural surpluses, and maintain a steady flow of the other resources necessary to maintain urban life.

I have just returned from one of my favorite places in North America, Chaco Canyon in the dry high desert of New Mexico. Around 800 years ago, the multi-story pueblo villages of Chaco Canyon seemed to be the hub of a network of Anasazi communities that stretched hundreds of miles. They were among the earliest permanent settlements in North America until their inhabitants suddenly disappeared. We don't know exactly what happened. There may have been prolonged droughts, or a greater population than their agriculture could provide for. Throughout human history, from the cradle of civilization in Mesopotania, to the great Empires of Rome, and Asia Minor, the story

> *What people think they need is constantly changing, culturally determined, and reflected by trend setting design.*

is the same. Basic environmental systems that support life are stressed through a domino effect of population pressure, deforestation, soil erosion, and poor water management, until the society collapses. In spite of our great technological advances, there is no reason to believe that we will escape a similar fate so long as present trends continue.

Ecological sustainability isn't possible in a planetary society of 5.5 billion humans living as we do in North America. At least a billion people have access to TV and either have, or dream of, a standard of living based on the Western ideal which is subsidized and entirely dependent on one million BTUs per capita per day energy consumption, the equivalent of six gallons of oil per person per day. The U.N. Commission on the Environment chaired by Premier Bruntland of Norway described sustainable development this way, "Sustainable Development meets the needs of the present without compromising the ability of future generations to meet their own needs." At a bare minimum, what this definition suggests is that the following three trends be reversed now:

1. The continuing conversion of prime agricultural lands and soil erosion.

2. The continuing deterioration of key biological systems: forests, grasslands, and ocean fisheries.

3. The continuing rapid depletion of oil and gas reserves before other alternatives are in place.

ECOLOGY, NEEDS AND DESIGN

What people think they need is constantly changing, culturally determined, and reflected by trend setting design. Most people use the word "design" to refer to style and styling, the visual properties of an object. "Design" is an active verb as well as a noun. Yet we most often use the word "design" in talking about objects rather than processes. This is a way of thinking related to the nature of our fragmented society which thinks in terms of pieces and fragments rather than in wholes or continuums. Even for many people aware of the planetary issues we face, their idea of what is desirable in their own environment is shaped by the images in *Architectural Digest*, the rest of the designer press, and the images produced by the fantasy factories here in Los Angeles.

Sustainability is an ideal against which to measure. In itself, it is not attainable within today's implicit assumptions of how we live our lives. Ecological design will require a rethinking of what we mean by "needs," socially, psychologically, materially. How do we merge our Western concept of individual needs for the commons and the needs of other Earth systems of life? We must develop concepts of "needs" that are grounded in the kinds of ecologically appropriate technologies, materials, and prototype designs that will be discussed here. We need concepts of quality and value that transcend today's materialist and visual image centered norms.

Ecology, as we learn about it in the earnest offerings of Public Television, or in the dramatic TV images of the latest eco-disasters, is different from what we learn as participants in real time ecological processes. Early in life, our culture teaches us to become obsessed with visual images, still and in motion. But the essence of ecology and sustainability are embedded in processes that are not often so visually accessible. They are processes that require deeper sensitivities and greater participation of all the senses. Once we are in contact, nature does not permit us our usual roles of passive observer or active performer. The natural environment is not a McLuhanesque "cool medium" nor does it

> *Sustainability is not attainable within today's implicit assumptions of how we live our lives.*

perform according to our mechanized sense of time. When, every so often, we come in contact with someone, something, or some place that is wholly beautiful and true, our minds stop, time stops, and our whole beings participate. What we experience is not so much the object but a flow, a force or energy. An ecologically designed living environment that interprets aesthetics, nature, and technology can produce this kind of response.

The strategies for selling and marketing ecology in a mass society may be effective to change buying habits and consumer behavior, but they may not change people or society as much as people changing things for themselves through their own experiences and perceptions gained through direct participation. The most profound ecological design concepts may be at a disadvantage in a speeded up, mechanical time based, visual image oriented society, an over-heated environment of mass media, marketing, and money. The Gulf War offers a perfect example. People were glued to the 24 hour coverage of the mechanical phase of the war. However, its ecological aftermath, in environmental and human terms, is more profound and complicated, occupies a longer time frame, and a diffused spatial context. So we don't get it, because in a result oriented society, if results are not quick, clear, and immediate, it's not news, it's not interesting, and it can't hold our attention. Ecological solutions grow out of needs to develop and take hold in diverse local community settings.

I look forward to the surprises growing out of what happens when people feel free to explore what they really want, what they perceive as important, not what the marketers, experts and politicians tell them they ought to want.

The uniqueness of people committed to improving their own local community, the spirit embodied in place, has the potential to shape an ecological future every bit as much as the experts, and currently, politically correct, green wisdom. Externally imposed centralized control and power, no matter how it is labelled, is the greatest enemy of an ecologically based redesign of culture.

> *Externally imposed control is the greatest enemy of an ecologically based redesign of culture.*

My compost looks beautiful to me, but when I show people photos of my worms, people squirm and squeal. Perhaps I need a compost stylist. Or perhaps, if people worked with earthworms they would grow to love them as I do. Our appreciation of the two dimensional beauties of nature has not prepared us for the smells of the earth, the constant cycle of death and decay, the surprises and uncertainties. For many, "eco-noia," or fear of living things and the changes that go with life, provides a static antiseptic certainty.

THE DIFFUSION OF CHANGE

Those who study the diffusion of change in cultures tell us that people adopt new ways of doing things when the perceived value of the new compared to the perceived value of the old is greater than the perceived cost of making a change. Notice that change is driven by the perception of value, which is subjective and non-quantifiable as well as objective and quantifiable. Personal habits and institutional inertia may keep people and organizations from doing things that make a lot of sense ecologically and economically.

Many improvements, particularly in energy efficiency which result from technical fixes, don't involve the user as a participant except in the role as consumer. Buying an energy efficient car, high efficiency lamps, or other green products is good for the environment, but involves only a minimal change in people's habits, perceptions, and life styles. They are transitional steps down the path towards sustainability.

The best and most powerful motivator for change is finding that another way of doing things, living, or being, is more deeply satisfying than the old way. People who live in radiant heated, passive-solar homes with thick walls never willingly go back to living in cracker-box houses with forced air heating systems. People who compost and garden become true believers, enjoying the process, the earthy smell, and the direct connection to a basic process of regeneration and renewal. Change and the adoption of an ecological way of life comes about through this level of participation. Teaching and preaching do not change people.

Guilt is not a good motivator for change. Economics is important but seldom primary, particularly for the prosperous trend setters in this society. A positive direct experience, and personal satisfaction that flows from doing something new and different can be the most important catalyst for change.

Ecological design proceeds from the premise that there is more than one right answer. There is a diversity of solutions springing from similar principles applied in different situations. Eco-design thrives on ethnic and cultural diversity. Eco-design puts its faith in people as equal to experts. Eco-design is grounded in incrementalism and a diversity of solutions and approaches, rather than grand design springing from the mind of the lone genius. Eco-design finds no panaceas or quick fixes.

> *Ecological design proceeds from the premise that there is more than one right answer.*

The most crucial change towards an ecological environment is design which makes nature and natural cycles and processes visible to urban dwellers and includes them as active participants. Spend one night under a clear black Sierra sky with billions of stars as companions and you understand just how deprived urban dwellers are of this most basic connection to the cosmos. Urban dwellers can't connect their daily actions, such as taking showers, turning on the air conditioner, opening a cellophane bag of carrots, or using the toilet, to ecological processes because they can't see or grasp the connections. Nature's complexity and flow have been tamed, harnessed and made invisible to the urban dweller.

KEY INDICATORS OF SUSTAINABILITY

Here's a list of seven key indicators:

1. Fossil fuel energy use. Look at the housing sector, building sector, and transportation sector, and, in addition to fossil fuel use, look at the CO_2 output.

2. Use of depletable materials, both local and external. I've used wood very wastefully over the years. I used 3" cedar industrial decking for my whole house in 1971. We can't do that any more. I'm using rammed earth now, using the local soil. Earth has lots of low-quality soil. Basically, you ram the material dry, with a small amount of cement stabilizer, into forms. This is a 3,000-year-old technology used in China and much of Europe. How are depletable materials like metal recycled? Rodale recommended rebuilding small appliances and reboring automobile engines. This is more feasible than sending them to the scrap heap. Instead of recycling to raw metal, why not recycle the machine and keep it running?

3. Conditions and integrity of natural systems: soil, air, water, plants and animals.

4. Human systems. Look at economy. How many dollars are produced and how many times are they recycled in the community or are they shipped out? Issues of equity are of human health. The fundamental issue is full use of human potential through communication and cooperation.

5. How much is locally produced? How much value is added locally? One of the real success stories in California of sustainability has been the re-emergence of organic agriculture. It started when I was in state government when we began direct marketing because the growers told us the stores wouldn't buy their stuff. So government facilitated the development of farmers' markets in urban areas. Now a smart grower can gross $60 - $100,000/acre.

6. How much money stays in place? All success stories are isolated here and there. We can't point to an integrated picture of success yet. Food is fundamental. If you're looking for a project, local food production is the place to start. That's something people understand; when things get tough it's important. Henry Ford decentralized his automobile plants very early, and one of the reasons was that he knew there would be business cycles and unemployment; his belief was you should have full-time workers and part-time farmers. I'm advising a prefecture in Japan where there are electronic firms and all the people are part-time farmers. As you know, Japan subsidizes, over-subsidizes, its small farms.

7. To what extent is intelligence shared and decentralized? Is there a common mind about the community? This is a critical ingredient. I want to emphasize the need in communities for a base of shared intelligence and then a process for doing things, rather than technical examples. Our planning processes remind me of what it's like to turn a supertanker. They're too cumbersome and too clumsy so they don't work very well. The kind of planning process that you need is more like white water kayaking. You can't negotiate a kayak unless you pay attention and get information all the time (what's the water ahead doing?) and then you respond.

Part of what I'm saying is we're clearer about the theory than the practice. I believe that people intuitively understand the value of sustainability, but that it involves making choices and trade-offs for this to happen. The technology and hardware are largely there to do all of this. The issue is integrating them into a coherent cultural and economic reality. Ten years ago, I designed a community of 5,000 using state-of-the-art technology. We showed we could get tremendous reductions in every indicator we could measure. The examples are all over and what we need is a process to integrate them.

How do we begin to do this? First create awareness and visibility. One tactic for local government is to acknowledge what's already going on. Start to inventory the community and make it visible. When I was in the California state government and set up the Office of Appropriate Technology, we had an instant printing place print up awards. We gave awards every week for something a community had done that was a move toward sustainability. Palo Alto put in a bicycle path. Mill Valley opened a farmer's market. A community up north turned off its gas for a week, because they were having a dispute with the gas company.

> *The most crucial change is design which makes nature and natural cycles and processes visible to urban dwellers.*

Secondly, there needs to be a belief that there is a necessity. In Marin County, which is often teased as the county of indulgence and hot tubs, we lived through two years of drought. People reduced their water consumption by 70% and it stayed reduced even when the rains came again. Why? Because people saw the need to do something and they saw it was going to be equitable. Whatever gets done needs to be fair and to treat everyone the same.

Third thing is the difficult one: the need to make the transition to an economy and institutions which reflect the true costs of using up the environment. We need to bend the market system to long-term sustainability. William Ruckleshouse, former head of the EPA said, "In violation of the core principle of capitalism, we refuse to treat environmental resources as capital."

Fourth, we need to design indicators into the community which visibly express sustainable values. It would be nice if you had an electric meter you could really read, somewhere you could really see it. Maybe there should be a big thermometer on City Hall which says, "Hey folks, this is how we're doing this month."

There are a lot of examples of sustainable design in terms of site planning. Village Homes, which is one of the most integrated examples of site planning, has all of the drainage on the surface instead of in pipes. I like to design in a way in which all our basic resource flows are visible. We've designed everything so it is clean and out of the way. Our electricity comes from some place, water comes from some place, and so on. We need to find ways of celebrating these resources and making them a visible part of the landscape.

The most important thing is to bring it all home . There's an interesting essay by the poet and writer Wendall Barry in which he talks about the futility of planetary thinking. What he means is that we all know about the fragile ball floating in space that we live on, but it's still pretty abstract. And the worst part is the bigger the scale, the worse it gets. When I read "Worldwatch" or the issue of "Scientific American" on "Managing the Planet," it all looks pretty dreary. Big numbers just are not sensible. What does one million mean? Or one billion? We have to get down to the home scale. We have to get down to what we literally can sense. And the best tool is honest information that's understood and believed. That's been my experience. And yet in this culture the burden is too much information, especially for decision makers. Endless reading, statistics, technical reports. How are we going to manage all this?

SUSTAINABILITY AND ORGANIC UNITY

A true "sustainable community" or "ecological city" is much more than a dense, efficient land-use pattern. It incorporates local food production, and waste recycling. Its size is limited to its watershed, and its capacity to recycle wastes without damage to the environment. Local economic value created stays largely in the community. Dollars are recycled locally.

Each designed component of an ecologically sustainable whole needs to be treated as a whole living system, like a cell or leaf. A simple leaf, a cell, a blade of grass, or tree is more complex than today's idea of a city. In a living organic form, consumption, food and energy production, recycling of by-products, the information that controls growth and response to change, are all connected in a seamless whole.

Sustainability depends on, and is linked to, organic wholeness. In other words, no amount of fancy design can turn a purse into a sow's ear, although a sow's ear can easily be turned into a purse. One is alive, the other is not.

> *A true "sustainable community" or "ecological city" is much more than a dense, efficient land use pattern.*

Consider a two billion year old life form: a single blue-green algae cell. As large and complex as Los Angeles is, it is less complex and evolved ecologically than this microscopic algae cell, an early building block of planetary sustainability that has been around for two billion years. Each cell is whole and complete, carrying a blueprint for its own growth and evolution. Each cell synthesizes its food from sunlight and the nutrients in the water. It exchanges wastes with the surrounding environment, without polluting it. As we move up the chain of life into greater complexity, we find the same organic unity, whether it be leaf, plant, or animal.

Vast cities are a short term aberration based on fossil fuels. We can make them more efficient, in terms of land and energy use, but in many ways this simply prolongs the destruction of global natural systems that are enslaved to the service of urban consumers. The size and design of a truly sustainable city must be ecologically balanced with water supply, waste purification, and basic food and raw materials production. What models can we learn from in designing new urban ecologies? The oldest and best is the garden, stable, and well-husbanded agricultural landscape. The most basic myth in

> *I want to emphasize the need in communities for a base of shared intelligence.*

Western culture is the expulsion from the Garden of Eden. The creation of botanical gardens in the late medieval period and early Renaissance were attempts to recreate the Garden of Eden in a material sense, and led directly to the development of modern science. Ironically, we still call industrial factories, "plants." The garden and traditional small scale agriculture represent a middle ground, a transformation of nature to human ends in a way that both people and nature are enhanced. In our search for solutions, we cannot do better than that.

TOWARDS SUSTAINABLE ARCHITECTURE (or) TOWARDS A NEW ARCHITECTURE OF SUSTAINABILITY

Richard Schoen, AIA

T he dual title of this article is intentional. The first title suggests that architecture as we know it can "become" sustainable. The second and more revolutionary of the two titles implies that a new architecture must, and is, about to be born, with its own rationale, theory of form, admirers, detractors, historians, theorists, and doers.

Each year, the present generation of architects and those working their way through the schools to join them, will create vast square footages of built environment, development, and entire new communities. Like it or not, all will have to function well into the next century. The world can ill afford for those buildings and communities to be environmentally non-responsive. For the full intent and incredibly challenging opportunities of sustainable architecture and planning to be realized, our structures must emerge as new, if not entirely radical, approaches to design, settlement planning, and city making!

One thing is certain. The way in which cities are planned, new settlements created, and buildings are built will all change. Many would argue that they already have. The real question is, will architecture change with it, or even, will architecture lead the revolution? Will architecture emerge once more as the life force it once was? Or will it continue to retreat to academic and intellectual havens, becoming the almost exclusive purview of the intelligentsia? Will it constrict to the point where it has about as much impact on the broad stream of contemporary life as painting now does? Will it become the private domain of the cognizant media? Will students continue to thrill to its abstract challenges only to continue to become evermore disillusioned with how little of what they dealt with in school has to do with the world they confront upon leaving it?

NEW KINDS OF LOADS: FORCES FOR SOCIO-INSTITUTIONAL CHANGE

One means of viewing forces for change is to see them as loads. Architects are intimately familiar with the concept of loads. We deal with them every day: structural loads, including vertical loads due to gravity, horizontal loads due to wind and seismic forces; circulation loads for adequate sizing of access and egress to buildings; parking loads, which so often dominate much of building design in Los Angeles. We deal equally with the two elements which both create and respond to loads: forces (of wind, rain, sun, earthquake), and capacities: the buildable envelope of a site, the number of seats in an auditorium, etc.

What follows are some numbers that describe forces which begin to define a whole new range of loads which need to be considered in planning and building for the future.

Time Magazine, in its *"Planet of the Year"* issue, told us that "through most of our two million years of existence on earth, humanity has thrived in earth's environment — perhaps too well. By 1800 there were one billion human beings

Richard Schoen is the co-founder of RSA Architects, the chair of the Los Angeles AIA Environmental Resources Committee and a Professor of Architecture at the UCLA Graduate School of Architecture and Urban Planning. His areas of specialty include energy/resource conserving design, building technology, and innovation and change in the building industry and design professions.

RSA Architects
6964 Shoup Avenue
Canoga Park, CA 91307
(818) 702-9654

bestriding the planet. That number doubled by 1930, and doubled again by 1975. If current birth rates hold, the world's present population of 5.4 billion will double again in forty more years. The frightening irony is that this exponential growth in the human population — the very sign of the homo sapiens' success as an organism — could destroy the earth as a human habitat." For example, "Mexico City has been described as the anteroom to an ecological Hiroshima. With 20 million residents, up from 9 million only twenty years ago, Mexico's capital is considered the most populous center on earth. Mexico City has been struck not by military weapons but by a population bomb.

"Ultimately, no problem may be more threatening to the earth's environment than the proliferation of the human species. Much of the next century's doubling will occur in poorer, developing countries (90%). During the next thirty years, for example, the population of Kenya (annual growth rate of 4%) will jump from 23 million to 79 million. Nigeria's population (AGR 3%) will soar from 112 million to 274 million. In the poorest countries, growth rates are outstripping the national ability to provide the bare necessities — housing, fuel, and food."

Thus, population pressures not only create almost non-respondable loads on the world's major cities, they call for unprecedented levels of new development at all scales, almost everywhere. This then is the issue, because geometric population growth in turn brings on, or at least contributes to, a host of other problems besetting the entire planet. And even though the impacts of first world lifestyles are currently more devastating than all the rest of the world's population combined, that equation will change radically as Third World development seeks to copy our unsustainable ways.

SOUTHERN CALIFORNIA: A THIRD WORLD MEGA-CITY

California is a microcosm of the world's growth. It is home to 30 million people, having added 6 million during the 80's, more than any other state has gained in one decade. About a third of the new people can be found in the Los Angeles area, which now holds more than 14.5 million residents - more than any other state except New York and Texas. California is almost certain to continue swelling twice as fast as the rest of the country until the state reaches 40 million... in about 2010. The continued population growth will affect the job and housing markets dramatically. Not surprisingly, overcrowding, insufficient amounts of potable water, polluted air brought on by an almost total reliance on the automobile as well as stationary combustion sources, polluted waters and soils, toxic waste dumps, rapidly filling landfills, and a significant urban heat-island-effect, all resemble similar problems being experienced by our colleagues in the developing world's major cities.

> *No problem may be more threatening to the Earth's environment than proliferation of the human species.*

If there is to be any hope at all of sustaining the basic needs of future Californians while still meeting current needs, all the while keeping the "Golden State" golden, sustainable development and architecture will be the key. With this in mind, we need then, to begin developing an architecture which can exist within the local resource base and as a result, 'live lightly on the land'."

The World Commission on Environment and Development in their report, *Our Common Future*, defined sustainable development as, "meeting the needs of the present without compromising the ability of future generations to meet their own needs."

In architectural terms, it would seem that sustainable architecture could best accomplish this by striving to live within the carrying capacity of the region, the local community, the site and place of building, and the land. To do so through design requires careful consideration and understanding of complex, systemic interactions between social-cultural, institutional, and technical considerations modified by program, environment, site, and climate — a deeper understanding of all contextual elements, beginning with watershed and ending with architectural detail.

> *Architecture now has this rarest of opportunities to give form to an entire new era.*

I believe that true architectural change, beyond mere stylistic fad or fancy, occurs only at times of great socio-institutional change. This is one of those moments in history. Architecture now has this rarest of opportunities to give form to an entire new era of peace, global awareness, and broad forces for change. If it misses this moment, it will perhaps never again recover from the place on the sidelines of a world in great flux where it will find itself.

SUSTAINABLE URBAN-RURAL ENTERPRISE EXPLORATIONS (SURE)

Andrew Euston, FAIA

Sustainability is the paradigm now and for the next millennium. It is the proper national purpose for the Untied States. We've led the pace for material progress. In our own self defense, we can and must build a path to ecological balance. The U.S. and humanity in general have become urbanized. If we ended war, urban ecological imbalances would remain to threaten all peoples. How to reconcile urban-rural patterns in the industrialized world of today is the core challenge of all politics, all humanitarianism, all enterprise. Sustainable enterprise will be the principal hope of this urban-dependent civilization humanity has come to depend upon.

At last, we can say we have a sustainable ecological cities movement underway. Now begun, it cannot afford to end unless, indeed, our urban civilization does. This historic conference, designed to help local leaders comprehend the overarching issue facing urban civilization — its sustainability — is one in a growing series of such conferences. The first one was convened in Richmond, Indiana, in 1989, entitled "Sustainable Urban-Rural Enterprise," or SURE. Since then, conferences on urban-rural sustainability have taken place in Berkeley, Chicago, the United Nations, Gainesville, Lincoln, Sarasota, Cambridge, Seattle and Amherst.

SURE LEADERSHIP IN RICHMOND, INDIANA

The Richmond/Wayne County, Indiana SURE conference of October, 1989 convened 40 out-of-state urban environmentalists, 40 citizens and officials and 20 Ball State University students and faculty. Its four day agenda has been translated into actions and further explorations. Eight topics were the focus of workshops to identify local options which have been pursued in varying ways since that conference. The eight topics are:

- Sustainable Enterprise Economic Models
- Water Treatment and Bio-mass
- Land Use Policies
- Energy Competitiveness
- Sustainable Enterprise Zones and Incubators
- Alternative Agricultural Production
- Communications Technologies
- Quality of Life

To give a sense of what has begun in Richmond/Wayne County, Indiana's SURE news coverage in the *Indianapolis Star* (11/10/91) is quoted here:

"In Indiana, the tomatoes in your salad might be from Mexico; the apples in your pie from Washington state; the broccoli on your plate from California. Though Indiana ranks about 23rd in vegetable and fruit production, out-of-

Andy Euston is Director of Sustainable Enterprise Explorations and Sr. Urban Design and Energy Program Officer, U.S. Department of Housing and Urban Development (HUD). Andy has been with HUD for 20 years, committed to sustainable design. He has established Sustainable Enterprise Explorations with HUD to function as a national networking and resource base for facilitating the nation's transition to ecological local self-reliance. He has written and talked extensively on the subject, including presentations to the Council on Environmental Quality, the Executive Office of the President and the U.S. EPA.

HUD
Room 7244
Washington, D.C. 20036
(202) 708-2504

state produce dominates menus and supermarket aisles here. That irks Delk [Bill Delk, a local restauranteur] and a handful of other people in Richmond who are trying to lessen the area's reliance on imports for even the humblest of veggies. They were surprised to find that the more than 50 restaurants, grocery stores and other food retailers in the Richmond area import $30 million worth of produce a year from far-away farms. And many of the items easily could be home-grown. Thus was born SURE, or Sustainable Urban Rural Enterprise. And from a slow start in 1989, SURE has made progress:

• The Richmond Farmer's Market this year added Tuesday hours and attracted an average of 34 vendors every Saturday, higher than in the past 10 years. A

> **Sustainability is the proper national purpose for the U.S.**

better site for the market, which used to set up on a city parking lot, was found last year next to the old train depot in the city's low-tax enterprise zone.
• A first-ever food show to encourage retailers to buy local produce was held in August. A larger show is planned next summer.
• Plans are under way to raise vegetables commercially in the winter in a greenhouse heated by steam from a power plant.
• A project with Richmond, Wayne County and Ball State University will use a computer to analyze three county farms to find alternative crops to grow and sell locally. "All these ideas have been done before, but to link all the ideas in a single community is a real jump Richmond is taking," says David Ferguson, a Ball State Associate Professor of landscape architecture.

CROP DIVERSITY VS. PROFIT

Ferguson has found 12 crops seldom grown in Indiana that he thinks Wayne County farmers could plant and market. They include asparagus, bamboo and mushrooms. An agricultural system set up to exploit economies of scale might increase profits, but it also limits diversity, he says. Indiana's two largest crops, corn and soybeans, account for 80 percent of the state's crop sales, and many Indiana grain farmers do not grow anything else. "As we made a push for commodity crops and mass crops, we squeezed out crops grown locally," says Ferguson. That limits choices for Midwest farmers and food handlers alike, who must rely on supplies delivered from across the continent in less-than-farm-fresh condition. Ferguson would prefer to see a profusion of crops on farms so an aerial view would look "more like a mosaic than a shag rug."

SUSTAINABLE ENTERPRISE CAN REBALANCE OUR CITIES

Today, all places are at risk as natural eco-systems relentlessly play by nature's rules in the brazen face of the human construct of urban civilization. What if, as is happening, the Third World blindly follows U.S. patterns and fatally magnifies our carbon burning, our toxification of earth's air, lands and waters as humankind consolidates its dependency upon urbanization and industrialization? Humanity is almost half urban already and world population will have tripled in this century. Science tells us that within decades, grave, increasing and irreversible human sufferings are the foreseeable outcome if we continue on our current unsustainable track.

Of concern everywhere, for example, is the health imbalance picture—its costs and causes. Decline in food's nutritional value (40% since WWII) and its chemical toxicity are two major health imbalance factors. Communities can rebalance the picture for themselves, if they choose, through urban organic, low-input, no-till agriculture enterprise. This is an urban planning, urban policy and urban sustainable enterprise agenda that could impact health and health costs in any community prepared to apply the necessary entrepreneurial correctives.

The average U.S. meal travels 1,600 miles to its destination. Citizens pay a fuel and transport premium for their impoverished diets. From the perspective of local economic health, virtually all fuel expenditures represent a hemorrhaging of local capital and its economic multiplier effects. Recognizing this, the energy directors for three West Coast cities—San Jose, San Francisco, and Portland—have generated the first urban energy efficiency options menu for addressing the hemorrhage. Their joint report is now available, as are a range of other insights that represent the emergence of an international Sustainable Enterprise Marketplace. The Harvard/MIT/HUD workshop report "Exploring Sustainability," San Jose's impressive action agenda "The Sustainable City," and the "Sourcebook for Environmentally Responsible Design" are among the current resources for exploring how sustainable enterprise can rebalance our cities.

SUSTAINABLE ENTERPRISE IS DIFFERENT FROM SUSTAINABLE GROWTH AND DEVELOPMENT

The phrase "sustainable development," like "sustainable growth," implies growth. For instance, the U.N. Brundtland Report of 1987, "Our Common Future," called for a five-to-ten-fold increase in global industrial output. Is this possible? Desirable? Inevitable? I propose here, as the alternative, "sustainable enterprise," which is process-oriented rather than product or production biased. It is a self-help, community focused corrective to conventional growth and development. A whole new pro-active potential emerges which concerned and innovative communities can begin to explore when the word "sustainable" is combined with "enterprise." It is up to communities to pursue their options, and that means entrepreneurship, an honorable and revered term in our culture.

We need to begin locally, within the existing marketplace, to help evolve a "Sustainable Enterprise Marketplace." Here and there, new modes of sustainable community governance are taking shape, which bode well for such objectives as retention of local capital, reduction of waste, improved environment and redefined options for improving the quality of life. In addition to places mentioned above, this new mindset is emerging in such diverse places as Lancaster, Pennsylvania; Sarasota, Florida; the Hopi nation in northern Arizona; Austin, Texas; Santa Fe, New Mexico; Cambridge, Massachusetts; and now, Los Angeles.

Whether we're talking about health efficiencies or fuel efficiencies or any number of related issues, communities can do better by and for themselves than they do now. Sustainable Urban-Rural Enterprise (SURE), and the concomitant global Sustainable Enterprise Marketplace imply new thinking. Wiser communities are beginning to mobilize the mindset required of this marketplace.

> *Virtually all fuel expenditures represent a hemorrhaging of local capital.*

Such places are shaping their own civic, nonpartisan, self-help approaches to building bridges from urban-rural-industrial civilization into the post- petroleum, post-war-production civilization ahead that peoples everywhere must eventually enter.

Americans are beginning to rebalance economics with ecology and thereby recast the flawed models being imitated by the masses of the globe. Three or four years ago, the local activity alluded to above would have seemed altruistic to me, beyond public acceptance, however valid its aims. But, the homily of "think globally, act locally," is gaining currency in all American communities. Individuals and their communities can indeed make new choices for themselves, discovering helpful linkages locally, as well as with other communities, in the process.

Usually the aggregated actions of science, commerce and nations remain at severe cross purposes with such a quest. "Sustainable enterprise" can serve to unify these actions into a more hopeful course of action overall. This will depend upon people acting at home and then aggregating their choices so as to induce new markets for authentically sustainable products and services.

In conclusion, there are specific steps to be considered, if a community chooses to gear up for sustainable enterprise. There is a modest literature to turn to for this purpose. There are formative meetings here and there. An informed network is in the making in which Los Angeles could play a role for the good of all.

RESOURCES:

An Energy Plan for Mission Bay, the first-ever urban design-scale guide for energy efficiency measures geared to larger urban projects. Conservation measures, marketability, affordability and high-priority and long-range elements are covered, 58 pp., available from the Bureau of Energy Conservation, City of San Francisco, (415) 864-6915.

A Sourcebook for Environmentally Responsible Design on Sustainably Developed Shelter, Land Use and Support Systems, 61 pp., available from the Boston Society of Architects: (617) 426- 0432.

Exploring Sustainability, conference report on current accomplishments by 14 pioneering specialists produced at MIT in 1988, 53 pp., available from Andrew Euston, FAIA, HUD, (202)708-2504, Room 7244, Washington, DC 20410.

Global Ecological Handbook, The Global Tomorrow Coalition, 414 pp., (202) 628-4016.

Heat, Plan and Heat Map, software computation systems for laying out district to citywide scale energy distribution networks for heating, cooling, thermal storage, waste-heat use, refuse-to-fuel, geothermal, cogeneration, renewable energy and other such urban energy systems. PC software and handbooks are available through Gordon Bloomquist, Washington State Energy Office, Olympia, Washington, (206)586-5000.

Remineralize the Earth Magazine, regenerating our soils, forest and health, recycling minerals with finely ground rock dust; quarterly, 50-60 pp., (413) 586-4429.

The Bottom Line: Restructuring for Sustainability, urban policy study, Gildea Resource Center's Community Environmental Council, $24, 930 Miramonte Dr., Santa Barbara, CA 93109, (805) 963- 0583.

The Sustainable City—A Revolution in Urban Evolution, presentation at Stanford in 1989 by City of San Jose officials, 25 pp., covers an outstanding public sector urban sustainability action agenda, available from Andrew Euston, FAIA, HUD, (202) 708-2504, Room 7244, Washington, DC 20410.

The Sustainable City Project, a 100-page report of a two-year joint effort by the Energy Offices of San Jose, San Francisco and Portland: strategic actions tied to prevailing city priorities for water, transportation, land use, waste, construction, etc. Available from Public Technology, Inc., Washington, DC (202) 662-2400.

ECOLOGICALLY INTEGRATED LAND USE PLANNING: A STRATEGY FOR SUSTAINABLE DEVELOPMENT

Jim Bell

Until recently, most urban planners have paid scant attention to the ecological aspects of the environment which their planning impacts. This is now changing to some degree but for the most part, plans designed to address ecological concerns have mainly led to cosmetic results. In other words, the projects that result from such planning may look good, but they contribute little toward making our society more ecologically secure. The reason for this problem is that planners, along with the rest of us, have very little knowledge about how our planet's life support system works, or what it costs us when our actions cause harm to it. Additionally, planners lack the critical tools which would help them present more ecologically sound land planning options.

To assist in addressing both of these problems, I am proposing a new approach to planning called Ecologically Integrated Planning or EIP. Basically EIP is a proactive planning method based on the premise that human built infrastructures are ultimately dependent on the ecological foundation upon which they literally rest. EIP also expands the venue of planning considerations beyond the boundaries of a particular project to include regional, national, and global concerns. The goal of EIP is to design communities that satisfy human needs and desires in ways which:

- Use local resources, like agricultural soils and groundwater deposits, sustainably.

- Maintain the integrity and diversity of local eco-systems by maximizing the preservation of native plant and animal communities.

- Use resources like energy and water as efficiently as possible.

- Minimize the use of imported resources and only use them if they are harvested, procured, and processed in ways that are ecologically sustainable.

To achieve its goals EIP examines land use considerations from three different infrastructural perspectives:

- The Ecological Infrastructure which encompasses everything in the natural environment including ourselves;

- The Human Support Infrastructure which focuses on the resources like agricultural soils from which humans benefit directly;

- The Human Constructed Infrastructure which is superimposed on the first two infrastructural levels.

Jim Bell is founder and director of the Ecological Life Systems Institute. He is a builder, planner, publisher, teacher and speaker on ecologically integrated design, and currently is Project Director for the Wastewater Treatment and Reuse Project in Tijuana, and Design Consultant for the East Lake Development Corp., the DeAnza Corp. and the Otay Ranch Joint Planning Project.

Ecological Life Systems Institute
2923 E. Spruce St.
San Diego, CA 92104
(619) 281-1447

The Ecological Infrastructure, in the broadest sense, includes everything in our planet's biosphere. It embodies the complex network of interrelationships and interdependencies which we, as a species, are part of and ultimately dependent upon for our survival. It is the underlying foundation upon which the well being of all life on our planet rests. Given this situation, the preservation and protection of our planet's ecological infrastructure is the primary consideration upon which all our planning decisions should be made. The planning processes related to the ecological infrastructure address a broad range of global concerns. However, from an applications perspective, a more localized ecologically defined planning area is needed. The most logical ecologically defined unit of space is the watershed or watersheds within which a project or mix of projects is to be built. This is because watersheds have an ecologically significant form and function relevant to the EIP process.

> *Preservation and protection of our planet's ecological infrastructure is the primary consideration upon which all our planning decisions should be made.*

In form, a watershed is a drainage basin composed of a valley and the surrounding slopes which funnel rainwater runoff into it. Because of its form, any heavier than air material that is introduced into a drainage basin will eventually impact lower elevations within the basin. Functionally, a watershed is home to a variety of multi-faceted and mutually dependent plant and animal communities. In addition to perpetuating themselves, these watershed communities benefit humans in a number of ways. For example, plant and animal communities build soil. They also protect watersheds from soil erosion and help them store water. Plant canopies and debris protect the soil from pounding rain. Root systems, in concert with tunneling organisms, make it easier for water to be absorbed into the soil and eventually into reservoirs and groundwater storage basins. The ability of healthy plant and animal communities to absorb rainwater also minimizes the problem of run-off.

The human support infrastructure represents the next level of relevancy in the EIP hierarchy. This infrastructure includes agricultural soils, stream and river channels, groundwater recharge areas, and groundwater storage basins. Although these elements of the human support infrastructure can be viewed as distinct physical features, it is vital to understand that their value as resources is almost entirely dependent on the health of the watershed community in which they lie.

The human constructed infrastructure which includes everything built by humans, is the third level of concern in the EIP process. Planners and members of the general public are relatively familiar with this level of infrastructure. But when it comes to making the connection between the human built infrastructure and its ecological supports, our understanding becomes a bit hazy. This haziness has, to a large extent, been the result of having access to cheap and abundant fossil fuels. Cheap, abundant energy has created the popularly accepted illusion that local ecological and human support resources have little value.

"Why not develop this prime agricultural site. It's more valuable to our community as a mall or industrial park than for growing food. Besides we can grow food other places and have it shipped here."

The preceding quote seems logical until we realize that it is based on the assumption that nonrenewable fossil fuels will last indefinitely. Currently around 8 to 20 units of fossil fuel are consumed for every one unit of food energy that ends up on our tables. Roughly 3/4 of this energy is consumed by non-farming activities like processing, packaging, and transportation. Clearly, in the long run, the validity of land use decisions based on the logic illustrated by the above quote will not hold up.

One way to bring into focus the connection between the human built environment and its ecological supports is to consider the ecological and the human support infrastructures from a global perspective. For example, world population is 5.4 billion and growing and there are only around 4 billion acres of reasonably fertile soil on the whole planet. Additionally, in the U.S. and planetwide, these soils are being rapidly degraded by erosion. The delivery of foods from distant sources is also dependent on the availability of cheap, nonrenewable fossil fuels. Given this national and global situation, over which we have very little control, is it not prudent to preserve the best agricultural soil in our local areas, places where we do have some control? Ultimately, these soils are our insurance policy for a food secure future. If these soils are preserved locally they can be used to grow food in the future if there is ever a serious breakdown in the current food production and supply system. If these soils are paved over or developed this option becomes seriously doubtful.

In order to take advantage of EIP principles, developing a new approach to mapping will be necessary to aid planners in integrating the three levels of infrastructure just discussed. In form, the maps will consist of base maps and overlays which delineate the various resources within each infrastructure level. Maps for a particular region will consist of a regional base map and maps for each major drainage basin within the region.

The formula for locating the boundaries of each regional map will be determined by the density and distribution of population within that region and the ecologically significant boundaries which surround this population. For example, using this method, the base map for the San Diego/Tijuana Region would encompass all the land south of the northern edge of the Santa Marguerite Watershed and north of southern edge of the Rio Guadalupe Watershed. In the east it is bounded by the Laguna Mountain divide which intersects the upper reaches of the Santa Margareta and the Rio Guadalupe watersheds. The region's western boundary is the Pacific Ocean. A number of other base maps would also be made to correspond with the major drainage basins of the region.

> *If soils are preserved locally they can be used to grow food if there is a serious breakdown in the current supply system.*

These base maps would have a series of transparencies or overlays for agricultural soils, flood plains, steep slopes, sensitive plant and animal habitats, wildlife corridors, and groundwater storage basins. An agricultural soils transparency might have several colors or patterns to differentiate the best soils from those that are less agriculturally valuable. Maps showing the location and type of existing development and zoning would also be prepared. These latter maps would help planners to assess the potential and cumulative ecological impacts of proposed and existing projects.

By laying the transparent maps over the base map it will be easy to see where the most ecologically and resource sensitive areas in a region are located in much the same manner as Ian McHarg has suggested in *Design With Nature*. It is obviously less desirable to develop areas where ecologically significant resources are present, especially where more than one of these resources occupy the same area. For example, flood plains, agricultural soils, and sensitive habitats often coincide. On the other hand, it would be logical to locate developments on sites where such resources are absent or where their value is marginal, i.e. it may make sense to locate development on marginally productive agricultural soils, especially if it would aid in preserving soils having more agricultural value. Along the same lines it is better to develop an area with marginal habitat value especially if it would take pressure off a habitat rich environment.

> *Most existing planning maps stop at property lines, no matter how ecologically arbitrary these lines may be.*

In addition to helping planners and the public easily identify significant ecological and human support resources, EIP maps can be used in at least two additional ways. First, EIP maps would simplify long term zoning decisions, particularly where the preservation of ecological and human support resources are concerned. Second, EIP maps that highlight existing development and zoning can help planners, developers, and policy makers evaluate a particular project's total impact on the watershed(s) it occupies.

In most jurisdictions today, large projects are already required to do considerable mapping. Unfortunately, the value of such maps is limited because they are site specific and do not normally extend to the boundaries of any meaningful ecological unit such as a drainage basin. Additionally, they do not usually include other existing or proposed projects. In most instances existing planning maps stop at property lines, no matter how ecologically arbitrary these lines may be. With such maps it is almost impossible to analyze the relationships between the various resources like agricultural soils, groundwater storage, and sensitive plant and animal habitats. It is also very difficult to gauge a particular project's impact in relationship to existing and proposed developments in the drainage basin(s) it will occupy.

The land use decisions we make today have a direct bearing on how secure our children will be in the future. The adoption of Ecologically Integrated Planning practices can help insure that the future we leave to our children will be a good one.

ECOLOGICAL DESIGN COMPONENTS

SOLAR DESIGN • WATER MANAGEMENT • URBAN LANDSCAPE • WASTE MANAGEMENT • TRANSPORTATION • SUSTAINABLE TECHNOLOGY

SOLAR DESIGN

SOLAR ACCESS

Ralph Knowles

T he sun is fundamental to all life. It is the source of our vision, our warmth, our energy, and the rhythm of our lives; its movements inform our perception of time and space and our scale in the universe. Assured access to the sun is thus important to the quality of our lives. Without this access, our perceptions of the world and of ourselves are altered. Without the assurance of solar access, we face uncertainty and disorientation, and we may lose our sense of who and where we are.

The natural world abounds with examples of arrangements based in some measure on exposure to the sun, but observations of the modern built world reveal that we have not followed nature's example in this regard. Our cities are nondirectional; our buildings are undifferentiated by orientation to the sun. They stand static, unresponsive to the rhythms of their surroundings. If we should wish to follow nature more closely, we must recognize the basic rhythms of solar change when we design and site our buildings. Hence, the concept of solar access must be defined by the paths of daily and seasonal variation in the sun's relationship to earth. For example, the length of our seasons may be determined by our latitude, but where we stand in relation to a tall building or hill that casts shadows can determine the perceptual length of our day.

A clear purpose is required to make sense of all this. Where and when we have access to the sun then becomes a matter of control, related to this purpose. If our purpose is to grow a summer garden, access must be provided from the east and west because most direct summer sun comes from those directions and from almost straight overhead. These observations, and countless others, remind us that the sun moves by day and by season. It is an ever-changing source of heat and light, a source that we can tap only to the degree in which we take account of its dynamic character.

SIGNIFICANCE OF SOLAR ACCESS

Without access to the sun, we cannot use it. Current discussions of solar access concentrate on the sun as a replacement for non-renewable fuel supplies and as a means for preserving our existing quality of life. Solar energy is a direct replacement for artificial light and heat, and through photovoltaic cells it beckons as a local alternative to electric power grids. In addition, the concept of solar access can support an improved quality of life.

Several components of our quality of life are related to the sun. The first is physical comfort, which may be the easiest to define. It is generally expressed in numerical ranges of temperature, humidity, air movement, light and other properties of the physical environment that impinge directly on our bodies.

Ralph Knowles is Professor of Architecture at the University of Southern California. His widely published work on solar policy and design has been recognized by awards of the AIA Medal of Research and by numerous grants from the National Endowment for the Arts. During 1993 he has been invited to teach and do research in a new program for ecological architecture at the Slovak Technical University in Bratislava, Czechoslovakia.

School of Architecture
University of Southern
* California*
Los Angeles, CA 90089-0291
(213) 740-2723

The second element, choice, is a harder element of life quality to define. For the designer, solar access provides a broader range of options because solar heat and light are assured for the future. For the user, solar access keeps future options open as changing technologies and aesthetics make the sun more valuable.

Comfort and choice are inextricably linked to the third element in the quality of life — a sense of well-being. Although somewhat difficult to define, well-being is nonetheless the reason we seek comfort and choice. Its superlative form is the fourth element in the quality of life — joy.

To the extent that solar access provides comfort, choice, and a sense of well-being, it provides the potential for joy. Perhaps joy lies in the sun's warm rays as they strike our outstretched bodies, or it may lie in reflections from a flower or a child's face. But in joy may lie the greatest justification for access to the sun.

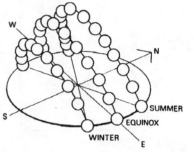

MEANS OF ACCESS

Solar access has come into focus as a topic of discussion in the United States because more and more we are turning to sunlight as a source of energy. A universal covenant has been sought that assures a right to the sun now and in the future. Alternative approaches to this problem have been explored but are largely untested in real communities. They fall into two main categories.

The first category includes a number of proposals to use permits, covenants, and easements aimed at guaranteeing solar access for energy conversion. An alternative to the permit system that applies to the same set of concerns is the "solar envelope." Several versions of this approach are being explored by cities, counties, and states throughout the country, but most share two characteristics. First, they are generally modeled on straightforward zoning regulations, and second, their intent is to assure future rights of access for land parcels.

The solar envelope has the additional advantage of being a more neighborly approach to the problem. Instead of restricting the development surrounding a given property, it constrains development on that property to protect the surroundings. The distinction may appear fine, but the ethical and legal differences can be significant.

The solar envelope is a container to regulate development within limits derived from the sun's relative motion. Development within this container will not shadow its surround during critical periods of the day. The envelope is therefore defined by the passage of time as well as by the constraints of property. The time involved would be a duration of solar access, a period of direct, line-of-sight approach to solar heat and light. The duration of access is determined by some segment of an arc drawn to represent the sun's path. If year-round access is required, two arcs may be used to represent paths of the sun during summer and winter.

> *The solar envelope is a container to regulate development within limits derived from the sun's relative motion.*

If the resulting angles of the solar azimuth and altitude are transferred to the edges and corners of a land parcel, the consequence is a set of geometric limits that derive their vertical dimensions from the sun's slanting rays. If the entire volume implied by the vertical limits is drawn as an explicit form, the result is a container with surfaces representing the three-dimensional boundaries of development. Depending on the duration of desired solar access, the land parcel configuration and surrounding conditions, the size and shape of the envelope will vary.

EXAMPLES FROM THE PAST

Built arrangements, like natural systems, should not use more energy than they exchange with their immediate environment. They must diversify to fit local conditions and not be dependent on large complexes of centralized energy supplies. The pueblos of America's Southwest provide a good example of how early settlements recognized natural rhythms in the adaptation of location and form for human comfort.

The location and form of buildings at Longhouse Pueblo, Mesa Verde, Colorado provided ancient residents with year-round comfort. The pueblo demonstrates a remarkable ability to mitigate extreme environmental temperature variations by responding to the differential impact of the sun during summer and winter, night and day.

The primary adaptation of the pueblo to the solar dynamic is in its location. The settlement is sited in a large cave that faces south, and the built structures are nestled within. The brow of the cave admits warming rays of the low winter sun but shields the interior of the cave from the rays of the more northern summer sun. Not only the orientation of the cave itself (which measures almost 500 feet across, is 130 feet deep and arches to 200 feet) but the juxtaposition of the structures within it are responsive to the solar dynamic. The interior structures stay within the summer shadow line, and they are arranged so that one structure steps up from another toward the back of the cave.

It is thus the location of the cave itself and the siting of the structures within the cave that ensured the comfort of the pueblo dwellers. Because of the orientation, the irradiation of the cave on a winter day is equivalent to that on a

All photos are of student projects from Ralph Knowles' University of Southern California design studio. Houses on this east slope capture winter sun through clerestories and channel it down through stairways into lower, and otherwise darker places. This project's Density Range is 20-28 du/a (dwelling units/acre).

summer day. The performance of buildings within the cave is 56% more effective as a solar collector in winter than in summer, providing winter heat and summer coolness with remarkable efficiency. Longhouse is one of many pueblos built after A.D. 1100 at Mesa Verde, but is one of only a few facing south. Those facing east are much colder in winter; those facing west are too hot in summer.

NATURAL VARIATION AND BUILDINGS

Form in nature bears the imprint of rhythmic variation. Buildings in our modern industrial cities are subject to the same recurring forces that act to structure nature. And yet despite this fact, we continue to build and perceive our cities as nonresponsive to recurring natural forces. There are few indications of natural rhythm in our urban forms. The modern city is a place where time is read from the face of a clock, not from natural cues. Days and seasons are counted along a single thread. They are not perceived as part of a deep tapestry of rhythms. The sun, for example, acts differently on the faces of a building, just as it does on the various slopes of a hill. James Marston Fitch, author of *American Building*, has asserted that the climatic differences between the north and south side of a building can be equivalent to 1,500 miles — the distance from Boston to Miami Beach.

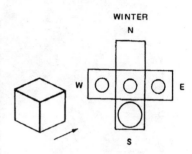

A cube-like building oriented on the cardinal points will receive different amounts of solar energy from one face to another. Over time, the irradiation levels upon any given face will vary. In winter, at 35 degrees north latitude, no energy will fall on the north face. The south face will receive the most energy, while east, west and top faces receive moderate amounts. In summer a small amount of energy will be received by the north face in the early morning and late afternoon and a small amount will also be received on the south face. But the lion's share will be received on the top face, with somewhat smaller amounts on the east and west. Overlay on this picture the variable impact of ambient temperature and wind, and the results can be startling.

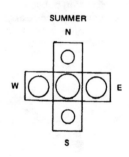

A warped and torn corner of a building near Anchorage is a good example of differential climatic impact. Constructed of metal panels, the building got only part-way through its first Alaskan winter. On a bright and windy November day, when the ambient air temperature dropped to about -30°F, the intense sun struck the south, west and top surfaces of the building. Where the panels met the southeast corner, the warming south face met the wind-chilled east. The combination of the expanding south and the contracting east literally exploded the corner.

The Alaskan case dramatizes the differential impact of sunlight and heat on the luminous and thermal state of the spaces inside buildings. How is it then that buildings usually look the same on all sides in spite of such differential impacts? For the answer to this question we must go back to conditions that followed World War II.

After World War II, rapid growth was the order of the day. The war years almost completely diverted our energy and resources abroad so that by 1945 there was a backlog of building need. The result was a postwar period of exuberant urban expansion. Such rapid growth could not really be planned. Changes took place so fast that planners could barely keep their maps up-to-date. We were busy applying American know-how, turning out buildings in assembly-line fashion,

When future conditions surrounding a building are subject to rapid change, and when the building cannot be fit to its environment with any certainty about its future performance, one solution is to build an indifferent box, seal it up, and supply it internally with life-support systems. And this is what happened. Based on a cheap supply of fossil fuels, such systems were developed and used to such an extent that today something in excess of 35% of our total annual energy consumption goes to light, heat and cool our buildings.

THE NON-IMAGE OF THE CITY

The American city's "legibility" (the visual cues by which we orient ourselves in a city) suffered during the thirty-year period of growth from 1945 to 1975. In great part this was the result of rapid development. We did not have time to plan. Rather than take the time to fit our development to a varied environment, we often modified the environment to fit repeated units of construction. Domi-

nation of nature was heady stuff, but it had at least one unforeseen consequence. Our urban environments became, in a sense, aspatial and atemporal. Our large buildings were often built to appear the same from side to side and from top to bottom. Large and small buildings were often built alike from block to block and even from one geographical region to another, regardless of energy.

Buildings took on a flat two-dimensional character that was repeated like the receding images between two opposing mirrors. Our buildings no longer responded architecturally to real time. They could mechanically peak-load off-site energy sources

Existing building stock in foreground allows neither view, cross-ventilation, nor daylight. The background design to the left combines apartments with townhouses around a south-facing, semicircular courtyard. The design to its right is split by a narrow N-S court that allows the midday winter sun to enter.

and be independent from the older adaptations of locations and form. Because designers depended almost exclusively on mechanical rather than architectural support systems, they did not often address the passage of time. As a result, time became non-imaginable. Only plate glass windows gave witness to daily and seasonal intervals. The location and form of buildings provided no cues. Our constructions stood faceless in their ranks, and still do.

Can our cities be transformed to use solar energy and thereby improve the quality of life? The answer is a conditional "yes." The condition is that we must spend more human energy designing a framework for urban growth so that less machine energy need be spent to maintain what we build. A part of the framework for urban growth is already in place, in the network of streets that define the urban grid. If solar envelope zoning provides another part of the framework, a careful look at street orientation is useful.

STREET ORIENTATION

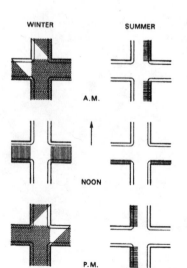

The solar envelope's size, shape, and orientation are greatly dependent on the patterns of urban settlement. In the United States, that context is usually influenced by orderly subdivisions that have geometricized the land. Typically, throughout the Midwest and the West, streets run with the cardinal points so that rectangular blocks extend in the east-west and north-south direction of the Jeffersonian grid.

Other grid orientations derive from climate, topography and geology. In Los Angeles, for example, the old Spanish grid is oriented nearly 45 degrees off the cardinal points. This diagonal orientation, an adaptation to sea breezes, was ordered by the King of Spain. It now extends from the old pueblo over the land that is modern downtown Los Angeles.

Before discussing the street grid's influence on the solar envelope, and hence on development, there should be some mention of the important qualitative differences of streets themselves as a result of their orientation. A comparison of the Jeffersonian and Spanish grids serves to demonstrate inherent properties related to shadows.

For example, streets that run east-west in a built-up urban area will tend to be shadowed during all of a winter day. In most parts of this country, including Los Angeles at 34 degrees north latitude, the streets thus remain dark and cold. By contrast, streets that run north-south are lighted and warmed during the midday and are consequently more pleasant during the busy noon time shopping period.

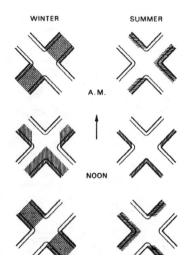

Summer presents an entirely different picture. Unlike winter, when the sun's rays come from the southern sky, the summer sun comes more directly from the east in the morning and from the west in the afternoon. At mid-day, it is nearly overhead. Streets that run east-west will receive a little shadow at mid-day, much less in the morning and afternoon — a critical factor on a hot afternoon. Streets that run north-south will be shadowed in the morning and afternoon, but will receive the full force of summer's midday sun.

From the point of solar orientation, the Jeffersonian grid leaves something to be desired. Its east-west streets are too dark and cold in winter; its north-south streets too bright and hot in summer. In Los Angeles, the older Spanish grid seems to have advantages regarding street qualities of light and heat.

During the winter, every street on the Spanish grid receives direct light and heat from the sun sometime between 9 A.M. and 3 P.M., the six hours of greatest irradiation. It is true that at mid-day all streets have shadows, but because of the diagonal orientation, the effective street width is very much increased, leaving more of the street in sunlight than would be the case for a street that ran directly east-west.

While every street in the Spanish grid receives direct sunlight and heat at some period of a winter day, every street has the advantage of some shadow during most of the summer day. Shadows are cast into every street all day long, with the exception of a short period during late morning and early afternoon when the sun passes quickly over the diagonal streets.

These differences in street quality that result from solar exposure are felt, if only subconsciously, by people, and they are even

This view from the north shows how separate designs seem to merge into a single form under the solar envelope. Also seen at closer hand are details of terracing and clerestories so characteristic of designs that take advantage of assured access to direct sunshine. This project's Density Range is 76-128 du/a.

acknowledged by real estate experts. But street orientation is almost never considered as a basis for land-use and planning decisions.

THE INFLUENCE OF STREET ORIENTATION
ON THE SOLAR ENVELOPE

Street orientation influences the solar envelope in two ways. The first of these has important consequences for development, the second relates more to issues of urban design.

The solar envelope over a city block oriented on the cardinal points will contain more developable volume than one over a diagonal block. Generally, the most height, and hence volume, are attainable at either of the two possible block orientations within the Jeffersonian grid, and the least volume is attainable at about the angular orientation of the Spanish grid. The street's gain in sunlight thus appears to be the developer's loss; this has made downtown Los Angeles a challenging problem from the viewpoint of development.

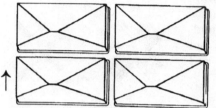

The urban design consequences of street orientation are important because they relate to legibility. Pathways, districts, and directions take on clearer perceptual meaning when the solar envelope becomes a framework for urban development.

These points can be demonstrated by the variations in solar envelope sizes and shapes that would result from different block orientations. These differences will result in street asymmetries, district variety and clear directionality along the streets. Such differences tend to occur systematically, not randomly, when designing with solar envelopes in mind. They therefore serve as dependable cues to orientation.

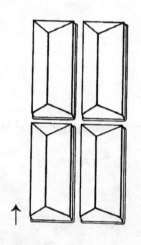

For example, solar envelopes over blocks that run long in the east-west direction contain the most bulk and have the highest ridges, generally located near the south boundary. Development that respects the envelope will occur symmetrically along the short dimension of the block, and asymmetrically on the long dimension, with high buildings on the north and low ones on the south to admit winter sun. Buildings along the north side of the street will vary in height. They will appear low at corners and gradually rise toward a high, level section at mid-block.

Solar envelopes on long north-south blocks will have less bulk and a somewhat lower ridge running lengthwise down the middle of the block. North-south streets will be symmetrical, while the shorter east-west streets will be higher on the north than on the south side. Those to the north will rise to an abrupt peak mid-block.

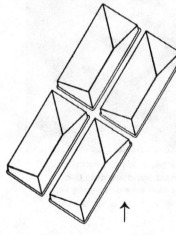

A third orientation, that of the diagonal Spanish grid as in downtown Los Angeles, produces envelopes with the least bulk and a ridge along the southeast boundary. All streets will be developed asymmetrically, with the northwest and northeast sides of the street higher, and the southeast and southwest sides lower to admit the winter sun all day long. Intersections will, where the envelope is respected, be marked with a high building on the north corner surrounded by lower ones on each of the three corners.

We thus see that development within the solar envelope is highly legible. Streets become qualitatively as well as quantitatively different. They have a predictable one-sidedness. Under the envelope, a change of street orientation always signals a change of aspect. Corners become unique events and are visually announced as one approaches by car or on foot. Street asymmetries, directional differences of streets, and differentiation along streets, all add to the definition of pathways, districts, and directions.

A DESIGN CHALLENGE

What has compelled me to explore the solar envelope so rigorously in all its diversity is that, more than any other means of regulation, it evokes form. The more diversified the context of its application, the richer the form possibilities become.

Where programmatic requirements of development cause the design to push against the limits of the solar envelope, the shape of those limits can play an important aesthetic role. If the designer values the sun as a basis for architectural and urban form, the envelope will be a tool that helps to translate that value into shapes, while providing neighboring projects with the opportunity to do the same. The photographs included here are from projects by some of my students. Their assignment was to create maximum density, while at the same time permitting solar access. Even when densities exeed 100 DU (dwelling units) per acre, these images convey a hint of the rich diversity possible when designing within the solar envelope.

A photgraph of the overall project, a detail of which is shown on page 86. This project's Density Range is 37-72 du/a.

Complex movements of the sun are difficult to see and impossible to quantify without a reference. The solar envelope provides both the reference and a formal expression of the effects of the sun's motion. It thereby introduces the designer to the concept of form in time and provides a basis for thinking of time as a medium of design. Time, as well as space, thus becomes the basis for a new aesthetic.

I hope that designers will rise to this challenge. At the same time, I hope they will not fail to understand the aesthetic, as well as the ethical and energic implications of this envelope, and to consider it not as a shackle on their imagination but rather as a concept that can help them to uncover unique, significant and beautiful architectural form.

PASSIVE SOLAR OVERVIEW: MINIMIZING MECHANICAL HEATING AND COOLING

Richard Crenshaw

Richard Crenshaw is an Architect and Landscape Architect who spent ten years in architectural practice, worked on the design of the New Towns of Reston and Columbia, spent 15 years doing research on performance standards, housing, and energy at the National Bureau of Standards and the Lawrence Berkeley Laboratory. He also taught environmental technology at Florida A & M University and is now drawing on these experiences to design a sustainable community for the Chesapeake Bay.

Managed Environments
940 Bay Ridge Ave.
Annapolis, MD 21403
(301) 268-3592

Over the years we have learned to use massive amounts of energy to create artificially conditioned spaces which overcome adverse physical situations so our species can live anywhere on the planet without adapting to the environment. Lately, however, we have discovered that all these artificially conditioned spaces are consuming a lot of high-grade non-renewable energy that could be replaced with low-grade solar energy or conserved by creating better enclosures. In this paper I would like to explore what we could do in the Los Angeles area to eliminate space conditioning mostly in homes, although the same principles apply to many other types of buildings.

To begin our effort to minimize, or maybe even eliminate the use of mechanical equipment like furnaces and air conditioners, we need to understand two concepts. The first is energy conservation and the second is passive solar heating and cooling. Energy conservation should be the first line of defense, and it refers to conserving heat in the winter and coolness in the summer. To do this we need to insulate a house very well, reuse extra heat and reduce heat losses due to infiltration in the winter and heat gains due to radiation in the summer. For example, refrigerators, stoves and other appliances, should be examined as a source of heat for hot water, thus reducing the heat they add to the house during the summer. Air which is exhausted to maintain indoor air quality should be vented through a heat exchanger in order to transfer heat in the outgoing air stream to cold incoming air.

Passive solar heating and cooling make use of natural forces in the environment to produce comfort rather than trying to overpower temperature and humidity by mechanical means. To accomplish this in heating and cooling, one has to be aware of natural climatic forces as well as one's own need for comfort. Comfort needs must be carefully considered so we don't use energy to provide comfort that we don't need. There is a lot of variation in the air temperature and humidity at which we are comfortable, depending on what we're doing, what we're wearing, how much breeze is blowing, and whether the sun is shining. Even though we set our thermostats at 68°F, 78°F is quite comfortable during the summer, 55°F is comfortable during the night when we are under the covers, 85°F can be comfortable when there is a breeze, and 45°F can be comfortable when we are skiing in a bathing suit on a clear sunny day.

So when we think of comfort, we have to be specific about the activities people are engaged in and the clothing worn. With this in mind we have an opportunity to save a lot of energy by making our bedrooms warm in the morning, cool during the day and cooler after we are in the bed, or by moving from room to room to take advantage of rising heat on the second floor in the evening during the winter, and the shade on the north side during the summer.

CLIMATE

To optimize the relationship between humans and our environment, we have to examine climate in some detail. In the example below I have used national hourly weather data for a typical year in Long Beach to represent only one of many microclimates that exist in the Los Angeles area. If you want to examine your area, you can get similar data from the weather bureau and follow my procedure. The results may be very similar, but there is still a lot to be gained from looking for the subtle differences. Beyond this, if you really want to be in tune with the weather on your site, you ought to install a small weather station to see if the temperature, humidity, wind, and solar radiation on the site roughly correspond to the weather data. They won't correspond exactly, because each year is different, but the overall trends ought to be the same. After you feel you have the best typical year weather data, put it into four weather graphs like those shown below so you can easily examine each component. The vertical axis represents hours and the horizontal axis represents months.

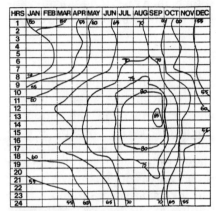

Temperature -- Long Beach

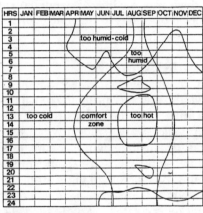

Temp. • Humidity

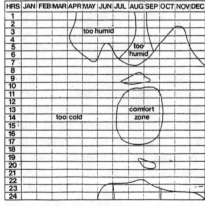

Temp. • Humidity • Wind

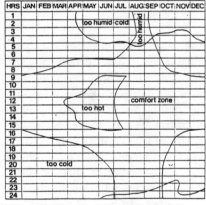

Temp. • Humidity • Wind • Solar

Fig. A 1

MICROCLIMATES

Looking at the data above, you can see that Long Beach is an ideal climate for human habitation and, if it didn't have air pollution, it wouldn't need any space conditioning. It gets a little warm in the summer and some times the humidity is a little high, but very warm in Long Beach is 85°F and very humid is 85%. Warm days are followed by cool, clear nights. There is usually a breeze off the ocean, and as the temperatures pick up, so do the breezes. With this overall understanding of your local climate, you can examine the mechanics of your microclimate so you can locate and orient your building properly. On the following pages described the mechanics of several microclimates are described, but the one we are mostly concerned in our example is the ocean microclimate.

OCEAN

During the day the air over land is heated more than that over water. The warm air over land rises, pulling cooler air from the water to create an on-shore breeze which may be felt 30 miles inland. At night the situation is reversed and the warmer air over the water pulls the air off the land creating off-shore breezes. The on-shore breeze starts out perpendicular to the land about sunrise and keeps swinging around to the northwest until it becomes off-shore breezes by sunset. Since the temperature difference between the land and the water is greater during the day, the off-shore breezes are stronger than the on-shore breezes. The on/off-shore breezes are a constant source of moving air, rather like a big fan that blows cool air during the day and warm air during the night. If one could figure out when a building was overheated and which way the breezes were blowing at that time, then one could orient ventilation openings to maximize air movement within the building when cool air was needed.

> *One could orient ventilation openings to maximize air movement within the building when cool air was needed.*

MOUNTAINS

In mountainous areas, variations in surface temperature tend to create local wind patterns. During the day if the upper part of the hills become five degrees warmer than the valleys, a slow up-valley wind develops along with a stronger up-valley-walls (slopes) wind. During the night the reverse takes place with the downslope winds being less than the down-valley winds. At night downslope winds are about 3 mph and the down-valley winds are about 5 to 8 mph. When the cool night air flows down into low areas, it lifts the warmer air above it. If this cooler air is not warmed, an inversion is set up and a frost pocket is created. At night the valley temperatures are 10 degrees less than the slopes and the humidity 20% higher, while during the day the valley is warmer than the slopes.

As the wind flows across the ridge, there is a point of separation. A zero wind eddy develops just downslope of this point of separation. If the wind is not strong enough, there is no point of separation, and the winds follow the slope. Most of the precipitation falls on the leeward or on the windward side at the top. Fog is thicker and more prevalent in valleys where colder heavier air tends to collect. Fog also occurs along the coast where shore breezes bring moist warm air into contact with colder land masses or bodies of water. It is important to understand that all these descriptions of typical conditions are idealized and really need to be checked with simple measurements like watching a string blow in the breeze. Despite the oversimplification, one can see what variations to look for and how important location is in the mountains or hills in order to maximize rainfall or daytime breezes and minimize frost and fog.

OPEN FIELD AND FORESTS

Open fields get warm during the day because of their exposure to solar radiation and cold at night because of their re-radiative losses to the clear dry Southern California sky. A forest is cooler than an open field during the day and warmer during the night. While it may appear that the forest is an improvement over the open field, Californians who live there often complain about long cold periods when they wish there were fewer trees so they could get warmed by the sun. With this in mind, it seems that the proper solution in Southern California is to surround buildings with a few carefully placed trees that provide shade when it is hot and sunlight when it is cold.

URBAN AREAS

Large urban areas like Los Angeles are great dry heat islands that evaporate much of the water that falls on them and are 4-5 degrees warmer than the surrounding area in both the summer and the winter. This occurs because urban areas are great solar collectors with more dark surface area and more conductive materials that have a greater thermal storage capacity than surrounding rural and suburban areas. In such an area, the orientation of the streets has a significant impact on how much solar radiation is absorbed and how much wind is available to carry excess heat away. By introducing pockets of green space the temperature in the city can be lowered and the relative humidity raised. In Los Angeles, we need to design a city that is more sensitive to our microclimatic needs. For example, we need to have the thermal mass of the city exposed to the sun from November to May when it is cold but not exposed to it from June to November when it is hot.

LANDSCAPE MODIFICATIONS

In addition to the mechanics of typical microclimates, one must understand how existing or introduced landscaping might modify these idealized microclimates. There are many opportunities to manage the microclimate around a building by using plants, fountains and fences. Comfortable living spaces can be created outside in partly or completely surrounded courtyards. Individual trees can be carefully placed to reduce cooling loads by 40% to 80% and to reduce heating loads due to nocturnal re-radiation in the spring, fall, and winter. Carefully selected trees can leaf and defoliate at just the right time. Dense shrubs not only shade part of the wall from solar radiation but also create a dead air space behind them which acts as insulation. Windbreaks can be used to

> *There are many opportunities to manage the microclimate around a building by using plants, fountains and fences.*

funnel air into windows or to reduce infiltration. Vines can be used to shade walls. Fountains or pipes dripping water can be used to reduce temperatures through evaporation. Ground surfaces around buildings can be used to reflect or store solar radiation thus causing local changes in outdoor air temperature which affect heat gains and losses through walls and windows. On a hot day in Los Angeles, for example, a typical temperature for grass is 89°F, for asphalt it is 106°F, and for concrete it is 111°F.

COMFORT CONDITIONS ON YOUR SITE

When you feel that the four basic weather graphs of temperature, humidity, wind, and solar radiation represent your best estimate of the conditions that will exist on your site after you have finished landscaping it, you are ready to evaluate whether or not the conditions on your site will make you uncomfortable. This is done by overlaying the four weather graphs (Fig. A1) to see when the combined effect of temperature, humidity, wind, and solar radiation match the condition Olgay describes in his human comfort chart as uncomfortable. For further information on these charts you should look at Victor Olgay's book *Design with Climate*.

Following are three Long Beach comfort graphs using Olgay's human comfort chart and the four weather graphs shown in (Fig A1). The first of these (Fig. B1) considers temperature and humidity and shows when uncomfortable conditions exist. The second (Fig. B2) considers temperature, humidity and wind, and shows when uncomfortable conditions exist. By comparing the first graph with the second, one can determine when it would be advantageous to let the wind into your building and when it would be advantageous to keep it out. In general, one can see that the wind can eliminate all the overheated periods, but, at the same time, can make periods that were comfortable too cold. In order to make best use of the wind, one has to find out which directions the wind is blowing from and orient operable windows in those directions when it is helpful.

The third graph (Fig. B3) shows how comfort is modified by solar radiation. Here again one can find periods where the sun is useful and when it is not. If we go back and examine the first Long Beach comfort chart in terms of how it was modified using wind and then solar radiation, we can see that the period of overheating during July, August and September can be brought into the comfort range by wind, and that cold periods between 8 am and 5 pm in November through April can be brought into the comfort range by solar radiation. The only periods which remain out of the comfort zone are evenings that are too cold. To bring these into the comfort range, use passive solar heating techniques which carry heat from the day over into the evening.

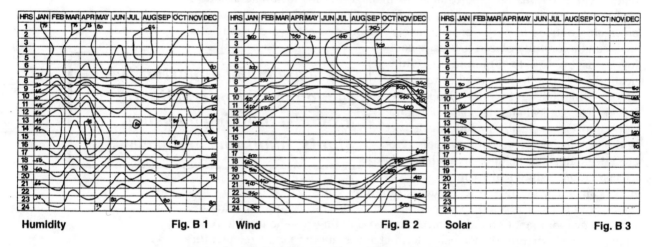

Humidity   Fig. B 1   Wind   Fig. B 2   Solar   Fig. B 3

STRATEGIES FOR MANAGEMENT

Based on the analysis above, we can see that there are four strategies that would be useful in Long Beach for making us comfortable. They are:

1. Use of solar glazing and shading devices to control solar radiation.
2. Carefully designed openings to maximize ventilation.
3. Use of passive solar heating strategies to carry heat from the day over into the evening.
4. Careful design of the roof.

In addition, two other techniques, night ventilation and radiant cooling, can be very useful as one moves inland away from the ocean breezes.

SOLAR GLASS

Three things happen to radiant energy when it strikes a window: part of it is reflected, having no thermal effect on interior spaces; part of it is absorbed and then dissipated to either side of the window based on the temperature differences between the glass and either side; and part of it is transmitted through the glass depending on the angle of incidence of the radiation and the spectral qualities of the glass. Regular glass transmits short wave radiation and absorbs long wave radiation. Heat Mirror, on the other hand, is a new type of glass that has been developed to reflect long wave radiation heat back into the interior of the building during the winter and back outside during the summer without reducing the transmission of light. Heat absorbing glass is much less effective, because it is designed to absorb long wave radiation and dissipate it to either side of the window. Heat reflective glass is a poor performer, because it is designed to reflect light and heat back into the environment, thus reducing heat gain not only in summer, but also in winter, and reducing the amount of daylight that reaches the interior of buildings all year.

SUN SHADING

Solar control is the least costly yet most effective means of passive cooling. Where monthly mean temperatures are less than 80°F, controlling solar heat gain can virtually eliminate the need for mechanical cooling. External shading devices are more effective than internal devices because they intercept the heat before it reaches the building. With external devices it is possible to eliminate more than 90% of the heat from solar radiation while with interior shading devices it is hard to eliminate more than 20-25% (Givoni, pg. 216). The west side of the building is the most important side to shade. East is next and then south. Dark external shading devices are more efficient than light ones on the windward side of the building, while lighter interior shading devices are more efficient than dark ones (Givoni, pg. 216). On the south, southeast and south-west sides, horizontal shading devices are more effective then vertical ones. While on the east and west exposures, egg crate shading devices are best, especially if the vertical members are oblique at 45 degrees.

The projection or overhang of the shading device in Los Angeles should equal the height of the opening divided by four (Mazria, pg. 250). The best way to evaluate how shading devices are working is to build a small model and then take it outside on a clear day and look at the shadows. To the right is a sundial that has marked on it the location and height (gnomon height) of the dial or pin. This sundial can be blown up in size and mounted on the base of your model with its arrow pointing south and a pin installed in the circle marked for it. After you mount it, if you take the model outside and point it towards true south, you can see on the sundial as you tilt it what time and date the cast shadows represent.

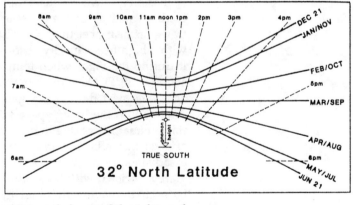

VENTILATION

Ventilation is dependent on the wind speed, the size and shape of the inlet and outlet, external architectural features, internal partitions, and the angle at which the wind hits the building. Overhangs, parapets, and wing walls can be used to force air into an opening. These are especially effective if the window is high. The principal requirement for satisfactory ventilation is an opening on both the windward and leeward side of a building. In the absence of cross ventilation, air movement equals 15% of wind speed. With cross ventilation, air movement equals 40% to 60% of wind speed. Velocity is maximized by orienting openings perpendicular to the prevailing wind and by locating inlets and outlets directly opposite each other with the outlet slightly higher to take advantage of the stack effect and 1.25 times larger to account for friction.

Distribution, scouring, and heat transfer are increased by turning the above configuration obliquely to the incident wind even though this lowers the velocity somewhat. Barriers within a space can serve to increase air movement patterns by creating eddies and secondary circulation loops pulled by suction. Air stream should be between 100-400 feet per minute (fpm) in the occupied zone in the summer in this climate. In a living room with people seated, air movement should be directed across heads and shoulders of the occupants. In a bedroom air flow should be directed just above height of bed in the part of the room where the bed is. In offices and schools, the air stream should be directed at head and shoulders of the occupants without disturbing the papers on desks. Fly screens reduce air flow by 50% to 60% at air velocities of 2 mph and 25% at 10 mph. Screened porches and balconies can compensate for this by increasing the ventilation area.

VOCABULARY OF AIR SPEED

Comfort Temp.
at 60%
Relative Humidity

Still air less than	50 fpm	76.7°	.6 mph
Pleasant	100 fpm	79.5°	1.1 mph
Aware air moving	200 fpm	83.2°	2.3 mph
Drafty	300 fpm	84.6°	3.5 mph
Disturbs papers	400 fpm	86.0°	4.5 mph
Breezy	800 fpm	88.0°	9.0 mph

DIRECT GAIN PASSIVE SOLAR HEATING

For solar heating, there must be south facing glass, thermal mass such as water or masonry, moveable insulation to keep the heat in at night, and a distribution medium such as air to move the heat around. Massive walls have the ability to transport heat over time. Dense building materials such as water and masonry with a high heat capacity absorb heat during the day, store it, and then release it during the night when temperatures get relatively low (daily temperature swing of 30°F). Once these materials have cooled they are ready to absorb heat again the next day. Direct gain solar systems allow solar radiation to enter directly into the living space where it is stored and used. The advantages to this are that losses due to heat transfer are greatly reduced, and room surfaces are warmed, allowing air temperatures to be comfortably lowered to 62°F. The disadvantages are that these living spaces tend to overheat, and there is a lot of glare associated with the south facing glass. Overheating can usually be solved by accurate engineering and by providing high and low operable windows, but glare is a more difficult problem and has to be dealt with on site to avoid cutting off needed solar radiation.

ROOF

One should be very aware of the roof. The roof is the part of a building that is most exposed to climate. It is the most important part of the building for protecting us from our environment. It is exposed to sun, wind, rain, snow and the cold night sky more than any other part of a building. It may be subject to the hottest and coldest temperatures and largest temperature fluctuations. The size of the roof is of first importance. The smaller the better. More wall area is a much better strategy than more roof area in this climate. The color of the roof is the second most important aspect of the roof. A dark roof will be 55°F warmer than a white one (Givoni, pg. 140). A double roof or a vented attic is also another very useful strategy for protecting the interior spaces from the extremes experienced by the roof.

PASSIVE COOLING WITH THERMAL MASS AND NIGHT VENTILATION

In areas where the night temperatures drop below comfort levels, and where mean daily temperatures are less than 60-65°F, cool night and morning air can be circulated through the building to draw heat from the thermal mass of the structure. Then the thermal mass can act as a heat sink during the day to absorb heat. This strategy is most appropriate in climates where large diurnal temperature variations exist of 30°F or more. Cooling capacity of this system is limited to the minimum outdoor temperature and how well the thermal storage is exposed to night air. An office building in Davis, California designed by Sim Van der Ryn et al. uses thermal mass with night ventilation to achieve indoor temperature fluctuations between 65-80°F while the outside temperatures reach 100°F.

RADIANT PASSIVE COOLING

It was noticed that a great deal of the heat gained during the day in a solar building was lost during the night unless a thermal barrier was dropped over the windows at night. This observation suggested that the night sky might be a reasonable source of radiant cooling. However, using the sky as a heat sink is questionable, because even with a completely clear sky, its temperature rarely drops below 20°F except in arid areas where the air is dry. Cloud cover severely reduces the sky's cooling rate, and a heavy overcast can effectively shut off the thermal view of the sky. Even with a clear sky the heat transferred to an object by moving air can offset that lost by radiation to the sky. A 3 mph breeze can halve the maximum clear sky losses and a 7.5 mph wind will reduce clear sky losses by a factor of 8.5. With this in mind, one could say that night cooling is only suited to regions where the summer skies are clear during overheated periods. Along with this, it is difficult to expose part of the building to the sky at night without exposing it to a solar load during the day.

> *Night cooling is only suited to regions where the summer skies are clear during overheated periods.*

Two approaches have been used to solve this problem. One is to place a pool on the roof for cooling during the night and then draw the fluid into the building during the day where it is protected from solar radiation. The other approach is to glaze the roof and open it to the sky at night to expose interior thermal mass to the night sky and then close it during the day.

CONCLUSION

Summarizing the Long Beach example for minimizing mechanical heating and cooling, we can conclude the following:

1. Once the site has been picked then the building and the spaces within the building have to be located and oriented to take advantage of the ocean breeze and other conditions that exist on the site. Avoid locating buildings in frost pockets and carefully evaluate the wind when a building is on the top of a hill.

2. Two types of outdoor spaces or courtyards are needed: one is exposed to the wind but protected from the sun for summer use; and the other is protected from the wind but exposed to the sun for winter use. Carefully placed trees and hedges can be used to block the breeze and to let the sun in from November to April and to keep it out from May to November. Fountains can be used in the summer for cooling. Windbreaks can be used to funnel air into a building. Walkways and paved courtyards should be explored as solar collectors to reduce the outdoor temperature swing between day and night.

3. Design houses with a small well-protected thermal core and a less-protected larger area that can be expanded into during pleasant weather. Take into account how one might move in the house during the day. Locate the bedrooms on the second floor where they will be warm in the evenings and locate the bathtub so you can get out of it into the sunshine.

4. The whole building needs to be well insulated. The roof needs to be light in color and have a well insulated vented attic with reflective foil placed on top of the insulation.

5. Evaluate solar shading devices using a model with a sundial. Be sure to include trees and their defoliation in your evaluation as a backup to solar shading devices.

6. Ventilation openings need to be oriented to the northwest to take advantage of the scouring effect of the on-shore breezes between 11 am and 4 pm in the months of May to November. Of course, you should check your site to see if the breezes come from the west between 11 am and 4 pm during the months of May to November. Most of the ventilation openings should be opaque and heavily insulated so they can be closed at 3 pm or 4 pm to prevent the setting sun from overheating the building. An equal amount of high openings need to be provided mostly on the north and south walls to create cross ventilation and prevent excessive heat gain. Remember that evening breezes will be off-shore and therefore from the east.

7. Glass openings for passive solar heating should be oriented south and have shading devices that protect them from May to November but let the sun in from November to April. This can be evaluated with a model using the sundial. Glass openings need to be covered with some type of insulation during the night to prevent heat collected during the day from escaping. Heat Mirror could be used on all orientations. The east and west walls should have minimal openings.

8. Calculations need to be done on the area of the following: ventilation openings and exits, solar glazing, and thermal mass. More in most cases is not better. Too much glass will overheat the building and too much mass will make it difficult to heat the building.

9. After you complete the building, put min/max thermometers in every room to see how things are going and call me if you need help.

REFERENCES

Givoni, B., *Man, Climate, and Architecture*, Elsevier Publishing Company Ltd., New York, NY, 1969.

Mazria, Edward, *The Passive Solar Energy Book*, Rodale Press, Emmaus, PA, 1979.

Olgay, Victor, *Design with Climate*, Princeton University Press, Princeton, NJ, 1963.

Watson, Donald, *Climate Design*, McGraw Hill Book Co., New York, NY, 1983 (see Bibliography pp. 251-273).

ECOLOGICAL DESIGN COMPONENTS

SOLAR DESIGN • *WATER MANAGEMENT* • URBAN LANDSCAPE • WASTE MANAGEMENT • TRANSPORTATION • SUSTAINABLE TECHNOLOGY

WATER MANAGEMENT

HOME AND COMMUNITY WATER MANAGEMENT

Bill Roley, PhD

Over 70% of the earth's surface is covered by water. Sea water comprises 97.6% of our world's most valuable resource. Of the remaining fresh waters, 1.9% is found in the polar ice caps while .02% is in our streams and lakes, and the remaining .48% is ground water (Enger et. al., 1983). Our present society still uses this water as if it is an unlimited resource. We have only recently come to understand water as a scarce resource. The drought has brought many to an awareness of the magnitude and proportion of the present crisis. Every major city on the west coast below Oregon imports much of its water. Orange County imports 60% of its water. The City of Los Angeles faces a long term water shortage due to many factors, including unpredictable rainfall and drought conditions, rapid growth, reduced water allocation from the Colorado River and a Superior Court mandate to stop the import of water from the Mono Lake Basin. Clearly, individual water-use habits need to be changed and water conservation and reclamation methods must become the norm at every level of our society.

LEARNING FROM HISTORY

By the early part of the 20th century, people were placing greater importance on cleanliness. Both water and the energy to heat it were relatively inexpensive, and so America used both in ever increasing quantities. However, the grim reality is that our Southern California bioregion gets a limited and unpredictable rainfall of 5-20 inches yearly, with 95% of it coming from December to March. We have a semi-arid Mediterranean climate from April to November. We are entering the sixth year of what appears to be an only slightly abated drought that is one of the worst to occur in the last 100 years. Prior to the European "invasion" of the continent, tree ring measurements indicate a twelve year drought cycle and anthropologists speculate that population changes in Mesoamerica before 1500 may have been due in part to prolonged drought.

Many cultures have existed on rainwater harvesting. (National Academy of Sciences, 1974; and Yeomans, 1981 and 1958). This almost 4,000 year old technology was practiced on thousands of acres and was essential for the development of many civilizations throughout the arid regions of the Middle East, Southern Arabia, North Africa and North America. The people who lived in these arid areas evolved techniques for capturing what little precipitation there was (Tohono O'adhan or Papago, Hopi and the people of the Negev Desert in Israel are some examples). Most methods centered around the use of special topographical and geological features, referred to now as macrocatchments, that slow and trap water on the landscape. By sculpturing the landscape (landform engineering), through use of swales or terraces, and check dams called weirs and gabions, precipitation is slowed to meander along natural patterns of the topography, thus increasing infiltration. These land alterations are currently used extensively in Europe, Australia, Sudan, the Caribbean Islands and Botswana. Their primary objective is the use, enhancement, and conservation of water supplies as well as stabilization and restoration of the landscape.

Bill Roley uses architecture, engineering, agriculture and ecology to weave restoration patterns into development. He heads the Permaculture Institute of Southern California, is one of the founders of the EOS Institute and has taught ecological design in all the educational forums from colleges to primary and secondary schools. Sprout Acres, his permaculture demonstration site, has been an inspiration for many years.

Permaculture Institute of Southern California
1027 Summit Way
Laguna Beach, CA 92651
(714) 494-5843

Sanitary engineering has been traditionally based on the adage that the solution to pollution is dilution. For centuries humans did not flush their wastes away; they returned wastes to the earth. As cities boomed, sewage related epidemics of typhoid and cholera became commonplace. As soon as the water closet was invented and the first sewers were built to take away our wastes, dilution became the solution. Each year in southern California, sewage treatment plants generate millions of tons of sludge and effluent (liquid that leaves the treatment facility) full of nitrogen and phosphorous, toxic metals, and chemicals. Making improvements in waste water quality with the mechanical and chemical technologies used in advanced treatment facilities is costly and in many cases requires the use of substances that are far more dangerous than the pollutants they're supposed to remove. The ultimate irony of conventional wastewater treatment is that the better the water gets, the worse the sludge problem becomes.

WATER QUALITY

Our limited supply of usable water is depleted by the many industrial, commercial and residential synthetic organic chemicals that are toxic to us and the environment. These poisons accumulate on our street surfaces and sewer outfalls through the "flush and forget it" philosophy. The advent of technological testing has brought the issue of our water quality to public attention. We are discovering that our water is being contaminated by agricultural practices, consumer and lifestyle habits, and industrial waste mismanagement. All life forms that use this water are affected as these toxins accumulate in the food chain. Industrial waste residue is now found in almost all living things. Newport Back Bay and Santa Monica Bay are specific examples of this concentration of toxins (The Santa Monica Bay Restoration Project, 1990). Chronic health problems are common in areas that have experienced toxic build-up, and are further born out by looking at a cancer map of the U.S. It is essential that we increasingly focus awareness and accountability for societal water use.

> *The ultimate irony of conventional wastewater treatment is that the better the water gets, the worse the sludge problem becomes.*

The mechanically engineered models of water management are in direct contrast to the biological methods that use nature's own purifying powers. Bioengineered systems can restore usable water to the environment, not just treat it, at a relatively low monetary cost. The immense quantities of sludge that contemporary systems generate can be the fuel that drives a polyculture of plants and animals in solar greenhouses like John Todd's New Alchemy model or Bill Woverton's constructed rock marsh wetlands (Garbage, 1990). These alternative natural sewage systems use marsh plants (cattails, hyacinths, reeds and rushes) as well as algaes and soil microorganisms to absorb and digest effluents. The plants themselves can then be harvested for feed and compost. (Note: Heavy metals are still a problem with these biological treatment systems.)

WATER QUANTITY

Water conservation is critical in certain geographical areas, especially here in Southern California where major political battles surround water rights. Two-thirds of the population of California is located in the southern half of the state, but two-thirds of the water is in the north. The majority of water in Southern California is pumped from Northern California and Arizona along an intricate aqueduct system of tunnels and canals. It is interesting to note that water transport is the single largest user of energy in the state, using 2% of California's energy (MWD [Metropolitan Water District] Plan). According toTim Brick, member of the Board of Directors of MWD, the power required to operate one pumping station pushing water over the mountains could keep the City of Seattle electrified for a year.

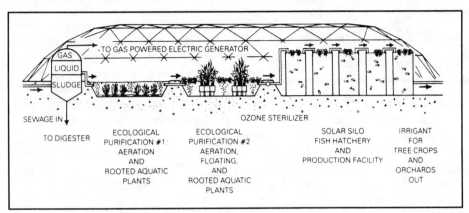

New Alchemy's Water Purification System (Reprinted from *Bioshelters, Ocean Arks, City Farming* by Nancy Todd and John Todd.)

Water supply is thought to be identical to water demand in Southern California. Water is in fact a limited resource, and we waste millions of gallons per year that could be available for agricultural and landscape reuse. Hydrologists and engineers have long been aware of the quantity of water lost each year due to runoff and evaporation. Most conservation plans seem to omit the potential water supply from both wastewater reclamation and storm water harvesting. The County of Los Angeles Sanitation Districts discharge considerably more than 486,000 acre feet per year (AFY) into the ocean (L.A. County Sanitation District, 1990). The intricate flood and storm management system channels carry hundreds of thousands of acre feet a year into our bays.

In the urban areas of the Los Angeles River watershed, only a small portion of the rainfall runoff is used for any beneficial purpose. Most of the water we use inside the home ends up in the sewer. That makes our chief use of water in urban areas to carry away wastes. All major urban areas in the United States are mandated by E.P.A. to develop comprehensive storm water management plans. These plans should use new and existing dams, flood control channels and percolation ponds to recharge groundwater. As much water as possible needs to be infiltrated at or near where it falls. The objective

> *Water supply is thought to be identical to water demand in Southern California.*

is to reuse all storm and wastewater. The potential for water recapture and reuse without importation of water could allow Los Angeles to have a surplus and even export water (Roley, 1991 and Wright 1991).

DOMESTIC WATER USE

Water requirements per family vary widely and are influenced by lifestyle, climatic conditions, household population, income, water price, and type of discharge system (sewer or septic tank). Typical water usage in a Los Angeles household of three is 135,000 gallons, or about 40% of an acre-foot, each year. An acre-foot is the amount of water required to cover an acre of land to a depth of one foot, or about 326,000 gallons. It takes many more acre feet to support this family with food, products and jobs. Water usage is reported in gallons per capita per day (gpcd). Sixty-five per cent of residential water use is divided among the kitchen, bathroom and utility room (L.A. Urban Water Plan, 1991). These figures vary from city to city and from region to region. Outdoor water usage increases once you get away from the coast and into more agricultural areas. Twelve times as much water is used in business and agriculture as in households.

> **Typical water usage in a Los Angeles household of three is 135,000 gallons per year.**

Changing lifestyle habits can significantly reduce water use. A simple turn-off at the shower head allows one to soap down, then turn the head back on to rinse. Water-conserving shower heads that aerate water have flow rates between 1.5 and 3 gallons per minute, instead of the 5 to 10 gallons-per-minute flow of standard shower heads. Besides the reduction of water use, a beneficial side effect of these conservation practices is the reduction of energy used to heat water. A family of four, utilizing these conservation methods and showering daily, may conserve up to 28,000 gallons of water and the energy equivalent to three barrels of oil in a year's time (DWR Bulletin).

There are graywater systems designed for toilet flush use. An average person uses 80 gallons of water inside the house per day. Of this, the toilet is the number one consumer of fresh drinkable water. In a single day, the average person uses approximately 27 gallons for toilet flushing, 3 gallons are personally consumed, 19 gallons for laundry and dishes, and 25 gallons for bathing and hygiene. If we assume a family of four is equipped with a conventional toilet using 5 to 8 gallons per flush, and each person flushes about 5 times a day, the toilet will utilize nearly 50,000 gallons of fresh drinking water in one year to flush 600 pounds of fecal waste into the sewer. There is a massive demand for water and energy to move this relatively small residue into our waterways.

Household indoor water use (not including business/commercial) including the bath, toilet, sinks, laundry and personal consumption accounts for 44% of the total water usage breakdown according to the L.A. Department of Water and Power Urban Water Management Plan 1990. The approximately 33.8% for outdoor usage varies with family income and availability of land. This water is used outside on the landscape for irrigation, for car washing, for pools and spas and for cleaning. There is a 7.2% factor that is unaccounted for in the audits due to leaks and unauthorized hook-ups.

Sprout Acres is the demonstration site for the Permaculture Institute of Southern California. Through the use of this site, we are able to evaluate the practicality and overall effect of implementing wastewater and rainwater harvesting systems that could supplement household needs. Two water conservation features at the field station are the composting toilet and a graywater recycling system which irrigates and fertilizes the landscape. I have experimented with harvesting rain runoff and recycling wastewater, the premise being that the outflow of water from the house and landscape is a resource and not a form of pollution (Roley 1984, 1983). This water reuse system taps into the unexploited wealth found when we view our sewage outfall from the house as a resource rather than a problem. Various physical, chemical and health considerations have been monitored to help evaluate the viability of this system. Careful attention has been directed to plant vitality and soil structure changes. I found that by recycling the nutrients commonly thought of as waste, the landscape can become an "outdoor room" which adds charm, character and energy efficiency to my house. The use of the nutrient cycling methods described in this paper can potentially create an abundant and robust residential atmosphere. More importantly, our water shortage could potentially be alleviated if we eliminate the "flush and forget it" philosophy of waste disposal and instead, recycle wastewater into the landscape.

GRAYWATER DEFINITION

Graywater reuse is potentially one of the solutions to the water quantity dilemma. Graywater generally refers to untreated water from washing machines, bathtubs, showers, and bathroom and kitchen sinks. It contains hair, soap, dead skin, small amounts of fecal matter, detergents, grease, oil, food particles, cosmetics, cleaning solvents and other household chemicals. Each section of the house generates waste water, each with different pollutants. The kitchen sink produces the most heavily polluted water (detergents, grease, oil, food particles and cleaning solvents); the shower and wash basin contain a minimum of suspended solids (hair and soap by volume) but are the most contaminated biologically, containing trace amounts of fecal matter, which potentially harbor pathogenic organisms (Farallones Institute). By contrast, blackwater is water that is flushed down the toilet. This water needs to be biologically treated in a sewer, septic tank, or other ecological treatment system. It is important to identify the various qualities of graywater depending on its source or origin. In a properly designed, nutrient recycling, wastewater treatment system, much of this water can be reused on the landscape.

GRAYWATER HOUSEHOLD USAGE

In arid regions like Southern California, most of the household landscape irrigation needs can be met utilizing only the graywater generated within the household. Sixty-five percent of the indoor household water outfall is graywater. It is roughly 29.4 gallons per capita per day but the volumes produced vary from area to area (L.A. Dept. of Water and Power, 1991). In Tucson, 31 gallons of graywater is produced per day per person totalling nearly 44,000 gallons per year for a family of four. In California, an individual uses 59 gallons per day while a family of four produces 1652 gallons of graywater in a week or 85,904 gallons per year. Any specific treatment system size and number of filtration components will depend to some degree on the size and occupancy of the home and waste generating activities.

> *Graywater reuse is potentially one of the solutions to the water quantity dilemma.*

GRAYWATER LANDSCAPE USAGE

Graywater can be incorporated into the outside irrigation system for landscaping and agriculture. If you are using the recycled graywater on the landscape you should not use detergents and cleansers which contain a significant amount of sodium, boron or chlorine because they can be damaging to the health of soil and plants. Some very acid-loving plants may be damaged by successive use of graywater since it has a tendency to make the soil more alkaline. Rainfall and fresh water will help leach the soil of excess mineral salts.

The long-term objective in agricultural use of graywater is to gain a degree of dilution, filtering and distribution over the garden soil. Adding gypsum and compost to graywater-affected soil will neutralize the detrimental effects of sodium, ammonia and phosphate salts. Limited use of toxic cleaning, hygiene and cosmetic products is advisable. Ammonia is preferable to cleaning products containing chlorine. Soaps and detergents containing sodium salts will create an alkaline pH condition in the soil; most plants prefer a neutral to slightly acid soil. Softeners, perfumes, colorings, lanolin and other additives found in household products need to be reduced or eliminated because they will be picked up by the plants in soil irrigated with recycled graywater. Water run through a sodium-based water softener filter is not advised for use in recycled graywater systems. The most important considerations here are to minimize bleach and absolutely avoid detergents or additives containing boron. Boron is incompatible with plant life.

Any extensive use of graywater for domestic irrigation will both reduce demand and provide some recharge to groundwater. It will also guarantee us a supply of irrigation water to be used on both ornamentals and fruit trees. So the collection and use of graywater may result in a significant reduction of freshwater consumption for residential irrigation in arid areas. Conserving water in this way will impact municipal water supply for home consumption and reduce an increase in capital investment in municipal water distribution and treatment and their respective energy costs.

GRAYWATER HEALTH CONCERNS

One of the most serious concerns in the use of graywater is its microbial content. Both the physical and chemical properties of graywater contribute to the growth of microorganisms. The increased concentrations of phosphates, ammonia and turbidity indicate that nutrients are available. By comparison, graywater has more usable nutrients that have not undergone biological degradation than blackwater components which have undergone microbial and enzymatic breakdown in the human digestive tract (Rose 1991).

The presence of Eschericia coli (E. coli) and other enteric organisms indicate fecal contamination and the possible presence of enteric viruses or intestinal pathogens such as salmonella. Fecal coliforms are pollution indicators and may be used to assess the relative safety of graywater. Generally, a high fecal coliform count is undesirable and implies a greater chance for human illness to develop as a result of contact during graywater reuse. The largest water user in the home after the toilet is the shower or bath which may also contribute the greatest number of microorganisms. Both total organism and fecal coliform concentration counts are greater in shower or bath water than in laundry water (Rose, 1991). Microbial populations in graywater increase over a 48 hour period and then stabilize for the next 12 days (Rose, 1991).

> *Extensive use of graywater will also guarantee us a supply of irrigation water to be used on both ornamentals and certain edibles.*

Public health officials have only limited data to assess the risks associated with graywater reuse. Regulations governing graywater reuse did not exist until recently except in Arizona. Many jurisdictions in California have or are now formulating such regulations. Wastewater reuse guidelines can reduce health risks associated with potential exposure (L.A. Office of Water Reclamation). In 1984, Arizona set graywater standards of 25 fecal coliform and 5 turbidity units. The turbidity and microbial contamination profiles vary widely according to family characteristics like number and age of children, hygienic lifestyle and activities such as gardening or washing cloth diapers. An index of contamination to assess treatment requirements prior to reuse of the graywater would measure: 1) indicator microorganisms 2) total bacterial populations (survival rates) for Salmonella and Shigella. Fecal coliform and total coliform counts are significantly higher in graywater from families with young children according to a study (Joan Rose et. al.) on the microbial quality and persistence of enteric (intestinal) pathogens in graywater from various household sources. The physical and chemical characteristics of the graywater change over time. Levels of ammonia and phosphate increase. A 100% increase in turbidity provides the new feed stock for the microorganisms that will grow if you store the graywater.

Design factors to eliminate potential health hazards, and aesthetic and management concerns for practical application of graywater reuse systems, include filtration, biological treatment and most likely some form of ecological disinfection. These are critical components in providing a reliable and consistent supply of graywater. The health risks vary according to the degree of contact with pathogenic organisms by humans or animals. These risks can be significantly reduced by following a few simple guidelines. In order to use graywater safely you must limit the level of pathogens. First, separate graywater and blackwater. Graywater can then be used in a subsurface irrigation system or mini leach field providing nourishment for shrubs and trees, including fruit trees. The graywater containing any fecal matter from washing soiled diapers or rinse water from the body or clothes of someone with an infectious disease should not be used in a recycled graywater system. The most sensible approach to using graywater seems to be the closed collection and underground distribution of wastewater in a mini leach field or drip irrigation system that irrigates mature fruit trees shrubs and groundcover. To reduce health risks, the recycled graywater should not be sprayed on vegetable gardens, lawns or other surfaces that come in contact with humans or animals.

> *Many jurisdictions in California have or are now formulating wastewater reuse guidelines.*

Health officials in Santa Barbara and San Luis Obispo state that graywater is a valuable resource that can be used for landscaping rather than allowing it to go through the sewer system. Their respective Building Departments approved a closed piping system to an underground mini leach field system that distributes the water in a subsurface irrigation pattern (City of Santa Barbara, 1990). This technique provides irrigation for fruit and other trees, shrubs and groundcovers. If water goes to fruit trees, one could develop a small orchard on four washing machine loads a week. Mature fruit trees need 75 gallons, while large shade trees may only need 50 gallons, and large shrubs can be maintained on 10 gallons a week (Kourik). Careful attention to native vegetation and bioregionally appropriate plants, their design and maintenance (xeriscape) can lessen your outdoor water budget by over half. So on-site water reclamation and reuse systems can be demonstrated to be environmentally superior and economically viable practices in our arid climate.

The use of these on-site recycling systems although successful and growing is relatively new and not yet widely known. In most areas a lack of experience with water reclamation and lack of specific standards and regulations have severely restricted the development of these systems. Systems also exist that can safely recycle all household wastewater, including toilets. Septic tanks with leach fields are designed to make partially treated wastewater move downwards, often contaminating groundwater. Newer systems can treat even toilet waste enough to use the water for irrigation. Ecologically engineered systems like John Todd's polyculture greenhouses and Bill Woverton's constructed rock marshes can restore water to drinkable quality. Perhaps urban neighborhoods of the future will replace many of their paved streets with such greenhouses and rock marshes.

GRAYWATER LEGAL CONSIDERATIONS

At present, plumbing codes do not allow a home owner to manipulate residential plumbing to extract wastewater. In some jurisdictions certain uses of graywater are not considered illegal, like washing machine rinse water reuse, and do not require a special permit. A California policy precedent for legal use of graywater dates back to 1970. According to the Office of Water Reclamation in Los Angeles, The Residential Water Conservation Tax Credit (Title 23, Subchapter 1.81) Government Code Section 11380.1, was enacted to provide incentives for individuals to install systems for collection, plumbing and distribution (and possible treatment) of graywater for subsurface irrigation. The incentive expired in 1983. Currently there is more of a political than a biological difficulty in dealing with graywater.

> *By far the largest percentage of household wastewater, about 35%, originates in our toilets.*

There is a need for consistent guidelines and regulations at all levels of government. Agencies from the federal, state, county and municipal level are involved in the creation of policies and directives. The present policy assumes that there are health risks involved in the use of graywater and blackwater. These risks can be dramatically reduced through controls placed on the source and type of wastewater recycled and the methods by which it is distributed and stored. The San Luis Obispo and Santa Barbara Health and Building Departments allow the sanitary distribution of graywater and define it as wastewater that contains no toilet discharge and no infectious contamination or unhealthy body waste. Graywater is defined as sewage by the State Health and Safety Code to be disposed of in a sewer to protect health.

In March, 1991 the State of California issued a statement entitled "Homeowner's Guide to Safe Use of Graywater in a Drought" which was signed by Governor Wilson and Kenneth Kizer, Director of Health Services. At least during the drought this announcement specifically overrides any other state pronouncement on the subject. Local jurisdictions apparently retain the right to regulate or forbid the use of graywater. The only thing that is clear at the moment about the legality of graywater reuse is that regulations are in flux. Health authorities have in the past often chosen either to demand "zero risk" or to ignore common practices thought to pose only minor risk. Now that almost all human activities are known to contain an element of risk, some formal or informal risk assessment must underlie any new regulations.

TOILETS

The City of Los Angeles 1990 Urban Water Management Plan estimated toilet flushing to use 27.4 gallons per capita per day (gpcpd). That is 15.5% of total water usage for the city. Replacement of older toilets with ultra low flush fixtures will stop leaks and excess water used in the older toilets. This can save 20.9 gpcd with no change in one's lifestyle. Many water purveyors now offer rebates for installing low flow toilets. Rebate programs for appliances have been very effective as a means of saving energy. As the motive for saving water grows, the chance to get widespread retrofits in place is excellent. The cost is far cheaper than building new dams, peripheral canals and wastewater treatment plants (Wright, 1991).

By far the largest percentage of household wastewater, about 35%, originates in our toilets. The subject of bodily elimination is so taboo that generations of engineers have been designing systems to treat a barely known commodity. About 27 gallons of water is used to flush away 1-1/2 cups of human feces and about four cups of urine a day. The organic nutrient "resource bank account" materializes when you multiply four cups of urine plus 1-1/2 cups of feces times 172 million people. The mean toilet volume is 5.48 gallons per flush, including leaks. The average person flushes five times per day for a total of 27.4 gallons per day. If we replaced every existing toilet in L.A. County with an ultra low flush model using an average of 1.3 gallons per flush, savings would increase dramatically. The total amount saved by replacing all L.A. County toilets would exceed 200,000 acre feet per year. That is enough to irrigate 165 square miles of forest. Since the predominant water usage in the commercial sector of offices and shops is flushing toilets, low-flow models can provide each building with major savings.

COMPOST TOILETS

One of the most critical criterion of a successful culture is a balanced relationship between growth and decay. Our society values growth but looks upon the processes and products of decay as waste. While the water toilet solved some major public health problems which are still being experienced in the rest of the developing world, it has also created a complex set of ecological and water quality problems (Santa Monica Bay in Los Angeles is a prime example of these complications). Because most of us in industrial societies were potty-trained on a porcelain bowl style, automatically clean machine (popularized by John Crapper), any other style of waste management is threatening. In our antiseptic, hygienic era, a major psychological shift is needed to switch from the waterborne systems of pumps and valves to a dry-toilet design that can recycle waste nutrients. Becoming responsible for our own waste is critical. The cliche "out of sight, out of mind" can no longer dictate our behavior. By returning our organic waste to the soil as nutrient compost, we could prevent the pollution of our waterways and we would not lose valuable fertilizer.

> *Our society values growth but looks upon the processes and products of decay as waste.*

The Enviroscope Carousel Composting toilet, field-tested for the past fifteen years at my Sprout Acres field station, is designed to decompose human excrement and organic household scraps in a safe and sanitary manner without the use of water or plumbing. The toilet consists of a commode in the bathroom and a digestion tank under the floor. A chimney going up the inside of the wall vents off excess gasses from the decomposition process, and insulation around the unit maintains a warm atmosphere for this "micro-biological restaurant." By following a composting recipe of multi-layers of organic material in the two 30-by-50-inch fiberglass holding tanks, a layered "pie" bakes in its own juices. After two years this mixture is ready for harvest and use as fertilizer. Studies at Sprout Acres have shown that an adult's yearly production of fecal waste and kitchen scraps, once decomposed by microorganisms in a composting toilet, will barely fill two five-gallon cans. The limitation of the compost toilet is the personal management of a complex biological machine that has moving parts. It requires personal attention and occasional monitoring for proper operation.

Dry composting toilets often bring to mind an outhouse: people may fear problems such as odors and pathogens. This fear is unwarranted, as many technologically advanced countries are using the biological process of aerobic decomposition in the composting of their household wastes (VanderRyn, 1978). Sweden and Norway have been testing composting toilets extensively for years, and many of these devices have been functioning safely for years. The United Nations and our own National Sanitation Foundation have sanctioned these units. It seems only reasonable that eventually these models will be found acceptable in the U.S. Presently, composting units have been installed in thirty-nine states but have received sanction for residential use in only four states. It is the politics and authority of pump-and-valve-trained engineers in decision-making roles, not the efficiency or feasibility of the composting toilets, that have hampered its growth. Composting toilets have been used in the wilderness by the National Parks and U.S. Forest Service. California is approving units, on an experimental basis, to collect data on their maintenance and operation.

A legitimate concern is the safety of this biological toilet in producing pathogen-free humus as an end product. The two-year-old compost from kitchen scraps and human excreta in the Enviroscope toilet at Sprout Acres has been combined with garden compost and put on test plots of vegetables with no negative results. Laboratory tests show that after two years of decomposition in the Enviroscope toilet, pathogens are eliminated. Apparently, any pathogens that may exist in composted material after two years do not adapt to soil life and therefore die or are ingested by other microorganisms within the first month in the soil; thus, they are not assimilated by plant roots nor translocated to the edible portions of plants. In fact, it seems that by combining the home and the landscape into a unified residential design, the rich source of nutrients from the toilet can be exploited while saving both the individual and society energy, water and money. Many municipal waste treatment plants are now recycling their sludge on landscapes and parks with excellent results.

> *The key to successful irrigation is to apply water slowly and let it soak deeply into the soil where the roots can use it.*

OUTDOOR HOUSEHOLD WATER USE

A high-income family with land and gardens may use between 300 to 600 gpcpd, while a low-income family in the same city may use only 25 gpcpd. Given both the semi-arid conditions that prevail throughout much of California, and our unpredictable levels of yearly rainfall, a proper water management design can save money without any additional expenditures. Large volumes of graywater could be available for reuse on the landscaping, lawns, gardens, pools and spas.

Water conservation begins with awareness. For example, brooms may be used rather than a hose to clean sidewalks. This saves water, as well as the energy it takes to pump the water to the home. Overwatering landscapes and lawns causes run-off on driveways, sidewalks and streets, as well as excessive evaporation. Over-watering encourages plant disease, and increases the need for fertilization, pesticide, herbicide and fungicide usage. All these additives eventually find their way into our waterways and enter the food chain.

The popular landscape term, xeriscape, or appropriate landscape plants, design and maintenance can be a beginning to water conservation and save over 50% of present water usage. The key to successful irrigation is to apply water slowly and let it soak deeply into the soil where the roots can use it. A drip system waters in gallons per hour rather than gallons per minute so the distribution rates are different. These systems water deeply and infrequently for as long as the soil can hold the moisture. If run-off occurs, the irrigation system needs to be adjusted. A controller and timer will help maintain a schedule of deep watering, but these electronic devices cannot take the climate into consideration. A better system employs a tensiometer placed at the plant root level; this device reads soil moisture and activates an irrigation system when the deeper soil that nourishes the plant roots is dry. A subsurface drip system can eliminate the evaporation from ground sprinklers. Mulching with a thick layer of leaves, bark, rock or other material placed on the soil surface will lessen soil evaporation and improve weed control. Composted material holds eight times its weight in water and contributes to the vitality of soil microorganisms and their home, the "humus-sphere". Tons of yard clippings in our communities are being put into landfills. About one-third of all material put in landfills is greenwaste. This material, properly composted, becomes black gold over time and is just waiting our proper resource management techniques to put it to productive use. All of the above suggestions can potentially save time, labor and money.

As much as 40-60% of outside ground space is taken up by lawn in suburban homes. The utility or expected return from the labor, money and other resources, including water, used in the maintenance of our home space is questionable. A lawn's major value seems to be aesthetic, based on a European bourgeois tradition of displaying open space not devoted to food production. It was a status symbol in the 17th and 18th centuries. Since today few of us are involved in the raising of our own food, the symbolic importance of a lawn is no longer appropriate. Practical alternatives to lawn grasses include drought-tolerant herbs like lavender, rosemary, savory or thyme, and all low-water fruits, like the citrus family, grapes, figs, almonds, guavas and loquats. These plants can provide an edible landscape to replace some areas of lawn. For

> *Water is our most precious resource. To conserve it is to support life.*

the more adventuresome and meditative, a vegetable or flower garden can replace lawn areas and provide savings of as much as 60% of your food budget, much of which goes into the marketing, packaging and transportation of commercial food products.

CONCLUSION

I have now discussed four primary areas that could aid the environmentally conscious homeowner of the future in conserving, recycling, reusing and restoring the water that is used in our homes and communities. It is imperative that we begin a unified water management plan that develops sustainable rainwater runoff harvesting this natural resource. First, by limiting construction in our upper watersheds and enhancing the biological diversity and complexity of the forest system, we can secure it as a biological sponge that slows runoff and stores the water in the ground. Second, natural systems have a remarkable ability to use the nutrients in wastewater, neutralizing and purifying the water enough so that it can be safely reused. These ecologically engineered systems can form a community wealth model that can restore and enhance our urban areas. Third, the conservation of outdoor water resources by using xeriscape techniques including planting design and sensitive maintenance practices like proper mulching and irrigation management. Fourth is the complete retrofitting of indoor water systems to conserve and reuse water.

These four elements can restore our urban areas to greater self-reliance. They can make our cities important sources of water rather than destroyers of the natural environment. Water is our most precious resource. To conserve it is to support life. I hope these ideas will give us more fresh water in our lifetime and provide it for our children for generations to come.

REFERENCES

City of Los Angeles, *Wastewater Facilities Plan Update*, Sept 1990

City of Los Angeles, Office of Water Reclamation, *Proposed Policy for Use of Graywater*, August 1990, 111 North Hope Street, Los Angeles, CA. 90012

City of Santa Barbara (Public Works and Building and Zoning Division with review and approval by the County Environmental Health Department), *Guidelines to the Approved Use of Graywater During the Stage III Drought Conditions*, April 1990

Department of Water Resources Bulletin, 1980-84, *Water Conservation in California*, July 1984

Enger, Eldon D., J Richard Kormelink, Bradley F. Smith, Rodney J. Smith, *The Study of Interrelationships: Environmental Studies* (Wm. C. Brown, Dubuque. 1983)

Farallones Institute, *Integral Urban House: Self-Reliant Living in the City*, Sierra Club Books, San Francisco, 1979

Kourik, Robert, *Graywater Use in the Landscape*, P.O. Box 1 841 Santa Rosa, CA. 95402, 1990

Los Angeles Department of Water and Power, *Urban Water Management Plan for City of L.A.*, March, 1991

MWD Plan, *The Regional Urban Water Management Plan for the Metropolitan Water District of Southern California*, Nov 1990, 1111 Sunset Blvd., P.O. Box 54153, Los Angeles, Ca. 90054. The document was prepared by Planning and Management Consultants Ltd., P.O. Box 1316, Carbondale, Ill. 62903

National Academy of Science, *More Water for Arid Lands, Promising Technologies and Research Opportunities*, Washington, D.C., 1974

Rose, Joan B., Gwo-Shing Sun, Charles P. Gerba, Norval A. Sinclair, "Microbial Quality and Persistence of Enteric Pathogens in Graywater from Various Household Sources," *Water Resources*, Vol 25, no 1, pp. 37-42, 1991)

Roley, Bill, Sprout Acres: "An Integrated Residential Energy Bank, Sprout Acres," *Elephant Ear, Journal of Public Opinion in Orange County*, Saddleback College, Spring 1983

Roley, Bill, "Household Water Management: A Lifestyle Change for the 80s", *Elephant Ear, Journal of Public Opinion in Orange County*, Saddleback College, May, 1984

VanderRyn, Sim, *Toilet Papers*, Santa Barbara, CA, Capra Press, 1978

Wright, Howard, Staff Report to the Permaculture Institute, *L.A.'s Water Surplus*, 1991

REMOVING INSTITUTIONAL OBSTACLES TO WATER RECYCLING IN THE CITY OF LOS ANGELES

Bahman Sheikh

Traditional obstacles to water reclamation such as costs, regulatory constraints and public perceptions are melting away in the face of long-term water shortages and short-term drought emergencies. The chief remaining obstacle is institutional: the inability of traditional institutions to adapt to change, to absorb new information and to effect revised protocols and processes needed to reuse water.

The City of Los Angeles has historically depended heavily on imported water for its growing needs. Those sources are now becoming more difficult to expand due to higher environmental and construction costs. Some of the imported water supplies will be reduced significantly in annual yield. For example, greater withdrawals by the State of Arizona are expected as the Central Arizona Project components are completed. Others have been cut back by court orders. The reduced water supplies will become even more stressed as regional and statewide water policies take effect, and as increasing populations demand greater volumes of water.

Water reclamation represents an ideal method of augmenting this increasingly scarce commodity. A primary goal of the City of Los Angeles is, therefore, to maximize its use of reclaimed water.

WATER RECLAMATION GOALS

The method chosen for quantifying the goals for the planning horizons of this study is to review the water supply and demand projections within the City of Los Angeles. In Table 1, a uniform 200 gallons per capita per day (gpcd) water consumption factor is used to project water demands into the future. Dependable water supply for the year 2010 is based on volumes deliverable with existing water supply facilities, while those for the year 2090 involve development of new sources and construction of new facilities. Interim supplies were obtained by linear interpolation.

STRATEGIES TO OVERCOME INSTITUTIONAL OBSTACLES TO WATER REUSE

Many of the traditional obstacles to water recycling have been overcome over the last two decades. Because costs of new increments of water supply have sky-rocketed, the relative costs of reclaiming wastewater have become increasingly favorable. As greater experience with operating water reclamation systems throughout the State of California have been gained, public attitude toward water reuse has become more positive. Regulatory constraints are also being gradually relaxed in light of the exemplary experience and performance record at existing water reuse projects.

Bahman Sheikh is the Director of the Office of Water Reclamation for the City of Los Angeles. Before joining the City, he spent 20 years as an international consultant planning water and wastewater systems, designing irrigation systems and developing water conservation and reclamation plants in countries which include Turkey, Korea, Egypt, Morocco, India, Kuwait, Sri Lanka, Syria and Jordan.

Office of Water Reclamation City Hall, Room 366 Los Angeles, CA 90012 (213) 237-0887

TABLE 1. CITY OF LOS ANGELES WATER RECLAMATION GOALS BASED ON BALANCING SUPPLY VS. DEMAND DEFICIT			
	Short-Term 2010	Mid-Term 2050	Long-Term 2090
Population, millions (a)	4.86	6.51	7.66
Water Demand, KAFY (b	1,089	1,458	1,716
Dependable Water Supply, KAFY (c)	893	997	1,100
"New Water Req., KAFY (d)	255	601	801
Reclaimable Wastewater, KAFY (a)	661	874	1,042
Percent of Effluent to Reclaim (e)	39%	69%	77%

(a) Population and flow data are based on the assumption of even population distribution
(b) Water demand assumed uniform consumption of 200 gpcd
(KAFY = thousand acre feet per year)
(c) Dependable water supply is based on current projections, excluding reuse
(d) "New" water requirement is the difference between (b) and (c), plus 30% to account for conservative flow estimates
(e) Portion of the wastewater effluent that would, if reused, supply the shortfall

Data in Table 1 point out that about 40% of the wastewater will need to be reclaimed to satisfy the City's short-term needs and 70% for the mid-term shortfall. For the long-term, this proportion increases to 77% or about 800,000 AFY (900 mgd).

The remaining major obstacle to water reuse is institutional and is indeed a difficult obstacle to surmount. It arises from the fact that existing institutions were not designed to perform tasks necessary for water recycling. In fact, the traditional mission of these institutions is to import water from the best quality source at the least possible cost. The stress to the environment that takes place at the source point as a result of importing this water is not yet fully recognized or acknowledged by these institutions. Water reuse as a new source of water supply is still too often met with less than an enthusiastic response.

> *The stress to the environment that takes place at the source point as a result of importing water is not yet fully recognized or acknowledged.*

To counter the institutional inertia and the resulting attitudes, the Office of Water Reclamation, in coordination with Council Committees and the Boards, conducts an information campaign, a political agenda and a legislative program. This three-pronged approach is integrated to focus the various institutions of the City on the need for permanent change in areas crucial to the achievement of the City's water reclamation goals. The approach is necessarily long-term, but is already bearing fruit. Cooperation of the operating Departments is ultimately essential to its sustained success. Modest beginnings are already evident and include:

- Acceleration of pace of development of several water reclamation projects by the Department of Water and Power.

- Introduction of ordinances to require dual plumbing in certain parts of the City, and banning the sale and installation of self-regenerating water softeners, because they introduce significant quantities of salts into the waste water which are very hard to remove.

- Heightened awareness of decision-makers regarding the impact of their actions on the City's water reuse prospects.

- Subtle changes in bureaucratic policies, organizations and procedures that are somewhat more favorable to water recycling than past policies and procedures have been.

- Commitment by the Department of Water and Power to spend over $500 million by the year 2000 toward achieving the water reuse goals of the City.

DESCRIPTION OF WATER REUSE CONCEPTS

The alternative concepts presented below are formulated recognizing the City's existing wastewater conveyance and treatment facilities and the potential for their future expansion and modification.

NEAR-TERM WATER RECLAMATION OPPORTUNITIES

Opportunities for future expansion of reclaimed water use in the City of Los Angeles are extensive, covering nearly all traditional reuse categories. Some of these categories are adaptable in the near-term and some in the long-term. The near-term reuse opportunities are essentially those identified and characterized in the *Orange and Los Angeles Counties (OLAC) Water Reuse Study*, 1982; and the JM Montgomery, *Financial Analysis of Reuse Projects*, 1980. Some of these opportunities are currently being translated into actual projects. With staged construction of needed distribution facilities, these and several larger projects are expected to be completed over the next 20 years.

> *Artificial recharge provides a means of balancing the high summer demands for water with the relatively uniform supply from wastewater treatment plants.*

MID-TERM WATER RECLAMATION OPPORTUNITIES

Even though the mid-term planning horizon is associated here with the year 2050, it is expected that different water reclamation opportunities and schemes will mature over several decades around the year 2050.

GROUND WATER RECHARGE AND SEAWATER INTRUSION BARRIERS

Artificial recharge of groundwater reservoirs with reclaimed water has been practiced for a long time in various parts of the country, notably Florida, Arizona and Texas. Artificial recharge provides a convenient means of balancing the high summer demands for water with the relatively uniform supply from wastewater treatment plants. Groundwater recharge usually involves introduction of water at some point into the aquifer and withdrawals at points some distance removed, after slow travel through the aquifer's porous media. A large-scale, long-term, controlled study was completed in Los Angeles County concerning epidemiological characteristics of drinking water from aquifers recharged with reclaimed water versus those receiving surface runoff. There were no detectable differences (Nellor, 1984).

Recharge wells specifically designed for injection of water along the coastline to counter inland movement of saline seawater are a special application. Such barrier injection wells using tertiary treated effluent are in current use in the coastal area of Orange County where highly treated water produced at Water Factory 21 is used to recharge the Talbert Gap Barrier Project. The potential for use of reclaimed water in these applications in the City of Los Angeles has been studied in the past, but a project has yet to be implemented.

In all likelihood, the *California Policy and Guidelines for Groundwater Recharge with Reclaimed Municipal Wastewater* will be published in its final form in 1992. These guidelines provide numerical criteria for input water quality, vertical distance from the water table, horizontal distance to nearest withdrawal wells and residence time in the aquifer.

Two of the City of Los Angeles' water reclamation plants are ideally situated for large-scale groundwater recharge operations. Although existing spreading grounds are located at considerable distances from these facilities, preliminary cost estimates indicate that groundwater recharge projects are more cost-effective than landscape irrigation or industrial applications of reclaimed water.

> *Costs of new sources of potable water supply will be so much higher, that the cost of treating existing water sources will no longer be an economic obstacle.*

SATELLITE PLANTS

This concept involves one or more treatment plants in upstream locations (in addition to existing upstream plants) to draw from major sewer interceptors and treat the wastewater adequately for reuse at locations near each "satellite" plant. Each wastewater treatment facility, whether existing, planned, or additional ones as needed, would be designed as a water reclamation plant, treating water to tertiary level, thereby meeting Title 22 requirements. The three stages of treatment include settling, biological treatment, and filtration and chlorination. Reclaimed water from these plants would be usable for a wide variety of landscape, industrial and recreational (including body contact) uses. Distribution networks, radiating from each water reclamation plant would serve the local water users, with adequate capacity for expansion, as demand increases and additional users are served.

LONG-TERM WATER RECLAMATION CONCEPTS

The long-term opportunities for water reclamation are expected to expand dramatically because of the anticipated trends and changes producing different future scenarios and conditions, e.g.:

- Population pressure will be greater and "drought" occurrences (deficit of supply vs demand) will be more severe and more frequent, giving rise to greater public and regulatory support for all reuse options.

- Costs of development of new sources of potable water supply will be so much higher that the cost of treating existing water sources will no longer be an economic obstacle.

- Wastewater treatment requirements and wastewater discharge prohibitions to receiving waters are expected to become so much more stringent in the future that they will play a significant part in: (1) making it necessary to place the effluents in environmentally acceptable locations (e.g., on the land), and (2) reducing the government's cost of incremental treatment, because those who create the contaminants will be mandated to remove them to a greater degree as a condition of discharge.

- Technological advances in water and wastewater treatment will increase the reliability of treatment and possibly reduce costs for advanced treatment processes such as nutrient removal, filtration, granulated activated carbon and demineralization. These advanced treatment unit processes will become more common at water reclamation plants of the future.

- The regulatory climate is expected to respond to the practically risk-free operational experience obtained at the over 850 locations in California reusing reclaimed water successfully, some for several decades. As a result, it is expected that there will be substantially less constraints to water reclamation.

GROUNDWATER RECHARGE

Various forms of groundwater recharge with reclaimed water are expected to become even more technically feasible toward 2090 than in the mid-term planning horizon. It is anticipated that the entire reclamation goal of the City of Los Angeles for 2090 can be met with use of the Central Basin and the San Fernando Basin aquifers for water storage. Unused capacity in these basins totals over one million acre-feet.

DIRECT POTABLE REUSE

Toward the latter part of the 21st century, it is envisioned that direct potable reuse will become relatively widespread in the dry areas of the United States and many other countries. Los Angeles and surrounding communities will probably be leaders in the scale of operation and the level of protection afforded for the health of the consumers. There are many types of treatment for taking tertiary treated water and rendering it potable. These include: reverse osmosis, aeration, granular activated carbon treatment (GAC), ozonation and ion exchange columns (which are used to modify the mineral content of the water if this is needed).

Currently, the Denver Water Board is conducting long-term animal feeding tests under Environmental Protection Agency (EPA) supervision and partial funding, using 500-fold concentrates of both reclaimed water and Denver's domestic supply. The concentrates magnify organic compounds remaining in the waters to estimate potential adverse health effects. Thus far, this renovated water, even in its highly concentrated form which should have tremendously magnified any problems, has compared favorably with the fresh snow-pack water it is being tested against.

A major advantage of direct potable reuse is that a separate distribution system is not necessary to convey the finished water to the consumer. It is envisioned that the product water would be released into the water reservoirs or raw water storage facilities for blending with treated water from imported sources.

> *Toward the latter part of the 21st century, it is envisioned that direct potable reuse will become relatively widespread in the dry areas of the United States.*

CONCLUSIONS

The unit cost spread among the near-term alternatives is narrow enough to make them almost equivalent. None of the alternatives has a "fatal flaw" for implementation in the near term. Furthermore, no one of these alternatives singly results in a major volume of water reclamation. Therefore, it is concluded that all available options should be implemented in parallel for the near term. Site-specific alternatives can be developed during facility planning.

A comparison of all the mid- and long-term concepts favors the satellite plants concept over all others. This is followed by groundwater recharge. Potable reuse is very close; it is second place in cost. The best immediate course of action, for the mid- and long-term alternatives, appears to be initiation of demonstration and pilot projects for both the groundwater recharge concept and direct potable reuse.

Ultimate success of water reuse in the City of Los Angeles depends on the survival of the new policies, procedures, institutional organizations and ordinances, beyond the life of the Office of Water Reclamation. Increased community awareness of the need for water recycling gives cause for optimism. Historical performance and back-sliding cast doubt.

REFERENCES

April 1982, *Orange and Los Angeles Counties Water Reuse Study (OLAC) Facilities Plan.*

Bruvold, William H., January 1988, *Public Opinion on Water Reuse Options.* Journal WPCF, Vol. 60, No. 1, pp. 45-49.

James M. Montgomery, September 1980, *Financial Analysis of Reuse Projects.* Orange and Los Angeles Counties Water Reuse Study.

Nellor, Margaret, et al., March 1984, *Health Effects Study Final Report,* County Sanitation Districts of Los Angeles.

WATER HARVESTING

Bill Roley, PhD

atershed management can provide long term water storage capacity, full-time wildlife habitat enhancement, flood control and water conservation in Southern California. Through the following methods, water is slowed down while soil and nutrients are held on the landscape.

Landform engineering is the act of using the natural movement of water while manipulating and enhancing the existing topographic conditions to improve a site's ability to catch, hold and absorb water. Reducing the velocity, or speed and force, of the downhill movement of surface water runoff will dramatically reduce erosion and increase fertility. The careful selection and planting of grasses, shrubs and trees within the "microcatchment elements" is an example of bioengineering (and we'll talk about microcatchments in a minute). The trees and shrubs are selected for their vibrancy in our Mediterranean climate. These mixed stands, or polycultures, are planted along swales which function as contoured terraces. The mixed stands are also planted along gabions, sand tanks, etc., and become a multi-use asset creating a park-like character referred to as a community's ecological wealth. The water from runoff catchments provides an acceleration of the natural forest formation. Water storage and nutrient collection processes contribute to forming a healthier ecological community within the landscape. This process allows water to infiltrate into the ground and enrich the life of the soil ecology. An oasis effect forms from the atmospheric moisture collection of the plants.

Following is a list of the microcatchment elements which should be integrated into the process of bioengineering. Several of the elements are discussed below.

WATER HARVESTING MICROCATCHMENT SYSTEM

- Mulching techniques
- Contour Trenches, swales and terraces
- Check dams - wattles (brush) and weirs (sets of gabions)
- Sand tank
- Dry wells and sand traps
- Parking lot and street runoff catchments
- Retention basins and diversion ponds
- Stripforest and understory

ELEMENTS OF THE MICROCATCHMENT SYSTEM

Mulching Techniques. Mulching is the easiest and one of the most effective methods in the microcatchment system to slow down water and hold it on the landscape. By covering the ground with mulch, straw, leaves and even branches, mulch forms a barrier of still air close to the soil, increasing the capacity to absorb water and slow the momentum of raindrops. Through decomposition, this material adds important organic matter to the soil, forming a basis for the

Bill Roley uses architecture, engineering, agriculture and ecology to weave restoration patterns into development. He heads the Permaculture Institute of Southern California, is one of the founders of the EOS Institute and has taught ecological design in all the educational forums from colleges to primary and secondary schools. Sprout Acres, his permaculture demonstration site, has been an inspiration for many years.

Permaculture Institute of Southern California
1027 Summit Way
Laguna Beach, CA 92651
(714) 494-5843

natural development of humus. Mulch shades the ground and keeps the soil moist, modulating its temperature so a soil community can form. Mulching is a very common method for promoting temporary protection of exposed erodible surfaces to permit the establishment of vegetation. Mulches are effective because when spread over the surface they protect it from splash erosion, retard runoff, trap sediment and create a more amenable microclimate to assist germination and early plant development. You can think of mulch as a condominium redevelopment project that enhances billions of soil microorganisms in the humus-sphere. Mulch then provides a nutrient-rich environment that creates a soil ecology of decomposers (fungi, bacteria, algae, actinomycetes and others) to exist. This thin environment is of vital importance to plant nutrient absorption, since the decomposers form a crumb soil structure which supports plant life. This crumb structure improves infiltration by adding airspaces to the soil particles. A layer of mulch then slows runoff and encourages soaking.

The mulch fiber acts as a sponge which quickly absorbs moisture. In fact, compost holds eight times its weight in water, making more water available to plants when needed, and strengthening plants against drought, stress and disease. A complex hierarchy of decomposers in the compost is an indication of soil fertility which is essential for the vitality and survival of most plants. This decomposition process creates humus which has the ability to hold four times more water than clay soils. This humus helps clay soils resist cracking, and in sandy soils holds onto moisture, slowing otherwise rapid drainage. So, thick mulch/humus acts as security from the fluctuation and unpredictability in rainfall, and adds drought tolerance to the landscape.

Contour Trenches, Swales and Terraces.   Swales are shallow hollows or steps built on the contour which create temporary pools of water on a level surface. These ditches or terraces cut along a hillside following the contour and

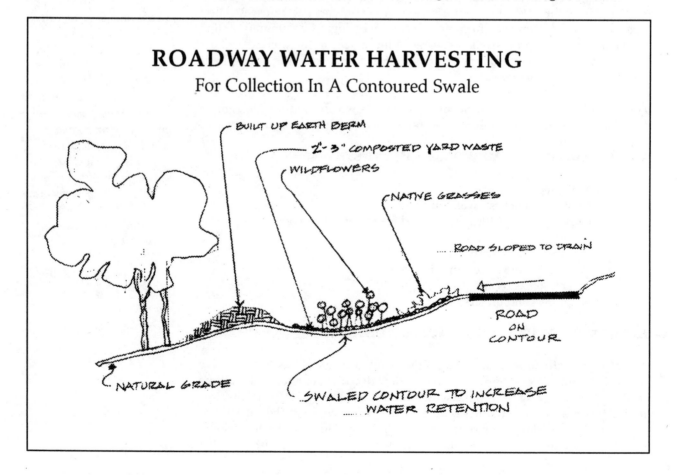

ROADWAY WATER HARVESTING
For Collection In A Contoured Swale

BUILT UP EARTH BERM

2"-3" COMPOSTED YARD WASTE

WILDFLOWERS

NATIVE GRASSES

ROAD SLOPED TO DRAIN

ROAD ON CONTOUR

NATURAL GRADE

SWALED CONTOUR TO INCREASE WATER RETENTION

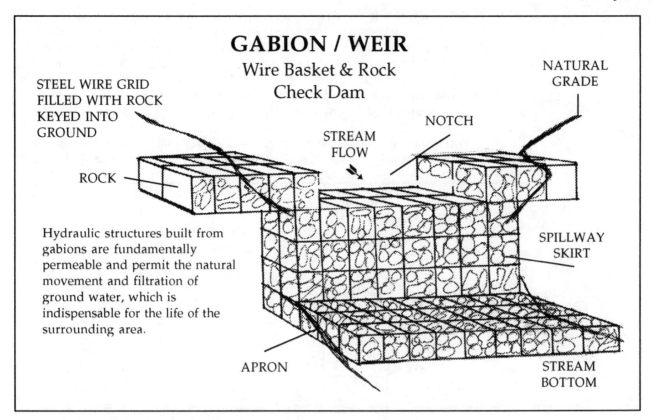

GABION / WEIR
Wire Basket & Rock
Check Dam

STEEL WIRE GRID FILLED WITH ROCK KEYED INTO GROUND

NATURAL GRADE

NOTCH

STREAM FLOW

ROCK

SPILLWAY SKIRT

Hydraulic structures built from gabions are fundamentally permeable and permit the natural movement and filtration of ground water, which is indispensable for the life of the surrounding area.

APRON

STREAM BOTTOM

run perpendicular to the downhill flow of water. They are just big steps that keep water and dirt from running downhill. Each swale slopes into the hillside with the high edge on the downhill side of the swale to further collect and hold the water. These trenches or ditches on the contour can then be mulched, graveled or sanded to improve rapid percolation as well as slow down the downhill movement of water. Landscape plantings are placed on the downhill side of the swale to further utilize and retard the flow of water down the slope.

It is interesting to note that if you grade the community roadway and golf course fairways along natural contours, these surfaces become water harvesting and retention areas also. The contoured swales are then planted in tree belts on the downhill side of the terrace to further reinforce these water catchment elements. The abundance of rain water that races off the roadways now can be used to irrigate the tree crops. It is important to facilitate the flow of excess runoff to protect the berms. Spillways or pipes need to be placed two or three inches higher than the growing plot. These overflow pipes or rock spillways must be installed to allow excess water to escape and bring additional water to lower catchment. Roadways can be laid out on the contour and provide a hard-surface water harvesting mechanism to collect water in a lower swale for a strip forest. The simplest version of this water catchment system is a net-and-pan system. Immediately up-slope from any growing area, a small holding basin is dug. It should be large enough to contain the rain runoff expected from an average flood event and contain enough water sufficient to wet the entire root area. The dirt from this excavation can be used to berm around the planting area.

Check Dams, Wattles (Brush) and Weirs (Sets of Gabions). If you use the indigenous landscape material found on the slopes high up in the watershed, you can weave branches, rocks and wire into forms called check dams. You want these dams to be small, tight and frequent. Check dams do not hold water, they are merely obstructions that dissipate raindrop energy and slow the water down. This gives silt which has become suspended in the water a chance to settle out. Clean, clear water percolates quickly into the soil and does not clog and seal the soil passageways. The goal here is to break up the swift movement of water over the landscape where gullies begin flowing into canyons. Gullies are a result of erosion, and mature watersheds covered with plants that intercept and absorb the water are the most effective means for controlling their destructive growth.

Wattles are permeable obstructions on hillsides that are constructed out of branches, brush or rocks found on the landscape site which are porous and

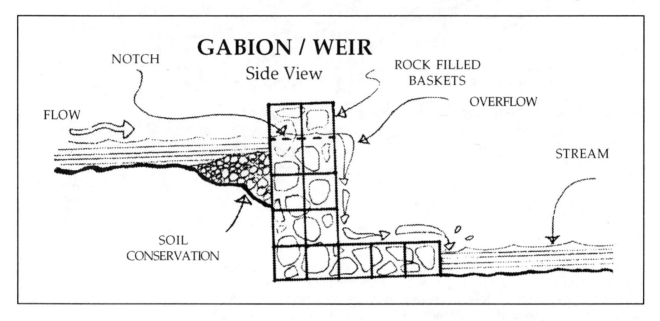

designed to delay the passage of water down the slope. Ground water infiltration and silt soil settlement are the benefits of such a design. Brush wattles have been used for erosion control in forestry and agriculture for many years. (Note: see *Trees and Shrubs for Erosion Control in Southern California Mountains* by Jerome Horton; California Forest and Range Experiment Station, U.S. Forest Service, 1949.)

Weirs are sets of gabions which use wire baskets filled with four to eight inch rocks. They form a flexible, permeable and durable barrier to slow down water running over the landscape. These water harvesting structures bend without breaking and increase in efficiency over time as silt and vegetation fill up the air pockets in the rock basket. The entire gabion solidifies into a permeable, monolithic unit and becomes part of the landscape. Plants can be placed behind the rock baskets further anchoring the weir in place. A weir provides a firm base below which the stream bed cannot be cut. Side slopes come to rest upon the material deposited above them and are supported by retaining walls at the base of the slope.

Proper design, construction and maintenance of check dams is essential if landform engineering is to succeed. By using the topography and geology of the watershed, the cost of constructing these microcatchment elements of flood control and water conservation strategy can be minimized.

Whichever material you chose must adhere to certain architectural principles of check dam construction. The most effective way to build check dams is with a series of head-to-toe alignments. These are constructed with the base of the upper dam on a level with the top of the lower dam. A notch where water can overflow the dam is essential. This will prevent the water from finding a line of least resistance to dig a path around the check dam. Building the dam over a number of rainfalls allows you to catch more sand, rather than silt.

By starting high up in the watershed, and using naturally stable points, you can divert small quantities of water into the landscape. This will eventually stabilize the whole gully by reducing the force and cutting action of the runoff. The plants will over time anchor the organic check dam in place. Plants suggested for gabion re-vegetation in dry areas include: Alyssum saxatile, Cistus crispus, Cytisus praecox, Echinum fastuosum, Lavandula, Portulaca grandiflora, and Jasminum officinale. The final outcome of this reforestation will further enhance the process of a climax forest and nature will take over flood control mitigation and water retention.

Sand Tank. Water is best stored in the ground in arid climates to avoid evaporation. Sand tanks have been used to supply drinking water to livestock in South and West Africa, Kenya, Australia and Arizona. Sand tanks store water in the pores between sand particles and release it over a long duration creating a life line (water vein) in the landscape. This increases the annual days of stream flow and its consequential effect on ecosystem vigor. Sand storage dams can be built only where the geology permits, usually across dry stream beds. The floodwaters must contain gravel or sand (course or fine granite, quartzite, microschist and dune sand all work well). The dam itself must be made absolutely water tight (cement-grouted or plastic sheeting to stop seepage).

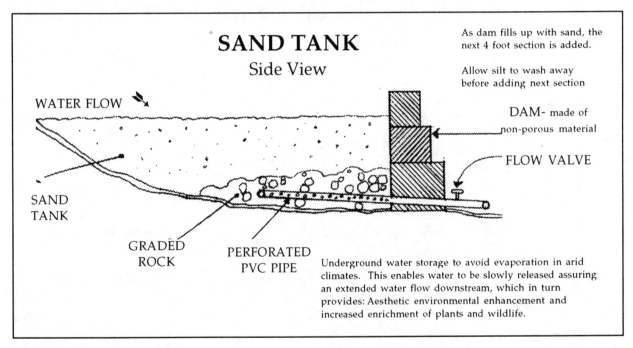

This water harvesting technique allows water to pool on the surface and percolate into the rock or sand storage medium. The captured water can be accessed by a pipe through the dam wall or by a well dug into the sand.

As sand builds up behind the dam, the water needs to be directed through a defined notch, forming a waterfall. A rock mattress or apron needs to be built to dissipate the water's energy so it will not dig out a pool and undermine the dam above. The easiest apron is a bed of rocks or stones where the falling water can simply knock itself out and flow tamely to the next check dam. Observation of clusters of rocks in the natural landscape can provide a model to follow. The water level in the tank should be kept more than 30 cm below the surface to shield it from evaporation. The rocks or sand reduce the volume of the tank by as much as 50% but they reduce evaporation by 90% (National Science Foundation, *More Water for Arid Lands*).

Once the dam wall is built across the riverbed during the dry season, the later storm flood will deposit the necessary sand and gravel for the storage well. Normally the soil carried by flood waters is 3/4 sediment and mud and only 1/4 sand and gravel. A dam trapping all this mixture would quickly silt up. To ensure that only sand and gravel are deposited, the dam wall is gradually heightened. After an initial wall of two meters is built, it can be raised in stages, one meter at a time. Then, flood waters will deposit heavy gravel and sand, but silt and soil are carried over the top by the speeding water. Each one meter stage is added when the dam is filled with sand and gravel until the operating height of six to ten meters is reached. Sand dams are particularly effective when built over fissures that lead to natural aquifers. Then, they not only control floodwater but redirect it into groundwater basins as well as extending the life of downstream flow.

Dry Wells and Sand Traps. Dry wells and sand traps can be used on golf courses to harvest water and avoid storm water flooding over the surface of the fairways. If the fairways are on the contour these injection wells replenish the ground water table.

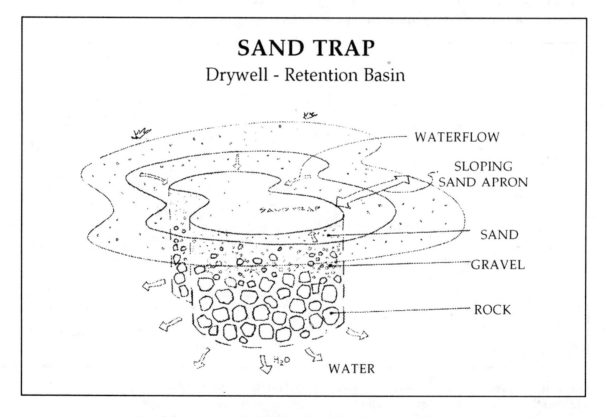

Parking Lot and Street Runoff Catchments. The objective is to use the hard surfaces to collect rainwater runoff and concentrate it on a planting strip. Water harvesting systems that transverse the contours of parking lots can direct runoff to frequent infusion sites that are planted with deep rooted and heat tolerant trees. This system could enable the homes in new and old developments to shade up to 60% of their hard surfaces, creating a rich habitat for humans and wildlife. This design will aid in cooling the parking lots as well as providing a natural edge to soften developed spaces. Streets and alleys could serve as water harvesting systems for the landscapes and produce shade elements and a microsite "oasis effect." Runoff from large roof areas could be stored in ground tanks to allow irrigation of these trees in drought periods.

Retention Basins and Diversion Ponds. These are flood water diversion and retention catchment basins that are constructed at optimal percolation sites along the water course. This water harvesting element only collects storm water and does not impede a natural river flow. A revised version could be used

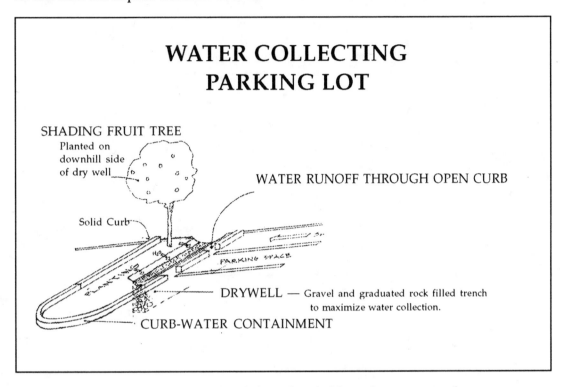

WATER COLLECTING
PARKING LOT

SHADING FRUIT TREE
Planted on
downhill side
of dry well

WATER RUNOFF THROUGH OPEN CURB

Solid Curb

PARKING SPACE

DRYWELL — Gravel and graduated rock filled trench
to maximize water collection.

CURB-WATER CONTAINMENT

to divert water on to swales on the slopes, thus holding the water on the landscape high up in the watershed. Examples of two such retention ponds are present on China Flats above Palo Comado Canyon. The silt found in these ponds at the head waters of the canyon could be blended with composted yard waste and used as a nutrient rich planting mix for all restoration work.

Stripforest. The following are some members of the natural plant community found in an oak woodland. The overstory is made up of Coastal Live Oak and Valley Oak. Present individually or together in the understory, depending on the particular microclimate and sun orientation, are: coffeeberry, ocean spray, blackberry, hazelnut and big leaf maple, braken fern, snowberry, madrone, toyon, California bay, ceanothus and redberry. These plant materials represent a first attempt at managing a landscape for a proposed village on the Jordan Ranch in Ventura County, CA. Environmental conditions within the planting area not only restrict the species that can be planted, but also determine their subsequent development. Understanding these conditions and using them to guide the selection of proper species and proper methods of planting are prerequisites for success. The survival and growth of these plants are affected mainly by five environmental factors: soil, temperature, exposure, precipitation and animal activity. By taking into consideration the habitat and requirements of the native vegetation, these plantings will establish vegetative cover and improve erosion control. Attention to these processes insures the maximum entry of water into the soil during heavy rains. The amount and velocity of water flowing over the soil surface can be reduced by our microcatchment strategy as well as the erosion caused by surface runoff.

ECOLOGICAL DESIGN COMPONENTS

SOLAR DESIGN • WATER MANAGEMENT • *URBAN LANDSCAPE* • WASTE MANAGEMENT • TRANSPORTATION • SUSTAINABLE TECHNOLOGY

URBAN LANDSCAPE

URBAN FORESTS:
THE LIFEBLOOD OF AN ECO-CITY

Andy Lipkis (edited by Katie Lipkis)

Andy and Katie Lipkis are respectively the President and Vice-President of TreePeople. Under their leadership, TreePeople has produced a continuous string of accomplishments including huge community planting projects such as the Million Tree Campaign, and innovative education programs like Citizen Forester training. The Lipkises co-authored **The Simple Act of Planting a Tree***, a book dedicated to the complex process of organizing community action and tree planting.*

TreePeople
12601 Mulholland Drive
Beverly Hills, CA 90210
(818) 753-4600

One hears "plant a tree" being used as a naive plea, as a band-aid for healing the environment. Who wouldn't be cynical? It's frustrating because the profound, sophisticated, even complicated way in which trees express their healing power is never expressed in this pat phrase. Trees are powerful not only for what they do physically but for what they achieve socially.

An individual tree can provide a home for abundant wildlife. A native oak can house up to 600 species of animals and bugs. One tree can shade a home to lower its energy bill and water consumption. One tree can raise not only property value but human spirits. A very special relationship can exist between one person and a single tree.

Nevertheless, trees in the city have a much broader effect planted in groups as part of an urban forest because the urban forest plays such a critical role in a city's life support system. Trees, used with precision, like acupuncture needles, can be true healers. Choose the right species, plant it the right place, take care of it and you have a real helper. (The opposite is also true. A pesky tree is simply the wrong tree in the wrong place.)

And what is the right place? A concrete-choked city, for instance, can be the perfect place for some trees. Trees can help break up urban heat islands and modify the climate. Scientists from Lawrence Berkeley Lab, among others, have proven that heat islands exist. Cities can be eight to twelve degrees hotter than surrounding countryside, because vegetation has been cleared to make way for heat-absorbing surfaces — parking lots, roads, rooftops — that store heat and radiate it, which raises the temperature even more. Updrafts of hot air from surfaces like parking lots are known to give pilots of light aircraft a bumpy ride as they cross a city.

The energy industry realizes that building power plants is not the best way to handle this increase in demand for cooling hot cities — that the more viable option is to efficiently save energy by planting trees to shade and cool parking lots, streets, school yards and buildings. Utilities like the Sacramento Metropolitan Utility District (SMUD) and all the utilities in Iowa, led by Iowa Electric, have launched aggressive tree planting programs. The City of Los Angeles Department of Water and Power (DWP) is working with TreePeople on a strategy for massive planting of the right trees in the right place, starting with the mountains around Los Angeles and coming right down into the neighborhoods. They recognize that trees equal "negawatts" or as Neil Sampson of the American Forestry Association puts it: "They are phantom power plants."

Carbon dioxide buildup is one of the major causes of global climate change. Trees are our prime absorber of CO_2 and, what's more, they can help prevent the buildup of CO_2 in cities by cooling the ambient air temperature and reducing the need for burning fossil fuels to make electricity for air conditioning.

AIR QUALITY

Trees produce oxygen. And yes, they do help reduce smog. They ingest some smog gases and their leaves filter smog particles from the air just like the filter on an air conditioner. Particles land on leaves or needles and eventually wash down in rainstorms. But even more significant is the heat island effect previously described. Trees can cool buildings, and trees can also cool the overall atmosphere. Smog is a byproduct of the cooking of the oxides of nitrogen and hydrocarbons and other stuff. By lowering the urban air temperature, trees lower the cooking temperature and, therefore, the smog level.

FOOD SUPPLY

A tree can feed you. A population that plants can help feed itself, establishing local food sources or local neighborhood food growing co-ops. TreePeople worked for years locating, preparing and distributing fruit trees through food banks to low-income families.

Liability problems do create restrictions. Most cities won't allow fruit trees on public property, particularly on parkways where fruit on the sidewalk could cause pedestrians to slip. But there are still plenty of potential locations. One can consider planting more than a household supply of fruit trees to provide an ongoing source of nourishment to a food bank or homeless shelter. One's own little piece of land can become something productive for others, as can church lands, parks and other public lands that present no safety hazards.

KILLER TREES

The "killer tree" controversy — that trees emit hydrocarbons and therefore produce smog — is a fallacious argument, the result of research having been twisted to create shocking headlines. Why is it that we've always had trees but haven't always had smog? To answer the question it helps to understand the fire triangle: air, fuel and heat. If you don't have one of these three ingredients then you can't have fire, so the firefighting strategy is to remove one of the three. It's the same story with smog.

> *Trees ingest some smog gases and their leaves filter smog particles from the air just like the filter on an air conditioner.*

Smog has three main ingredients: hydrocarbons, oxides of nitrogen and ultraviolet light. Federal standards demand the reduction of both hydrocarbons and oxides of nitrogen. Original research revealed the constant presence of naturally-occurring hydrocarbons. The object of this research was to demonstrate that regardless of the effort to reduce hydrocarbons, they will always be present from their biological source. The suggestion was made that standards should be switched to focus on oxides of nitrogen (NO_X), a small but powerful agent in the production of smog, because it is completely human-sourced and its eradication is therefore entirely within the power of humans.

When the media discovered one of the basic premises of the original research — that trees produce hydrocarbons, the story became "trees make smog." In fact, some researchers argue that the turpenes and hydrocarbons produced by trees actually digest human-produced hydrocarbons. So one can see there's still much research to be done.

THE CITY AS AN ECOSYSTEM

When we study a forest ecosystem, we see cycles: the energy cycle, the water cycle, how nutrients move through the chain. There is no waste, no energy shortage, no water shortage. Nature in balance is a closed loop.

If we overlay this notion on a city — the urban ecosystem — everything we've done wrong will be dramatically revealed. Like it or not, the city is a living ecosystem and responds just like a forest ecosystem. By ignoring this fact, we've engineered systems that defy natural cycles and we're paying a very high price for violating the laws of the ecosystem.

> **The city is a living ecosystem and responds just like a forest ecosystem.**

Consider energy. Consider the energy we humans eat, the energy dumped on fields to grow our food, and the energy it takes to get the food to our table. We use some of this energy after it's eaten, but a portion we give back as sewage which, instead of being returned to cropfields, is sent to pollute our oceans. It's just as the scientists describe: pollution is wasted energy. All ecosystems depend on recycled energy in order to stay healthy and unpolluted.

THE WATER CYCLE

The annual normal rainfall in Los Angeles could meet the entire city's irrigation needs, even though it totals only twelve inches per year. We have paved two-thirds of the city. If we could capture and store all that falls on the paved two-thirds, we would have the equivalent of *twenty-four more inches of rain*. But we have ignored that we are an ecosystem and have spent billions of dollars on a storm drain network that sends water (along with toxins from the street) efficiently to the ocean.

We have so overpaved ourselves that, when the Army Corps of Engineers discovered recently that the L.A. River (which was designed to handle all the water this city could ever produce) can no longer hold a hundred-year flood, they proposed a one billion dollar project to raise the river walls six to eight feet from downtown to the ocean. Their solution is to pour more concrete to deal with the fact that we have poured too much concrete. Nowhere in the one and a half inch thick Environmental Impact Report is there mention of solving the problem by managing the watershed.

> **The annual normal rainfall in Los Angeles could meet the entire city's irrigation needs, even though it totals only twelve inches per year.**

If we apply the forest ecosystem model to the city, we won't need to pour that concrete. When it rains in a forest, trees catch and slow the raindrops. By the time rain hits the forest floor, its velocity is diminished. What's more, it hits a sponge: the mulch. One of the main energy byproducts of the forest is mulch. It's made of all the "waste" products of trees. The mulch slowly releases the water into the soil where it feeds everything as it percolates down to rivers and the ocean.

The trees in our urban forest produce the same mulch material: branches, leaves..."trimmings". What do we do with it? We send it to landfills where it accounts for 35% of the waste stream. If we mulched it and used it on our gardens, we would hold and slow that rainfall, helping avert three problems at once: floods, trash and the pollution of Santa Monica Bay. If we planted more trees and used the mulch, we would be doing even better. And that's low tech. Technical fixes like removing concrete or making areas of concrete permeable to water would truly start addressing the problems we face.

In Australia, Israel, or as close as Arizona, water is trapped on-site in cisterns and used for irrigation. Imagine subterranean tanks made of recycled plastic and powered by solar-powered pumps to meet existing irrigation needs and to water even more trees.

One can only understand integrated urban ecosystem management when one can see the cycles of a healthy forest.

WHY ARE TREES NECESSARY TO MAKING ECO-CITIES?

Studying an ecosystem means studying the dominant players and their interactions. The dominant players in the urban ecosystem are humans. But when we talk only of planning and policy, we leave out the dominant players. We leave out the players who can make an informed choice to clean up their collective act. This is the major omission of decades of environmental law that turned out to be insufficient or unenforceable. While necessary, policy and law alone will not get the job done.

We are a population not of citizens but of consumers. We're the problem. This society has become so accustomed to *receiving* that we don't know how to *give*, so accustomed to being told what to think that we don't know how to act as individuals, as problem-solvers. We don't know the pathways. There is this whole realm of human participation that needs rehabilitation.

> *The importance of trees to the making of eco-cities is that they provide a common point from which all people can gather to move into action.*

Here we are, the dominant players in this living ecosystem called the city. We're given physical, creative, intellectual and spiritual energy. When we don't recycle it, it goes the way of all wasted energy: it becomes pollution. What does it look like? It looks like frustration, alienation, pain, disturbance. How does it manifest? Graffiti, suicide, murder, drugs, gang violence, overconsumption.

The dominant players have a lot of energy. They live in an ecosystem just like a forest. Doesn't it make sense that to teach people how to be citizens, we need to teach them how to consume less and how to link up the cycles again, how to recycle their energy to keep their city healthy? The importance of trees to the making of eco-cities is that they provide a common point from which all people can gather to move into action. Nobody needs to change who they are — for starters. They can participate now. They can understand that basic concept. It's probably the value of the naive "plant a tree" plea. Nobody need have a change of political heart. No one needs enlightenment first. Everyone can make a positive contribution right where they stand.

Once people have moved into healing action, they are fed by it. It recreates neighborhood. It makes citizens. We've seen communities built when people started planting their streets. Soon it's Neighborhood Watch, then the neighborhood gets a name, and before you know it, adults and kids are working together in a positive way, taking pride in what they've created. Urban tree planting can profoundly move our society and create lasting commitment because of the quick physical results it can produce — a sure sign of the power of individual action. And of course, the game only works if everybody plays. Twenty years of legislative action — since the first Earth Day — won't do it alone.

You see, not Washington, nor the state legislature, nor even city hall have the intelligence that each person in each neighborhood has. Only *you* know that graffiti-covered wall on your corner that needs vines growing on it so it's no longer a target. Only *you* know that vacant lot, or that place where people wait for the bus that should have a tree shading it. You're the one who will benefit by doing something about it — not just physically but spiritually and emotionally. You get the identity and the strength. It's that dynamic relationship between people and trees that's critical.

The notion that humans operate only via the fight or flight syndrome is not accurate. We've been undersold. We're much more powerful and capable than that. I think our response is: fight, flight or heal. I believe that we have the intelligence and the ability to correct our mistakes and re-connect nature's cycles, or even engineer new cycles that can mimic nature's patterns in order to make our eco-cities work.

THE ROLE OF URBAN AGRICULTURE IN RECLAIMING THE URBAN ENVIRONMENT

Brenda Funches

The concept of urban agriculture is not new. Certainly the idea of growing food in the city has been with us since the first Europeans migrated to major urban centers and grew herbs and plants specific to their cultures in small spaces. In the early part of the century the most visible form of urban agriculture was the "victory garden" movement which sprouted during both World Wars I and II. During the last two and a half decades, urban ecologists, environmentalists and those who promote the concept of "organic living" advocated planned communities that were self-sustaining and which helped protect and conserve natural and/or non-renewable resources.

As we move toward the 21st century, Los Angeles and other major urban centers have begun to grapple with the challenges created by decades of unplanned or poorly planned development, significant changes in their tax revenue bases, profound changes in not only the labor pool but in resident populations, and ever more urgent concerns created by a deteriorating environment.

Where and how urban agriculture will play a role in meeting these challenges could be discussed through consideration of four broad questions. What is urban agriculture? What are some compelling reasons to consider its role in the cities of tomorrow? What are the potential benefits to be gained? And finally, what are some systemic obstacles and challenges facing urban agriculture, and what can we do to overcome them?

WHAT IS URBAN AGRICULTURE?

There is still a great deal of dialogue over whether there is indeed such a thing, and if there is, how should it be defined. John Lyle of Cal Poly, Pomona, has been looking into this question as part of a major applied research effort. In California, we focus primarily on commercial ag-producers and allied industries as part of the $17 billion or so credited to the state's annual GNP. These include the farm equipment retailers and manufacturers, brokers of both vegetable and animal crops, processors and packagers, and wholesalers.

Until recently, little attention has been paid to the economic contributions of small scale production in essentially backyard plots, and its impact on neighborhood economic systems. Just as commercial agriculture has a "ripple effect" on the macroeconomic level, small scale food and specialty crop production have the potential for the same effect on the micro, or community level. Too often we think only of immediate tangible cash or bottom line results when speaking about urban agriculture, and not enough about its potential for ecological cities of the future. For our purposes here, let us define urban agriculture as "any and all enterprises, commercial and non-commercial, related to the production, distribution, sale or other consumption of agricultural and horticultural produce or commodities in a metropolitan/major urban center."

Brenda Funches is the Cooperative Extension Advisor for the Common Ground Garden Program. She operates 15 community and 34 gardening projects throughout L.A., benefiting 450 families, and nearly 1,200 children. She is Co-founder of L.A. Harvest, a non-profit organization which will develop urban agriculture projects to increase entrepreneurial and farming skills among jobless inner city youth and adults.

Common Ground Garden Program
2615 South Grand Ave., #400
Los Angeles, CA 90007
(213) 744-4342

Commercial urban agriculture in Los Angeles County consists primarily of wholesale nurseries producing woody ornamental plants. These are grown primarily under power lines and along freeway frontages. Next are small farms and specialty crop producers. Small farms are found mostly in the high desert and along contiguous borders with San Bernardino, Ventura, Kern, and Orange Counties. Specialty crop producers usually have less than five acres of land and specialize in so-called "baby vegetables," herbs, and organically grown vegetables. In the aggregate, these activities contribute approximately $260 million annually to Los Angeles' GNP, and have maintained Los Angeles County as 16th in the state in overall agricultural production.

> *Little attention has been paid to the economic contributions of small scale production in essentially backyard plots.*

Frequently overlooked, but significant in terms of its impact on primarily low income neighborhoods, is the strong, well-established community food gardening movement. There are between 90 and 110 active community vegetable gardens in the greater Los Angeles area at any given time. Collectively, these gardens account for approximately 1.25 million square feet, or 29 acres under production year-round. Using a conservative USDA formula, the value of these gardens is nearly $900,000 annually. Other food access groups such as End World Hunger, and the American Community Gardening Association have preferred to calculate the value of community food gardens based on actual retail prices a family of four would need to pay to purchase fresh produce regularly. Their estimates range from a low of $1.8 million to $3.7 million grown in 6,200 plots of 200 square feet each.

Clearly, the economic impact of urban agriculture in the greater Los Angeles area alone is significant. And the entire field needs to be studied as an entity unto itself, much as John Lyle at Cal Poly is doing. David Campbell, U.C. Davis Economics and Public Policy Analyst concurs. He asserts that "...traditional farming research methods, grounded in narrowly conceived cost-benefit accounting, fail to adequately account for the impact of farming...on the environment, public health, worker safety, and...community development...."

WHAT ARE SOME COMPELLING REASONS TO CONSIDER URBAN AGRICULTURE'S ROLE IN THE CITIES OF TOMORROW?

As the European-American population ages in major urban centers, we have witnessed the crumbling of the entire fabric of the so-called "American way of life." As voters, these mostly white middle class individuals have refused to tax themselves for any but the most basic public services, e.g., police, fire, and public safety programs.

At the same time the infrastructure is crumbling, entire school systems have become bankrupt, primary health care and mental health services are out of the reach of most Americans, and at least one week of each month in the United States of America, most families in poverty go without food.

A poorly educated, mostly minority and female population is the largest sector of the urban labor market. Unlike their predecessors, these groups do not have the resources necessary to support the coming essential increases in personal tax revenues, nor will they account for the growth in the corporate and business tax revenues needed to support further population expansion in our area.

The fastest growing segment of the economy is in the "service sector," consisting of those jobs which pay the least and have the fewest opportunities for occupational and wage mobility. Women and people of color comprise 80% of the employees in these occupations; by the year 2000, 85% of entry level jobs will be held by these groups.

Among people of color in Los Angeles, immigrants from Southeast Asia, Asia, and Latin America account for the most growth, with the African-American population being relatively stable.

We make these points because what is most often overlooked in rosy projections about the growth of the labor market and the Los Angeles area economy is that the people who account for that growth are the same people who draw upon overburdened public health, welfare and education services that were designed to meet vastly different needs than we now require of them. New value systems and agendas have replaced those of the once-dominant white cultures, with few or no financial resources or political power attached to those agendas.

Finding resources for these groups is one of the major issues for our future. Growing one's own food may be such a key resource when one considers the cost of food for a family of four ranges from a low of $309 to a high of $680 monthly (USDA, 1991). Most lower income families, even two wage-earner families, net a low of $900 to a high of $2,200 monthly for a family of four, and spend from 40% to as high 75% or more of their incomes on housing.

> ## At least one week of each month in the United States of America, most families in poverty go without food.

So urban agriculture may not only represent better food for the disadvantaged but also an annual increase of 5% or more in their income. However, the role of urban agriculture in the future must not be allowed to evolve by happenstance and serendipity as has happened in other aspects of urban development. Small scale ag-production for both personal and commercial purposes has a vital place in the economic infrastructure of the future and should be included in the city's general and community plans with protective zoning designations.

FROM FOOD CO-OP TO URBAN FARM

David Cundiff, MD

The Long Beach Organic Food Co-op existed in the Belmont Heights area of Long Beach, California for over ten years before we switched to buying organic food in late 1990. Half a year later, I hired a Mayan Indian vegetable gardener to begin producing some of our own food. He works in my backyard on weekends growing tomatoes, corn, beans, lettuce, and several other vegetables.

On my recommendation, a local urban organic food producer hired this Mayan gardener to supervise three vegetable gardeners working on a 50 x 100 foot lot. Our food co-op now buys lettuce, cabbage and apricots from this local producer and soon will buy tomatoes, beans, corn and strawberries. We hope that eventually, the local organic food producer, the Mayan gardener and his colleagues will produce half or more of our produce.

This local vegetable gardening project benefits a Third World farmer whose people have long been exploited in the production of inexpensive food for export to the United States. As our food co-op membership grows, we plan to support more gardeners and expand the area of food production.

From an ecological perspective, organic food co-ops save topsoil lost in non-organic food production and reduce petrochemical pollution from pesticides, chemical fertilizers, gasoline and packaging. Our co-op also provides teenagers with jobs that teach them about organic food and business skills, but what makes this urban venture more unusual is tying it into locally grown produce. Since the co-op required no initial financing, any small group of people can find local growers to commit all or portions of their crop to a co-op.

Contact phone #: (310) 438-9000

HOW CAN THE CITIES OF THE FUTURE BENEFIT FROM URBAN AGRICULTURE?

Stating the obvious, planned integration of urban agriculture into the cities of the future has one immediate benefit: a significant reduction in our dependency on the massive non-renewable, petro-dependent production, processing, packaging and transportation of agricultural products and commodities. Economically distressed communities would benefit from job training and development of transferable entrepreneurial skills among jobless adults and youth. The entire chain of production, processing, distribution and consumption of food alone would generate new sources of income in local communities and thereby increase disposable income in these communities. Families growing $300 to $600 worth of fresh produce each year may not be burning up the produce section of the grocery store, but will certainly be freeing up significant income for other needs and desires.

One of the most outrageous conditions impacting American citizens at the dawn of the millennium is hunger among the poor and the working poor. According to a 1986 United Way study on the food distribution system in Los Angeles, as much as 20% of usable food never reaches the potential consumer. This loss comes from the inability of large farm equipment to harvest entire planted fields, damage during processing, culling produce considered cosmetically inferior, and spoilage. These loses could be almost eliminated in community gardens.

Consider the cost/benefit ratio of healthy, well fed low-income families, mothers to be, children, and working adults: fewer missed days of work and school due to nutrition-related illness, less drain on an already overburdened health care system, and greater contributions to the tax and business revenue base. Planned urban agriculture activities could help reverse the continued economic decline in real estate markets by creating communities where visual blight would not exist. Trees and drought-tolerant ornamental planting could improve the quality of the air, and reduce temperatures during heat waves.

If the concept of urban agriculture were seriously implemented, we might even have a good chance of reaping some of the rewards associated with a small farming community. In a landmark study, Walter Goldschmidt found that one such town supported by small farms had more institutions for democratic decision-making, broader citizen involvement, and that about 20% more of the people were supported at a higher standard of living than those living in a town supported by a single large corporate farm.

Another important potential benefit of community-based urban ag-production is that organic community gardening groups and small businesses may choose to take responsibility for helping to safeguard the world's depleting bank of regenerative seeds. By maintaining seed diversity at the community level, we help the whole planet ward off potential devastation caused by the patented non-regenerative seeds commercially available.

WHAT ARE SOME CHALLENGES AND OBSTACLES, AND HOW MIGHT WE OVERCOME THEM?

What needs to be considered in the whole discussion of urban agriculture are the realities experienced by small family farmers with a gross of less than $50,000 annually. The impact of bad weather, drought, disease or pestilence on these individuals is devastating. Consider then what the impact might be on a small enterprise on just a vacant lot or two? Even now, because of the vulnerability of small enterprises, large-scale commercial agriculture can and does hold urban ag-activities hostage to its agenda. Recent decisions to eradicate

Medfly infestations damaged more than automobiles and lungs here in Los Angeles. Backyard, community, and small scale commercial gardeners report that delicate micro-environments were severely damaged. In addition, the prospect of 14 to 16 hour days to possibly earn $50,000 annually might appeal to some, but not most urbanites, even if they currently earn minimum wage.

There are also the obstacles and barriers in the infrastructure. Zoning laws and permit processes are prohibitive. The whole issue of seed capital and financing from urban banks is difficult. Farm finance institutions are unfamiliar with urban enterprise while urban trade financiers are unfamiliar with small scale agriculture. Add to this the need for urban ag-producers to be able to provide business plans, and have a proven track record to obtain loans, and what you have is a series of obstacles which may be too difficult for even the most intrepid small business person. Pragmatically speaking, we believe that the concept of urban agriculture, in its early stages, would be most beneficial if it were considered an augmentation to a more stable income source.

While the challenges we face in Los Angeles are difficult, there are some active projects and models from which we can draw information and encouragement. Sim Van der Ryn suggests that government subsidies to agriculture be redirected, and urges research, development and education on small scale ag-production. Such a policy could and should lead to the support of small scale ag-production through an Urban Agriculture Extension Service, with the emphasis where it should be, on service. Other suggestions include shifting research subsidies and efforts from chemical fertilizers and pest control to composting, mulching and integrated pest management, moving agriculture away from petrochemical dependency. Presently, this type of applied research

is being conducted by specialists at U.C. Davis and at U.C. Santa Cruz through the Agro Ecology Department. At Common Ground, we are currently cooperating with our consumer marketing/public service advisor to study the impact of compost, mulches and organic fertilizers on tomato crops and will consider other crops in future research.

The question of support through adjustments in the infrastructure offers some engaging scenarios. Creation and sales of urban ag-bonds is one concept that is being explored in a small community in New York state. Many other urban groups across the country are engaging in what has come to be known as Community Supported Farms. Households and groups of friends, church groups or other community groups buy "shares" in a small farm which entitle them to a portion of the harvest. The farmer, in effect, pre-sells their harvest. Low-interest credit and seed capital programs for small scale producers is another possibility.

While these concepts are helpful, the process needs to be adjusted to allow for the culturally induced small-scale farming expertise of immigrants, and at the same time provide assistance in the development of skills needed to apply for a loan, and manage a business. Major incentives for water reclamation to support increased urban ag-efforts; and expansion of urban ag-land trusts are other growing concepts which warrant further study.

A recent article in *American Demographics* magazine indicated that while more than 78% of Americans acknowledged a need to improve the quality of our environment, fewer than 11% are willing to make significant changes in their living habits. Another 11% are willing to pay more for environmentally friendly products, but would not give up free time or convenience; 26% are ambivalent about the trade-offs necessary between economic development and environmentalism. Some 24% believe that they should not be asked to "bear the burden alone." 28% have almost no pro-environmental leaning and feel that one person's actions cannot make a difference anyway.

Perhaps it is not surprising that this 28% share the characteristics of those individuals who are economically, socially and politically disenfranchised — poorly paid service economy workers. Change must not just start with the 11% of the population who are already committed to major change in their lives. All of us must take responsibility for expanding our vision. We must find ways to bridge racial and cultural gaps in order to involve, educate and support economically stressed minority communities. In moving to a future where urban agriculture plays a meaningful role in reclaiming, revitalizing and renewing urban environments, perhaps our greatest challenge lies in the need to capture the hearts and minds of those disenfranchised people who would then have the political and social will to act on the moral imperatives inherent in the preservation of the planet.

RESOURCES FOR FURTHER INFORMATION

American Community Gardening Association, c/o Philadelphia Green, 325 Walnut St., Philadelphia, PA 19106, (215) 625-8280 National membership organization for professionals, volunteers and supporters of community gardening and greening, preservation of open space, and land use management.

"Earth's Best Friends"; *American Demographics Magazine*, February, 1991. An analysis of consumers and their attitudes toward environmentalism, recycling, waste management, and personal involvement.

Canine, Craig, Arvin, and Dinuba; "A Tale of Two Towns". *Harrowsmith Country Life Magazine*, May/June 1991. Highlights some of the benefits that accrue to towns built around small family farms, and compares them to the disadvantages of towns developed for large-scale corporate farming.

Grough, Trauger and McFadden. *Community Supported Farms, Farm Supported Communities: Farms of Tomorrow*. Subscription farming programs in communities across the country allow consumers to pay organic farmers in advance for a portion of the annual harvest.

U.C., Cooperative Extension; 2615 South Grand Avenue, #400; Los Angeles, CA 90007; (213) 744-4341 for Community Vegetable Gardening, (213) 744-4851 for Farm Advisor for Specialty Crops and Small Farms, (213) 744-4340 for L.A. Harvest: Urban Horticulture and Community Greening, sources of information on small farms, urban agriculture, community gardening, and inner city revitalization.

U.C. Sustainable Agriculture Research Program; U.C. Davis; Davis, CA 95616; (916) 752-7556. Newsletters and research information on sustainable agriculture and integrated pest management.

Van der Ryn, Sim, and Calthorpe, Peter. *Sustainable Communities*. San Francisco: Sierra Book Club, 1986.

XERISCAPE

Julia Scofield Russell

Julia Russell is Founder and Director of the Eco-Home Network and the Eco-Home demonstration home for ecological living in Los Angeles. Since 1985, she has been appearing on radio and television and has given lectures and workshops on the importance of living in balance with nature. A frequent spokesperson at City Hall for integrating environmental systems into our city infrastructure, she was one of the three principal planners of the First Los Angeles Ecological Cities Conference initiated to bring ecologically sound design principles and practices into mainstream development and redevelopment.

Eco-Home Network
4344 Russell Avenue
Los Angeles, CA 90027
(213) 662-5207

"Steal my horse, carry off my wife, but damn you, don't touch my water!" This old frontier saying, as emphatic as it is, hardly expresses how precious water is when there isn't enough. Gold is a paltry, superfluous thing in comparison.

It's easy to forget that Los Angeles County is semi-arid desert country. Our lush, tropical vegetation here is artificially maintained through regular supplemental watering. In fact, it is estimated that about 50% of water for home use is employed in maintaining lawns and gardens.

Since the early 1900s, when local water resources threatened to become insufficient for the very rapid growth of Pueblo de Nuestra Señora la Reina de Los Angeles, it's been suffering from an unquenchable thirst. First, it coveted the abundance of Owens Valley, and through some dubious transactions of a handful of enterprising men managed to obtain virtually all the water rights in the valley. Bill Mulholland built his celebrated Los Angeles Aqueduct and the dehydration of Owens Valley began.

Once a prospering agricultural community, Owens Valley now chokes in alkali dust storms that blow up off the parched basin that used to be Owens Lake. In 1970, a second Los Angeles aqueduct was completed and by 1976, the L.A. Times reported that the Department of Water and Power was pumping 90,000 gallons per minute of underground water from Owens Basin. The water table has been lowered. The springs of Owens Valley flow no more.

But all the water in Owens Valley couldn't satisfy the needs of Los Angeles for long. Soon the water resources of the Mono Lake Basin, north of Owens Valley, were tapped, threatening the integrity of the unique ecology of that region as its fresh water supply was depleted.

The Metropolitan Water District was formed in 1928 for the purpose of bringing water from the Colorado to coastal southern California cities, Los Angeles among them. The 242-mile Colorado River Aqueduct was completed in 1941.

Two separate water systems, the federal Central Valley Project (CVP) and the State Water Project (SWP), pump 4,479,455 acre-feet of water per year from the Sacramento-San Joaquin Delta. The SWP reaches as far north as the Feather River to bring its water more than 600 miles south to our faucets and hoses here in Los Angeles.

As our population continues to grow, so does demand for water. Because of two lawsuits, one filed by an association of California water agencies and contractors and one by northern California counties and timber companies, the Klamath, Smith, Eel, Trinity and lower American rivers were removed from the Federal Wild and Scenic Rivers System and are subject now to damming and pumping.

The Colorado River Board of California proposes cloud seeding in the Colorado River Basin headwaters, combined with clearcutting timberlands and other so-called "vegetative management," to increase run-off into the Colorado River.

There are proposals to build an aqueduct to the Snake River in Idaho and even the Yukon and other Alaskan rivers. How much more of the rest of the Earth are we willing to desiccate and disrupt to keep our Los Angeles lawns green?

Unless we learn to curtail it, there is no end to the growth in need but, despite the best efforts of our water companies, and they have evidently been considerable, there is an end to the resource. And the plight is not exclusive to California. The prospect of water shortage is being faced nationwide. Water consumption in the U.S. is expected to nearly triple within 35 years, reaching 880 billion gallons a day by the year 2000.

In California, according to our Department of Water Resources, approximately 85% of the water is used for agriculture and 14% in urban areas. Government, industry and commerce account for 32% of water use in the cities. Sixty-eight percent goes to residential use and 50% of that, as mentioned above, goes for landscape maintenance.

Water reclamation is high priority now, and much has been done and will be done to recycle waste water. An Office of Water Reclamation has been established within the structure of Los Angeles city government. Reclaimed water is a key to ameliorating our water problems, but a long-term one. Though many large projects are on the books, it will still be years before they can play a critical role in the water resources picture.

Water conservation is the only means which will be effective immediately as well as in the long run. There are conservation measures to be taken within the house in dishwashing and toilet flushing, etc. Information on indoor household water conservation can be obtained from the water company in your district. But since 50% of our residential water is used outdoors for our landscapes, that is where we can make our biggest saving. We can, and must, drastically reduce the water we use in our lawns and gardens.

Are we left then with dusty, brown lawns and burned out flower beds? No. There is an alternative, and it is called a xeriscape. A xeriscape garden is one that does not require supplemental watering to thrive all year long. The native vegetation of our region is beautiful and varied, and in addition, we have available to us introductions from other "Mediterranean climates" that are adapted to our semi-arid climate. A natural garden of climate-appropriate plants in southern California need lack nothing in grace and diversity.

In addition to a new palette of water conserving plant materials, we have a new technology of irrigation to learn

Xeriscape scene by Allison Starcher

about. Forget sprinklers that disperse gallons of water per minute into the air where much of it evaporates onto saturated soil, from which it then runs off into our gutters. Drip irrigation is a water conserving technology imported from Israel, that releases a gallon of water, not per minute, but per hour, directly to the root zones of your plants, eliminating evaporation and run-off.

California Bush Sunflower by Melanie Baer-Keeley

The California Landscape Contractors Association, the California Department of Water Resources and the Metropolitan Water District of Orange County sponsored the first conference on the subject in 1983. They coined the word *xeriscape* (zer´-i-scap), derived from the Greek word for dry, for the title of their conference. Conference attendance grew quickly, from a few hundred to thousands within a decade, attracting landscape architects, contractors, horticulturists, nursery people, gardeners, irrigation engineers, writers and environmentally concerned individuals. The agenda ranges from the history of California water development to the technical and horticultural specifics of water conservation in the landscape, all accompanied by illustrative slide shows. Xeriscape conferences are now given semi-annually, one in northern California and one in southern California.

Two Orange County development companies have been pioneering the use of drought-tolerant landscaping in their planned communities. Hundreds of plants are being tested at the Mission Viejo Community Drought Tolerant Test Site and the Irvine Ranch Test Station for their performance under varying degrees of water deprivation. Through successful demonstration and education, including proof of significant cost savings, the companies were able to convert resistant home owners' associations into enthusiastic supporters of xeriscaping.

Years ago, as a lone hunter stalking the wild fennel, sage and manzanita to herd into my home garden, I dreamed that one day every garden would be climate-appropriate, a garden that didn't need to plunder another's resource to flourish. It isn't happening overnight, but the progress within a decade is impressive.

Rancho Santa Ana Botanic Garden in Claremont, the Arboretum in Arcadia and the Theodore Payne Foundation in Sun Valley, California are great resources for information and appropriate plant material.

Two books that have been helpful are: *Trees and Shrubs for Dry California Landscapes*, written and published by Bob Perry, and *Plants for Dry Climates*, by Mary Rose Duffield & Warren Jones, published by HP Books. (See Resource Guide for additional books on xeriscape.) Also, California State Polytechnic University at Pomona, Office of Continuing Education, offers courses in xeriscaping.

The Municipal Water District of Orange County has available a very comprehensive flyer on xeriscape, including a list of 80 drought-tolerant plants, a sample landscape design, information on drip irrigation systems, planting techniques and other guidelines.

PLANTING HINTS

Plants which are adapted to long, hot, dry summers and cool, rainy winters are called "Mediterranean zone" plants. These include plants which are native to California, as well as those which originate in other Mediterranean climates around the world, such as regions around the Mediterranean Sea and some areas in South America, Africa and Australia.

When planning a new garden or changing the one you have, plan for water conservation:

- Cut back on the lawn areas. Lawns need great quantities of water, especially in the summertime.

- Wait until fall or winter to install a new garden. New plantings take more water than established ones.

- Keep low-water plants away from thirsty plants. Mediterranean zone plants will suffer from too much summer watering.

- Install a drip irrigation system or buried soaker hoses for efficient watering instead of conventional and wasteful sprinkler systems.

- Mulch your planting areas. Mulch is a layer of stones, compost, bark, leaves or even plastic on top of the ground. Mulch prevents water from evaporating from the soil and moderates soil temperature, protecting the roots of plants from extreme heat and cold.

- Create a shallow basin around each plant for water collection.

- Keep shade plants in the shade and place water-loving plants at the bottom of slopes.

The following are a list of the plants in the Eco-Home Xeriscape:

TREES:
Almond 'Nonpareil'
White Sapote, *Casimiroa edulis*
Loquat - *Eriobotrya japonica*
Piñon Pine, Pinus *cembroides edulis*
Golden Medallion Tree, *Cassia leptophylla*
Jacaranda, *Jacaranda mimosifolia*

SHRUBS:
Prostrate Rosemary, *Rosemarinus officinalis prostrata*
Wild Fennel, *Foeniculum vulgare*
Oleander 'Petite Salmon', *Nerium oleander*
Lantana, *Lantana camara*
Mahonia 'Golden Abundance'
Creeping Mahonia, *Mahonia repens*
Lemonade Berry, *Rhus integrifolia*
Wild Buckwheat, *Eriogonum fasciculatum*
Red Buckwheat, *Eriogonum rubescens*
Manzanita, *Arctostaphylus* 'Howard McMinn'
Australian Grass Tree, *Xanthorrhea quadrangulata*
Rock Rose, *Cistus*
Australian Tea Tree, *Leptospermum*

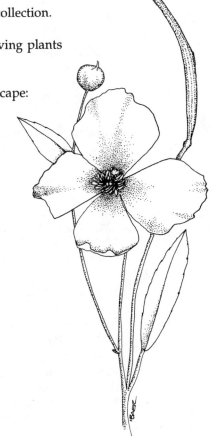

Tree Poppy by Melanie Baer-Keeley

**FLOWERS AND
GROUND COVERS:**
Lantana, *Lantana montevidensis*
Fortnight Lily, *Dietes vegeta*
Yarrow, *Achillea taygetea*
Red Yarrow
California Fuschia, *Zauschneria*
Scarlet Pimpernel, *Anagallis arvensis*
Ice Plant

SHADE PLANTS:
Braken fern, *Pteridium aquilinum*
Calla Lily, *Zantedeschia*
Pacific Coast Iris, *Iris munzii*
Heucheria

More and more nurseries are now
stocking collections of drought-tolerant plants. Ask your nurseryperson
to show them to you.

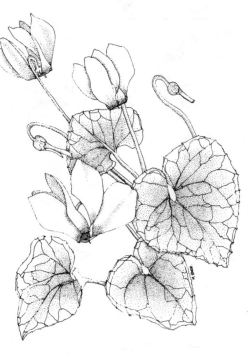

Cyclamen by Melanie Baer-Keeley

**LOS ANGELES AREA
NURSERIES CARRYING
NATIVE CALIFORNIA PLANTS:**

Boething Treeland Farm, Inc.
234/5 Long Valley Road
Woodland Hills, CA 91367
(818) 883-1222

Chatsworth Nursery
10538 Topanga Canyon Blvd.
Chatsworth, CA 91311
(818) 341-5600

Glendale Paradise Nursery
11249 Wheatland Ave.
Lakeview Terrace, CA 91342
(818) 899-4287

Hewlett's Coastal Zone Nursery
31427 Pacific Coast Hwy.
Malibu, CA 90265
(310) 457-3343

Mockingbird Nursery
1670 Jackson St.
Riverside, CA 92504
(714) 780-3571

Rancho Santa Ana
Botanic Garden
1500 North College Ave.
Claremont, CA 91711
(714) 625-8767

Sassafras Nursery and Farm
275 N. Topanga Canyon Blvd.
Topanga, CA 90290
(310) 455-1933

Sperling Landscape Co.
24460 Calabasas Rd.
Calabasas, CA 91302
(818) 340-7639

Theodore Payne Foundation
10459 Tuxford St.
Sun Valley, CA 91352
(818) 768-1802

Tree of Life Nursery
P.O. Box 736
33201 Ortega Hwy.
San Juan Capistrano, CA 92693
(714) 728-0685

Weber Nursery
237 Seeman Drive
Encinitas, CA 92024
(619) 753-1661

Wildwood Nursery
3975 Emerald Ave.
La Verne, CA 91750
(714) 593-4093 or
(714) 621-6675

Las Pilitas Nursery
Star Route Box 23X
Santa Margarita, CA 93453
(805) 438-5992

**SOME LANDSCAPERS
SPECIALIZING IN XERISCAPE:**
Ilene Adelman
(310) 470-2295

Robert Cornell
Cornell & Wiskar
(213) 731-0858

Susanne Morelock
P.O. Box 7626
Jackson, WY 83001

**WILDFLOWERS
BY THE POUND:**
Environmental Seed Producers, Inc.
P.O. Box 5904
El Monte, CA 91734
(818) 442-3330

**DRIP IRRIGATION
CONSULTANT:**
Bob Galbreath
Garden Technologies
P.O. Box 7322
Culver City, CA 90233

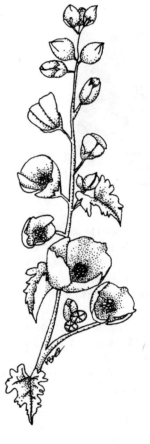

**Desert Mallow by
Melanie Baer-Keeley**

ADDITIONAL BOOK LIST:

Taylor's Guide to Water-Saving Gardening (Houghton Mifflin Company, N.Y., 1990).

Southwest Gardening, Rosalie Doolittle (University of New Mexico Press, 1968).

Waterwise Gardening; Beautiful Gardens With Less Water (Menlo Park: Sunset Publishing Corp., 1989).

Water-Conserving Plants & Landscapes for the Bay Area, Barrie Coate (East Bay Municipal Utility District, 1990).

The Xeriscape Flower Gardener, Jim Knopf (Johnson Publishing Co., 1991).

OUT OF PRINT — AVAILABLE IN ECO-HOME LIBRARY

Successful Gardening with Limited Water, Wheatly (Woodbridge Press Publishing Company, Santa Barbara, 1978).

Native Plants for Use in the California Landscape, Emile L. Labadie, (Sierra City Press, 1978).

Gardening in Dry Climates, Cedric Crocker, ed. (Ortho Books, 1989).

GARDENS IN THE SKY

Bob Walter

Bob Walter is the President of the Los Angeles based Eco-Home Network, and was one of the three principal planners of the First Los Angeles Ecological Cities Conference. He is an environmental writer and consultant who co-edits the Ecolution magazine/ newsletter and writes the New City Living column for The City Planet.

Eco-Home Network
4344 Russell Avenue
Los Angeles, CA 90027
(213) 662-5207

othing could have prepared me for my emergence into Shirley Robinson's garden. I climbed the staircases of the large old heart-of-Hollywood apartment house with its long history and longer halls, and faithfully followed her through a doorway onto the building's parking structure roof. The reality shift was like entering the Starship Enterprise's holodeck in the middle of somebody's jungle fantasy.

Here on this baked, forsaken surface, a massive burst of healthy plants trailed and intertwined across the roof. Profusions of huge red cabbages, squash, corn, pole beans, cucumbers, raspberries and blackberries trailing up trellises, melons of all sorts, bananas, apricots, apples, guavas, thirty fruit trees in total. Everything looked so healthy in this large organic garden made of individual planting containers. Clearly, Shirley was not your ordinary gardener. Plants paid attention. Insect pests need not apply.

Hidden away here from the sight of passersby, Shirley's garden, during the eight years she tended it, greened the souls of all whose windows looked down on this oasis from which her small family derived virtually everything they ate.

Bob Gordon manages an apartment house in West Hollywood. His rooftop garden is more modest. But it is a special place where he can look out across the city, tend his garden, and try to figure out whether he or his carefully cared for plants receive more nurturing from this symbiotic mid-city experience. And when his reveries subside, he can walk downstairs carrying fresh organic lettuce, tomatoes, radishes and dill for the dinner salad.

Jeff Tucker has a private home in Santa Monica with beautifully landscaped grounds, including an edible landscape, but to expand his growing space, he has put some barrel planters and drip irrigation on the flat part of his roof to grow some extra food.

Shirley, Bob and Jeff are pioneers who represent the first wave of a movement which has relevance for a great many of us city dwellers. We have a vast, untapped growing space above us, but most of us just haven't realized that it's there. The roof is a perfect spot for growing food. It's a private place that's quick to get to and, in our immediate environment, there is no other location as likely to receive extended sunlight.

> *Rooftop greenhouses will offer lush spaces filled with the fragrance of flowers and earthy scent of plants and soil, a place of solace and reflection.*

Planting a rooftop garden is something you could start small and increase in size as your interest grows, but it must be approached with a bit of thought. There are potential problems. Most roofs are not really made to have gardeners tromping around on them, and most are not structurally prepared to support the weight of a great amount of soil. But these concerns are addressable.

If you or the building owner are worried about the roof being walked on, you can build decking so the roof itself does not absorb the ongoing impact of the added foot traffic. Wooden pallets make an inexpensive decking substitute, and their modular nature makes them ideal if they have to be removed for any

reason. The weight of soil can be mitigated by using carefully spaced planters, (the heaviest being placed directly above structural columns) and irrigation can be done with mini drip hoses so there is no excess water build-up.

LESSONS FROM NEW YORK CITY

In New York City, Paul Mankiewicz, from the Gaia Institute, has spent seven years testing and perfecting a super lightweight growing medium called Solid State Hydroponics™, in order to promote intensive rooftop agriculture. This substance uses recycled Styrofoam shredded into small particles to replace the sand and fill that makes up at least 80% of standard soil. Vermiculite is another option being considered by certain growers as a soil substitute to reduce weight. An average roof can handle thirty to forty pounds per square inch. A cubic foot of soil weighs about a hundred pounds, but the Gaia Institute material only weighs nine to twenty-two pounds per cubic foot.

Mankiewicz's plan is to build greenhouses that cover the entire rooftop garden area. This not only extends the growing season, but also keeps the light planting material from blowing away. By coating the rooftop with a squeegee-applied thermoplastic sealant and covering the whole roof with eight to twelve inches of his special soil, he will take care of drainage problems, provide a buffer against foot traffic and maximize his growing space.

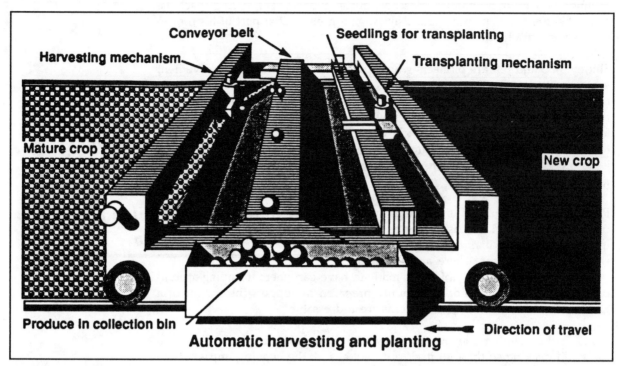

Conveyor belt

Seedlings for transplanting

Harvesting mechanism

Transplanting mechanism

Mature crop

New crop

Produce in collection bin

Direction of travel

Automatic harvesting and planting

The Gaia Institute's motorized gantry system for intensive roof top agriculture.

Every aspect of the system is designed with two design parameters: light weight and maximum production potential. The greenhouse structure, designed by Advanced Greenhouse Systems, uses a thin film glazing technology that allows a lightweight steel framing system to be used that is less rigid and less expensive than that which is needed for standard glass. Part of its design includes the ability to attach this structure to existing rooftop parapet walls.

While less intensive community gardens that permit individuals to walk up and down through the garden can and should be promoted, the idea of rooftop farming can be taken all the way to high tech industry. To increase the usable productive area by 30-90%, individual pathways can be removed. This is made possible by incorporating a motorized gantry system, designed by William Kinsinger Associates. Rolling on tracks and spanning a width as wide as 20 feet, this gantry allows access to the planting area from above.

In manual configuration, people lie on the carriage as it rolls across the gardening area. Paul indicates that this system could eliminate much of the fatigue associated with the "stoop-work" of agriculture. This new type of planting/harvesting experience would be more like lying on an air mattress in a swimming pool and could even allow elderly and handicapped individuals to take part.

In its more high tech configuration (see illustration), this gantry, with the appropriate attachments, would be amenable to automated planting and harvesting techniques being developed in the United States and Japan, and, according to Paul, would be much less capital intensive than the sensing/harvesting systems being developed for ground-level use.

The perforated underground tubes that comprise the Pulsed Nutrient System is more sophisticated than simple drip irrigation because of a central set of valves that can pipe either liquid or gas through the soil. Water, nutrients in solution, microbes, carbon dioxide, or high concentrations of oxygen are piped through as needed to enhance plant growth, control predators and regulated soil temperature.

According to Paul, this type of technology, which permits plants to be grown very closely together, can make the difference in the economic success of a rooftop farming operation. An 8000 square foot greenhouse could net 40 to 70 pounds of produce per square foot per year. At the American average of 150 pounds per person, this garden could provide produce for over 3,700 people per year. This is a yield 30 to 50 times more than that of field crops.

There are a number of benefits that can result from this proposed new agriculture industry. Growing food this close to consumers would eliminate the high costs of transportation which either could be passed along to the customer or provide increased income for the grower. Air quality is improved not only by the plants' ability to remove air pollutants and generate oxygen, but fewer produce-carrying trucks moving in and out of the city would also help to improve the air.

Covering a roof with this type of greenhouse would extend the lifespan of the roofing material by protecting it from large temperature variations. The blanket of soil would also serve as insulation which protects against ultraviolet radiation and cuts down heating and cooling expenses. Paul also points out that the greenhouse structures and increased human presence would cut down rooftop access for burglars. Lastly, Paul says:

"Rooftop greenhouses will offer lush spaces filled with the fragrance of flowers and earthy scent of plants and soil, a place of solace and reflection. Such healthy environments encourage the spirit of cooperation, as do community gardens, by making the common good more tangible."

Imagine flying over city rooftops and looking down to see a vari-textured patchwork quilt of different color greens. providing food, making oxygen, allowing people to feed their families. Think of a market displaying organic produce that has been harvested on its roof literally moments before you buy it. Paul's

Business Incubator with built-in rooftop agribusiness designed for the City of Bell Gardens by David Harper & Associates.

vision is to see 10% of all city roof tops intensively farmed in this manner. He sees this not only as a way to green the city but also to provide healthy food and provide employment for lower income households.

THE CHOICE IS OURS

While a bit of caution is necessary to garden on older buildings' rooftops, new structures can be built so they accommodate the extra load. If building codes were changed to stipulate sufficient structural integrity, railings, drainage, access to water and designated planting areas, then garden beds could be awaiting owners or tenants when they move in. Cal Poly Pomona's Institute for Regenerative Studies has made rooftop gardens an integral part of their village's building design and the City of Bell Gardens is planning a business incubator complex that will include a rooftop urban farm.

Whether it's a hobby, a job, a participatory ecological act, or a way to augment income, there is something uniquely satisfying about eating food that we have grown ourselves. It puts us in touch with nature's cycles and a connection with the Earth that most city dwellers are lacking.

Breaking an ear of corn off the stalk, husking it and eating it right in the garden is an experience impossible to duplicate with produce trucked in from distant farms, because the sugars have already begun turning to starch in the first five minutes after you harvest, and that elusive taste is lost. By and large, our urban lifestyle has cut us off from these sorts of experiences. But if we want them back, they could be as close as our rooftops and gardens in the sky.

RESOURCE CONTACTS:

Gaia Institute; 1047 Amsterdam Avenue; New York, NY 10025; (212) 295-1930

David Harper & Associates; 8221 E. Third Street, Suite #300; Downey CA 90241; (213) 869-9816

ECOLOGICAL DESIGN COMPONENTS

SOLAR DESIGN • WATER MANAGEMENT • URBAN LANDSCAPE • *WASTE MANAGEMENT* • TRANSPORTATION • SUSTAINABLE TECHNOLOGY

WASTE MANAGEMENT

INTEGRATED WASTE MANAGEMENT FOR NEW DEVELOPMENTS

Chip Clements

PLANNING FOR WASTE REDUCTION

S olid waste management has come to the forefront in the last few years as a key issue to be addressed in all types of development. We have worked on a few projects lately, one in particular, where the ability to recycle, compost, and reduce the waste stream were critical elements in whether the project was going to go ahead. Across the nation and more so every day here in Los Angeles, we are facing a severe scarcity of landfill space. Because of this, new developments need to minimize the generation of waste that has to be disposed in a landfill and maximize the ability to reuse and recycle.

The basic programs we can use to reduce the amount of waste requiring disposal include backyard composting, centralized composting facilities (depending on the size of the development this could be something sited within the boundaries of the development), and curbside recycling programs for items such as newspaper, mixed paper, cardboard, metal cans, glass, PET, HDPE and film plastic. Some types of programs are branching out to take any type of plastic, from plastic toys to detergent bottles.

We are going to be seeing more and more mixed use developments that include not only residential but commercial and recreational uses. In these situations you can also include programs like office paper recycling and bar and restaurant glass recovery. Certain developments may have some type of hotel or resort, and these present other recycling opportunities for office paper, cardboard, and recyclables now thrown away in the individual rooms.

With enough planning early in the design process, new developments can have all waste management components working together in a web or network. They could even include a biological waste water treatment system where waste water treatment is done using aquatic plants to achieve purification, and when those plants are harvested, they in turn can go into the composting system. Of course the final compost product is something you can use on home gardens as well as public landscaped areas.

So what we try to do with the solid waste stream is put as much as possible into a loop, into a conservation and reuse mode, rather than just generating more materials that put further strain on the landfills. The old style of dealing with solid waste by simply throwing it out is unacceptable now.

We can still have development but we need to do it with ecologically conscious design that works using sustainable, circular cycles. In the future, I believe any type of development, whether office tower, hotel, residential or recreational will be required to absolutely minimize the waste stream and to have recycling and other environmentally sensitive programs in place in the design phase of the facility, not after it has been built.

Chip Clements is a registered professional civil engineer, Founder and President of Clements Engineers Inc., an environmental engineering firm that has completed over 100 solid waste management projects for municipalities, private waste managers and development corporations in Southern California. He has presented papers and spoken nationwide on the subject of waste management.

Clements Engineers, Inc.
6290 Sunset Blvd. Suite 1223
Los Angeles, CA 90028
(213) 469-4406

The first thing to do with solid waste is not generate the material in the first place. We call it source reduction. In a typical residential development, yard waste will run anywhere from 20-40% of the total waste stream. All the projects we have designed include the space for people to simply and efficiently do backyard composting.

COMPOSTING

Our first level priority should be to start with backyard composting because we can use kitchen scraps as well as yard waste, thereby reducing garbage pick up and transport.

Backyard composting is a program that is really gaining in popularity. There are many types of bins available and many different programs. In the design of homes, we try to have composting systems built-in near the kitchen where food waste can be moved from kitchen counters through chutes down into a composting bin. Beyond that, you can designate a composting area in one suitable part of the yard. This way you encourage people to generate their own compost.

> *We can still have development but we need to do it with ecologically conscious design that works using sustainable, circular cycles.*

The next phase is to set up a centralized composting facility within the boundaries of your development or shared with a neighboring development. This is a good idea because it can handle the larger, bulkier wood items as well as the material of those who, for whatever reason, choose not to process their own compost. If you have recreational areas such as golf courses, they can be prime candidates to house this centralized composting facility because they are major contributors of materials as well as users of the finished product.

Gardeners and landscapers servicing the area as well as individual homeowners can bring their yard waste and tree trimmings to a centralized drop-off facility. Although there are many different types of facility design, they usually include a chipping and shredding operation and space where debris can be composted in windrows. Animal manures might be included as well as more elaborate systems of in-vessel composting for rapid production and odor control, although this type of technology is usually very expensive.

Developments which contract with a single landscape maintenance service for a majority of the homes are ideally suited for recycling green waste. Using the idea of circular patterns and sustainability, they can generate compost from the green waste and return it to nurture the landscapes they are working on.

Another waste stream reduction process is curbside recycling. Each home is given one or more bins that are put out on the same day as the regular trash collection. It is best to work closely with the refuse hauler because it is important to coordinate curbside recycling with regular refuse collection. Some haulers are now using dual-purpose trucks to pick up recyclables at the same time they are picking up solid waste which reduces air emissions and noise that would otherwise be generated by separate trucks.

MATERIAL RECOVERY FACILITIES

When planning a development, it is important to locate the nearest Material Recovery Facility (MRF). Some MRF's have the ability to separate mixed commercial loads of waste and pull out cardboard, wood and high grade paper.

Most of the MRF's have the capability to separate glass by color, to separate the different grades of plastic, and to sort newspaper for contamination. In fact some of the very new MRF's being developed now are able to process totally mixed waste streams. That is really the new horizon for these facilities, but we are going to have to see how well this works in terms of recycling the different elements of the waste stream without contamination.

Another part of the waste that MRF's are starting to handle is demolition and construction debris. In an urban area like Los Angeles, about one-third of the waste stream is construction and demolition debris including concrete, asphalt, rubble, wood, and bulk metal. What we are seeing is recycling programs at the construction site which will put different boxes out for dirt, broken concrete and asphalt. These materials will go back to the MRF, which will chip the wood, send concrete and asphalt to crushing plants, and pull out bulk metal to be recycled. MRF's that are taking this kind of material already recover 50 to 60 percent of construction and demolition loads. This is a very promising area for future efforts.

SOURCE SEPARATION AT THE BUILDING SITE

Depending on your ability to separate the material at the building site, there can be great savings in disposal. Now, instead of drop boxes going to the landfills where you are charged to dump them, you may have no charge or even receive some money for the materials depending on the cleanliness of the load. Also, if some of these recycled materials can be used in the project, you will be helping to develop a market for them, creating another benefit in the construction of your development.

We are looking for a hierarchy of programs starting with reuse and recycling in the home, then pre-separating and then the larger facilities to separate out even more. In fact, in cities like San Diego and Portland, we are seeing yet another level of facility that can compost the rest of the waste stream after all of the other sorting and removal stages have been completed. This final stage could take us into the 75-80% range of waste reduction.

If you are creating an extremely large development which is generating in excess of 100 tons of material per day, you could put in your own MRF that would greatly minimize waste stream impacts. This could become a very valuable feature in making a positive presentation of your project to the city or county.

> *In an urban area like Los Angeles, about one-third of the waste stream is construction and demolition debris.*

On an overall basis, we are looking for a sense of how convenient all this will be for the individual homeowner. What really gets people involved is how convenient their backyard composting can be and how convenient their curbside recycling program is. In addition, the developer would want to know what the benefits are of going through the effort and expense of putting in these various waste management components.

I think that in the near future these types of programs are going to be mandatory in order to even get permits to do development. So if you are going to plan such a project, you should think about putting in these types of waste minimization and recycling programs, because most cities are soon going to require them.

Beyond that, by reducing the amount of waste that needs to be collected there can be savings in refuse collection fees for the homeowner and for the community. Right now in commercial situations you pay for refuse collection service according to what you generate. This is a trend that is beginning to affect the residential waste stream.

Lastly, most developments are going into areas where there are already existing communities, so by presenting your project as having these types of waste management programs built-in, you will score points not only with local government but also with the surrounding populace. This makes it much easier to get through the permit process and it makes you a good neighbor from the outset.

Saving money in the construction process and ongoing waste management savings once the community is operating, when combined with the good will gained by being environmentally responsible, adds up to an attractive win-win scenario that very shortly will become the norm rather than the exception in development and planning, The message is: why not start now?

HOME AND COMMUNITY COMPOSTING

Howard Westley

*Howard Westley is one of the
leading advocates for
composting in Los Angeles. He
was consultant on the city of
Santa Monica's composting
project, has studied with the
UCLA Municipal Solid Waste
Management program and has
consulted and spoken on the
subject of compost throughout
Southern California.*

*525 Gretna Green Way
Los Angeles, CA 90049-4011
(213) 472-9965*

W hen first observing a European colonist turning over the sod with a mold-board plow, his Native American friend muttered: "White-man turns the earth up-side-down!" The "civilized" philosophy of "conquering nature" runs like a thread through the litany of dire global trends. The problem of soil erosion cannot be corrected without nurturing the life in the soil. Any soil becomes impoverished when crop after crop is removed, material that nature would have returned to replenish its life. Chemicals and pesticides add insult to injury, and death to the soil biota. Overuse of fertilizer and water has contributed to the pollution of half of the water wells in the United States. The process that can take the place of these destructive methods and heal our ravaged topsoil is composting.

In community composting programs across the country, bagging grass clippings in plastic facilitated handling, until it came to getting the grass out of the bags and the bags out of the compost. In Fort Worth, the Texas Agricultural Extension Service, with turf-grass specialist Dr. Bill Knoop, implemented a *Don't Bag It* pilot program to educate lawn-owners to leave grass clippings on the lawn. Mowing height and frequency along with fertilizing schedules were prescribed for each type of grass. Free fertilizer and free use of 100 Toro mowers were added incentives for the 190 home-owners who joined in the project its first year. Watering schedules recommended one inch of water every five or six days. But thriftier lawns can thrive with far less watering, less fertilizing, and less mowing. The Professional Lawn Care Association of America has coined a new word: "grasscycling," and are conducting a nationwide campaign to publicize the benefits and techniques of lawn care without collecting the cuttings.

Grass clippings left on the lawn, if in small enough pieces, will fall between the standing blades of grass where they serve as a mulch while being slowly devoured by soil biota microbes and macrobes. Pesticide use will halt or reduce this process and is not recommended. Dried grass clippings, spread an inch or two deep on other parts of the garden, will shade the surface from sun and wind, conserve moisture, feed creatures in the soil (earthworms, pill-bugs, etc.), and in the process add nitrogen and other organic matter to enrich the soil.

Leaves and other yard trimmings can also serve as mulches. Their utility is often improved and decomposition sped up by shredding, chopping up, trampling, having a rotary mower chew them up or piling them up for children to play on. Certain wood chips will add their own distinctive and pleasant aroma when used in a mulch.

Wood, being high in carbon content and low in nitrogen, can serve to counterbalance the high nitrogen content of green grass. Wood chips also tend to trap air and moisture in a composting mix. Too thick a layer of grass, on the other hand, tends to mat down, suffocating the air-breathing microbes. Anaerobic microbes, however, are free to multiply under these circumstances, producing acids and gaseous odors which neighbors may not appreciate.

Some purposes in landscaping may best be served by lawns and some lawn grass varieties are less demanding of water than others. But in parts of the country that receive low amounts of rain, xeriscaping practices and drought tolerant plants often can serve better than lawns. Perhaps the ultimate solution will be to build permaculture, to serve the new patterns of human community that cities must develop.

Although there are many other uses for post-consumer paper, it is quite compostable, the more so if shredded. More edges mean easier access for the microbes to reach all cells in the material. Many farmers have welcomed shredded newspaper for use as bedding for animals at $25 per ton, replacing straw at $60 per ton. The paper is more absorbent, and the animal urea improves the nitrogen content, counterbalancing the high carbon in the paper. Shredding, moistening, and fluffing up all enhance the paper's compostability. The lignin of the paper, and of the wood and sawdust paper is made from, is an excellent chelating agent in the soil, making the soil minerals available to the plant.

MUNICIPAL COMPOSTING PROGRAMS

Encouraging people to make and use their own compost and mulch on-site can reduce collection and processing costs while conserving valuable resources for our topsoil. Gardeners take naturally to composting and mulching. But since not everyone can or will compost their own, communities furnishing curbside collection of "clean green," or providing drop-off sites for compostables, widen the options for allowing people to take responsibility for their own trimmings and discards.

> *Encouraging people to make and use their own compost and mulch on-site can reduce collection and processing costs.*

The trimmings which are placed at the curb in specially designated containers are taken to the centralized facility where the material is heaped into long piles called windrows. There are a number of machines now on the market designed specifically to turn and aerate these windrows to speed the composting process. Although the mass of the windrows is reduced by one-half after only about a month, a program looking to produce a top quality finished product will let the compost cure for another month or so before putting it on the market.

Illinois, one of 15 states to ban yard trimmings from the landfill or incinerator, promotes a *Y-Baggit* program, but has had start-up problems including lack of experience and facilities, and lack of a stockpile of dry leaves to mix with the grass as they collect, leaving the mountains of grass to turn anaerobic and offensive. But the law that bans yard trimmings has gotten government, industry and citizen alike to persist in working through to solutions for the operational, financial, and public relations problems. (*Resource Recycling* magazine, Feb. 1992.)

New Jersey, Connecticut and Pennsylvania banned only leaves from landfilling and incineration. But legal and economic incentives, including high tipping fees, have powered rapid development of composting facilities.

In New Jersey, Woodhue Farm made available dumping space for 250,000 cubic yards per year of leaves, lawn clippings and other plant waste of the state's home owners and food companies. The people trucking the raw material were able to tip it for a fee of $10 per cubic yard versus the $40 dollars per cubic yard at the landfill, so it was a great savings for them to drop it off at Woodhue. Woodhue used the finished compost on their own crops and felt they were being paid to have the raw materials for their fertilizer brought to them. It was a win all around. (See *New Farm Magazine*, July/August 1988: "$2.5 Million from 126 Acres.")

In Europe, development of large-scale bio-gas production and composting are yielding rewarding results.

Denmark mandates separation of food discards by restaurants, public institutions and catering centers producing over 100 kg/week which is collected in 16-gallon drums for composting, and ultimately bio-gas production (*BioCycle*, November 1989, p.70).

Since 1969, Zurich, Switzerland has run a greenhouse-compost facility which accepts 60-70,000 cubic meters per year of yard discards, and sells finished humus and woodchips. Starting in 1985, Zurich started to encourage multi-unit dwellings to adopt decentralized composting projects which now number in excess of 540. The programs include food discards and working with neighbors. In December 1990, the citizens overwhelmingly voted for the composting of all organic waste. Waste reduction rates of 10% to 40% are estimated. Closed vessel composting combined with bio-gas production are planned. Apartment dwellers are cooperating in the collection and composting work because of reduced trash collection bills and the ability to use the finished compost in their window boxes, and ties within the community are strengthening.

> *Legal and economic incentives, including high tipping fees have powered rapid development of composting facilities.*

An example of composting on this scale is provided by Ocean View Farms, a seven-and-a-half acre community garden near Santa Monica, California with 260 members who pay $20 per year to use a small plot of land and participate in work projects, pot-luck lunches and other events. An active composting committee has succeeded in reducing waste-hauling fees from $2,500 down to $1,200 per year by banning organic material from the dumpster, and building a compost pile every Saturday instead. They used the savings to purchase a shredder, which they use to size-reduce the material brought by wheelbarrow from the entire garden to the central composting area. A base layer of loose branches in a shallow pit is established, and upon that a layer-cake compost pile is built each Saturday, incorporating food discards from local restaurants and members' homes, elephant and horse manure, and spent sprouts, one ton at a time. Any dry material is well-watered and the finished pile is covered with the straw (elephant bedding) for insulation. A stake driven into the top of the pile bears the date, the names of the pile builders, and some fanciful name for the pile itself. Temperatures are measured at weekly intervals and marked on the stake. When indicated, the pile is aerated or turned, and that is noted on the stake as well.

Washington state has awarded $600,000 in grants for studies in food waste composting in the Seattle area. Assessment of backyard food waste systems, and funds for on-site composting facilities (non-residential), are parts of the plan (*BioCycle*, January 1992, p.61).

From April, 1991 to the end of January, 1992, Riedel Oregon Compost Company, Inc. (ROCC), a subsidiary of Riedel Environmental Technologies, Inc. (RET) accepted up to 600 tons per day of municipal solid waste (MSW) for composting at the 600-tons-per-day facility they owned and operated, using their Dano drum system.

They were unable to finance the estimated $3.5 million for the modifications required to meet the environmental standards their permit required for odor emission and finished compost quality. Credit Suisse, as guarantor of $25 million of a total $30 million in municipal bonds issued to build the plant, then took ownership, releasing RET from responsibility for all but $5 million of bonds issued by another bank. The overall plan is to find the funding so solutions for these problems can be implemented and the program can continue.

According to John Roulac of Harmonious Technologies, it is generally agreed that the end product of MSW composting is a lower grade of compost. Although giant magnets pull out the metal, and even though the majority of plastics and other impurities are removed by hand, Roulac says that critics of this process are still concerned about contaminants from inks, batteries, plastics, industrial chemicals and other pollutants that enter the waste stream. This type of composting was started in Europe but so far most plants have been unsuccessful in marketing the final product. Europeans are now moving toward source separation with separate collection of compostables, to produce a safe, stable and nutrient-rich compost.

For the sake of fairness, Roulac notes that proponents of MSW composting contend that it is more sanitary than landfilling and that the final product can be used on degraded lands or in the horticultural industry.

Many municipalities across the United States are considering or beginning to institute composting programs. The key to their success is for them to study the matter carefully and obtain the advice of consultants with sufficient expertise and no hidden agendas. For example: while it is very simple to keep a home composting operation smelling sweet, there is no easy way to keep large-scale municipal operations from receiving lawn clippings that have spent a number of days in a tight container and have begun to go anaerobic and smell bad. A properly sited and constructed composting facility can minimize or control such problems, but proceeding without the proper design could result in the same problems as those experienced by the Riedel Oregon Compost Company mentioned above.

THE ESSENTIALS OF COMPOSTING

Most mulching material will break down, given enough time, and can be raked, tilled or mixed into the underlying soil. Apply a heavier layer of mulch material, and the process is called "sheet composting." But whether the gardener's purpose is simply to dispose of organic materials or to transform them into useful soil amendments, composting speeds up and enhances the process by providing the structure.

> *It is generally agreed that the end product of MSW composting is a lower grade of compost.*

1. MATERIAL: Mix woody and soft, dry and wet, carbon and nitrogen. Equal volumes of brown and green is a good rule of thumb. The smaller the pieces, the easier access both moisture and microbes will have to the cells that are their food. However, pulverizing material into pieces too small can exclude air. Microbes for the process come with the material, the soil, and the air. It is not necessary to buy inoculants.

2. MOISTURE: 50-70% by weight is optimum. Dryness slows population growth, wetness can crowd out necessary air. A handful of material should adhere when squeezed in the hand, but not yield dripping water.

3. AIR: Too much air will dry and cool down the pile. The desired biota need air or they will suffocate, leaving the process to become anaerobic. The gases then produced can be offensive, and valuable nitrogen can be lost in the escaping ammonia.

4. TEMPERATURE: This is one good indicator of the level of biological activity producing it. It also varies with the amount of heat being lost from the pile. Material in a closed bag, can, or bin will retain the heat produced, while more open or loose piles may keep giving off the heat as it is generated. In my latest test, 12 pounds of grass clippings placed in an open 32-gallon plastic trash can quickly reached above 100°F. One composter of horse manure for mushroom-growing revealed a process reaching 170-180°F. High temperatures will kill weed seeds and pathogens such as protozoa, bacteria, helminths.

> *In the cooler stages of a composting process , worms can produce castings which add a fine quality to any soil.*

If you wish to cater to worms, Mary Appelhof, in *Worms Eat My Garbage*, suggests many techniques for managing a worm/composting process, hints on fly control, and uses of castings. She warns that worms will die or leave if they run out of food, or if the temperature of their substrate gets too hot or too cold or too dry. A viable range is 50-84°F, optimum for waste conversion is 55-77°F.

In the cooler stages of a composting process, worms can be useful, chewing and digesting the material, and producing castings which add a fine quality to any soil. Fallbrook Sanitation District in California uses large-scale vermicomposting to transform sewage sludge into marketable castings. When food discards are incorporated into a compost pile, proper management can usually prevent the intrusion of scavenging mammals or flies. But for tighter control, some composters prefer to use worm bins. Some even keep their bins inside the house, where better access and climate are advantages. An occasional sprinkling of high-carbon material such as wood chips, shredded paper, or sawdust, can enhance the carbon/nitrogen balance and prevent the escape of odors.

SIX STEPS TO COMPOSTING:

1. Choose locations and stockpile, provide structure.

2. Inoculate—sprinkle material with earth, compost, "starter."

3. Mix, and build the pile in thin layers.

4. Water each layer, leaving no pockets of dry material.

5. Aerate by turning and "fluffing" lumps, to avoid piles from becoming sour.

6. The active pile is fun to watch and monitor. A thermometer would add precision to your observations, but is not necessary. A sharpened broomstick inserted into the pile for a minute will reveal heat and moisture. Shrinkage of the pile, its aromas, and your calendar records will tell you much more.

FIVE ELEMENTS TO GUARANTEE SUCCESS IN COMPOSTING

1. No matter what mistakes you do make (barring catastrophe) expect to make reasonably good, useable COMPOST.

2. Develop a basic understanding of its life forms and processes.

3. Have a willingness to experiment.

4. Exert a little effort.

5. Develop a little artistry and create your own recipes for compost. You can develop an enjoyable process that can be altered to fit your changing needs, your materials, and your physical limits. You may wish to try including a little shredded paper, human hair, vacuum cleaner dust, or what organic material you will. I found my neighbors quick to share their bags of leaves or grass to help me balance the menu for the teams of microbes and worms and pill-bugs that work in my compost piles.

USEFUL TOOLS IN STRUCTURING SOME COMPOSTING SYSTEMS

HANDLING TOOLS: Kitchen caddy, pails, boxes, bags, bins, wheelbarrow, cart, dolly, trash cans, canvas (or plastic) tarps for covering or bundling and dragging material, compost fork, shovels, trowel, spading fork.

SIZE-REDUCING TOOLS: Knives, choppers, blenders, machetes, pruners, hedge-clippers, saws, axes, chopping blocks, garbage disposers, food processors, rolling pins (to crush items such as egg shells), car or foot traffic to crush leaves, or kids to romp in piles of them. Shredders are easily oversold! Be aware of function and load limits, safety, maintenance, noise, pollution and costs. A rotary mower ejecting against a wall or barrier can shred large volumes too.

HOLDING STRUCTURES: Barrels, corrals or wire-mesh, fencing, chicken-wire, bins of wood or brick.

WATERING TOOLS: Hoses, soaker hoses, sprayers, sprinklers, buckets, kitchen caddies, and tarps which prevent loss of water by condensing moisture on their undersides, especially in hot or windy climates.

ACTIVE PILE, LOCATION & MANAGEMENT: Piles should be accessible, but unobtrusive, in contact with the earth where possible. Sunny places are preferred in cold climates, shade in hot climates. Piles should be located so as to not invite structural rot of a fence or a building. And piles should be placed not too near neighbors — your "cooking" odors may offend some. If odors trapped inside the pile will be released upon opening, turning, or manipulating the pile, or if shredding noise is loud, be a good neighbor and time your

> *Develop a little artistry and create your own recipes for compost.*

operation with weather and social conditions in mind. Your whole initial design may not be "idiot-proof." Be alert to modify and improve your procedures.

INFORMATION: Develop a network of friends, acquaintances, neighbors, etc. A library, a bibliography, a hotline, the *Rodale Complete Book of Composting*, numerous states' and manufacturers' manuals, gardening and farming periodicals and bulletins, and your own records in journals and calendars.

SOME OPTIONS FOR ORGANIC DISCARDS

I might keep a pig, a goat, chickens, rabbits, ducks, or geese. They could eat my food scraps as might raccoons and opossums. Many leaves and lawn sweepings end up rotting in street gutters and storm drain catchments, along with some non-organic discards. The magnolia leaves I sweep, shred, and compost are diverted from that process, and become soil conditioner.

I use two or three half-gallon frozen yogurt containers for scrap storage on the kitchen counter. I also use them for taking graywater to the flower bed. I might add a Kitchen Komposter (centrifuge/filter) to the disposer system. This saves none of the water, but allows the pureed food scraps to be removed and used as soil amendment. For now, I bury the food discards 10-12 inches deep in my composting active pile without the aid of such water-wasting kitchen machinery.

> *Piles should be accessible, but unobtrusive, in contact with the earth where possible.*

The makers of the Green Cone Composter also make a 1.45 gallon Kitchen Caddy, with bail handle and tightly fitting lid for about $6. Other buyable bins: Soil Saver, Gedye Compost Bin, Ringer, City Gardener, Growmaker, all plastic, under $100.00. Wood-slatted bins such as Cedar and Evergreen are both much cheaper, but are more liable to dry out the pile they contain. A homemade bin can be constructed from a 32-gallon plastic trash can. Perforate the sides as desired, cut a 12-inch hole from the center of the 18-inch bottom, and place it on the earth, or on a box of sand or dirt on the balcony of the apartment or condo. Earth furnishes biota, and the soil also filters odors and allows the can to breathe. This model easily adapts to service as a worm bin. After repeated failure to get any composting action on his ranch in the dry desert, one determined gardener closed his compostables in a metal trash can, tied a rope through its handles to hold the lid on, rolled it daily with a kick, and, voila!

REFERENCES

Backyard Composting, Harmonious Technologies, Harmonious Press. (1992) 96p.
The Ecology of Compost, Daniel Dindal, SUNY 12 p.
Permaculture (One & Two), Bill Mollison, Australia. (1987) 128 & 150p.
The Basic Book of Organic Gardening, ed. Robert Rodale. (1971)
Sunset Guide to Organic Gardening, ed. Philip Edinger. (1973) 72 p.
The Complete Book of Composting, J. I. Rodale & Staff (1975) 1000p.
Composting, Process & Principles, Clarence Golueke (1972) 110p.
Composting Municipal Wastes, Biocycle Staff (1989) 166p.
Yard Waste Composting, Biocycle staff (1989) 197p.
Municipal Composting Handbook, (CWMB) Gibbs & Hill (1983) 45p.
Leaf Composting Manual for New Jersey Municipalities, Rutgers (1985) 40p.
Mulching & Composing: Resources, ILSR (1980) 45 p.
Eight Yardwaste Composting Programs, EPA, Taylor (1988) 49p.
Yard Debris Composting Program Design, Seattle, (1988) 124p. (Also 4p. summary
    and recommendations)
Composting & Mulching, U. of Minnesota Extension (1988) 8p.
Soil Management: Compost Production & Use, FAO #56 (1987) 177p.
On-Farm Composting Conference, MA & USDA, etc. (1987) 94p.
Don't Bag It, Lawn Care Plan (TX AG Ext Service (1990) 52p.
Worms Eat My Garbage, Mary Appelhof — Kalamazoo, MI (1982) 100p.
Let It Rot, Stu Campbell, Garden Way Publishing (1975) 152p.
Harnessing the Earthworm, Thomas J. Barrett (Bookworm Publ.) (1976) 150p.
Resource Manual, (Source reduction, recycling) CWMB (1989) 3 Lbs.
The Solid Waste Dilemma: An Agenda for Action, (EPA) (1988) 2 vol. 4 lbs. (Also,
70p. Draft Report/Summary of the above)
Long Term Viability of U.S. Agriculture, (Report # 114) 48p.
Magazines of interest: *BioCycle; Organic Gardening; Resource Recycling; New Farm
Magazine; Sustainable Agriculture News; Garbage; Sunset*

DOING THE RIGHT THING CAN COST LESS: A RE-EVALUATION OF PUBLIC WORKS

Arthur Jokela

Los Angeles is in the difficult situation of having served for decades as the world capital of conspicuous consumption, although many other urban centers are not far behind. Our large scale public works projects are, in some ways, the most evident and "proudest" aspects of this overconsumption. These freeways, long distance aqueducts, remote power plants and other facilities symbolize our technological and economic authority, our ability to overpower nature and our endless ambition to settle together in large numbers.

Therefore, if we are serious about our role in the global community of providing beneficial world leadership and improved physical examples, our objectives need to include reducing our continued reliance on such imports, particularly of water and power. The extended drought in California and the resulting turmoil in state and local water policy have provided an opportunity to reconsider how our basic plumbing systems are organized. Here are some perspectives on the subject:

The Metropolitan Water District (MWD) is in the process of spending $11 billion to build facilities to deliver water supplies that might not even be available. This is a cost of over $700 per capita for the 15 million MWD residents.

The City of Los Angeles is spending $3.5 billion, $1,000 per capita, to improve the quality of sewage effluent discharged to the ocean. The project includes a substantial increase in capacity of the treatment plant, from about 400 million gallons per day (mgd) to about 500 mgd. The plan is based on an assumption that per capita daily water demand will remain stable at about 180 gallons per capita per day (gpcd), about 120 gpcd of which is residential use. Actual demand has dropped abruptly, however, due to voluntary conservation by the public; much more reduction could be achieved through aggressive measures such as system-wide conversion to low flush toilets, and incentives for local recycling in new construction. The chances are good that the sewage system is being built up for delivery and treatment of increased municipal water that may not be needed, even if it were available. The County Sanitation Districts face a similar situation in planning the improvements of their large plant in Carson. If we spent money on small measures, we might avoid having to spend it on these large ones.

If $1,000 per capita (or even $1,000 per household) were to be spent throughout the city for conservation and reuse measures, rather than for centralized sewage facilities, we could be confident that the need for large-scale plumbing would abate on both the water supply side and the waste disposal side of the system. The reduced demand for imported supplies could, in principle, add a few billion dollars of metropolitan capital funds to the kitty, assuming that MWD could be brought into the rosy future of seeing its role differently: as a total water supply system manager and not primarily as a builder of large, centralized facilities.

Arthur Jokela served for 17 years as principal scientist in the graduate program in landscape architecture at Cal Poly Pomona as part of his contribution to the evolving "institutional ecology" of environmental planning and management. He directs the newly formed Southern California Institute of Natural Resources, which is engaged in planning, technology, education and public policy reform for state resource management.

Southern California Institute of Natural Resources
One West California Blvd.
Suite #124
Pasadena, CA 91105
(818) 793-0877

Meanwhile, the real water quality problem in our local ocean is increasingly recognized to be due more to polluted storm-water runoff than to sewage outfall discharges. For example in Santa Monica Bay, runoff water contributes twice the amount of particulates per year and five times the amount of heavy metals compared to the outfalls. The County of Los Angeles and the cities are now subject to federal E.P.A. National Pollutant Discharge Elimination System (NPDES) permits requiring substantial cleanup of runoff water over the next several years. This is virtually impossible to achieve through centralized treatment facilities for stormwater. To be successful, a collection and treatment program must be dispersed as widely as possible, preferably to every house lot. The City of Los Angeles is spending about $40 million this year on stormwater quality control, mainly for centralized efforts. This is a large number for a new program, but still a modest $12 per capita, a very small number compared to the water and sewer capital facilities budgets mentioned earlier.

Before there was imported water, individual homes in Los Angeles collected rainfall from their roofs in cisterns—the best quality, low-salinity water available. Runoff water was collected purposefully and impounded for later direct use or infiltrated into the ground. By contrast, our practice today is to pave half the land area and to compact much of the rest that is not covered by buildings. The objective seems to be to get rain water off the land and into the ocean as fast as possible (with incidental speed that gives the water its maximum ability to carry detritus with it to the sea). The subsoil is largely sealed off and deprived of natural moisture, causing "urban desertification" as a consequence of development.

There are alternatives: Porous pavement is common in Europe, for example, and is virtually unknown here. There are "Dutch drains" and "French drains", and a variety of natural-quality swales and terraces that can cause "running water to walk," and give it a chance to be put to use. Such measures are easier to install at the time of development. Failure to do so has added greatly to the downstream risk of floods. The types of on-site facilities needed include "dry wells" to convey rooftop and pavement drainage water into the subsoil instead of to the flood control channels; trees and shrubs to replace grass, and to make better use of the resulting deeper, enhanced subsoil moisture; and graywater systems to supply certain qualities of household water to particular uses outdoors, such as direct irrigation of tree roots.

> **The real water quality problem is due more to polluted storm-water runoff than to sewage outfall discharge.**

Howard Wright has shown that an intensive program of water conservation indoors and out, together with runoff control measures such as on-site filter strips and dry wells for infiltration could have a major effect in reducing demand in Los Angeles for imported water. Surprisingly, the import demand can be reduced to zero, by his reckoning. With an aggressive program of water recycling, L.A. could actually be a net exporter of water. I have confirmed this by a simple calculation of my own family's experience. In 3-1/2 years on an ordinary house lot in L.A., maintaining a green outdoors, we averaged 40 gpcd (about 1/3 the average residential use) with surprising little discipline and no major retrofits. With a foot of average annual rainfall, it would require only 1/5 of an acre of total catchment control to fully supply our five people from local water alone.

Compost and mulch are valuable to loosen the soil, while reducing the need for chemical fertilizers and pesticides, thereby improving runoff water quality and stormwater infiltration. Diverting organic matter out of the waste stream addresses a further, hard-to-solve environmental problem, the 30% organic fraction in landfills. This is the most troublesome fraction, due to its compactability, and its role in the production of leachate and fugitive gases. Larger scale use of compost can be important in reforestation. It's hard to grow trees in the desert without organic matter; if we were serious about restoring the natural environment to the way it was before the colonizers arrived, we would experience a net deficit of organics, rather than a surplus causing a problem of waste disposal.

> **With an aggressive program of water recycling, L.A. could actually be a net exporter of water.**

Conservation and reuse of water and organic matter can have important bearing on air quality of the region, and on the billions of dollars of capital investment and related high operating costs now projected for conventional air pollution regulation. The important, key feature is maintaining evapotranspiration and environmental cooling of the urban area. According to Lawrence Berkeley Lab, our urban area is hotter than a "natural" landscape by several degrees, which has a major impact on the rate of pollutant-forming chemical reactions. Air pollution would be much worse if we stopped irrigating and allowed the ambient temperature to rise further. Maintaining a lower temperature would also reduce the power needs for air conditioning and if this is accomplished by irrigation with reused water, it would decrease the amount of water we need to import.

THE NEED TO GET IT RIGHT, HERE IN PARTICULAR

A great many of the examples we Americans set in our lifestyle, our environment and our physical facilities are transferred to the rest of the world through personal and business contacts abroad and by visitors who come to the United States. Motion pictures and TV shows produced here reinforce those images and examples. Engineering services, finance and other forms of worldwide institutional support carry our models directly into practice elsewhere, sometimes whether wanted or not by the local people.

The approaches and conditions enumerated above are all conducive to the support of community-based employment and the development of independent local enterprises. Through capitalization of such enterprises and employment opportunities, rather than the continuation of conventional investment in single-purpose capital facilities, we can have a positive worldwide economic and environmental impact.

ECOLOGICAL DESIGN COMPONENTS

SOLAR DESIGN • WATER MANAGEMENT • URBAN LANDSCAPE • WASTE MANAGEMENT • *TRANSPORTATION* • SUSTAINABLE TECHNOLOGY

TRANSPORTATION

HOW ALTERNATIVE FORMS OF DEVELOPMENT CAN REDUCE TRAFFIC CONGESTION

Joel Woodhull, PhD

Joel Woodhull is the manager of the Environment and Joint Development Section in the Planning Department of the Southern California RTD. He has a PhD in Transportation Engineering from Rensselear Polytechnic Institute and his primary interest is in humane urban development which he believes will only come about if walking, bicycling, and transit are placed on an equal footing with the private auto.

Southern California Rapid Transit District Planning Department Environment & Joint Development Section 425 S. Main Los Angeles, 90013 (213) 972-4850

We are hearing more and more about PFDs, TODs and TNDs. What are they, and how can they help us deal with traffic congestion and related problems of air pollution and energy consumption?

PEDESTRIAN FRIENDLY DEVELOPMENT (PFD)

Even if we can't think of many examples of pedestrian friendly developments, it is easy enough to imagine what they might be like. One would feel safe walking around or having one's children out on their own. Being on the street would be interesting, even pleasant. "Interesting" means there would be variety over short distances, not 50 single family detached houses all in a row, and not monolithic blocks of office buildings, and certainly not large parking structures, however well disguised. Trip origins and destinations in a PFD would be close enough that one would be willing to walk.

TRANSIT ORIENTED DEVELOPMENT (TOD)

A transit oriented development is a PFD with a high enough population density to justify connecting it to other places of high density, and arranged so that transit routes can be reasonably direct and well-connected to each other and to the places they serve.

TRADITIONAL NEIGHBORHOOD DEVELOPMENT (TND)

A traditional neighborhood development is a place with characteristics that prevailed when walking and transit were the primary means of getting around. The premise of using TND as a model for modern urban planning is that they would still be well suited for walking and transit. Their transportation-related features are in stark contrast with Conventional Suburban Developments, (CSDs). The streets are narrower. The blocks are smaller. The streets are in grids that are more or less continuous. There is parking on the streets. There are alleys for vehicle access, so autos needn't cross sidewalks. Front yards are shallow, and lots are narrow. There is more mixing of land uses.

TRAFFIC CONGESTION, WHY HAS IT BEEN GROWING?

The simple answer to why there is growing congestion is that there are more people, with most doing a lot more traveling, and road capacity hasn't been keeping up. But the simple solution of building more roads isn't a very good one. Car availability has been growing faster than the population. We have gone from the family car to the personal car. According to the 1983 National Personal Transportation Study, 84 percent of all persons over 16 years of age had driver's licenses, and the number of home-based motor vehicles almost equaled the number of licensed drivers (Lowry, 1988). From that same study it was determined that the average person with a driver's license travels 30 miles a day (Reno, 1988).

Much of the disproportionate increase in travel has come about because a significant percentage of the population has gradually shifted their residence locations from urban to suburban, where a car is a virtual necessity for all trips and where the marginal cost of each car trip has intentionally been made as low as possible.

Typical of the nation as a whole, the Los Angeles area has been moving away from PFDs, TODs and TNDs for the last 40 to 60 years. While there is some new interest in these models, and some projects are in the works that embody their principles, what is actually being built today seems to continue the Conventional Suburban Development trend. This trend is based on a cycle of neighborhood encapsulation and arterial congestion which can be briefly described as follows:

Due to growing traffic congestion on the main arteries, drivers detour through residential neighborhoods (the British call it "rat-running"). As a defense, residential streets are arranged to inhibit or prevent such detours. This causes further congestion of the arterials, which now must be widened. The widening is done either by pushing back front property lines or by narrowing the sidewalks within the existing right-of-way. Where the sidewalks are narrowed, it leaves existing land users closer to the increased flow of traffic. This additional noise and reduced quality of life often causes the property to be sold and adapted to another use. The new owner is then forced to conform to zoning requirements and expand the shrunken sidewalk which decreases their buildable square footage. Most of this happens without environmental impact reports.

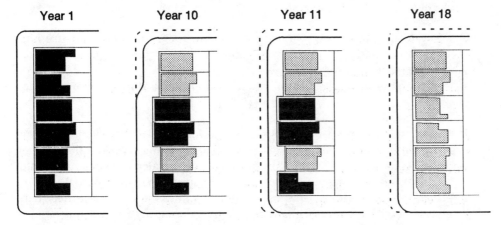

The sidewalk as future storage

Since the residential neighborhoods usually have nothing but residences, everybody has to leave the neighborhood for everything. They are all forced into their cars and out onto the arterials. Walter Kulash calls them the "urban sellscape". With everyone having to pass by, and moving much slower than the road designers intended, what better place to sell them all those things they can be induced to want (Kulash, 1990).

The Porter Ranch development in southern California's San Fernando Valley is an example. Although there was an attempt to balance land use activities in a general way, the balancing is still done at such a gross scale that most people will be forced to get in their cars for almost everything they do. So, recognizing the growing congestion on the arterials and freeways, what is to be done about it? Among transportation professionals, the current hot topic is IVHS, Intelligent

Vehicle Highway Systems. If you can't find a place to build more roads, and widening is meeting resistance, electronics will allow more cars into the same lanes. It is but the latest manifestation of attempting to cure the problem by doing more of what caused the problem in the first place.

A NEW PARADIGM

If we want to break out of this trend before it does us in, we must stop accelerating the same kinds of actions we have taken in the past. It is not simply a matter of building lots of mass transit that will carry us faster than the car. We need a new paradigm.

> *The key to integrating our thinking about transportation and land use is to focus on access rather than mobility.*

In a research paper on urban growth, Sherman Lewis describes three paradigms for discussing land use and transportation. The first, which he calls the *capacity paradigm*, is based on the assumption of car dependency and subsidies for car use. The presumed goal is the pleasant suburb, with density being an unwanted condition associated with many urban problems. The second is the *congestion paradigm* associated with more compact European and Asian cities. High density encourages pedestrians and transit and discourages use of cars. It is a response to the dominant *capacity paradigm*. It is better, Lewis says, but it can fail where a city lacks sufficient density, and development can be pushed even further into the hinterland. He argues for a third paradigm: *"compact, mixed use, transit-served, balanced cities* which decrease congestion through pricing and land use reforms" (Lewis, 1990).

The key to integrating our thinking about transportation and land use is to focus on access rather than mobility. Mobility means going faster and farther. Access means getting to more places conveniently. With access, the focus is on places. Mobility focuses on paths, often to the neglect or even the destruction of places.

When we begin to think of integrated solutions, we will think in terms of systematically solving multiple related problems. Rather than simply focusing on traffic congestion, we will make sure that we are also correcting air pollution, global warming, resource depletion and petroleum dependence. When we apply electronics to transportation, we will want assurance that the systems really are intelligent, rather than the mindless pursuit of speed and vehicle throughput. We will strive instead for traffic calming, preservation or creation of pleasant places and reduction of the stresses that our mad preoccupations with mobility have inflicted upon us.

DENSITY

Density has a marked effect on the number of vehicle miles traveled. Analyses based on averages often miss some important relationships between density, structures of land use, and transportation. An exceptional study was done by John Holtzclaw. He used actual mileage records of vehicles owned by residents of high and low density areas in the San Francisco Bay area to determine the relation between Vehicle Miles Traveled (VMT) and urban density. He found a consistent relationship: per capita VMT is reduced 30% by a doubling of population density (Holtzclaw, 1990). The extremes in his study were Nob Hill and Danville-San Ramon. Nob Hill has 26 times the gross population density of San Ramon, and Danville-San Ramon has 5.4 times as much vehicle mileage per capita.

There is an undeniable, widespread disdain for high density; the capacity paradigm is still deeply ingrained. Especially in California, it is said, people just wouldn't accept the densities that people elsewhere accede to. Sometimes we even hear analogies of rats crowded in cages, suggesting that our anxieties, and even the crime rate, are largely a result of this urban crowding.

Unconsciously we do as much as we can to make high density living unbearable: we put it next to freeways to shield the low density neighborhoods and we don't provide adequate services, or open park land and green space. Since the majority of people live in single-family, detached housing, most of the advantages flow to those households.

What people seem to dislike most about high density is the auto traffic associated with it. The problem suggests the solution. By converting a significant portion of the space resources taken by the automobile to other land uses, the population density can be raised significantly while reducing the negative impacts of density. Urban space hasn't been considered a resource, so a space-wasting transportation system — the auto — has been substituted for a space-conserving system.

How high does density have to be to promote walking and riding transit? A case could be made that in many areas, we are already at the upper limit of what can be supported by an auto-dominant transportation system. Fortunately, this positions Los Angeles near a density that could support excellent transit service. The average density of the City of Los Angeles is 7300 persons/sq. mi., and the average (weighted) population density served by RTD buses (throughout its service area in Los Angeles County) is about 10,000. Wherever the population density is 15,000 or so, there is no difficulty attracting people to bus service, as evidenced by the overcrowding that exists on some bus lines. With a density three times that of Los Angeles, one could have a walking city.

So the task before us is more a matter of local arrangements of density than increases overall. We need open green spaces for ourselves as much as we need higher densities for effective transit.

SOLUTIONS OFFERED BY PEDESTRIAN-FRIENDLY TRANSIT-ORIENTED TRADITIONAL NEIGHBORHOOD DEVELOPMENT

There is much that these new/old forms of development can offer in humanizing the environment of the pedestrian. They can serve the traffic that is really necessary without promoting excess. And they can allow for better transit.

> *Unconsciously we do as much as we can to make high density living unbearable.*

THE STREET NETWORK — In the new paradigm, we should think of the street network as providing just the capacity necessary for access. Wherever pedestrians are insecure, there is probably something wrong with the network. We have to examine the process of neighborhood encapsulation and arterial enlargement that has led to our present congestion. The wider the streets become, the more of a barrier they present to easy pedestrian movement.

STREET PATTERNS — People will always insist that vehicles shouldn't speed through their immediate neighborhoods and will find ways to prevent it if they have the power. Encapsulation has been the solution in the CSDs; within the superblocks formed by the arterials, many streets are terminated in cul-de-sacs so no one can travel through the superblock. This design also has the effect of minimizing the developer's road construction costs, and transferring street costs outside the immediate development. This solution has been bad for public transit, an inhibitor of pedestrians, and has made auto traffic worse.

Walter Kulash makes a good case for the street patterns of the TND: "TND streets are narrow and connected into dense networks. On these streets, there is an emphasis on non-motorized travel and on the overall quality of travel for the automobile traveler. There is, at the same time, a de-emphasis of the narrowly defined performance standards (mainly travel capacity and speed) that are dictating what our streets and suburbs look like today" (Kulash, 1990).

Kulash shows how the key to the success of the network, even in regard to auto traffic, is the size of the intersections. The sparser the network, the larger and more complex the intersections, the slower they work, until at some point, the whole network bogs down.

The dense network of the TND is clearly more friendly to pedestrians and bicycles than the sparse network of the CSD. Kulash explains why it will also work better for auto traffic. The key is the left turn. If there are many comparable paths between origin and destination, as is the case with a dense grid, the number of vehicles turning left at any one intersection is fewer. If one intersection is temporarily blocked, the driver has more freedom to take the next one.

Since the streets of a TND also have fewer lanes, left turns can be made more quickly and safely because the driver has only to consider gaps in a single lane of oncoming traffic. When multi-lane streets cross, a left turn across two or more lanes with heavy traffic usually means that no gap will appear simultaneously in the oncoming lanes before the signal changes. Then two, maybe three cars can turn. Persistent long queues often lead to a separate left-turn signal phase, which limits the time available for the majority of cars moving straight through the intersection.

the larger and more complex the intersections, the slower they work, until at some point, the whole network bogs down.

In a paper addressing the walkability of urban areas, Alan Jacobs focuses on the network density in terms of the numbers of intersections per square mile. He presents simple black-and-white maps of public rights-of-way for selected square miles in each of several very different cities, as well as an historical comparison for Boston. In Boston, he notes that for "efficiency", some of the streets have been eliminated over the years in order to assemble superblocks. In the examples cited, there would be little disagreement on which areas would be interesting to a pedestrian and which would not. He concludes that blocks should be small if the streets are to be pedestrian oriented. He speculates that this may represent an issue of human freedom and decentralized power, because the more intersections per square mile, the more choice for the pedestrian (Jacobs, 1989). A high density of intersections is, of course, one of the characteristics of TND street patterns.

STREET WIDTHS — The sizes of blocks and the continuity of the network, interacting with the intensity of land use, largely determine the widths of streets. When people talk about the "nice wide streets" they are obviously speaking from the vantage point of the motorist. Over the years we have tended to favor wider lanes for safety and more lanes for capacity. Wider lanes have encouraged higher speeds, and the numbers of lanes have had the detrimental effects on the network noted in the previous section on Street Patterns. The fact that wider streets take longer for pedestrians to cross means that traffic signal cycle times ultimately get stretched beyond the standard 60 seconds. Long cycle times are bad for transit and bad for pedestrians.

ONE-WAY STREETS — One-way streets have merit in certain situations, like limiting traffic in residential neighborhoods or providing acceptable street conditions for transit and bicycle operations. Their use for increasing street capacity is questionable. One research report (Harwood, 1990) notes that earlier beliefs that one-way intersections were more efficient, which were included in the 1965 Highway Capacity Manual, were contradicted by later research. One-way streets should not be used where they result in one-way routings of transit service.

MODE MIXING — While there are frequent requests for transit-only lanes and other separations of modes, there are some possibilities for more civilized sharing of road space. The *woonerfs* of Holland are perhaps one of the best examples of pedestrian friendly street treatments. In a *woonerf*, the street is shared by vehicles and pedestrians, with clear indications to drivers that they are on pedestrian turf and have to behave accordingly. Curbs are eliminated and there are changes in direction, plantings and street furniture acting as obstacles to vehicles.

> *One of the reasons we build subways is because people are unwilling to give appropriate priority treatment to transit vehicles running on roads.*

Where buses need to be given traffic advantages, bus-only lanes may be "too good". They allow the buses to move freely, but total prohibitions of autos arouse so much opposition over property access that few bus-only lanes will ever be implemented. Another option is the combined vehicle access and transit lane, where cars are permitted on a street for the purpose of access, but cannot continue straight through an intersection. This is a way of permitting the most critical uses while minimizing optional uses.

SIDEWALKS AND OTHER PEDESTRIAN WAYS — The TND will do a better job in protecting the pedestrian's own space, the sidewalks. TNDs rely on alleys for access to space within the block, rather than driveways across the sidewalks, to avoid unnecessary conflicts with vehicles. Sidewalk widths are considered as important as roadway widths in a TND. Sidewalks are not just a space left over after the roadway is constructed. Smaller curb return radii at the intersections limit the right-turning speed of autos, and enhance the safety of pedestrians stepping off the curb. It might help even more if right-turn-on-red were to be eliminated in high pedestrian use areas. And what about the crosswalk in these areas? By raising them to the level of the sidewalk and giving them texture, they signal to the driver that the area is primarily for pedestrians. Raised crosswalks have the further advantage of making corner curb cuts unnecessary for wheelchair accessibility.

PROVIDING FOR TRANSIT — What makes a development transit-oriented? The considerations are: how the transit vehicles are treated relative to autos; and the provisions made for transit passengers when they are getting to and from their stops, moving between transit vehicles, and waiting at the stops.

TREATMENT OF TRANSIT VEHICLES ON ROADWAYS — One of the reasons we build subways is because people are unwilling to give appropriate priority treatment to transit vehicles running on roads. Zurich is an outstanding example of a city that refused to bear the expense of subway construction, yet had the will to give priority to transit wherever necessary. As a result, although there are only about half a million people in that urbanized area, Zurich has one of the highest transit riderships in a Western city, 430 transit trips per year per capita, as contrasted with Los Angeles, which has only about 55 trips per capita. Its efficient system, primarily trams, has enjoyed a continuous incremental improvement effort since 1975, when its city council issued the following policy statement:

"In accordance with the city council's repeatedly stated wish to give priority to public transport when weighing up various transport interests, the city departments are hereby instructed in principle to give preferential treatment to public transport. Moreover, reasonable provision must be made for the needs of pedestrians, disabled people, cyclists and delivery vehicles. The environment, the quality of life in the city's residential areas and the townscape must also be taken into account."

> *Transit can only be fully competitive if the conditions at bus stops are someone's responsibility.*

Implementation measures that have been taken are based on studies of delay, which identify causes and recommend remedial actions such as left-turn restrictions, traffic lights controlled to favor trams, parking restrictions, redistribution of the street surface area in favor of trams, or eliminating car traffic altogether in some transit line segments (Joos, 1989).

TRANSIT PASSENGER WAITING AREAS — With good reason, waiting at the bus stop has become a metaphor for delay and misery. Transit can only be fully competitive if the conditions at bus stops are someone's responsibility. Typically, if there is a bench to sit on, it is placed too close to the curb. There is usually no shade or protection from the elements, except where the site has sufficient advertising potential to warrant a shelter.

Sidewalks at bus stops are no wider, or even narrower, than sidewalks elsewhere. A study on transit crime in Los Angeles pointed out the need to allow some segregation of people waiting for buses from people passing by, to minimize conflicts between waiting passengers and the other users of the space. This suggests, at a minimum, some widening of the sidewalk at intersections.

It must be conceded that what usually gets widened at the intersection is the roadway, usually at the expense of the sidewalk, and sometimes at the expense of the fronting property owner. Such widenings are often in the form of a bus "cut-out", a bay for the bus to pull into that gets it out of the stream of traffic. This speeds up the auto traffic at the expense of the buses, and gives additional encouragement to motorists to turn right in front of the bus. Where the aim is to give transit priority, transit "pop-outs" will be used instead of cut-outs. Pop-outs are extensions of the sidewalk out to the travel lane. They give additional sidewalk width for waiting passengers and permit the bus to stop in the right-hand traffic lane. When the bus resumes travel, it doesn't have to swing into traffic, and it can make good time, because something of a gap builds up ahead of it when it stops for passengers.

PARKING

TNDs not only have far less parking than CSDs, the parking is differently arranged. The trend over the past 40 years has been to integrate more parking into the land use, whether residential, commercial or industrial, and to favor off-site parking over on-street parking. So much is typically required, that if any charge were to be made, many empty spaces would result. In the Los

Angeles area, this has resulted in the peculiar situation in which Air Quality Regulation 15, limiting the number of vehicles used to bring people to work, now creates an imbalance in which the parking spaces required by most zoning codes are not all used. If carpooling is to be encouraged, then this should be reflected in regulations that call for fewer employee parking spaces.

ON-STREET PARKING — While some circumstances warrant prohibition of on-street parking, it can often be more pedestrian-friendly to have it serving as a protective barrier and spacer between the pedestrians on the sidewalk and the moving vehicles. Unless parking is approached via an alleyway, which is a rarity, off-street parking generally requires the cars to use driveways to cross the sidewalk, a decidedly unfriendly arrangement.

PARKING CONSOLIDATION — To the extent that off-street parking is needed, it would be better to consolidate it in one or two sites on a block instead of dispersing it across every lot. Having parking convenience more comparable to the transit riders' access to bus lines would be an encouragement for transit use as well as an inducement to walk or cycle for short trips. Less land would be wasted, because consolidation would permit sharing of parking between complementary uses, such as residential and commercial. Housing could be constructed less expensively, and non-parkers wouldn't have to bear the cost of parking spaces they don't use. Consolidated parking would also facilitate arrangements for co-operative sharing of vehicles, such as short term auto rental. Appropriate charges for on-street parking could assure that whenever there is a real need for proximate access to dwellings or businesses, it would be available.

ANGLE PARKING — This practice, which is almost universally used in parking lots, has been in disrepute until recently for streets. It is coming into favor once more, where there is a need to provide more on-street parking and reduce traffic speeds and/or volumes. While traffic engineers often dislike it, believing that it causes accidents, the driver's perception of potential danger is a large part of its effect on traffic speeds. It has the further virtue of reducing the hazard for pedestrians entering the street between parked cars; they enter at an angle to face oncoming traffic, and their presence is more easily noted by drivers because they can usually be seen over the trunks of cars.

> *Within the block, the scale of land uses is important in fostering pedestrian activity.*

DEVELOPMENT PATTERNS

The most distinguishing feature of TNDs, according to Kulash, is its "continuous fabric of intimately blended land uses, arranged so that travel between them can be made by a variety of methods." Mixed-use is the only way to achieve jobs/housing balance in a way that would make a significant difference in vehicle miles by giving more opportunities for people to walk to their jobs, and more importantly, to the market, the child care center, church, restaurants, etc. Within the block, the scale of land uses is important in fostering pedestrian activity. Alan Jacobs suggests that there needs to be many entrances onto the sidewalk, as well as visibility of what is behind the walls. It is important to provide interesting interior views for pedestrians. Banks, for example, have been shown to actually cause people to turn away because their interior vistas are boring. Street edges need to be well-defined.

ECONOMIC INCENTIVES

Urban transportation is much more expensive than it needs to be. Many of its problems are created because of the money poured into the automobile system. For the last 70 years, a wide variety of subsidies, both public and private, have been devised to support the automobile, most of which are not even apparent to the auto driver. Since much of the subsidy is channeled through development itself, in the form of parking requirements, fees and property dedication for roadway enlargement, etc., the TND offers a means of taking the car off welfare. In other words, the best way to bring balance to the economic incentives in the transportation system is to remove them from the auto system.

If areas are dense enough, and autos are not subsidized, transit services can be economically healthy. Transit needs subsidy today in high density areas only because the auto is very heavily subsidized in those areas. Simply withdrawing auto subsidies over a period of time would assure transit competitiveness and economic self-sufficiency. The financial resources that are saved can be redirected toward solving some of the more pressing problems of the poor.

COMMUNITY INSTITUTIONS

Perhaps even more than we need better regional planning, we need more local governance. The problem is not so much that there is a conflict between levels of government as it is that decisions are often made at the wrong levels. Cities today engage in fiscal zoning because there are not adequate mechanisms for funding government services. On the other hand, decisions on localized issues are often made outside the community affected, because there is no community governance mechanism at all.

Many of the deficiencies in our urban transportation environment have been recognized, even if there is no clear consensus on what remedies to apply.

By granting local communities the rights and responsibilities of decisions with truly localized impacts (e.g. what street trees will be allowed on my block?), city and county government can focus their attentions on problems of a more distributed nature (e.g., water, power, regional transportation).

Neighborhood parking could be a good first issue for local community management. The primary responsibility for deciding how much parking there should be (and what the charges should be) could be assumed by a duly constituted Neighborhood Association. The Association would bear the costs and take the revenues. Chances are that parking would be managed much differently than it is today.

COMMENTS ON PROCESS

PFDs, TODs and TNDs have much to offer in solving our traffic congestion problem. How can their development characteristics be introduced into an environment that has been evolving for seventy years in the wrong direction?

Many of the deficiencies in our urban transportation environment have been recognized, even if there is no clear consensus on what remedies to apply. Some of the mechanisms for discussing them are community plans, environmental impact reports, and recently, congestion management plans (CMPs). These instruments will not solve the problems themselves, but they do furnish an opportunity for fruitful public involvement.

Transportation elements in EIRs often confuse mitigations with problem causes. They have inconsistencies and internal conflicts. In particular, they commonly portray congestion as an environmental impact to be remedied by more road capacity, parking and, ultimately, more cars. The fact that they typically fail in this respect doesn't mean they couldn't succeed. But they, and the CMPs just now coming on line need some clear-thinking public citizens to involve themselves seriously in the process.

We have gone through a period of lean years for infrastructure construction; some call it disinvestment. We may look back twenty years from now and view the hiatus as a blessing. This period gave us a chance to change directions. Now we are building rail systems and perhaps bolstering other elements of the transit system. That is good, from the standpoint of having a balanced system of transportation with enough options to represent a real choice. But, unless we are careful, we could still lose sight of the need to develop from the community outward.

REFERENCES

Ira S. Lowry. *Planning for Urban Sprawl. TRB Special Report 220, A Look Ahead: Year 2020.* Transportation Research Board. 1988. p. 305.

Arlee T. Reno. *Personal Mobility in the United States. TRB Special Report 220, A Look Ahead: Year 2020.* Transportation Research Board. 1988. p. 373

Walter Kulash. *Traditional Neighborhood Developments: Will the Traffic Work?* Paper presented at the 11th Annual Pedestrian Conference, Bellevue, Washington. October 1990.

John Holtzclaw. *Explaining Urban Density and Transit Impacts on Auto Use,* Paper prepared for the State of California Energy Resources Conservation and Development Commission by the Natural Resources Defense Council and the Sierra Club. April 1990.

Sherman Lewis. *Managing Urban Growth in the San Francisco Bay Region,* Center for Public Service Education and Research. Department of Public Administration, California State University, Hayward. October 1990.

Alan B. Jacobs. *City Streets and Their Contexts,* Proceedings of the Tenth Annual Pedestrian Conference. Boulder, Colorado. September 1989. Pp. 41-61.

Douglas W. Harwood. *Effective Utilization of Street Width on Urban Arterials.* NCHRP Report 330. August 1990. p. 14.

Ernst Joos. *The Zurich Model,* Modern Tramway. March 1989. Pp. 75-82.

THE ROLE OF BICYCLES IN ECOLOGICAL CITIES

Ryan Snyder

Ryan Snyder is President of Ryan Snyder Associates, Inc., a transportation planning firm. He received his M.A. in urban planning and B.A. in economics from UCLA. He specializes in commute programs for employers and large new developments, and in planning for bicycles as a means of transportation. He is Executive Director of Citizens for the West L.A.Veloway, member of the City of Los Angeles Bicycle Advisory Committee, the Westwood Design Review Board, and chairs the L.A. Business Council Transportation and Planning Committee.

Ryan Snyder Associates, Inc.
1015 Gayley Ave. #1248
Los Angeles, CA 90024
(310) 824-9931

Many of our environmental problems are transportation-related. Transportation consumes the largest single portion of the energy we use and, in many cities, comprises the largest single source of air pollution. Global warming can also find many of its roots in the way we now travel. The bicycle is the most energy-efficient form of transportation known. For 350 calories (a bowl of cereal), we can travel ten miles. An average auto uses about 18,000 calories for the same trip. The bicycle creates no air pollution. It takes up very little space.

The bicycle also offers point-to-point flexibility and flexibility of time departure, making it faster and more attractive than public transit for many trips. Roughly half of all commute trips in American cities are currently within reasonable bicycling distance, and most shopping and recreational trips are short enough to be done on bicycle. In the ecological city of the future, where land uses are closer together, the bicycle would be suitable for most trips. Its potential has barely been tapped.

LIVING IN A BICYCLE-FRIENDLY COMMUNITY

What would a bicycle-friendly community be like to live in? Imagine your daily life beginning with a three-mile bicycle ride to work. You have the option of getting ready for work by putting your work clothes in a special garment bag which attaches to your bicycle. You retrieve your bicycle from the secured storage area near the entrance of your home. There is a short route to work, which has light motor traffic, because barriers restrict through-travel to motor vehicles while allowing bicycles to pass through. The street is quiet and well-landscaped.

You arrive at work and ride into the bicycle parking area of your office building conveniently located just off the street. You roll your bicycle into your own bicycle locker and take your garment bag with you. Next, you go to the locker room, next to the bicycle parking area. You take your morning shower, put your bicycling clothes in a locker, and dress for work. Now you're ready to walk up to your office, relaxed and refreshed. You have received your daily exercise without the need to go to a gym after work. Your employer gives you $50 per month in commute allowance, which you use in part to cover bicycling expenses, while the rest is your reward for bicycling to work.

At the end of the day, you can look forward to the ride home. Along the way home, you stop at the bank and at the market to do some shopping. Convenient, secure parking is waiting for you near the storefronts. Autos are no longer allowed in the downtown area.

A network of bike routes covers the city. Some are "bicycle boulevards" with barriers preventing through-traffic. Others are exclusive bicycle paths with scenic routes along the beach, a stream bed, or an old railroad right-of-way. Some of the routes consist of striped lanes. All of the streets are wide enough to allow bicycles safe passage.

For those commuting longer distances to work, park-and-ride stations allow bicyclists to ride a short distance from home, park securely all day long, then hop onto public transit, a carpool or vanpool. The buses and trains allow foldable bicycles to be carried on. Buses have special racks on the front for bicycles, and trains allow bicycles on a special car. Bicycle lockers at all stations allow commuters to keep a second bike at their destination stop so they can ride it the rest of the way to work. Transit stations and downtown areas have bicycle parking, rental, and repair.

The community has a bicycle coordinator to oversee program and planning efforts. City staff in the Planning, Transportation, Parks, Police, and other departments have been trained to consider how bicycles interrelate with other means of transportation. A citizens' committee advises the city on the needs of bicyclists. Education programs in city schools, at the local college, and at companies teach people how to ride bicycles safely in traffic.

Land use planning mixes housing with retail uses, employment, health care, child care, and recreation so that most destinations are within convenient bicycling distance.

WHAT'S ALREADY HAPPENING

In today's cities where we have planned for bicycles, there are already good results. In California, about one percent of all work trips are made by bicycle. In Palo Alto, which has a good network of bike routes, public bicycle parking, amenities requirements in work sites, and education programs, over ten percent of all work trips are made by bicycle. In Eugene, Oregon some eight percent of all commute trips are done by bicycle. Other communities have achieved much more than the average, including larger cities such as Seattle, Tucson, and San Diego. It is realistic to set a goal of planning for bicycles in all cities and to achieve a five percent share of all trips by the year 2010 and ten percent by 2020.

> *New legislation adds flexibility to federal highway funds, leaving more eligible for bicycle facilities and programs.*

In the Los Angeles area, the bicycle revolution is underway. In 1991, the City of Los Angeles became the nation's first large city to pass an ordinance requiring bicycle parking, showers and clothing lockers in new work sites. Also added in 1991, the revised Air Quality Management Plan for the South Coast Air Basin includes requirements for all cities in the Basin to have similar ordinances by 1993, and to include bicycle routes in their general plans. This same year, the Southern California Rapid Transit District initiated a policy to allow bicycles on Blue Line light rail cars during certain hours, and began a bike-on-bus program. Also approved are lockers and racks for bicycle storage at park-and-ride sites along the Metro Blue Line. Many companies required to have ridesharing programs by the South Coast Air Quality Management District have opted to provide facilities and financial incentives for bicycle commuters.

Funds have been allocated to pave a bicycle route along the Los Angeles River to complement the existing network of flood-control channel bikeways in the region. Plans are moving forward to build an elevated bikeway into UCLA.

State legislation is pending to increase annual funding for bicycle projects, which will help to expedite implementation for expansion of local bike route networks. New legislation adds flexibility to federal highway funds, leaving more eligible for bicycle facilities and programs. It will be up to bicycle advocates, planners, and policy makers to see that more funds are spent on bicycles to help speed the realization of a bicycle-friendly region.

PLANNING FOR NEXT STEPS

The highest priorities for cities are to:

- Plan and implement complete numbered bicycle route networks
- Produce bicycle maps
- Pass ordinances requiring bicycle parking, showers, and clothing lockers in new work sites
- Provide secure parking in retail and recreational areas
- Hire bicycle coordinators to advocate, promote, and manage bicycle planning and awareness
- Provide safety education
- Zone for compact, mixed land use
- Maintain streets well
- Provide access to public transit.

The highest priorities for counties are:

- Using more of their flexible transportation funds for bicycle facilities and programs
- Coordinating planning of regional bike routes
- Coordinating bicycle links to transit.

The highest priorities for state activity are:

- Providing more money for bicycle facilities and programs
- Organizing statewide bicycle education
- Setting road width and design standards that are bicycle-sensitive
- Statewide planning, coordination, and research.

The highest priorities for the federal government are:

- Providing more funds for bicycle facilities
- Providing more funds for education programs
- Conducting research.

Additionally, transit agencies need to provide access to transit as well as park-and-ride stations. Regional planning agencies should coordinate efforts among cities. Air quality districts can require bicycle amenity ordinances and bike route networks for local cities.

ELECTRIC CARS

Michael Hackleman

L os Angeles is mandated by the Air Resources Board to have zero-emission vehicles make up 10% of total automobiles sold per year by the year 2003 (an estimated 200,000 vehicles). By the year 2010, the target is to have 17% of our entire automotive fleet made up of electric vehicles. This would translate into about 1.3 million automobiles. Many car companies are in development on vehicles that will enable them to compete for a share of this market, and since other cities will likely enact similar rulings, it is important to have a basic understanding of what exactly is involved in switching over to electric cars.

The general public rarely has the opportunity to observe an electric vehicle up close. Most cars registered as EVs still look like regular cars. When you do manage to corner an EV owner, it is unlikely that a brief exchange will adequately answer your questions — IF you even know what questions to ask! What follows are answers to the most frequently asked questions about electrics.

WHAT IS AN ELECTRIC VEHICLE?

An electric vehicle, or EV (pronounced eee-vee), is one that uses an electric motor instead of an internal-combustion (IC) engine, and batteries instead of a fuel tank and gasoline. The motor is a larger version of the one that powers your hair dryer, or the refrigerator in your kitchen, or the tape player in your car. The batteries are similar in size and shape to the one used to start your car's engine — only there are many more of them. The energy of the battery pack is routed to the motor through an electronic controller. Housed in a small black box, this works like a light-dimmer switch (or the speed control on the electric drill in your garage) — smoothly delivering power to the motor and controlling the EV's speed.

*Michael Hackleman is the author of six books on alternative energy and has built a sola-and wind-generated electricity research center as well as his own solar home. He is President of the Electric Vehicle Association of Southern California, Editor and Publisher of **Alternative Transportation News**, and President of the Board of Earth Mind, a non-profit corporation specializing in alternative energy design and research.*

Earth Mind
P.O. Box 743
Mariposa, CA 95338

The Impact is General Motors' highly publicized electric car which quotes impressive acceleration statistics but derives its power from a fairly exotic and expensive battery array.

HOW IS AN EV BETTER THAN A CAR WITH AN ENGINE?

There is a long list of advantages to be found in the EV. Since no fuel is consumed, there is no exhaust pipe — and no pollution wherever an EV is operated. The requirement for a smog certificate is a thing of the past.

EVs require little maintenance and repair. Parts that move wear out. Engines have hundreds of these. The electric motor has ONE moving part. And this motor does not use gasoline, lubricating oil, or coolant. Also, it doesn't need to be tuned, timed, or adjusted. There are no points, plugs, carburetors, oil pumps, fuel pumps, oil filters, air cleaner filters, fuel filters, fuel injectors, water pumps, generators, voltage regulators, starter motors, starter solenoids, or fan belts. In a gas-powered car, these take a bite out of your pocketbook.

There's no more waiting in lines at gas stations, either. Or wondering what gasoline will cost tomorrow if there's a crisis halfway across the globe today.

IF ELECTRICS ARE SO GOOD, WHY CAN'T I BUY ONE OFF A SHOWROOM FLOOR?

The answer to this question is complex. The automotive industry says that electric vehicles are low-performing and limited in range. They claim that, since the battery pack must be replaced every 2-3 years, electric vehicles are too expensive to be competitive with gasoline-powered cars. They claim that technological breakthroughs in batteries and motors are required before the electric vehicle will meet the performance standards that the driving public has come to expect from automobiles. There are many people and groups that do not share these views. In fact, Green Motor Works the first electric car dealership in Los Angele, opened to the public in April 1992.

WHAT ABOUT PERFORMANCE — ACCELERATION AND SPEED?

Driving a car that has been converted to electric propulsion is virtually identical to driving one that has a gas-powered engine. The same operator controls are used — accelerator and brake pedals. So, your foot pushes on the accelerator to control the speed of the vehicle, and pushes on the brake pedal to stop it. A good EV will accelerate quickly and reach freeway speeds. The experienced EV owner avoids jackrabbit starts and high speeds, knowing that this affects range. Still, if you get stuck in traffic or are stopped at a signal light, enjoy the idea that the electric motor is not running and, therefore, not consuming or wasting power!

WHAT ABOUT RANGE?

At this time, range is the biggest handicap in an electric vehicle. Standard conversions — gas-powered cars that are converted to electric propulsion — will only get 70-90 miles at low speeds and 40-50 miles at freeway speeds. Lightweight and aerodynamic prototypes double these figures. While this is a discouraging point — it is obvious that you can't drive an EV all day long — realize that this is well within the average daily trip length for cars. Think about it!

The Destiny 2000 is available today from Solar Electric and in electric car showrooms like Green Motor Works in North Hollywood, CA. It is based on a Fiero chassis, and has solar panels on its hood and rear deck to help charge its batteries.

The daytime range of the electric car is easily doubled by worksite recharging. A range of 100-120 miles, then, will meet all of the daily needs of more than 80 percent of the driving public, and a large portion of the daily needs of the remaining 20 percent.

WHERE DOES THE ELECTRICITY COME FROM?
Utility power is the primary source of electricity for EVs at this time. A battery charger at home will recharge the battery pack in an electric vehicle directly from house current in 8-10 hours. You just plug it into a standard wall socket. High-rate chargers use a plug similar to the one on your clothes dryer, and fully charge the vehicle in 6-8 hours. Many conversions have the equivalent operating cost of a vehicle that gets 30 mpg.

Overnight charging is the best way to re-plenish battery packs. While you sleep, your car is recharged. This process can take advantage of cheaper utility rates. Cities like Los Angeles value electric vehicles so much that they will give all owners a special rate, 1/4th of the standard rate, for the amount of power that the EV will need daily! Southern California Edison estimates that it can absorb 800,000 EV's on the grid before this load will begin to impact their power plant capacity.

The Doran is a 3-wheel vehicle with a 60-mile range. It can be built from a 96-page manual offered by its designer, Rick Doran.

The battery charger can be carried on board the EV, too. So, wherever you go, you can plug in to charge. Many businesses permit on-site recharging — and a dedicated parking space! This way, an overnight charge gets you to a work as far away as 50-60 miles, and the recharge performed during work hours gets you home.

POWER PLANTS MAKE SMOG TOO. HOW IS THIS BETTER?
Utility-scale power plants operate 2-3 times more efficiently than car engines. Thus, for each barrel of oil, three electric vehicles can be powered over the same distance as one gasoline-powered car when the oil is burned in a utility-size power plant to produce electricity. Smokestack emissions decrease proportionately. It is also much easier to monitor and control the pollution of a single smokestack than tens of thousands of tailpipes.

Finally, EVs can be recharged from ANY source of electricity, including privately-owned wind power and solar-electric power systems. The recent demonstration of utility-scale solar-powered plants indicates that grid power can also use sustainable and non-polluting sources of energy to generate electricity instead of oil, coal, and nuclear power.

HOW CAN I GET AN EV?
A number of car manufacturers have expressed interest in producing electric vehicles for the general public. Some even have impressive prototypes. However, all of them seem to be waiting for someone else to test the waters. At this rate, the first ones won't appear until sometime around the mid- to-late 90s.

The easiest way to own an EV is to buy or perform a conversion. If your car qualifies as a cost-effective vehicle to convert to electric propulsion, you can obtain plans and books that will guide you in this venture. Armed with this information, a good mechanic can do the job in a modest automotive garage. Also, there are businesses that will do this job for you. There are a growing number of entrepreneurs who are buying up vehicles that are in good condition, converting them, and offering them for sale.

The Lightspeed is an extremely light (850 pound) sports car with solar panels built into the roof. It claims a range of 100-150 miles on its nicad batteries, a top speed of 85mph, and 0-60 in 8.5 seconds.

While almost any vehicle can be converted, car models that demonstrate good aerodynamics (streamlining) and are lightweight and small will give you the most performance for the dollar invested. Currently, vehicle-specific plans are available for: VW bug, VW Rabbit, Honda Civic, Chevy Chevette, Datsun B210, and Fiat 128. While other vehicles can be converted (and have been!), plans help you avoid pitfalls and costly mistakes, and result in successful projects. Also, the conversion hardware is available off-the-shelf for these cars.

(Conversion plans, publications on prototypes and hybrids, and component sources are available from EARTHMIND. Send for a free publications list at: P.O. Box 743, Mariposa, CA 95338.)

When you make the decision to convert, invest the money for a good brake job, new shocks, and any other repair that will make the car "like new".

HOW MUCH DOES IT COST TO CONVERT A CAR?
There is an old saying, "The more you know, the less you pay." If you just "order" a conversion done, you can pay as much as $9K, and more than half of that is labor.

Electric propulsion is fairly simple and intuitive, so don't discount the possibility of doing some or all of this yourself. EV clubs are good places to experience an EV, to get help in selecting the right system, and to get the inside scoop on hardware and people experienced in doing conversions. In the L.A. area, the Electric Vehicle Association of Southern California is a good start.

The motor, controller, and battery pack for a modest conversion will cost (early 1991) about $3K. Package deals (i.e., conversion kits) might be cheaper, but don't count on it. Control accessories and other conversion pieces can add another $1K. Labor varies considerably; this is a good time to nurture relationships with people who are mechanically-inclined!

IS THERE A WAY TO EXTEND THE RANGE OF AN EV?
Adding more batteries may increase range, but it also results in a heavier vehicle. An alternative is to use an extra power source. An EV that uses two or more power sources (one of which is a battery pack) is referred to as a "hybrid" EV. The power produced by the extra energy source will vary considerably with the type and design, but it is designed to augment the power from the battery pack, adding to overall range, performance, and other operational characteristics.

The most common hybrid EV is one that uses a genset, or engine-driven generator. Imagine a lawn mower engine connected to your car's alternator or generator through a V-belt. This would be a low-power unit, but when added to an EV, it becomes an on-board charging system. The engine itself can be fueled with gasoline, propane, alcohol, hydrogen, or diesel, depending on the type and your own preference of fuel.

In the genset, the engine is relieved of the task of producing PROPULSION (as in standard cars) and assigned the task of producing POWER. Electrical power. This goes toward the propulsive effort, battery storage, or both. When the auxiliary charging unit (ACU) is operational, the power it produces is never wasted. It's used or stored. Compare that to an IC-engined car stuck in a traffic jam or waiting for a signal light!

Hybrid EVs address two fears held by the driving public concerning electric vehicles in general: low performance and getting stuck somewhere with a dead battery pack. City driving favors use of the battery pack; freeway driving favors ACU operation.

Use of an ACU increases overall system complexity and initial costs. It may increase overall vehicle weight, too. Hybrid EVs are really a transition technology. Eventually, we will outlaw most kinds of combustion technology, since this is at the root of the greenhouse effect.

WHAT ABOUT OTHER FUELS FOR ENGINES?

There are alternatives to gasoline and diesel for engines in cars, i.e., methane, propane, methanol, ethanol, and hydrogen.

• Methane comes from biogas, a fuel derived from the decomposition of manure and biomass, but requires large amounts for operating a car, is corrosive, and requires 2,500 psi to liquify for storage.

The Epic is an electric vehicle concept car designed by Chrysler.

• Propane is a clean-burning fuel but the conversion kit costs $1.5K, and its price is tied to oil prices.

• Methanol is derived from oil and shale, but is also tied to these prices, and formaldehyde is an added toxin to the exhaust emissions. When made from agricultural waste, it avoids sulphur emissions and increased CO_2, but needs industry-scale plants to make it efficient and economically viable.

• Ethanol is alcohol distilled from biomass (crops), but requires a lot of biomass to fuel even modest driving habits. Has similar limitations noted for methanol.

• Hydrogen is the most promising of alternative fuels, since it is produced by breaking down water into hydrogen and oxygen. When burned, water is the main byproduct! Solar and high-temp processes (i.e., electricity, laser) may be used to split water molecules to obtain the hydrogen. Fuel cells powered by the hydrogen produce electricity directly. Storage is an issue, as is the complexity and cost of the production process, but this is rapidly becoming viable and affordable.

All fuels suffer the same bottleneck — the inefficiency of the internal combustion engine itself in converting the energy into propulsion. Furthermore, with the exception of hydrogen, combustion technology gulps oxygen at enormous rates. Gasoline makes up only 8 pounds of the 20 pounds of exhaust produced when one gallon of it is burned in an engine. The other 12 pounds comes from oxygen. How much oxygen is 12 pounds? It is the same amount of oxygen consumed by 30,000 people breathing for one hour!

WHAT ABOUT SOLAR-POWERED CARS?

A solar-powered car is an EV with a big solar panel on it. The solar panel is made up of solar cells that convert the sun's energy into electricity to help run the motor or increase the energy stored in the car's battery. Officially, then, a solar car is a hybrid vehicle.

Putting solar modules on an electric vehicle doesn't make the car a solar-powered vehicle. To achieve any real benefit, thousands of cells are required at enormous expense. This makes the vehicle fragile, bulky, and prone to theft. A better plan is to put the solar cells on the roof of the owner's home and to charge the vehicle from them. Grid power exchange, alternate pack charging, pack-to-pack charging, and pack exchange are all possibilities for making this work.

Solar cars are important. They demonstrate the practicality and simplicity of electric vehicles. It gets people to look at alternatives and to ask questions. It's amazing what one horsepower can do when weight and streamlining are factored into vehicle design. And, of course, it demonstrates that solar is a power source that works anywhere under the sun.

HX3 us a General Motors hybrid electric concept vehicle whose small internal combustion engine is only used to charge the batteries.

WON'T WE STILL HAVE CONGESTION WITH EVs?

Yes! Electric vehicles are only a PART of the solution to today's transportation problems. We really need an arsenal of transportation methods — rapid transit, carpooling, telecommuting, bicycling, phone and delivery service.

Rail technology, particularly light rail and electric rail, is improving overall and is the heart of a good transportation system. Carpooling most of the time saves fuel, fatigue, money, and hassles with parking. Telecommuting, or working at home through communication lines, works for a large number of jobs and minimizes unnecessary commuting. Bicycling and walking are underrated components of a solution puzzle — and as a nation we need the exercise. Mopeds and scooters are good fair-weather options as gasoline prices climb, and are less expensive to maintain and insure than automobiles. Telephones and mail service deliver direct to the front door of most homes. Planning ahead eliminates the thoughtless abuse of ANY transportation mode.

HOW CAN EVs WORK IN THIS DECADE?

Transportation today is a matter of convenience. We want what energy does for us — heat, light, power, water, food, and fast wheels. We haven't paid much attention to how it was done. And at what price. Do you want it to change? Look at the way you use your own car. Also, support sensible projects, even if you don't use them right away.

How can what you do matter? The REAL vote each individual holds is the dollar. Spend a dollar on gasoline and you vote for it and for whatever policies the people who sell it to you choose. To change these policies, move toward a mode that decreases and minimizes your consumption of oil. Increase your awareness of the issues and technology in transportation. Buy, construct, use and support alternatives!

HOW CAN I LEARN MORE ABOUT EVs?

Check the local library for books on these topics. Another option is to attend a meeting of a local EV club. Clubs like the EAA and EVA exist throughout the country and often meet monthly. There is merit to the idea of experiencing an electric vehicle first-hand.

The BMW electric prototype is significant as an example of a prestige company starting to gear up for the turn of the century when they feel a real market will have developed.

ECOLOGICAL DESIGN COMPONENTS

SOLAR DESIGN • WATER MANAGEMENT • URBAN LANDSCAPE • WASTE MANAGEMENT • TRANSPORTATION • *SUSTAINABLE TECHNOLOGY*

SUSTAINABLE TECHNOLOGY

SUSTAINABLE ENERGY OVERVIEW

Bob Walter

H ow we generate our energy is one of the most critical elements in the successful formula for sustainable cities, because fuel refining and energy production add up to our second largest source of air pollution. These processes, plus the motors that drive our industrial operations and propel our vehicles, foul the air and impact our health and the health of our planet. In addition, enormous amounts of non-renewable resources are consumed along the way at an alarming rate.

If our current level of consumption continues, the easily accessible worldwide supply of oil may last another 30 years and our easily accessible natural gas should keep us supplied for another 50 years. Ecological city designers are looking at scenarios stretching out over 100 years and longer, so if we are really planning for the future, revamping the means and methods by which we heat, cool and power our lifestyles is not an option to explore but a vital necessity.

The simplest set of criteria for what makes an ideal energy source is that it should be renewable, non-polluting, locally produced and economically viable.

RENEWABLE POWER

Renewable energy production is becoming an increasingly viable option. We are making progress both in the area of large energy plants that transmit energy over long distances and in the area of technology with much more localized application. Advances are being made in hydroelectric power generation with the advent of much more efficient generators than those installed decades ago when most of our major dams were built. Wind power is going through its own technological overhaul discussed below, but the field of renewable power generation undergoing the biggest revolution involves direct processing of sunshine.

How we generate non-polluting energy is certainly the key issue, but another almost equally important question must also be answered, and answered early in the process, before we commit huge sums of money, time and effort to particular courses of action. It is: do we build big plants far away from our cities or lots of little local energy sources?

Energy expert Michael Hackleman is one of a growing number of people who feel that what is most appropriate is for each bio-region to take care of its needs with what it can produce within its geographic boundaries. Keeping this paradigm in mind, importing resources from distant locations whether they be food, materials, or energy, works against achieving sustainability.

This is a pivotal point in time for us because major utility companies are starting to address both the questions of non-polluting power and that of decentralization versus centralization. Because of the large time and money investments involved,

*Bob Walter is the President of the Los Angeles based Eco-Home Network, and was one of the three principal planners of the **First Los Angeles Ecological Cities Conference**. He is an environmental writer and consultant who co-edits the **Ecolution** magazine/newsletter and writes the **New City Living** column for **The City Planet**.*

Eco-Home Network
4344 Russell Avenue
Los Angeles, CA 90027
(213) 662-5207

we should be sure we don't let our pressing need to develop renewable energy resources keep us from making the most appropriate choices. What follows is a look at a few of the programs taking place in the Southern California area.

SUNSHINE PROCESSING AND "TOTAL COST" PRICING

Sunshine processing is being developed on two fronts simultaneously. One is the planning of large-scale power plants out in the desert under optimal sun conditions. The other is improving photovoltaic panels to be installed on individual homes.

In the latter part of 1991, Luz, the most successful solar power firm in the United States, declared bankruptcy. Backed against the wall by the low post-Persian Gulf War oil prices, the company foundered. Although their plants will be reorganized and continue to operate, the development and construction divisions of the business ceased doing business.

Newton Becker, the Luz chairman, feels that if they had been receiving the same level of subsidy as fossil fuel and nuclear energy, or if subsidies were removed from these other forms of energy, the company would not have had to enter bankruptcy. Another way to establish a level playing field would be if the cost of remediating the effects of the pollution caused by fossil fuels were added to their cost. Under these circumstances, solar power facilities would not only be competitive, they would be the power plants of choice.

This concept of "total cost" is gaining momentum, because communicating to people through their "pocket book" is the most direct way to change people's buying habits. In Germany, a study determined that the direct social costs attributable to electric generation are about three cents per kilowatt. This accounts for medical expenses, loss of pay due to sickness, repairs required to buildings, and loss of forest revenues, but little or nothing for the more intangible but no less real losses of pain and suffering, bereavement, or loss of scenery. In fact, according to Lorin Vant-Hull, of the University of Houston Physics Department, the German study's estimates of the actual expenses of acid rain and air pollution were on the low side.

Vant-Hull has estimated social cost fees for coal fired plants at seven cents per kilowatt

> *Major utility companies are starting to address both the questions of non-polluting power and that of decentralization versus centralization.*

and four cents per kilowatt for natural gas plants. He has included two cents per kilowatt for a CO_2 tax and a sinking fund in the same amount. (A sinking fund is an amount of money held in escrow to be used for the eventual replacement of fossil fueled electrical generation facilities.)

This "total cost" pricing is leaving the realm of theory in Europe where, in mid-December 1991, the 12 European Community nations approved in principal an energy tax designed to cut down on carbon dioxide emissions. This tax would increase Europe's average price of gasoline by 6% and their price of electricity by 14%. (If the percentage of gasoline tax seems low, remember that the price of gas in Europe is over $4 per gallon.) Although they only produce 13% of the CO_2 made from energy production, they hope this will send a message to the United States, which produces twice as much as Europe does.

CENTRALIZED SOLAR OPERATING PROCESS

The basic operating method of the centralized solar electric plant is to use the sun to heat a liquid that can be taken to an extremely high temperature, which in turn is used to convert water into steam. This steam then drives a generator which produces the electricity.

Luz's technology involves trough-shaped mirrors that focus solar rays on a tube of oil which flows along the focal line that runs the entire length of these long rows of mirrors. This special oil, which is heated to 750° F, flows to a central location where it is used to generate steam.

The newest technology that a consortium led by Southern California Edison will spend 39 million dollars to test, involves using molten salt instead of heated oil. This molten salt is heated in a central receiver on a tall tower, surrounded by a field of thousands of large, nearly flat tracking mirrors called heliostats, which follow the path of the sun and focus it onto the central receiver where the sunlight's heat is concentrated.

Once the molten salt flows through the central receiver and is heated, it is stored in tanks capable of storing the salt at maximum temperature for up to several weeks with only extremely minor heat loss. From there it is drawn on as needed, to heat water and create the steam that drives the electricity generating turbines.

> *If molten salt plants are built in sufficient numbers, they could produce electricity at a price within 10% of a standard fuel burning plant.*

Luz has proved that large-scale solar energy generation can be produced commercially were the game to be played on an even economic playing field. Whether its technology or the newer molten salt process will win the day remains to be seen. But, thanks to Luz, the technical feasibility of providing large-scale solar power is no longer a question.

It is estimated that if molten salt plants are built in sufficient numbers, they could produce electricity at a price within 10% of a standard fuel burning plant. If the standard plant is assessed the true "total cost" of its process, then the solar plant's cost may be as much as 60% below a gas burning plant's cost.

Although the solar plant does not generate pollution per se, there is some pollution created in the process of manufacturing the materials that go into its construction. It would take this plant about fourteen months of operation to pay its pollution debt. Thus, it would operate the remaining 29 years of its life as a pollution free source. The savings in CO_2 alone is about 25,000 tons per megawatt of installed capacity over this time.

A previously existing 10 megawatt central receiver plant called Solar One is being converted to molten salt technology by Edison in a cost sharing agreement with the U.S. Department of Energy. The plant will be renamed Solar Two, and will serve as the test for this process that Edison believes holds more promise than the heated oil pipes used by Luz.

Lorin Vant-Hull is working with Edison on this new design. He feels there are several benefits that warrant its development:

First, it is capable of building up more heat than the Luz plants (1050°F versus 660°F) enabling it to work at greater efficiency. According to Vant-Hull, while

Solar One plant, which will be converted to molten salt technology.

the Luz plants are capable of generating electricity with solar power alone, in many cases — even under optimum conditions — some natural gas is burned to run the turbines at maximum efficiency. The Solar Two technology makes it possible to run efficiently without resorting to a natural gas boost because of the extreme heat of the molten salt. Although Luz uses natural gas to meet contractual agreements when inclement weather threatens production, Solar Two does not since it is a pilot demonstration rather than a commercial plant.

The second benefit of the molten salt process relates to storage capability. Molten salt is far less costly then the special oil which courses through Luz's pipes. This makes it financially feasible to create large storage facilities. By designing a plant that can heat 1.8 times more salt than the plant is capable of using during daylight hours, a six-hour backlog of molten salt can be heated and stored. This means that this plant can go on generating electricity on "solar" power for six hours anytime after sunset.

In addition to operating at a higher rate of efficiency, the central receiver plant will be simpler to maintain because the mirrors are nearly flat rather than concave. Not only does the shape of the reflectors make them easier to clean, but the fact that one doesn't have to work around a pipe carrying super-heated oil also makes for a faster and safer maintenance process.

If there is a spill, the salt would harden and it could be much more easily cleaned up than oil.

> *If there are feasible local solutions to our energy problem, then these should win hands down as the plan of first choice.*

After the 10 megawatt Solar Two is tested, the plan is to either build one or a few 100 megawatt stations and follow that with a 200 megawatt facility that may be the first of many. The 200 megawatt facility is being looked at as an optimum size. Able to generate power for about 12,000 homes according to Vant-Hull, it is neither so large that a failure would result in a major power outage or so small that its maintenance and monitoring staff becomes a top heavy portion of its operating expense.

The central tower of the 200 megawatt plant will be 896 feet tall (the Eiffel Tower, as a point of reference, is 984 feet tall). The motorized heliostats that individually track the sun and focus it on the top of this tower will be distributed over an area just under three square miles. The actual focal point for these mirrors will be 74.5 feet wide by 93.2 feet tall.

Aside from the vastness of each location, energy expert Michael Hackleman has some serious questions about this type of installation. Luz's installation is simpler to build. A single stepping motor can take care of moving one of the long mirror troughs. This is far less complex than the Central Receiver arrangement, where each 100 square-meter separate mirror requires its own motor and its own set of computer instructions so it can track the sun and reflect its rays on the Central Receiver. Multiply this set-up by the literally thousands of heliostats needed, and you have a greatly increased margin for failure. On the plus side, even a few hundred heliostat failures would only reduce energy collection by 10%.

A 200 megawatt power plant is not that big when compared to large-scale 500 to 1000 megawatt fossil fuel plants. It will take a lot of them to replace the fuel burners we currently have in place. It could be argued that a relatively small piece of our vast desert is a small price to pay when, on the other side of the ledger is a list of items that includes burning up our limited supply of fossil fuels, the pollution generated in that process as well as the thousands of acres strip-mined to provide a 30 year fuel supply. In addition, a lot of people might say that a piece of the desert that they have no intention of ever seeing would be a readily made sacrifice. But many people feel passionate about protecting the desert environment, and would not have large pieces of it built upon. Sometimes, the answer that first comes to mind is not always the best solution. If there are feasible local solutions to generating renewable energy, then these should win hands down as the plan of first choice.

CALIFORNIA WIND POWER PLANTS GENERATION

SOURCES: CEC; CEC PRS; OTHER
1991 Paul Gipe & Assoc.

WIND POWER

Wind power is another method of generating clean, renewable power that is usually done in centralized production facilities called "wind farms". It is easier to understand why these large turbine arrays are built, because there are far fewer places where the wind blows continuously and strongly enough to warrant wind farming, than there are places where the sun shines sufficiently to generate efficient solar power. Even so, Paul Gipe, of the American Wind Energy Association, points out that, particularly in areas such as the Great Plains states, privately owned wind turbines are an extremely viable energy option that is currently underutilized.

As with many fledgling industries, wind energy has had its own learning curve, rife with the sort of mistakes one expects under such circumstances. European wind turbines, designed for constant wind, broke down under the varied wind conditions of the California passes and could not produce energy for significant portions of the year. Quick-buck operators with no real environmental concern overemphasized the investment potential of wind turbines, and in some cases, investors, and the tax payers who provided the funds for the investment tax credits got burned. Unfortunately, these early negatives have been perpetuated in people's minds, and so this negative press is something the wind industry is just climbing out from under.

The modern crop of wind turbines are much more reliable. Surveys have shown that these turbines are available for operation more than 95% of the time compared to 50-60% in the early 1980's. New designs and refinements of existing technology have resulted in turbines that perform 46% better than earlier turbines, according to the California Energy Commission (CEC).

The U.S. Department of Energy (DOE) has identified 37 states with sufficient wind resources to support development of utility-scale wind power plants, and there are ample winds for small, residential-size wind turbines in all 50 states. Battelle Pacific Northwest Laboratories, in a study for the DOE, estimates that the wind resources in the lower 48 states could meet 27% of the nation's electrical needs even after removing many areas because of environmental sensitivity. The American Wind Energy Association believes that, realistically, between 10-20% of the nation's electric supply could be met with wind power if "federal policy placed the proper emphasis on renewable energy development."

California is the wind capital of the United States. The state's wind turbines generate enough electricity to meet the residential needs of about one million people. By the mid-1990's the American Wind Energy Association states that wind-generated electricity sales to the state's largest utilities are expected to approach three billion kilowatt hours per year.

More than half of current wind-generating capacity has been installed without the incentive of federal energy tax credits. The wind industry is fond of pointing out that although there is a high initial installation cost, wind plants are less costly to operate, maintain and fuel than conventional power plants, to say nothing of the environmental benefits of completely clean power. Wind power is currently the closest solar technology to being economically competitive with fossil fuel power according to *Scientific American*, even when factoring in the initial investment. By late 1990,

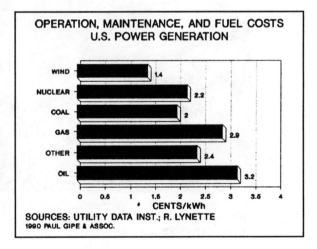

the cost of wind power had dropped to less than seven cents per kilowatt hour, compared to a new coal-fired plant costing about five cents per kilowatt hour in the United States. This is one very obvious place where "total cost" pricing would make wind power a real hero.

In fact, wind power meets many of the basic criteria for an ideal power source, except that most large urban areas do not have sufficient wind to generate significant amounts of electricity. The other challenge with integrating wind power into our energy plans is that supply does not match the demand. With sun power the peak generating ability occurs on hot days when energy demands for air conditioning are greatest. But in the case of wind power, since electrical storage is impractical and very expensive, electricity must be used when the wind blows, and not necessarily when it is most needed.

HOME SOLAR POWER

Heating a liquid or other material to extremely high temperature in the fashion of a Luz or Solar Two plant is not really an option at this time for electric power generated in the home, although the latest model of rooftop solar hot water heater features a parabolic tracker that super-heats oil, which in turn is used to heat hot water for radiant heating or washing water.

But photovoltaic panels that convert the sunlight into electricity can be placed on any south-facing roof not blocked from the sun. While these panels have been around for a good number of years, we are on the verge of some serious breakthroughs. One of them is being created by Southern California Edison.

There are three factors being addressed by those who work on advancing photovoltaic panel technology: efficiency, durability, and cost. Southern California Edison, in conjunction with Texas Instruments, has made major strides in the latter two categories.

A conventional photovoltaic panel is made from ingots of high-grade silicon which is sliced into thin wafers. These wafers can be easily broken, and the ingots from which they are made cost up to $35 per pound, with 30-50% of this material getting lost in the slicing process. According to Nick Patapoff, a Senior Research Engineer with Southern California Edison, the Edison/TI breakthrough involves converting metallurgical-grade silicon which costs about $1 per pound, into tiny solar beads.

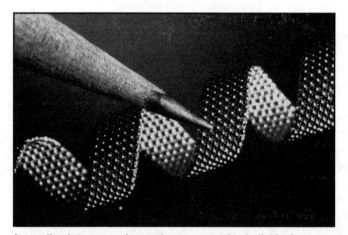

A pencil point appears large when compared to individual spheres that make up Texas Instrument's and Southern California Edison's new solar photovoltaic technology.

About 17,000 of these little spheres can be packed into a four square-inch area. They are embedded into four-inch squares of thin perforated aluminum foil and are bonded into place by heat and pressure. A second layer of foil without holes is then bonded to the bottom of the spheres. Each one of these beads acts as a separate solar cell. The beauty of this design is that the four-inch panels can be ganged together into something that resembles a roll of roofing material. It is extremely flexible, and if one solar bead does malfunction, all the rest of them continue working, so the overall unit continues without any significant measurable loss. In addition to upping the durability, the low cost of the metallurgical-grade silicon could bring the finished cost of these panels down to one-fifth the cost of panels currently on the market.

The one area this technological breakthrough does not address is greater efficiency. Patapoff estimates that it will take about 100 square feet of the new panels to generate about 2000 kilowatt hours of electricity per year which is about one-third the annual consumption of an average Southern California residence.

Edison's plan is intriguing. Once the "solar spherical" technology is perfected (commercial availability is predicted as early as 1994), they are proposing to place 100 square feet of these new pan-els onto the south-facing roof of every new building that is constructed and every old building when it is re-roofed. These panels will be connected directly to the grid instead of being hooked up to batteries as is the case with most current privately owned systems. Power would automatically flow back and forth between the house and the utility. Any energy not re-quired by the home would flow into the grid and at night "conventional power" sources would take over to supply our needs.

Revolutionary rooftop solar cells developed by Southern California Edison and Texas Instruments.

What makes this strategy so appeal-ing is the underlying logic. Edison is taking the view that all the south-facing roofs in the city are potential compo-nents of a power plant that would dwarf any huge plant that could be built out in the desert.

From the consumer viewpoint, this is a very easy way to get involved with solar power. The utility company installs the panel and you get your electric bill as you always have. One concern is that it is almost too invisible a process. This could be easily taken care of by an education campaign so that people really get to understand they are participating in achieving local energy self-reliance.

The down side of this system is that it doesn't involve any storage per se and needs to be augmented by conventional power, which in most cases means burning fossil fuels. There is no reason that this solar energy could not be stored in batteries other than the high cost of our current battery technology. Also, this creates a whole new billing problem for the utilities because they won't necessarily know how much electricity each home is using unless they install another metering system.

Batteries are another link in the photovoltaic chain that needs to be strength-ened. While off-the-shelf battery systems can be purchased that, although costly, work just fine, there is a sense that breakthroughs in greater efficiency and less toxicity are close at hand. The surging interest in developing effective electric vehicles is stimulating new interest in battery research. Once batteries are de-veloped with greater capacity and reduced cost for electric vehicles, they can also be placed in homes.

If Edison is successful with their plan, there is nothing to stop individuals from using this new technology to get further off the grid, clearing the way for greater independence from the utility companies for those ready to take the initiative. Other companies are also working on photovoltaic breakthroughs. Sanyo is rumored to be working on a roofing tile that is also a photovoltaic panel, and the British magazine *Nature* reported that a Swiss company is also on the verge of a significant advance in photovoltaic design. If 100 square feet of the Edison panels will generate one-third of the power for an average home, then 300 square feet should handle most of a family's needs, particularly in combination with other energy conserving measures and a lot of batteries.

Another application of solar power that can be effectively installed by individuals is solar-heated hot water. Solar panels have been installed on roof tops in Los Angeles since the early 1900's. With a backup gas heater for those days when it is too cloudy to generate sufficient hot water, this is an excellent way to conserve natural gas. The main problem with these systems is shared by owner-installed photovoltaic systems: they have a fairly large price

> *All the south-facing roofs in the city are potential components of a power plant.*

tag attached to them, and sometimes it is tough to see beyond the initial cash outlay to that point a number of years down the road where these systems have paid for themselves and are now making us money because of reduced utility bills.

FUEL CELLS

There is another localized form of energy generation which one of our major utility companies is actively beginning to promote. The Southern California Gas Company is installing fuel cells in ten selected locations, including a South Coast Air Quality Management office, a Kaiser Permanente medical center, and a Rapid Transit District Blue Line office. This is a technology first developed for the Space Program which is now coming down to earth in price. Although their cost is still quite prohibitive, the Gas Company feels that with increasing production volume and continued research, the price of cells will continue to drop until these units will be economically competitive with current means of electrical generation.

The fuel cell works like a battery with one exception. Instead of electricity, it needs to be supplied with hydrogen fuel in order to work. There are three sections to the fuel cell, which from the outside simply looks like a metal box. The first is the *fuel processor* in which natural gas reacts with steam to create the hydrogen gas needed for the actual energy production, which is accomplished in the *power section*. In the *power section*, an electrochemical reaction takes place between the hydrogen and oxygen to produce electricity, steam and heat. The fuel cell recycles the steam back to the *fuel processor* to be reused to make more hydrogen, and the heat can be used to heat buildings and water. Once the electric power is generated, it goes to the *power conditioner*, where the direct current is converted to alternating current (AC).

THE FUEL CELL POWER SYSTEM

One of the major benefits of the fuel cell, aside from being a power source that the South Coast Air Quality Management District says produces up to twenty times less air emissions than conventional power plants, is that it is also a great deal more efficient. A standard gas burning power plant, for example, operates at about 30% efficiency, while current fuel cells have an efficiency rate in excess of 80%. While the electrical efficiency of fuel cells is around 45%, the additional 40+% efficiency comes from making use of the heat and steam that the *power section* generates.

Fuel cells also produce electricity more cheaply, and supply power without the surges and drops of the standard power grid. This makes them ideal for installations with lots of computers and other delicate equipment. In addition, fuel cells have few moving parts, are quiet and require little maintenance.

Fuel cells, like batteries, have a replacement aspect to their operation. Every five years the cell stack needs to be replaced. David Moard, the Fuel Cell Market Development Manager for the Gas Company, estimated that if the cost of a 200 kilowatt fuel cell could be brought down to around $300,000, then it would cost about $75,000 to replace the cell stack.

At the present time, the 200 kilowatt fuel cell is being installed by the Gas Company in businesses whose electric draw is large enough so that the power the fuel cell generates represents only the amount of power needed by the business during its time of lowest electrical use. In this way, the fuel cell can be utilized round the clock, and operating in this peak efficiency manner can pay for itself in the

A typical fuel-cell installation for larger businesses.

shortest time possible. Currently, the 200 kilowatt fuel cells cost around $500,000. It is hoped that by the mid-1990's, the cost of this unit will come down to around $200,000. As the cost of the fuel cells goes down, there will be less of a concern about the unit sitting idle or operating at less than maximum capacity.

The Gas Company is planning to make fuel cells an extremely attractive energy buy. Its customers don't have to pay for the hardware, and compared to the price of the electricity they regularly purchase, they will end up paying 10-15% less for the electricity that the fuel cell generates. The South Coast Air Quality Management District anticipates saving about $10,000 on their total electric bill. With savings like this, it is not surprising that the Gas Company has a long waiting list of those interested in having fuel cells installed.

Small-scale fuel cells (two-foot cubes) are also being considered for the home and even smaller models for powering automobiles in conjunction with standard batteries which may be needed to supply the necessary bursts of energy for quick acceleration and hill climbing,

The fuel cell looks really good on first and even second glance, but when we peer at the whole picture, this is another of those situations in which present state of the art technology is an improvement over past technology, yet doesn't quite meet all of the criteria for "sustainable" energy. The Gas Company says that the power section of the cell is essentially pollution-free if its heat is being utilized as a benefit, and that the fuel processor only produces 40% of the CO_2 a gas burning power plant does, but that doesn't change the fact that CO_2 is still being generated.

Of more concern, is that this process is currently very strongly tied into using natural gas to make the hydrogen necessary for fuel cell operation. But we are facing a 50-year limit of easily available natural gas at the current projected use rate. This availability span will shrink even further if we start using natural gas as an increasingly popular means of generating power. Switching to coal or fuel oil as a source for hydrogen presents the same problem.

Using methane (natural gas is 95-100% methane) generated by this country's 3500 landfills could produce 20,000 megawatts of power, the equivalent of ten Hoover Dams, according to Tony Henrich, Manager of Marketing at Pacific Energy (a subsidiary of Pacific Enterprises). But this now reintroduces the problem of having to inefficiently transmit the power to the end user, and if we start composting larger amounts of the organic materials currently going into landfills, methane production from this source will be decreasing.

What needs to happen to make fuel cells really viable is an efficient, renewable method of hydrogen production. Electrolysis (making hydrogen from water) is not the answer using present technology because of the amount of electricity needed to separate the hydrogen atoms. At the moment it is more efficient to use the electricity directly, rather than using it to manufacture fuel for a fuel cell which in turn makes more electricity.

One scenario in which hydrogen production from electrolysis might make sense is if we create such an abundance of solar power that it can be used to generate the hydrogen through electrolysis. In this case, we would be producing the hydrogen in a non-polluting manner and would also be circumventing the need for batteries, because we in effect, store energy in the hydrogen where it would stay indefinitely until used in the fuel cell.

> *The fuel cell produces up to twenty times less air emissions than conventional power plants.*

Alden Meyer, of the Union of Concerned Scientists, views fuel cells as an energy source that could be an important interim strategy in our transition toward renewable power. He feels a key to fuel cell development is not to let natural gas supplies dwindle and become too expensive before seeking alternative means to produce hydrogen. The optimum scenario would be for the people who are intensely developing cost-efficient fuel cells to make sure equal amounts of effort are devoted to researching renewable and inexpensive hydrogen generation. This would help insure that we don't find ourselves, a few decades into the future, heavily committed to another energy generation technology which must be shut down and replaced.

INTERFACING WITH THE GRID: WHERE THE TOTAL DESIGN COMES TOGETHER (OR FALLS APART)

In working to transform our energy system into one that is renewable, it is important to have a basic understanding of the technical problems utility companies find themselves up against as well as some of the financial pressures they face.

One reason Southern California Edison is planning to provide sufficient capacity for each household to generate only one-third of its power via their new solar panels is that if Edison generated more energy via these panels, this solar power would start to put more electricity into the grid than we are capable of using.

The most obvious solution would seem to be shutting down the non-renewable fuel source power plants during the day and starting them up in the evening when the solar energy drops off. But this is by no means such a simple task to accomplish. Were one of these plants to be shut down, the potential is there for the turbine blades to sag and bend out of alignment due to the sheer mass of their own weight. If they need to be shut down, they are put on a turning gear which keeps them moving very slowly so they don't sag out of shape. This is done if there is a need to cool off the turbines, but if these plants are stopped and started up more than about ten times, the stress involved in that procedure marks the effective end of that plant's operating life-span.

It is also possible to feather these turbines and operate them at as much as 70% beneath their most effective rate and then dissipate the power being produced so that the grid is not flooded with excess current, but this presents two large problems. The first is that non-renewable resources are still being consumed and pollution created. The second is a powerful economic issue.

> *Utility companies think of non-renewable resources as a way to store energy easily and efficiently.*

These very expensive facilities are designed to provide a payback over a certain number of years. If they are operated in "neutral" and are not generating any revenue, this could have serious financial consequences for the company which borrowed the money to build that plant. It is easy to say that mere financial issues like these should not be allowed to become part of the renewable energy equation, but try to imagine yourself being confronted with losing 100% of your investment's earning power.

Even trickier than the financial minefield is the question of storage. Utility companies think of non-renewable resources as a way to store energy easily and efficiently. They can use just as much as they want, when they want. It is simple to store, lasts indefinitely in storage and is easy to handle. As we move toward renewable energy, storage becomes a much more complex question.

A solar generating plant, such as Solar Two, can store energy in its molten salt. Batteries are capable of storing any excess solar energy that is not being used. However, both of these are expensive storage alternatives to chucking a few tons of coal into a bin. The current Southern California Edison thinking does not involve providing batteries along with their new solar panels. This means that the 24-hour grid is still of great importance. What will a household do for electricity at night or during an extremely cloudy day?

One method of storage which has not been widely used involves a partnership with hydropower. Instead of one dam, two get built. The water from the higher holding area is allowed to flow into the lower dam, generating electricity as it passes through turbines. If excess solar or wind energy could be used to pump that water back into the upper dam, then that water could flow through the turbines in an endless cycle, generating yet more hydropower.

In Austria, according to Lorin Vant-Hull, one of these double-dam installations buys standard, cheap night-time power from Germany and uses it to pump water into the upper dam. The hydropower this water makes is then sold back to Germany during peak hours at triple the original price.

Dams are long-term, vast undertakings but they may provide a partial answer. Batteries certainly work well for individual homes, but one has to be willing to maintain them and use one's store of electricity wisely. The utilities supply power so effortlessly that we have come to accept it as one of the aspects of urban life we need not think about. This take-it-for-granted approach does not marry well with the care and maintenance a large number of batteries need. Either the public can become more aware and involved, or it has to be prepared to pay the utility companies to supply this kind of maintenance service. Both options are possible, but they mean life-style adjustments that will require some significant re-education.

> *We need to look at each energy strategy to see if it conforms to the criteria of being renewable, non-polluting, locally produced and economically viable.*

Whatever the means, we will not be ready to shift toward large-scale renewable power generation until we come up with the capability of storing sufficient renewable power to take care of peak demands and non-sunny or windy conditions. There is the feeling that the basic parts and pieces are available to us, but the experts have not yet assembled them into the ultimate renewable energy plan.

CONSERVATION

Amory Lovins is a physicist, a co-founder of the Rocky Mountain Institute, and one of the leading proponents of energy conservation in the United States. His message is very simple: If this country starts to put into place all the energy conservation measures we have currently developed, we can cut down on our energy consumption by 75%. This country has already put into effect many energy conserving methods over the last few decades; so to think that we have in our hands the knowledge to improve our efficiency to the point where we are only using one-quarter of the electricity we now generate is staggering.

Some of the main components of Lovins' implementation plan include a new generation of electrical motors that are much more efficient than those we currently employ, designing our buildings to make much better use of sunlight for indoor lighting (see articles on passive solar: pgs. 82-98), and using compact fluorescents which need only one-quarter of the power that our incandescent bulbs draw. The Rocky Mountain Institute puts out regular bulletins that detail state-of-the-art advances in conservation technology, and on a consultancy basis is helping government and industry realize our full potential for conservation.

We need to look long and hard at each energy strategy before us to see if it conforms to the criteria of being renewable, non-polluting, locally produced and economically viable. If it doesn't measure up, and another course of action does, then re-evaluation is in order.

It is tempting to start moving in every direction that looks promising. But what we need now is to step back, marshall all the knowledge we have at hand, and take a very long-range view that weighs all the factors. While we are in this for the long run, the few decades we have to achieve energy sustainability are very short.

RESOURCES

Rocky Mountain Institute
1739 Snowmass Creek Road
Snowmass, CO 81654-9199
(303) 927-3851; fax (303) 927-4178

American Wind Energy Association
208 South Green Street #5
P.O. Box 277, Tehachapi, CA 93581
(805) 822-7956; fax (805) 822-8452

Southern California Gas Company
555 West Fifth Street, Los Angeles, CA 90013-1011
Mailing Address: P.O. Box 3249
Los Angeles, CA 90051-1249
(213) 244-3030; fax (213) 244-8253

Southern California Edison
2244 Walnut Grove Avenue
Rosemead, CA 91770
Information # (818) 302-7946

Michael Hackleman (Earth Mind)
720 Brooks Avenue; Venice, CA 90291
(310); 396-1527

Lorin Vant-Hull
University of Houston, Energy Laboratory
Houston, TX 77204-5505
(713) 743-9126

Electric Power from Concentrating Solar Thermal Systems:
An Environmentally Benign and Viable Alternative,
Lorin Vant-Hull, World Clean Energy Conference.
Geneva November 1991

A TELECOMMUNICATIONS STRATEGY FOR SUSTAINABLE CITIES

Walter Siembab & Bob Walter

Walter Siembab is an urban planner and economist specializing in communications planning. He was formerly Chief of the Policy and Planning Unit for the Department of Telecommunications, City of Los Angeles. In that capacity, he managed the City's telecommuting pilot project and was responsible for assessing the communications needs of City departments. He is currently Director of the Telecommunication for Clean Air technology demonstration project.

5944 Sheraton
Los Angeles, CA 90056
(310) 649-6326

elecommunication is becoming an important environmental issue. The choices made today about telecommunications technologies, public policies, and social applications will significantly influence the extent to which our cities and metropolitan areas are sustainable in the 21st Century.

Now that there is beginning to be some movement toward a pedestrian-oriented urban design strategy, it makes sense to identify the major challenges that must be faced before we heavily invest our expectations and our capital in this "neo-traditional town design." There are at least four planning guidelines for transforming our cities to a pedestrian orientation:

1. We need to accomplish the restructuring of our cities in the shortest time possible.

2. We need to create the maximum beneficial effect for a minimum price.

3. We need to substantially retrofit the existing built environment, not just plan for new development.

4. Access must be provided to a sufficiently extensive range of goods and services so that people will find it attractive enough to change their automobile oriented habit patterns. This means not only retailing and office based job centers, but also a range of health care, education, governance and social services.

TELECOMMUNICATIONS STRATEGIES FOR CITIES

Our most effective response to the challenges identified above requires institutional decentralization as well as physical retrofit of the existing built environment. The main question involves implementation. How can land use patterns be changed to support a more decentralized city and how can institutions adapt to this new decentralized structure?

Since this approach will create communication needs while reducing transportation needs, the best response is a telecommunications plan that integrates fully with the mixed-use cluster town designs.

We believe that the key institutions for implementation of this telecommunications strategy may be city and county governments. Local governments control land use, they are large employers (about 40,000 work for Los Angeles City and 80,000 for the County); they have police powers that can provide incentives for telecommuting programs. They have corporate powers which can pay for telework centers and their own telecommuting programs; they are large consumers and users of telecommunications; they have some regulatory powers over telecommunications markets, and they are, at least nominally, democratic.

IMPLEMENTATION VISIONS

With a more advanced system of telecommunications, our telephone service, our cable TV and our computers will start to overlap and interrelate. This means it would no longer be necessary to make employees drive long distances to congregate in a huge office building in order to perform efficient and coordinated tasks for a specific company.

Smaller, very localized branch offices of a large company or a City Hall could be opened that are accessible without having to go downtown. Staff meetings would be possible with the participants spread out in all different parts of the city. Individual computer interactions between branch offices would take place as easily as if they were all connected by the file server down the hall.

> *With a more advanced system of telecommunications, our telephone service, our cable TV and our computers will start to overlap and interrelate.*

We can see the beginnings of this already. When you go into a local office to pay your phone bill, that transaction is immediately available to the computer terminals at offices all over the city. The same is true with airline reservations. There are certain stores that ring up a transaction at the cash register and an inventory deduction is made at a central headquarters computer across the country.

Conference calls can now be set up by anyone who wants to pay for the service. In the future, instead of carefully arranging for them ahead of time, an office could bring up a number of different parties not only on the telephone but also on video screens. Information that any one office is displaying on a computer screen would appear simultaneously on screens in all the conference rooms tied into that meeting.

Many of us have experienced the power of this kind of communication when we fax someone something while we are speaking on the phone with them. There is that amazing sensation of handing somebody a piece of paper even though they are perhaps thousands of miles away.

This is not a call for dehumanized work situations where you sit isolated in a cubicle with only your computer and a video monitor hooked up to the phone line for company. Each localized office will have its own staff and there will be even more reason to work closely with one another because, in a localized office with fewer employees, each person will have to be less of a specialist in order to provide the full range of services expected by their customer or client.

All of a sudden, that compact, mixed-use-cluster town center, in addition to shops, restaurants and other localized businesses, will become part of a series of giant communication webs that are connected by very long hallways which can be negotiated by very short trips.

At home, a certain small segment of the population has been using their personal computers to make bank transactions and order goods from catalogues. This potential for home shopping will only expand. It would be possible to inquire about a certain item and then watch a short informational video piece about it on your television. In addition, the same kinds of service available in the work place could be set up in home offices so that even more people could make their living without having to burn non-renewable fuel and waste valuable time in an arduous commute.

POLICY CONSIDERATIONS AND CONCERNS

Not only is this potential for reshaping our institutions possible, it is cheaper than implementing mass transit. The cost of satisfying transportation needs by building new facilities has become prohibitive. Heavy rail costs in excess of $200 million a mile and light rail about $40 million a mile. With high capacity coaxial cable or underground fiber plant costing less than $100,000 a mile, telecommunications is a relative bargain.

As a matter of national policy, telecommunications markets, once a public utility, are becoming competitive. Because of this, new products and services are exploding out of the research and development labs. There are voice processing, optical storage, video conferencing, cellular telephones and personal communications networks. With the telephone industry wanting to develop a national infrastructure consisting of fiber optics to the home at a cost of approximately $500 billion, an opportunity exists to move ahead rapidly toward reaching certain telecommunication goals.

But despite the major benefits that telecommunications advances may provide, there are matters of concern which must be taken into consideration. Without the appropriate planning and education, this array of new technology could result in large-scale consumer confusion.

> *All of a sudden, that compact, mixed-use-cluster town center will become part of a series of giant communication webs.*

The loss of the internal subsidies that have traditionally kept telephone services affordable to residences and low-end consumers may make the average cost of these new services unaffordable to lower income consumers.

Since the affluent will be the first to afford this new technology, the rural wilderness may increasingly face suburban style development by people who mistakenly feel that these telecommuting links can take the place of town centers.

The key to achieving success and avoiding these pitfalls, is to carefully manage the burgeoning technology at this early stage so that it fits in as part of a well thought out overall eco-city strategy.

CONCLUSION

Cities cannot be physically rebuilt to make them sustainable in the next century without a simultaneous willingness to revamp some of our current institutions. This revamp can be significantly aided by using telecommunications technologies to deliver a broad range of services to one community which are produced in another community with a minimal level of automobile transportation involved.

The challenge is to make cities sustainable by changing the "software" — the behavior of institutions. The "hardware" — the physical buildings and transportation system — should be re-used with a minimum of expensive new development. This "software" rather than hardware oriented solution can be both affordable and timely. For these reasons it is important to incorporate an understanding of the potential of telecommunications into our design strategy if we want to be successful at retrofitting localized urban districts to be truly self-sufficient.

GEOGRAPHIC INFORMATION SYSTEMS: COMPUTER-BASED TECHNOLOGY FOR ENVIRONMENTAL MANAGEMENT

Carol Houst

Geographic Information Systems (GIS) are powerful tools for the creation of a sustainable world. As an integral part of the environmental program for a planned development, GIS are computer-based mapping systems that can allow developers of land-based resources to play interactive "what if" games, simulating proposed changes to the environment and the effect of those changes over time. GIS are used to create the natural-resource data base as well as the human mapped and constructed infrastructure data base, and then clearly display their relationships in beautiful graphic form.

Such an interactive tool can be used to identify ecologically important areas for protection and restoration as well as to analyze the development potential of the terrestrial environment so that appropriate zoning maps and master plans can be generated from real data. The GIS thus are invaluable assets not only for organizing and analyzing spatial data but also for presenting information and ideas in easy to understand graphic form to concerned publics — a critical aspect of the development process.

GIS typically provide graphic representations of multiple data layers such as aquifers, geology, wildlife habitat, vegetation patterns, slope, watershed flows, demographics and built infrastructure such as pipelines and roads. When clearly displayed through a GIS, the proposed development's ecological impact is demonstrated to all concerned and thus becomes vital to helping the community have the informed input it needs to analyze and review the proposed project.

The use of GIS for education, research, and management in government, industry, and higher learning has exploded in the last decade. GIS-related employment opportunities already outstrip the pool of trained individuals, and the number of these positions will continue to increase. For the general public, GIS has vast inherent educational potential with its computer-based representation and analysis of geographic data. It is increasingly used as a basis for interactive, computer-based games and participatory "real world" planning as mentioned above.

Cities, counties, and utilities worldwide are turning to computerized GIS to automate everything from simple mapping functions to complex land-use analysis, site selection, and network modeling. GIS has not only created a new dimension in map-making, it has opened new frontiers in how we plan and manage our cities and natural resources, including such features as land holdings, social services, vehicular traffic and utility distribution systems.

GIS unites computerized mapping and database management so users can capture, display and edit environmental and urban databases in ways that just were not possible before. Because of this, GIS are tools for accessing, integrating, sharing or distributing large spatially referenced sets of data such as socioeconomic surveys, scientific field and lab studies, and satellite imagery.

Carol Houst is President, of Nippon Mortgage Corp, a company arranging debt and equity financing for large-scale socially and ecologically responsible real estate developments. She is also Director of the Ecological Entrepreneurs Network, a non-profit networking forum which assembles design teams for ecological city development and does ecological building and environmental consulting for developers. The EEN also helps start businesses creating environmental products and services.

Ecological Entrepreneurs Network
11212 Tujunga Canyon Blvd.
Los Angeles, CA 91042-1250
(818) 353-7459

GIS use is multipurpose. Recent issues of the trade journals "GEO Info Systems" and "GIS World" have included articles on such diverse applications as:

- EPA using a GIS to study and map soil and ground water contamination.

- The US Forest Service and private forestry companies using GIS to monitor timber resources and to study fire damage.

- Marketing firms analyzing the extensive U.S. Census Bureau database with GIS in demographic studies.

- Transporation agencies using the systems to plan routes or keep maintenance records.

- Assisting in the speedy reconstruction of Kuwait infrastructure destroyed in the Gulf war.

- County land management agencies turning to GIS as the mode of interaction with land owners.

- Extensive use by political parties in redistricting for analyzing the potential results of gerrymandering and other maneuvers.

These examples demonstrate how GIS applications will become apparent to the general public. As the nature of decision making evolves to include this technological innovation, the impact on our daily lives is increasingly evident.

The design of a useful and efficient GIS begins with a very simple concept. That is, in a single geographic location there are layers of map information available. These include environmental data such as soil types, vegetation and geology, and area data such as political boundaries, school districts or zoning classifications. These layers can also encompass demographic data which might include characteristics of people in the cities or wildlife in the environment. The various layers of mapped information can be worked interactively to reveal key relationships among the layers.

> *GIS unites mapping and database management so users can display and edit environmental and urban databases in ways that were not possible before.*

Organizations acquire a GIS for a variety of reasons, so the system must be tailored to meet individual needs. This personalized approach is built around several essential components including procedures for operating and managing the system, a database of information, the hardware it runs on and the software which provides the tools for meaningful analysis.

The most important component of any GIS is the people who need to use the technology. They might be faced with a challenge of improving services with shrinking budgets, or trying to eliminate the inefficiency and expense of an overburdened manual system of mapping and analysis.

Essential ingredients for the success of any GIS in the development process are the procedures for how the database will be designed, updated and accessed. This is critical, for example, in a city government where there are between 200-300 separate definable tasks involved in gathering, entering and distributing geographic data. Everything from land use planning, issuing building permits, managing roads and traffic, routing vehicles and infrastructure management to policy making. Although the activities are different among departments, they share a common jurisdiction and therefore can utilize a common, integrated database and "base map."

Problems surface in a manual system when data needed to execute any of these tasks is located in a single department, making access difficult. Conversely, if each department maintains its own data it can mean duplicated effort and inconsistent files. A properly planned and implemented GIS can eliminate these problems, thus providing easy access and consistent data to all.

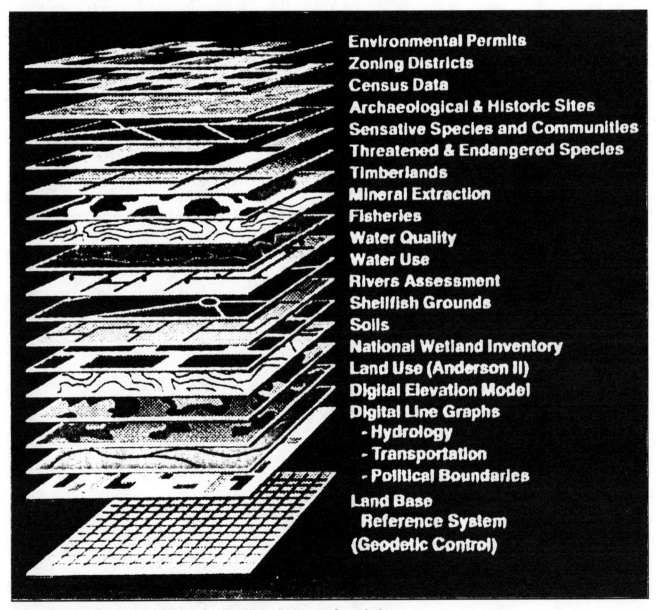

Environmental Permits
Zoning Districts
Census Data
Archaeological & Historic Sites
Sensative Species and Communities
Threatened & Endangered Species
Timberlands
Mineral Extraction
Fisheries
Water Quality
Water Use
Rivers Assessment
Shellfish Grounds
Soils
National Wetland Inventory
Land Use (Anderson II)
Digital Elevation Model
Digital Line Graphs
- Hydrology
- Transportation
- Political Boundaries
Land Base
Reference System
(Geodetic Control)

A sample GIS produced by the South Carolina Water Resources Commission showing how layers of information can be simultaneously tracked.

The rapid developments in GIS are changing the way some institutions function and are changing the institutions themselves. In time, they will change the ways that we think about our personal and public environments, as GIS become as commonplace as word processing in computer systems.

The Ecological Entrepreneurs Network through key member affiliates is able to offer access to the types of products and services described in this article. We are committed to making low cost GIS widely available to assure the support of environmentally-responsible development and participatory planning.

RESOURCES:

Major GIS systems include: GRASS (public domain), Arc/Info, EPPL, ERDAS, GeoVision, Intergraph, MOSS, Atlas and SAGIS.

BOOKS AND PERIODICALS:

The Local Government Guide to Geographic Information Systems: Planning and Implementation; ICMA, 1991; ICMA Distribution Center; P.O. Box 2011; Annapolis, MD 20701; (800) 745-8780

GIS World
2629 Redwing Road, Suite 280
Ft. Collins, CO 80526
1 (800) GIS WRLD

GeoInfo Systems
195 Main St.
Metuchen, NJ 08840
(908) 549-3000

GRASSClippings Newsletter
U.S. Army CERL, P.O. Box 4005,
Champaign, IL 61824-4005
(217) 878-7220

ECONOMIC STRATEGIES

THE ECONOMIC POWER OF SUSTAINABLE DEVELOPMENT: BUILDING THE NEW AMERICAN DREAM

Joseph Smyth

HISTORICAL ROOTS OF SPRAWL

Joseph Smyth, President of the Joseph Smyth Company, is a visionary and imaginative planner who, since 1971, has designed and developed ecological communities on both East and West Coasts. Currently planning pedestrian-oriented urban and rural villages, Smyth has pioneered a participatory planning process to create a financially and environmentally sound master plan for Ventura County.

Joseph Smyth Company
509 Marin Street #134
Thousand Oaks, CA 91360
(805) 373-3712

Before World War II, many Americans lived in small towns and villages, and dreamed of owning their own farm or homestead. After the war ended, more and more Americans moved to the larger industrial cities, bringing with them these visions of home ownership. The factories that had been expanded to supply the war effort were being reconverted to peacetime production, and jobs were plentiful. Americans were proud of winning the war, and there was an optimistic mood in the country. The economy was booming, and everybody wanted a piece of the good life.

In 1947, east coast developer William Levitt had a dream of his own: to build affordable homes away from the congested cities. Brooklyn-born Levitt bought acres and acres of potato fields on New York's Long Island. For no money down and $65 a month, a $6,900 Cape Cod home could be bought, and bought they were! Levitt's dream was so successful that he built and sold thousands, completing as many as 36 a day. Levittown and the suburban tract home and lifestyle were born, and the new form of The American Dream took hold.

At first, this form of land planning and building worked. Large numbers of people found themselves homeowners, with a yard where they could plant a garden reminiscent of the farms and country villages from which many came. Land was plentiful, and with cheap oil and labor, it appeared the answer had been found: one could work in the city and "live in the country". Cars were also cheap, allowing workers to drive to town and be home by sundown.

THE PROBLEMS WITH SPRAWL

In 1992, some 44 years later, tract housing, suburbia and automobile-centered transportation are no longer seen as a solution. Rather, they are seen as part of a complex problem which affects all aspects of our lives from environmental to economic and social conditions.

An example of one of the many environmental problems has been identified by the American Farmland Trust, a national organization representing the interests of farmers. The Trust found that since 1980, 11 million acres of farmland nationwide have been lost to suburban sprawl. That is one million acres consumed each year. In addition to the loss of farmland, entire ecosystems are being disrupted and lost to this expansive land use pattern.

Examples of some of the many economic problems relating to suburban sprawl were the subject of a cover story in the *Nation's Business* (Sept., 1991). Author James Drummond states: "Americans lose more than 2 billion hours a year to traffic delays [not counting commuting time, just delays in commuting], according to the Federal Highway Administration. It says that figure could increase to almost 7 billion hours by 2005. One estimate pegs the current yearly cost of those delays at $34 billion. Truck delays alone add $7.6 billion a year to the cost of goods that Americans buy, according to the American Association of State Highway and Transportation officials."

The local transportation commission in Ventura County, California (a semi-rural county with a population of approximately 600,000 located just north and west of Los Angeles County) found that the County will need to spend $1.35 billion over the next 8 years to widen roads and build interchanges just to maintain and slightly improve the current level of service. That equals over $168 million per year starting this year and going for another seven years. Where will the money come from to pay for the needed maintenance and improvements, and what happens after that? Imagine the advantages of putting that kind of money into sustainable transit development in the County.

Examples of some of the many social problems relating to current development patterns have been noted by Marcia D. Lowe, researcher at the Worldwatch Institute, an independent think-tank that analyzes global problems. Ms. Lowe notes that low density, single-use land planning has contributed to a series of social problems, all stemming from an increasing breakdown of community. She says this breakdown of community is brought on, in large part, by the physical separation and dispersion inherent in suburban sprawl planning. She also explains that geographic isolation reinforces and encourages exclusionary land-use controls and social attitudes, dividing entire communities along economic and social lines. In addition to a breakdown in community, exclusionary land-use controls tend to create a limited range of housing types, resulting in among other things, a jobs/housing imbalance.

> *This breakdown of community is brought on, in large part, by the physical separation and dispersion inherent in suburban sprawl planning.*

In summary, low-density single-use suburban tract housing builds in massive losses of farmland and open space, increased automobile dependency, growing operation and maintenance costs resulting in unsustainable economics, pollution, and a spreading sense of physical and social isolation. All of these factors contributed to the breakdown of the environment, economy, community and our overall quality of life.

ESSENCE AND FORM AND THE AMERICAN DREAM

The question is, what do we do about it? Recently a city councilwoman asked me: "If we give up the single-family tract home, what will happen to The American Dream?" Indeed, what will happen to The American Dream? Before we look at possible answers to the councilwoman's question, it is important to make the following distinction that can get things going in a productive direction. In the dictionary, the word "essence" is defined as "inward nature, fundamental or most important qualities", while the word "form" is defined as "shape, outline, configuration and arrangement".

The single-family tract house is not the essence of The American Dream. It is only a current form, which can change without altering or compromising the essence of The Dream. In fact, a change in form can be for the better in bringing forward more of the important qualities of The Dream. The essence of The American Dream has never changed: open space, freedom, opportunity for personal expression and a place we can call our own. The form, on the other hand, has changed and is currently changing again.

As mentioned, an early form of The American Dream was the family farm, which changed over time. As the desire for social interaction, specialization and creative personal expression grew, and as cities were formed, new forms of The Dream were called for. As we now know, the most popular new form was suburbia and the single-family tract house. Built into this form, however, was a whole series of problems, such as high infrastructure and maintenance costs, loss of open space, massive pollution, traffic congestion, and the breakdown of community and the sense of place. It's time we take a new look to re-evaluate what is truly important to us as individuals, as families and as communities. It's time once again to look beyond the present form of The Dream to its essence, and draw out a new, more complete and satisfying form.

> *It has been estimated that in conventional land use planning, 40% of the initial cost of development is automobile-related.*

Part of the answer to the councilwoman's question is to ask another question: How can we create a lifestyle that offers more of what is important to us? The answer is manifold: clean air; beautiful views of permanently protected open space; clean and ample water; fresh food provided from local sources; safe, friendly and beautiful surroundings; safe places to walk and bicycle; places to get to know our neighbors once again; a lifestyle that offers more opportunity for a larger percentage of the population to pursue personal, professional and business interests; a lifestyle where people of different income levels have a choice of owning their own living spaces, and where these living spaces are conveniently located within a short distance of work, school, shopping, services and recreation.

THE PROCESS OF CITIZEN PARTICIPATION IS HELPING TO REDEFINE THE DREAM

There is a growing awareness that we must leave the earth to our children and all future generations, knowing that the planet is in at least as healthy and beautiful a state as we found it. To assist in this objective, a group of citizens and environmental planners have come together in Ventura County, California, to form an organization called Citizen Planners. The group has recently published a document entitled *Ecological Planning Principles For Sustainable Living In Ventura County*. The following is a list of those principles:

1 - Protect, Preserve and Restore the natural environment
2 - Establish true-cost pricing economics
3 - Support local agriculture & local business products & services
4 - Develop clustered, mixed-use, pedestrian-oriented eco-communities
5 - Utilize advanced transport, communication & production systems
6 - Maximize conservation, and develop local renewable resources
7 - Establish recycling programs and recycled materials industries
8 - Support education for participatory governance

Of the list of ecological planning principles, Principle 8 is actually the starting point for changing the way we live. We must, as individuals, families and communities learn to understand and appreciate each other's points of view. It has been said that the greatest number of individual perspectives reveals the common ground and the larger truth. Recently, J.W. "John" Ballard, co-founder of Leadership Santa Barbara County and president of a company called Winning Teams, made the following statement:

Master Plan for an Urban Village where residents live, work, shop and play without a car. 1438 residential units surrounding a large, 16-acre central park. Perimeter structures, 3-5 stories high, create a sound dam and visual boundary.

Central quad features a resort hotel on its northern side. A three-story complex with a food store, cinema and roof-top tennis stadium sit in the northwest corner. Northeast corner holds a health spa with olympic-size pool.

In the northern end of the central park lies a three-story fine arts museum with central atrium and rooftop sculpture garden. Also in the northern section of the park is a formal, walled Japanese garden.

Office and residential units line the west side with a central-town square, university extension facility, and chapel.

A residential hotel with potential retirement and convalescent center is situated on the eastern side.

Aviary and children's amusement areas lie in southern end of central park. The southern end of the village complex contains a three-story covered shopping mall, an open 1/2 circle court of outdoor shopping and 2,000-seat amphitheatre. Moving sidewalks within a covered bridge span the freeway, and connect to a circular light rail station, southernmost in the plan.

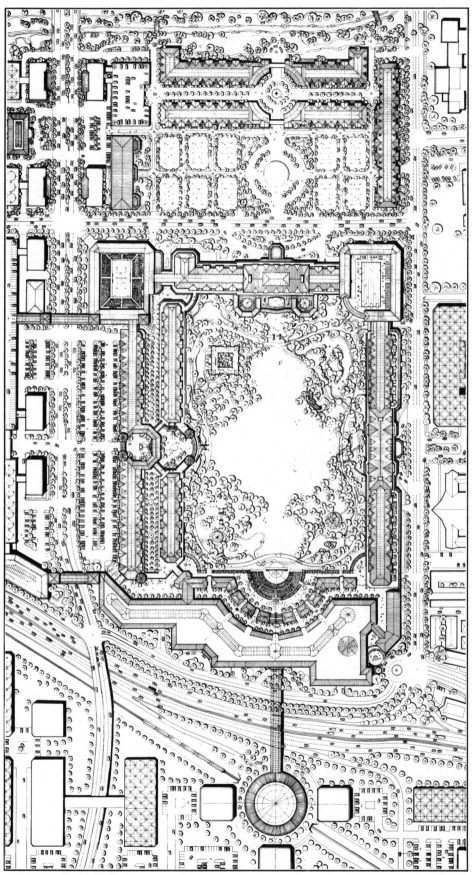

Anaheim Mall Proposal

Existing Anaheim Mall

"The people we have the most disagreement with are probably the people from whom we can learn the most, and with whom we can be the most productive, when we can find that common ground. The common ground is always there, it already exists."

The challenge is to uncover it together. Once we have uncovered the common ground, the new forms of The Dream will emerge quickly and, through mutual cooperation, turn into reality.

THE ANAHEIM MALL PROPOSAL: AN URBAN VILLAGE CONCEPT

The preceding principles, steer us in a new direction, away from "sprawl" and toward "clustering," thus preserving open space, supporting rail transit, and creating mixed-use pedestrian-oriented communities or "Urban Villages."

One possible answer to the councilwoman's question is a proposed Urban Village on a 72-acre site located in the City of Anaheim, California. By Urban Village, we mean a place where a person and a family can live within walking distance of work, schools, shopping, services, entertainment, recreation and cultural facilities, while having easy access to mass transit traveling to other communities. At the present time, in its center is a city block occupied by an old mall with a high vacancy rate and no improvement in sight. The proposal is to take down the mall and build in its place a 16-acre central park surrounded by 3- and 4-story structures composed of the uses mentioned above.

A detailed description of the structures and their uses is listed alongside the master plan. The circular building located at the bottom of the drawing on the south side of the freeway, Interstate 5, represents the transit stop. The plan is to develop a public transit system from the site to Disneyland,

Urban renewal clustering: A neighborhood block BEFORE conversion

1.3 miles south of the mall; the center of Anaheim, 1.2 miles east; and the planned mass transit hub located near Anaheim Stadium, just south of downtown. The key is to create a lifestyle opportunity and living arrangement that is convenient, spacious, beautiful and much less dependent on the automobile.

The Urban Village creates economic savings in every way. It has been estimated that in conventional land use planning, 40% of the initial cost of development is automobile related. In other words, the money goes to pay for freeways, streets, stoplights, parking lots, driveways, garages, parking structures, and the land they cover. And that is the cheap part. The increasing operational and maintenance costs of suburban sprawl make continuing this pattern more and more costly. A specific example of the economic savings coming from the Urban Village Plan described above is the cost of parking.

Currently, according to code, the City of Anaheim would require 11,000 parking spaces to serve the Urban Village project. Because of the mixed-use aspects of the project and the rail transit orientation, we propose the parking be cut in half, saving some 5,500 spaces. If parking structure spaces cost $10,000 each, 5,500 spaces will save $55 million. Instead of building concrete parking structures—a permanent problem—a better investment is to contribute that money toward building the rail line—a permanent solution. Due to the mixed-use aspects of the project, economic savings also come through faster absorption, allowing the project to be finished sooner. Also, savings come through multi-story construction, which reduces infrastructure costs and operating and maintenance costs to the city and property owners over the short and long term.

URBAN RENEWAL CLUSTERING

On a smaller scale, another example of urban renewal clustering involves the renovation of an inner city neighborhood block. The objective is to bring the property owners within the block together, creating a common goal. In other words, encourage cooperation to improve the quality of life in an economically viable manner for all of the block's inhabitants.

The first drawing shows the block in its present condition, and the second shows it transformed into a mixed-use pedestrian-oriented neighborhood center. As you will note, in addition to extensive renovation of existing buildings, there is one new large apartment building proposed for the block. Not only does this new building provide much-needed affordable housing, but it also provides the additional capital required to improve the land forming the community's central park, shown on the second drawing.

In other words, through cooperation and a pooling of resources of both land and capital, all of the property owners benefit economically, environmentally and socially.

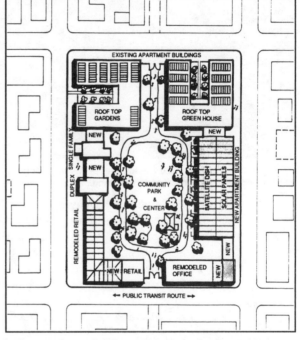

Urban renewal clustering: A neighborhood block AFTER conversion

RURAL CLUSTERED COMMUNITIES

Mixed-use pedestrian-oriented clustered communities are also being planned for rural areas. The same principles apply, but with one additional advantage: the advantage of permanently protecting vast amounts of farmland and open space. The protection of the open space is made possible by the transferring of development rights to one area of the property, where the clustered community would be built. In most cases, the clustered communities would only occupy 10% to 20% of the property, leaving 80% to 90% as permanent open space.

The following scenario and calculations are an example of how the mixed-use clustered concept works in a rural setting. Start with a purchase of 3,000 acres of rural property at a

McCrea Ranch Village — Town Square & Main Street

cost of $30,000 per acre, or a total land cost of $90 million. Now using the mixed-use clustered concept, plan a village to occupy 300 acres (10% of the 3,000 acres). This leaves 2,700 acres as permanently protected open space.

The residential units within the village will be structured in the form of townhouses and condominiums, all adjacent to parks, plazas and pedestrian pathways leading to near-by work places, schools, shopping, services and recreational and cultural facilities. The obvious question is: how to pay for leaving so much land within the village and surrounding the village (2,700 acres) as permanent open space?

McCrea Ranch Village — 300 Residential Units on 37 acres with 300 acres preserved as permanent open space.

If we assume the village will contain 6,000 residential units with an average unimproved land value of $20,000 per unit, the total residential land value once the village plan is approved will be $120 million (6,000 units times a land value of $20,000 per unit). Now if you add in the land value set aside for commercial space ($80 million), the total undeveloped land value after approvals and before development has risen from $90 million to $200 million. If the land cost is subtracted, $110 million remains after paying for the land. A major portion of the remaining $110 million will be used for primary infrastructure components, such as water reclamation, refuse recycling and composting, transit connection and communication systems. The point is that the clustering concept can pay its way as it creates a beautiful, clean, safe, convenient community, surrounded by over 2,000 acres of permanently protected farmland and natural open space.

A NEW DEFINITION OF INFRASTRUCTURE

President Bush has stated that if we are going to contribute and play a healthy role in the global economy, we must rebuild our infrastructure nationwide. He emphasized the need for improving and expanding our freeway systems. We propose a broader definition of the word infrastructure. We see the entirety of human habitat as infrastructure and, yes, it must be rebuilt. When infrastructure is looked at from a whole systems point of view, our investment choices will be based on permanent long-term sustainability. Choices from this perspective will ensure a better quality of life for current as well as future generations.

It's time that the form of The American Dream change once again. Like William Levitt, we dream of creating housing that is affordable, where it's safe and healthy to raise a family. We know we can build clustered communities utilizing advanced transportation, communication and production systems for less cost than current developments, and end up with a healthier environment, economy and society; a place where we once again can get to know our neighbors. The question is: will we do it before we disrupt and destroy the remaining natural beauty of the planet? The key to speeding up the change is to get involved, to take part in creating the new form. If you are interested in your community and County creating a similar program, we encourage you to contact the Citizen Planners Project of Ventura County. Call or write us at 509 Marin St., Suite 134; Thousand Oaks, CA 91360; (805) 495-1025; FAX (805) 373-3809.

HOW TO USE THE MARKET TO REDUCE SPRAWL, CONGESTION, POLLUTION AND WASTE IN OUR CITIES

William K. Shireman

We think of cities as collections of buildings and houses and roads and people. But in reality, cities are just legal constructs, through which human behavior flows, to create systems of commerce and housing and transportation that reflect the underlying legal orientation. So, in talking about how to build eco-cities, it is not enough to talk about what they should look like when they are done. For if our vision of an eco-city contradicts something deeply ingrained in the legal traditions of cities, then all the rules and incentives and traditions will be against eco-city ideas, making them unworkable. Instead, we must first look to the city on paper: what are the rules that shape the way people design, build, work, and engage in commerce in the city? Are these compatible with environmental needs? If not, how should the rules change, to cultivate the growth of eco-cities?

Today, economic development is certainly a leading objective of a city. But industrial development of the type we saw in the 1800s through the 1950s is not so much what people have in mind any more. Nevertheless, once rules are written and on the books, they gain a certain momentum. Everyone's interests, if only their sense of order and conservatism, seem tied in some way to these rules. But there come times in the history of cities and of all governments when the basic conditions of living have changed, when new imperatives emerge, and when old rules need to be rewritten to meet those new imperatives.

Before 1880, access to water was the founding principle that underlay the rules of city development. Then, the emergence of the fossil fuel industrial economy changed the nature of cities, in three successive steps. First, around the turn of the century, steam power created huge, centralized cities. Then, the electric power station exploded the densely populated core of the industrial cities, spreading them like shrapnel over the surrounding countryside. Finally, of course, petroleum and the internal combustion engine led to an unprecedented sprawl of cities, and the development of the suburb, the archetype of development in the latter half of this century.

Los Angeles is a good example of a city built by old rules, moving into a century that will be forcibly shaped by new rules. Los Angeles is the product of a late industrial economy, one founded on cheap energy and the illusion of free air, water, materials, and land. In an economy like that, we achieve something that appears to be economic growth, by very rapidly consuming as much of what is valuable, yet free, as we can. As a result, L.A. and hundreds of other cities designed from 1900 through 1970 and after, are designed to produce what used to be maximum economic growth: they are designed to be a conduit for the rapid consumption of resources.

When we designed and built L.A., we did so according to a set of rules that no longer bear a close relationship to our goals. We divided it into zones: some for industry to build things, some for commerce to sell them, and some for the residents who consume them. We built power plants to provide electricity to

*Former Director of Californians Against Waste, in 1989 William Shireman founded California Futures, a consulting firm that designs legislation, utilizing market incentives to protect the environment, and designs programs that promote sustainable economic development. His monthly newsletter and reports include **Profit the Earth**, which tracks trends in the environmental and green business movements.*

California Futures
8498 Sunblaze Way
Sacramento, CA 95823

all these entities. We constructed roads and highways to connect these zones, which could be miles, even hundreds of miles, apart. We built systems to bring in water, and systems to dump it out. And with all of that, we built houses, businesses, schools and universities, shopping centers, parks and every other form of development, all as if the only cost of air, water, energy, land and raw materials was the cost of using it—never the cost of creating it.

Then, about 1974, the catalyst for growth in the economy shifted from resource consumption to resource efficiency. In the process, we found that the economic development practices that made sense before had now, in many cases, been carried way beyond the point of diminishing returns. Traditional zoning put homes far from stores and jobs. Traditional property taxation may have discouraged redevelopment, encouraged speculation and sprawl. Subsidies for water, energy and transportation led to waste, pollution, congestion, and depletion. In many communities, this fact of life has led to the emergence of new, post-fossil fuel, post-suburban forms of development.

> *There come times in the history of cities, when new imperatives emerge, and when old rules need to be rewritten to meet those new imperatives.*

In Sacramento, for example, a major developer is building what is called a Pedestrian Pocket community—a 1,000-acre community built to de-emphasize the car, by placing people and houses near stores, jobs, parks, and, eventually, transit. But we can't build eco-cities within a structure of rules that makes them more expensive, less convenient, and less satisfying than their old suburban counterparts. Nor can we compel the development of eco-cities by somehow banning those aspects of traditional suburbia that we don't like. To build eco-cities, we need to develop new rules with which to define cities; rules that seek not the rapid depletion of material resources, but which fully integrate the proliferating information explosion, with seasoned knowledge and wisdom to cultivate the new building blocks for a sustainable future.

DISTINGUISHING BETWEEN GOALS AND POLICIES

Following is a short menu of possible "new rules" for eco-city development. Some are in use today; others aren't, although they seem capable of adding to the eco-city reality, because they are both economically and environmentally proactive. Before going into these new rules, I will make a few overarching points. It is important to distinguish between goals (what we want) and policies (how to get it). I have a new baby, and she is the most wonderful person in the world to me. And when she wants something, she demands it, and I give it to her. That works when you are ten months old. But it doesn't when you are 33 and operating in a political world. Yet, often, we as environmentalists seek to get what we want by demanding it directly. That leads to political palliatives— policies that seem to reach for what we want, but not to solutions.

Solutions require more organic, holistic thinking, like the thinking that nature produces when she designs an ecosystem, with its careful integration of causes and effects. We ignore the lessons of nature, of how nature grows, when we demand growth control for its own sake. Growth control is a policy, a means to an end, perhaps, but not an end in itself.

Political opportunism and organizational self-interest often lead to policies that are more symbolic than substantive. We need to be wary of fulfilling the political needs of politicians who create the rules, commissions and procedures that have the mere appearance of improving the environment. More often than not, political solutions make for disastrous policies: they delay the emergence of legitimate solutions by creating the illusion of progress, and increase the transitional pain and suffering that are the inevitable byproduct of substantive policy improvements. Getting tough isn't necessarily the same as being effective. Rules create incentives for state officials to look for infractions involving faulty filing of paperwork, rather than serious environmental damage. The clearest example taken for granted today, is zoning. Zoning encourages the most egregious forms of corruption at the local level. The power to control the value of land is as close to the power of God that most local officials will ever achieve. It creates temptations, "political realities," which are often too great to ignore.

ECO-CITY GOALS

Let's clarify what our goals in the development of eco-cities may include:
1. Using land more efficiently in order to:
   - Reduce need for cars
   - Preserve land at urban fringe
   - Reduce tax revenues spent on infrastructure
   - Minimize loss of farmland and wetlands
2. Using energy more efficiently in order to:
   - Prevent climate change
   - Avoid depletion of resources
   - Reduce dependence on foreign oil
   - Reduce air pollution
3. Improving transportation in order to:
   - Reduce time spent in transit
   - Reduce pollution from cars
4. Reducing taxes
5. Making production sustainable
6. Increasing the supply of affordable housing
7. Improving the quality of community and family life at all income levels.

Distinguishing between goals and policies permits recognition of trade-offs, for example, between affordable housing and efficient land use. More important, it helps enable us to take advantage of synergy: to design policies that achieve multiple goals.

> *Growth control is a policy, a means to an end, perhaps, but not an end in itself.*

For a telling example, let's look at land use. Rather than thinking of land merely as a physical entity, land is also an object of economic value. Unlike other entities, location has no value in itself. The value of a particular parcel of land is determined in the market entirely by demand, by the amount that people are willing to pay for it. As a result, land is subject to speculation. This can be decried but not denied. So, rather than preaching against land markets or attempting to prevent speculation through regulations, environmentalists would be well-served to learn how taxes could be used to limit the gains from speculation.

MITIGATING LAND SPECULATION THROUGH LAND TAXATION

The most important tool that exists for that purpose may be the concept of benefit assessment districts. The Mills Act authorizes the use of these districts to finance public transportation; but it has never been used, largely because of the lack of understanding of how it functions. Quite simply, a benefit assessment district raises money to build transit lines, by taxing increased land values in the vicinity of transit nodes. To understand the significance of this form of taxation, we must consider the effects of transit systems on land values and development. If an urban mass transit system is built, land values in the vicinity of stations skyrocket. Thousands of people pass through the area each day, giving nearby landowners the chance to charge higher rent to businesses on the property. In the absence of a benefit assessment district, all of this land value increase amounts to a windfall profit for the lucky landowners.

The same is true of a freeway exit. Landowners near an offramp benefit from the multiplying traffic that increases the value of the land. This can form the basis for a well-known and often-ignored source of political corruption. If someone knows in advance where a transit stop or a freeway offramp will be located, they can buy the land cheaply, and can profit from the increase in value. This creates an incentive to induce local government officials to release information on development plans, or, somewhat more elegantly, to actually design local developments, drawing out the plans oneself, and becoming politically active and generous in their promotion. This is called speculation. As a matter of equity, land speculation of this sort involves a transfer of wealth from those who pay taxes to build the road or the transit system to landowners near its nodes. Having to raise money from general revenues also decreases the number of mass transit lines that can be built.

Environmentally, it is important to encourage high-density development in the vicinity of transit nodes, to reduce demand for land farther away from the transit line, and to encourage pedestrian use. This can be achieved by increasing the tax on the land that increases in value. That is the effect of benefit assessments. They give landowners around the station an incentive to build as densely as possible. Benefit assessment districts should be combined with zoning policies that permit greater development in the places where land values increase. This increases the effectiveness of both policies.

The Mills Act was passed specifically to permit benefit assessments to be used as a financing mechanism for BART, but it was not adopted. Instead, BART was paid for with sales taxes, thereby giving a windfall profit to some landowners. To counter that inequity, Berkeley down-zoned the land in the vicinity of some stations. In other words, that city encouraged sprawl for the sake of equity, when it could have had both.

> *Environmentally, it is important to encourage high density development in the vicinity of transit nodes to reduce demand for land farther away from the transit.*

New York City is perhaps the best example of successful use of benefit assessment districts. The subway system was largely paid for by using this technique, and development around the stations increased more than enough to pay the cost out of land value increases. Benefit assessments were also used to provide irrigation to farmers on the eastern side of California's central valley in the early part of this century. Farmers paid for their share of the water out of the increases in land values that the added water caused. No one got rich in land speculation, the farms were of moderate size, and the irrigation systems required no subsidy from others. This is quite different from the later federal and state water system that provided huge subsidies and produced large corporate farms in the Westlands district. If the same policy had applied to the water imported into Los Angeles, it is likely that the San Fernando Valley would have been much slower to develop, and that no one would have made a fortune from land speculation. Perhaps Mono Lake would have been better preserved.

Ideally, this principle should be extended to the entire urban area, since transit systems are not the only projects that affect land values. The policy that would increase the efficiency of land use more than any other would be to eliminate the tax on improvements (buildings), and raise the tax on site values. If it were raised high enough, it would be possible to eliminate the sales tax. But most important, a high tax on land values would encourage full utilization of land within existing urban areas, and would reduce leapfrog development and sprawl.

Contrary to some fears, site value taxation would not lead to wall-to-wall development within cities. There would still be a reason to leave room for parks, purely for fiscal reasons if no other. When a city creates a park, the neighboring land values typically increase more than the lost revenue from the park. If those land value increases were captured in site value taxes, it would be easier to gain support for parks, because they would actually add to the overall tax base.

> *A high tax on land values would encourage full utilization of land within existing urban areas, and would reduce leapfrog development and sprawl.*

The major losers from site value taxation are owners of underutilized land. That includes land that has been left vacant, land used for parking lots, land used for warehouses in the vicinity of office buildings, and land occupied by slums. Part of the reason that landowners do not improve buildings that are deteriorating is the tax on improvements. Several cities on the East Coast have increased the supply of low-income housing without spending a dime: instead, they have taxed the land under the deteriorating buildings to give an incentive to rehabilitate them.

Many people invest in real estate with the expectation of making money from the sale of it. Even if society would be better off with a tax that encourages more efficient land use and more affordable housing, in the short run, a large increase in site value taxes would reduce the value of the land on which people's houses rest. The tax could be set low enough to avoid that problem, but then the major land use benefits would be lost. In this respect, there is a clear trade-off between short-run personal gain and long-run environmental benefit.

The same is true of transportation policies aimed at reducing car use, and encouraging the use of buses or rail systems. Charging a toll on highways would raise the price of driving and encourage car-pooling, generally much more than the diamond lane does. Raising parking fees to between $5 and $10 per day would also encourage commuters to car-pool or use mass transit. But these policies are not popular, because of the widespread view that driving alone without paying the social cost is an inalienable right. Nevertheless, if we could raise the price of driving by 30 or 40%, that would affect the decision that some people make about where to live. Since people's residential choices balance the cost of housing with the cost of driving, raising the cost of driving would encourage everyone to live closer to their job. That is also why taxing the most valuable land is important, because, in tandem with higher transportation costs, it can alleviate the jobs-housing imbalance without any further regulation.

ZONING REFORMS

Euclidian zoning was originally justified as an extension of nuisance law, to separate noisy or otherwise disruptive activities from one another. Now, however, combined with other policies, present zoning policies tend to increase congestion, pollution, and the imbalance of jobs and housing.

Houston has never adopted a zoning ordinance. To an extent, restrictive covenants have served similar exclusionary purposes to euclidian zoning — including keeping poor people out of rich neighborhoods. But in the lower-income areas of the city, a sort of jobs/housing/commerce balance has been reached: numerous small shops and in-home businesses are interspersed with homes, reducing dependence on automobiles to get to stores or work.

Fort Collins, Colorado created a system they call Performance Zoning. Rather than mapping predetermined development densities and uses, the city uses a points system. Developers compete with one another to earn the most points by meeting various social and environmental objectives laid down by the city. This makes for more flexible zoning, and allows developers greater certainty in advance about what requirements they must meet. Some analysts have also proposed the establishment of "neighborhood amenity rights," as an antidote to NIMBYISM. Under such a system, when someone buys property, they would also gain title to some of the amenities that make the purchase worthwhile: such as unobstructed views or clean air and water. If someone wanted to obstruct their view or build a landfill across their fence, they would have to pay for that right, through a system of amenity rights marketing.

> *Transportation subsidies often cause congestion, pollution, higher costs of living, and higher taxes.*

In Pennsylvania, Australia, Canada and Denmark, a number of cities have modified their property tax system into the system of Site Value Taxation, similar to that mentioned earlier. By raising the tax on site values, and lowering it on improvements, this system has reportedly reduced the incentive for developers to hold high-value urban land in speculation, while developing land further and further out, at great cost to the city. Advocates of the system say that it is reducing housing prices and business rents, accelerating the redevelopment of declining neighborhoods and business districts, slowing suburban sprawl, reducing transportation distances, and bringing a better jobs/housing balance. A Site Value Taxation systems would require study and planning, and Constitutional amendments. It may be one of those ideas that will be politically incorrect, and politically naive, until it becomes absolutely unavoidable.

In Sacramento, county planners are working with environmentalists and developers to remap the county into a series of Transit-Oriented Developments, or TODS. Within each TOD would be a mix of housing, stores, and jobs, many within walking distance and accessible to transit. The first 1,000-acre development on this model is about to be opened. Finally, the State Office of Planning and Research, a decade ago, suggested the increased use of standby charges by local government. Cities and counties would levy fees against vacant or underutilized lots that have access to public services, such as sewers and roads, to pay the capital costs of the city.

TRANSPORTATION

Transportation subsidies (free roads, use of sales taxes for transportation, and all the public safety and health expenses incurred due to roads and highways) were originally intended to enhance economic growth. Today, however, they often cause congestion, pollution, higher costs of living, and higher taxes.

CalTrans and local agencies often seek to reduce congestion by encouraging carpools, and, building carpool and bus lanes. Most environmentalists support these efforts. But some oppose carpool lanes, because they increase the total volume of traffic and discourage more comprehensive approaches. Many transportation analysts suggest Congestion Pricing Systems, such as imbedded electronic tolls that would charge vehicles a fee for using congested roads during rush hours.

To enable our cities to expand public transit at a lower cost, one free market think tank has proposed Peak Load Shedding, where the city contracts for private transit services only during peak hours, paying them the same subsidy per-passenger-mile that they incur on traditional roads and transit. To begin to internalize transportation costs, analysts have long suggested that we impose all such costs through gas taxes, rather than through sales taxes or general revenue sources that encourage further sprawl and reduce competitiveness.

ENERGY

Finally, in the energy field, most people are aware of the idea of Rate-Basing Efficiency. Energy efficiency improvements typically have payback periods of just two or three years. New power plants to generate the same amount of energy can take twenty years to pay off. Utilities like PG&E, DWP and SCE have profited by financing energy efficiency improvements, and by adding the costs to their rate base as if they were building a new power plant. The result is lower costs to energy users and higher profits to utilities.

WATER

Local government power is largely restricted in its ability to control the supply of water, since the state and federal governments operate subsidized water projects. However, local governments can significantly reduce water use, simply by charging users according to the amount they use.

Sacramento, for example, still does not have water meters at individual homes: people pay $10 a month or so, no matter how much water they use. Surveys of 37 cities show that 20 to 55% of local water is saved when meters are installed and people are charged according to how much they use. Most of the savings come painlessly from cutting back on unnecessary landscape over-watering. To reduce groundwater depletion, the Political Economy Resource Center has proposed unitized groundwater property rights, similar to pumping rights in multiple-owner oil fields. In the area of water quality, local businesses and communities are spending billions of dollars to build tertiary water pollution control facilities to further clean up water discharges from point sources. Meanwhile, water quality is declining, since non-point sources like agriculture and urban runoff are uncontrolled. Denver, Colorado

> *None of these policies demands that people as a whole do something that is against their economic or environmental interests.*

and Fox River, Wisconsin have begun to market water pollution rights that enable point-source polluters to pay to prevent non-point pollution, rather than spending the same amount to clean up a much smaller amount of their own waste.

SOLID WASTE

Traditionally, local governments have subsidized waste disposal, by charging residential generators less than the actual cost of collection and disposal, and charging a flat fee, regardless of how much is thrown away.

In Seattle, the garbage utility recently switched to a variable can rate-system. Residents pay for every can of waste they generate. They even pay by the pound in one section of the city. The result is a 60 percent decline in the number of cans set out for disposal. Most of the reduction has gone to recycling and composting; the rest has gone to compaction and source reduction. Some communities are considering establishing Advance Disposal Fees on products containing unnecessary wastes from packaging, or where the product itself is non-recyclable, non-reusable or non-compostable. In this way, wasteful products would be discouraged. Assemblyman Byron Sher is proposing a statewide system of ADFs this year.

CONCLUSION

None of these policies demands that people as a whole do something that is against their economic or environmental interests. They merely refine the rules, so that the most beneficial environmental and economic opportunities overall also make the most sense at the individual level. When considering how to solve the economic development and environmental challenges we face, there is a tendency to re-travel well-worn paths, to use familiar tools to try to solve new problems. But building eco-cities that serve human needs will require new, innovative approaches by cities, developers, and activist citizens -- not more efforts, but different ones. The menu of approaches that can be used by cities is increasing. Not all of them will work. But once applied, refined, and improved, they hold the potential to create an engine for the emergence of eco-cities, as machines that don't burden the environment, but benefit it.

THE CO-OP APPROACH TO NEIGHBORHOOD DEVELOPMENT

Lottie Cohen

Since I'm a long-time member of the cooperative movement and want you to join in too, I would like to address you as cooperators. That is what people in the cooperative movement call each other. Many recent movements and trends have come out of the co-op movement. In the 1960s, "socially conscious", "health conscious", "feminist conscious", "anti-war" and "free speech conscious" people started to take control of the resources that surrounded us.

In addition to housing cooperatives, communes and intentional communities, we, the cooperators, established consumer food cooperatives. I was on the formation board of the Cambridge Food Cooperative, now almost 20 years old. At first, the food co-ops were exclusively member-owned and managed and catered only to the demands of the member customers. This was the source for organic produce and the widest assortment of health foods, recycled products and, in addition to consumer goods, a base for information dissemination (now called "networking") about other similar cool and groovy movements.

FOOD COOPERATIVES

Look at the power and changes of what food cooperatives have wrought. In California, the food co-op movement has been the seed in changing many laws that make our world healthier. First, there was a clamor for a way to certify that organic produce was truly organically grown, with specific limits on chemicals and pesticides. This was a co-op movement clamor that resulted in the first State law defining "organically grown", and was written by California co-op activists. (See California Code of Health and Safety, Title 41, 26469, and 26569.11 -26.569.16.)

Then cooperators preferred to buy and sell in bulk bin containers, which reduced the use of wasteful packaging, because virtually all cooperative shoppers recycled their plastic and paper bags. This resulted in the bulk bin law. (See California Food and Agriculture Code, Title 31D, 42501 et seq.) The co-op movement also was seminal in the truth-in-labeling movement, which requires food packagers to accurately label the contents of foods. (See California Food and Agriculture Code, Title 31D, 42514.)

Now you see organic produce, health foods and bulk bins mainstreamed (what we used to call "co-opted") in supermarket chains. But in the early 1980s when the health food craze sprouted, co-ops were the only place to find these special foods. It forced prosperity on those food co-ops which opened their doors to the public, such as Co-opportunity in Santa Monica and Venice-Ocean Park Food Cooperative in Venice.

Other outgrowths of the food co-op movement include the farmer's markets and small food buying clubs. The farmers' markets are another avenue for bringing direct benefits from farmer to urban consumer, and creating a

Lottie Cohen is a real estate, tax and business attorney who represents many housing, consumer and worker cooperatives. She has been involved in the co-op movement for 20 years and is currently writing **The California Cooperative Housing Compendium** *under a grant from the California Center for Cooperatives.*

9841 Airport Blvd.
Suite 900
Los Angeles, CA 90045
(213) 215-9244

community gathering place each week for many neighborhoods. Many small organic food buying clubs throughout California range in size from 3 or 4 households to 30 or 40, and build a sense of community while neighbors purchase inexpensive organic food cooperatively.

HOUSING COOPERATIVES

Now let us look at the current status of the housing cooperative movement in our society. On a national and state-wide scale, even though legislation permits housing cooperatives certain tax advantages and access to low and moderate income housing development funds, there has not been a tremendous housing cooperative movement. There are perhaps a half million housing co-op units in the U.S., that is, ownership apartment units. Then, there are thousands of intentional communities and shared housing communities, including rental and ownership units. All have homeowner associations and/or social governing structures. And among existing housing co-ops, there are several membership organizations or federations, such as the National Association of Housing Cooperatives, the California Association of Housing Co-ops, Twin Pines Co-op Housing Institute, the North American Students of Cooperation, the Fellowship for Intentional Communities and many others. These organizations of co-ops provide education, training and technical assistance to emerging and established co-op groups.

What is needed is a cooperative housing movement that assimilates and integrates all the ecological, environmental, economic and social resources into a Mutual Housing Association (MHA) that will generate multi-unit housing that will be a pleasure to live in. The time is ripe and people know that the need for cooperative housing development is now.

MHA developed co-op housing can take a variety of design forms, from apartment buildings to townhouses to cohousing (that is, where a group of pedestrian oriented households owns a common house), to other forms of collaborative housing, such as the urban village cluster, SRO's, go-homes or condominium type structures. The legal and economic framework for the on-going development of co-ops is now available through the MHA concept. This MHA co-op structure can provide substantial economies of scale for all types of sustainable building technologies and materials.

> *What is needed is a cooperative housing movement that integrates all the ecological, economic and social resources into a Mutual Housing Association.*

The reason it is so much more difficult to sustain the housing co-op movement than it is food co-ops is that the food co-op is a central member-run store to which the members (and now public shoppers) have a place to go to make their purchases of specialty natural and health food items. In contrast, the housing co-op movement has no central store of co-op housing stock, of co-op housing funds, builders, developers, planners, or organizers, to which the public can come, explore and meet other co-opers or existing groups planning for their future co-op housing. All of these elements can be provided by an MHA organization.

In several European countries, MHAs are being used effectively to facilitate the co-op housing movement. If we cooperators could adapt one of the European MHA models, we could develop sustainable cooperative housing for members and groups who had contributed to the MHA, and had participated in the development of their homes and neighborhoods.

HOW MUTUAL HOUSING ASSOCIATIONS CAN WORK

The MHA can be comprised of individuals, professional groups, and other housing and food co-ops who deposit their savings into the MHA's cooperatively owned credit union or bank for a revolving source of funds. The MHA could buy land and place it into a community land trust which is a legal entity that prevents resale of the land and maintains, by permanent legal controls, the continuing affordability of the cooperative housing built or leased on that land.

The MHA could operate as a central clearinghouse for potential members, with provisions for facilitating each co-op group's understanding of the rights and responsibilities of cooperative ownership and shared living. For it is only when we drop our psychological barriers (what we used to call "hang-ups"), and learn to accept the sacred space of other people's lives, that we can truly live closer together, in a cooperative, healthy environment.

Professional staff of an MHA can help facilitate an interactive planning, financing and development process among co-op groups that approach the MHA, or the MHA could organize such groups.

As an example of an American MHA, the National Association of Housing Cooperatives has formed a subsidiary called the Center for Cooperative Housing (CCH) which will focus on the creation of home ownership opportunities through the development of housing cooperatives. The initial project for the Center will be to serve as the first national technical assistance advisor to the Resolution Trust Corporation. The RTC is disposing of the real estate assets of failed savings and loans across the country. CCH will evaluate multifamily properties, and will determine which ones

> *... it is only when we learn to accept the sacred space of other people's lives that we can truly live closer together, in a cooperative, healthy environment.*

have the potential for successful conversion to cooperative ownership by the tenants. Properties in New Orleans, Houston, Denver and Phoenix will be among the first to be studied.

With all the housing stock in California controlled by the RTC, it would be great to create a local MHA to organize existing or prospective tenants to buy the multi-unit buildings (and even single-family homes) and divert them into cooperatives. This would provide, at last, the "central store" approach to the cooperative housing movement. Another emerging MHA opportunity is one that the Cooperative Resources and Services Project is planning as the non-profit developer for the Los Angeles EcoVillage. Finally, there is a statewide task force of affordable housing activists who have started the California Mutual Housing Association.

In conclusion, it is a fact that the ongoing cooperative movement is a powerful and organized resource with which all ecologically-minded people should join forces. The people involved in the food, housing, child care, credit union, agricultural and worker cooperative sectors already are socially conscious people who have taken control of some aspect of their lives. The MHA model is an ideal umbrella organization for those involved in the housing aspect of building ecological cities. However, in true cooperative activism fashion, we can have any number of fantastic conferences, but unless a centrally organized and mutually funded MHA is created in California, the co-op housing movement will be slow-paced in our state. The task of forming an Ecological Cities MHA belongs to us, now.

CHANGING LENDING POLICIES

Carl Hanson MBA

Carl founded Urban Lending Associates, Inc. (ULA) to design single-family afford-able housing finance pro-grams for implementation through mortgage banking clients. ULA is organizing Eco Framing Associates to design cellulose-insulated panels for the California and Mexican markets. Carl is a board member of the Los Angeles Community Design Center and of the San Diego/ Tijuana chapter of Habitat for Humanity.

*Urban Lending Associates
1509 Continental Street
San Diego, CA 92173-1737
(619) 661-2510*

We often refer to the jobs/housing imbalance. We know the social and personal costs that result from long commutes between home and job. Traffic congestion, air pollution, stress on the commuter and stress on the family are obvious costs, but the loss of community, creation of racial and economic ghettoes, and "Desert Storms" resulting from energy dependence are equally real costs. The issues are serious! Correcting the jobs/housing imbalance involves numerous land planning, transportation planning, taxation and financing issues. I will develop a narrow focus on the role some home lending policies play. I will also discuss how these lending policies contribute to the jobs/housing imbalance, and how these policies might be changed.

America has developed some of the most efficient housing finance mechanisms in the world. Local mortgage lenders have a whole array of these mechanisms at their disposal:

1. FHA, VA, FNMA and FHLMC all represent national lending standards and procedures. Local lenders use computers to appraise, package, underwrite, document and service home loans according to these standards.

2. A secondary market allows lenders to originate and resell their loans. Mortgage insurance, mortgage-backed securities, national intermediaries such as FNMA and FHLMC, statewide housing finance agencies such as CHFA, and local agencies such as City and County Housing Finance Agencies (HFAs) all support the secondary market.

3. Deposit insurance from FDIC and FSLIC allows local thrifts to gather savings nationally to invest in housing.

4. Tax-advantaged mechanisms such as interest deductions, tax exempt bonds and mortgage credit certificates provide public support to homebuyers.

I have assisted numerous homebuyers who work in Los Angeles to purchase an "affordable home" in San Bernardino or Riverside County, perhaps 70 miles away. Let's review how American housing finance mechanisms make affordability possible for a typical buyer, the Smiths.

John Smith, a Los Angeles school teacher, his wife and their two children, saved $10,000 as a down payment on their first home.

Meanwhile, Eco Builders planned a community of 500 "energy-efficient" homes in Moreno Valley. The detached homes have an energy-saving package at the affordable monthly cost of only $10, which is almost saved on utilities. The homes include an optional garage to house the buyer's current car, and a new car purchased to navigate the 150 mile round trip to work in Los Angeles or Orange County.

Eco Builders are conscious of the importance of financing for affordable homes, and every available program was arranged by their Mortgage Banker to assist first-time homebuyers to buy with affordable payments.

When the Smiths visited the project, they fell in love with their home, and appreciated the energy-saving package but, most importantly, the homes were affordable. John was concerned about the two-hour commute each way daily, but there was no convenient public transportation. His school provided parking for every teacher (through school bonds), and this was the price several other teachers were paying for a slice of the suburban dream.

The Smiths bought the home after the Eco Builders salesperson explained the financial benefits of their purchase. I will describe how we, the taxpayers, pay one-half of the Smiths' housing interest costs. Later we can ask ourselves whether this is the type of housing development we wish to support.

1. The Smiths' family income was under $45,000 per year, and their First Time Homebuyer status qualified them under the Riverside County 20% Mortgage Credit Certificate program. The MCC provides a credit against their Federal income tax, and effectively reduces the interest rate from 10% to 8%.

Mortgage Revenue Bonds (MRBs) and Mortgage Credit Certificate programs both cost the Federal Government in lost taxes, and represent one of the few remaining subsidies for first-time moderate income homebuyers.

2. The mortgage interest and property tax are deductions from income for purposes of Federal and State income taxes. This further reduces the remaining interest from 8% to, say, 5.5%.

3. The Smiths' down payment was 5%, and Mr. Smith was driving four hours daily to and from work. FHA mortgage insurance was required to ensure that the mortgage investor would receive the payments, in the event that the Smiths ran into financial difficulties.

4. Mortgage investment is a complicated process. The GNMA Mortgage-Backed Security program was developed to allow investors to invest in "handy" bonds secured by pools of FHA-insured and VA- guaranteed loans. These bonds are backed with the "full faith and credit of the United States Government," and marketed to investors worldwide, including Japanese banks and FSLIC/FDIC-insured American institutions.

5. FDIC and FSLIC guarantee depositors in banks and Savings and Loans. These institutions often purchase GNMA securities.

Measuring the FHA, GNMA and FSLIC/FDIC mechanisms' combined impact is beyond the scope of this discussion. Let's just imagine that the combined impact will reduce the effective remaining interest rate from 5.5% to about 5%.

> *Housing finance mechanisms are within our political control, and can be reshaped to serve our will.*

The combined total effect of the housing finance mechanisms mentioned above was to reduce the effective interest rate burden from 10% to about 5%, or a reduction of 50%.

These mechanisms are in our political control, and can be shaped to serve our will. None of these support systems, including the mortgage interest deduction, is cast in stone. We must reshape them as our ecological awareness develops.

The Smiths have an "affordable" home, but can the community afford the "total costs" of pollution, congestion and segregation created as a by-product of the Smiths' "affordable home"? What does this imbalance between jobs and housing cost? These additional costs of air and water pollution, health and social isolation should be added to the 5% housing subsidy before we proclaim "affordability."

The lending institutions and related governmental agencies in the Smith case were efficiently performing the roles society has assigned to them. Do we like the results? These mechanisms were developed to encourage affordability. Restrictions were imposed regarding family income and home sale prices. We can also develop appropriate environmental restrictions that address the jobs/housing balance. As examples of environmental restrictions or incentives, guidelines could be developed that restrict the subsidies provided to the Smiths to:

- Homes located within 1/4 mile of shopping or public transportation.

- Borrowers who work within 10 miles of their home or provide some proof that they use public transport.

- Borrowers who work at home offices, telecommute, or walk to work.

- Other indicators of balance .... what do we want?

The question is, "How can we help the Smiths get a home without polluting the rest of us?" Housing finance institutions must be recruited to assist in implementing a new "jobs/housing balance." These include dozens of types of banking, finance and securities institutions, primary and secondary, both private and public.

> **As agencies develop new incentive programs, builders, borrowers and lenders will respond to environmental goals.**

Business excels at implementing established programs, while government is often best suited to setting social policy. In the housing finance industry, business and government support each other. Government agencies at all levels establish programs and incentives for business. Local lenders and builders conduct their business to utilize the available programs.

As agencies develop new incentive programs, builders, borrowers and lenders will respond to environmental goals. But first, environmentalists and whole systems thinkers need to become actively involved in providing information to the finance community, which will help them to change their lending criteria to stimulate the new jobs/housing and other environmental and social goals.

LENDERS CAN DO CERTAIN JOBS VERY WELL

The costs of disseminating information on loan incentives can be very substantial. Lenders can provide program information and conduct seminars for borrowers, brokers, builders, appraisers, the home buying public and others, because the lenders have the infrastructure of local offices and staff.

Program demonstration costs are great within large agencies and firms. Lenders might subsidize the effort if planned volume can justify their private costs. Patents are unavailable for lending program innovation, but geographically exclusive forward commitments can create sufficient market opportunity to justify their investment.

Lenders will not form the initial impetus for changed lending policies, but they will be able to monitor changed regulations at low cost, underwrite loans against transport and energy considerations, and verify income, first time status, and occupancy, and approve loans for families that qualify. Lenders can also provide monitoring services for the life of the loan.

FNMA has new employee-assisted housing programs that allow the employer to determine where the assisted employee can live. The lender can assist FNMA in administering this and other employer-sponsored initiatives.

Lastly, lenders can arrange construction loans and equity capital for development of marketable projects.

WHAT MOST LENDERS CANNOT DO WELL

Social interest programs must define the incentives to lenders and buyers carefully. We will get what we pay for. Lenders cannot establish progressive social policy, but they can implement the programs once established.

Lenders have a hard time determining when a project is ecologically beneficial. Any definition of relevance may be slippery, and lenders need very well-defined standards. Such standards must be created in a whole systems context by carefully evaluating the

> *An ecological lending movement should take its place alongside the affordable lending movement.*

situation from social, financial and ecological perspectives. For example, policy formulators need to answer questions such as "Is a 1500-square-foot 'affordable' home for a family of two appropriate?"

Secondary markets have standardized high-volume lending. Some variety is possible with mortgage insurance, but non-conforming portfolio loans will be made at higher cost by local thrifts. Many lenders will only make loans to sell.

ECOLOGICAL LENDING: A NEW MOVEMENT

Non-profits over the last 10 years have taken the forefront in affordable home lending. Groups such as the Local Initiative Support Corporation (LISC), the Enterprise Foundation, Habitat for Humanity, the Los Angeles Community Design Center and other community development corporations, SAMCO and CCRC have created new models for others to follow in California.

An ecological lending movement should take its place alongside the affordable lending movement. Eventually these two movements should combine their energies to provide resources and advocate projects that are affordable both for the family and the community.

Initially a non-profit lender can create an ecological lending niche in the following activities:

- Take time with financially marginal (low-origination fees relative to effort) but ecologically significant loans.

- Originate loans of experimental or social funds to allow priority for experimental technologies, small builder access to foster innovation, and, test market incentive programs before mass introduction.

- Provide expert testimony for environmental review of Community Reinvestment Agency (CRA) statements of lenders, CRA hearings at bank merger applications, California-based tax incentive programs combining lending and tax incentives, such as California Housing Finance Agency-funded programs, and, with practice, HUD, VA, FNMA, etc.

- Refer environmentally motivated professionals and interns to job opportunities with lenders as advisors and/or loan officers.

Non-profit groups might develop a California Eco-Lending program as:

- An independent non-profit with initial support from environmental groups and a board combining ecologically-oriented and like-minded lending leaders.

- An existing non-profit, such as a community design center or community development group, with a grant for this specific purpose. Rural Community Assistance Corporation based in Sacramento, and the Los Angeles Community Design Center, are regional groups that serve other focused non-profit groups.

- A lending industry-sponsored group with an environmental focus. The Savings Association Mortgage Company (SAMCO) is owned by 48 S&Ls that participate in affordable home loans. The California Community Reinvestment Corporation is a non-profit mortgage bank formed by 26 banks in 1989 to make loans on affordable housing projects.

- A nationally recognized environmental group with a local office staffed both by paid employees and volunteer experts.

OTHER POTENTIAL AREAS FOR ECO-LENDING

The jobs/housing imbalance in our story is only one example of an issue that can be developed into environmentally responsible lending policies. Still other issues that merit a brief mention as the basis for potential development into eco-lending practices include:

> *The jobs/housing imbalance in our story is only one example of an issue that can be developed into environmentally responsible lending policies.*

- Resource conservation. How can we more effectively recycle, reuse, and limit consumption? Can we create more satisfaction with less material? How can we move our resource consumption closer to global standards? For example, housemoving keeps buildings out of the landfill. How can the high cost of packaging HUD 203k- and CDBG-assisted loans for move-ons be reduced? While rehab lending preserves communities, it also creates gentrification. How should HUD 203k, HUD Title 1 and FNMAs Rehab programs be targeted?

- Create sharing systems within extended families, and between nuclear families, persons, groups, and neighborhoods. Land-sharing innovations such as granny homes, co-ops, cohousing, community land trusts and second units reduce sprawl and the speculation that drives sprawl.

- Produce variety *vs.* large-scale monotony, enable self-design and construction *vs.* programmed design and professional construction, i.e., opportunities for mutual self-help and individually expandable homes.

The California Housing Finance Agency could be allowed to fund self-help housing organizations. The National Housing Agency in England operates a separate self-help housing fund. Wadsworth Partners in the UK manages for-profit self-help housing projects funded by Building Societies. Our S&Ls say self-help lending is too risky, but they invest in junk bonds.

> *Eventually eco-lending divisions of banks, S&Ls, or mortgage bankers will develop as they find sufficient opportunity to support for-profit programs.*

- Protect environmental quality of water, air, trees, etc.

- Help grow whole people and a good society, while avoiding crime, greed, inadequate education, etc. by prioritizing construction programs that help to integrate "at risk youth" into the life of the community.

- Recognize the importance of what buildings do, and let the aesthetic follow.

- Support building of eco-sensitive new towns. HUD Title X created many problems. Rouse's Colombia, MD was a joint venture with two lenders.

- Resolution Trust Corporation (RTC) sale of properties to community groups can provide opportunities for people to invest in their own neighborhoods. This will help ensure that properties are properly maintained and ecologically retrofitted, as neighborhood groups become more aware of eco-retrofitting.

- Energy-conserving home loan underwriting with FHA/FNMA programs for superinsulated homes, as well as homes that use recycled cellulose, passive and active solar energy systems, composting, roof gardens, etc.

- Redevelopment agencies have access to tax revenues that can combine with private capital to redevelop areas. A 20% set-aside for low to moderate income housing is mandated by the law. A 20% eco-set-aside can be developed to projects that actually begin to reverse negative environmental impacts. Publicly funded community redevelopment agency projects can become models for public eco-developers in our cities.

- Tax-exempt mortgage revenue bonds and mortgage credit certificate programs are the main federally-sponsored single-family housing subsidy delivery programs. The income credit could be supplemented with a community credit or a fossil-fueled car credit. The sales price credit could be supplemented with a pollution reduction credit.

Eventually eco-lending divisions of banks, S&Ls, or mortgage bankers will develop as they find sufficient opportunity to support for-profit programs. Following the necessary interim phenomena of "Eco-Lending" divisions, eco-lending will become so mainstream that no special distinction will be needed!

THE HUMAN COMPONENT — CITIZEN PLANNER INTERFACE

CHANGING POLICY TO MAKE WAY FOR ECO-CITIES

David Mogavero

THE ENVIRONMENTAL COUNCIL OF SACRAMENTO

I n the Sacramento area, we have been successfully articulating a vision for our future. Even more important, we have had success in transmitting this vision to public officials and developers so that a perceptible change in the overall city design process has occurred. I believe that beyond the specifics of our particular locale, there is a basic process we have employed which will stand citizens in other urban areas in good stead.

At the heart of our activities is a loose organization called the Environmental Council of Sacramento. When I first became its President, I wanted to tighten it up, but after a while I began to understand why it worked loosely very well. It's about 17 years old and dates back to when the State mandated that communities do general plans. It has sometimes been casual and at other times aggressive — it's ebbed and flowed in terms of what it's accomplished.

As President of the Environmental Council of Sacramento, David Mogavero has led the structuring of the Sacramento County General Plan Update around pedestrian and transit-oriented mixed-use development. He is the principal of Mogavero Associates Architects, which has had an emphasis on in-fill housing and the design of several midtown "institutions".

Mogavero, Notestine Associates
2229 J Street
Sacramento, CA 95816
(916) 443-1033

Until the past few years it was a coalition organization only. It was composed of the local chapters of the Lung Association, the Audubon Society, and the Sierra Club, as well as a bunch of neighborhood associations (which is the way I became involved) and local environmental groups that focused on specific parks or creeks or open space amenities. Now we have some housing advocates in it, and we're also in the process of pulling in the Social Service Planning Council, the organization which is responsible for coordinating all of the social services in the region.

We restructured the Environmental Council so it could be not only a coalition organization but also a membership organization, which would attract more individual volunteers because, naturally, the coalition members had primary responsibilities with their group of origin. Now we have some at-large positions on the Board, and an opportunity to reward people with nominations to these positions when they're doing good work at the committee level.

BEER-AND-PIZZA PLANNING

One of our strategies has been that when there is a major project, we will actually prepare our own plan. We call these our "beer-and-pizza plans". Under the CEQA law, there are circumstances where the municipality is required to incorporate citizen-based alternatives in the EIR; but that's not always clear due to various legal aspects. However, we pulled a bunch of architects and planners together — sometimes just for one night — and we would sit down at 5 p.m., get a couple of 6-packs, and crank out a concept of how that project should be developed.

In fact, one of these plans actually turned into the Laguna Creek project that ended up being a commission for Peter Calthorpe. The old master plan was for a 5000-acre development of all single-family homes. We didn't get everything we wanted, but we got everything on one side of Laguna Creek dedicated to open space over the long term; and we got the concept of "Village-Oriented" development incorporated for a major component of the plan.

To make this happen, we did a lot of research all over the country. There were no Pedestrian Pockets. Duany and Plater-Zyberk had done Seaside, and that's all there was at that particular time. We drafted a very simple eight-page document,, and it clearly articulated a vision simplified to four or five basic principles. Amazingly, we didn't end up going under the heads of the professionals, the policy people, the people that are supposed to be more sophisticated, although we really targeted lay people in terms of our projection of the basic concept.

Most importantly, this particular plan was a precursor to our entré to the general plan process — we went in to prime the pump with the Board of Supervisors with this plan, which was to say, "We want you to not only consider this at the 'micro' level, but we also want it to be considered in the general plan at the 'macro' level" — and, we won! The end product is a general plan which is now in the environmental review process that is, in my opinion, a monument to planning in the United States. Peter was hired to develop the design guidelines for the plan,

> **In my opinion, the Sacramento general plan is a monument to planning in the United States.**

and the general plan staff wrote the plan themselves. This has been a significant victory for us in Sacramento, and has really made the going much easier in many other communities in the Metropolitan Area.

DEVELOPING CLOUT

So, why do we have clout? Well, I think the litigation has a lot to do with that. There have been times when we've been willing to go to the wall, empty that bank account, and work out pro-bono deals with attorneys. CEQA law does not say that a governmental body has to "do the right thing" — it just says they have to tell everybody about how bad a project is. So I think what we've accomplished through litigation on that level has been marginal.

But litigation has been powerful in conveying to the development community that, if necessary, we're willing to put it all on the line and hold them up for two or three years or whatever; and it costs them money. The other reason we're effective is that our resource base in Sacramento is very professional — we have many environmentally knowledgeable State workers, particularly in the Resource Departments, so we usually come forward with a well-documented, well-thought-out, well-organized analysis filled with the latest thinking.

Some of the specific actions we took, which I believe are necessary to succeed in making the community's voice have actual impact on the overall process, include:

1. Working hand in hand with Planning Staff. Develop a good relationship with Planning Staff. Get in there every week. Talk to them, bug them, drive them crazy, and make them your friend. Take them to lunch like the developers do.

2. Working directly with receptive developers to obtain implemented examples as soon as possible. And this may involve compromises. A lot of people are poo-pooing Laguna Creek right now, because it doesn't encompass a broad enough vision of the Eco-City. And we recognize that, but it was a knowing compromise on our part. We actually went to Phil Angelitus, who was a young liberal Democrat friend of ours. He had taken over the resources of this development company, and Phil asked us, "What do I have to do to keep you off of my back during the approval process?" So we told him. We wrote a little five-page paper describing what Laguna Creek should look like and, by the way, we told him, you should probably hire a professional from this list (which included Peter Calthorpe), to get somebody to help you make it more concrete.

So we ended up going arm in arm into the county, and together rolled over every ounce of opposition that the Public Works staff had. There was a compromise to it, but we needed a practical real victory, so that the development community would stop saying, "Oh no, this isn't practical." And it worked. And I think that the Laguna example has been the seed that has nurtured this new sort of development in the real estate community, all through the western United States.

3. Working with the second-tier policy planning people. We sponsored a variety of different forums that were focused on different constituencies in the community that participate in the planning process. We started out with the second-tier planners, because they were the ones who were providing most of the feedback to the supervisors for the General Plan process, and that included people who sit on the neighborhood Planning Advisory Councils that advise the Board of Supervisors. So we took them through the process of conceiving how pedestrian-oriented development would be applied in various kinds of existing neighborhoods, and various kinds of undeveloped areas.

We did another kind of forum for developers, where we brought five in-fill developers from around the country to Sacramento. We charged the development community $150. We had almost all of them there that day. And we had them listen to other developers there talk about how they are making money doing in-fill development. You have to show people how they are going to make money doing this stuff, or forget it! The essence of life is ending your day with a little left over for yourself every single day.

4. Working directly with elected officials.

5. We created a forum for architects, engineers and planners, where we let the technicians who implement these things get their hands into it, and actually help us write a document about how some of the principles might be applied in Sacramento County. A few of the ideas left something to be desired, but others were great. Many germs of wisdom came out of that process.

It's often the young architects and planners charged with lots of idealism and altruism who are primed to contribute, because they are stuck in these funky offices doing work they don't necessarily believe in. Architecture and Planning is about hope, and people going into these professions are hopeful, and they want to do things that validate their hopefulness. So tap into that by going to the local AIA chapter or the associates group within the AIA or APA chapters. It's a matter of taking a few weekends and putting together your own concept and getting it into the CEQA process.

> *Architecture and planning is about hope . . .*

In general, what has been powerful for us is getting out there ahead of the public process, and being pro-active instead of just being heel-nippers. We planted the banner in the ground and raised it up in the air, and started heading in a direction. You can do this too.

Articulate a vision that's simple enough so that a lot of people can participate in it and appreciate it. There are enough information and resources out in the community, so it's just a matter of getting those organized and getting pro-active. We are all heroes. If we get out there and do everything that we can on every level, we can succeed.

PARTNERSHIPS FOR SUCCESS

Jane Blumenfeld

This city is a built-out place. It is a maturing city, and so we have to address the problems we have now by working with the existing infrastructure. We are not going to build more roads. Population growth will continue. Resource and fiscal constraints will continue. So, balancing priorities is increasingly important, and that is why creating consensus and ecologically sound development are receiving greater attention as time goes on.

By examining different ways of building consensus and involving communities, it can be seen how various ways and attitudes towards development can produce quite different results. I will take four case studies of projects, which people from L.A. are probably familiar with, and compare the way each of them was done, looking at the process of arriving at a plan for development. Some of these are almost mini-cities, and one of them is a smaller project.

From a regulatory point of view, there are lots of ways to plan a major project, and there are lots of ways to approach the processes you have to go through in the City. I believe that good development will also be good business. If the project is well-thought-out, if it's conceived of as part of a community and as an asset to a community, then, even if it costs more to plan and build, ultimately it's going to be better for the community and also for the developer. You will see this in the four projects I am going to discuss: Porter Ranch, Central City West, Farmer's Market, and a little bit about Playa Vista.

THE PORTER RANCH PLAN

Porter Ranch comprises 1,300 acres in the western San Fernando Valley at the edge of the City. The property is a large vacant piece of land owned by a single individual. The Porter Ranch Plan is the City's first attempt to engage in a public-private partnership for a large-scale planning effort. The private and public sector joined forces here to do what up until that time had been done only by the public sector, namely, the Planning Department.

Public-private partnerships are not inherently good or bad. They can be achieved in many different ways. I want to describe how this one was structured, and how the public was involved, and how this affected the final product.

The Porter Ranch developers agreed to fund the Planning Department for the staff, the consultants, and the equipment to prepare a specific plan for the 1,300-acre site. Without this funding arrangement, the plan still would have been created, but the Department might not have assigned staff to it for months or years, depending on the priorities of the Department's overall work program. So this was a way to pay for the needed extra staff so that they could begin sooner. This in itself was not a problem. The problems began when the details of this public-private arrangement were structured.

As the Planning Advisor to Los Angeles' Mayor Tom Bradley, Jane Blumenfeld is responsible for tracking major development projects and developing land use policy for the City of Los Angeles. She spent 11 years as a planner for the City. Her particular interest is formulating policy that effectively channels growth, such as the development of mixed-use projects and the integration of land use, transportation and environmental planning.

Office of the Mayor
Room M1
200 North Spring Street
Los Angeles, CA 90012
(213) 485-6301

In discussions with the City Council and the Planning Department, it was agreed that the developer would put an amount of money into a special account to pay for the staff and equipment. The fund was controlled exclusively by the developers. They decided how it was spent; they signed all the checks for the expenditures. As a result, the types of consultants who were assigned to plan this mini-city were decided on by the developers. The developers also selected the specific consultants to be hired, and wrote their paychecks. A majority of the consultants who ended up being picked to design this project were engineers, although there were also economists, transportation consultants and architects.

Another problem that arose as a result of this arrangement was that the developer had a plan for this project before he even began this process. In fact, his entire stated motivation for the process was to write an ordinance legitimizing his intentions, since the plan he had drawn up was not allowed under the existing rules. So, the process that was decided upon to carry this out was the Council appointing a citizens' advisory committee which had monthly meetings run by the developers and their consultants. This was a process of very limited involvement by the broader community. No real alternatives were explored, only minor differentiations within a very small range of possibilities.

For example, at the first meeting, the developers came to this community group with a plan. At the second meeting, they had a full-scale model. So, not unexpectedly, the plan that emerged from the 15-month process was almost exactly the plan that the developers had originally conceived of before the public process had even begun.

A specific point of controversy was the design of the Porter Ranch regional center, which is to be a mall that is very discrete and segregated from everything else in the project. People in a residential section located only a few feet from the mall will have no way to get there because of the curvy streets, and walls that will be constructed in order to segregate uses and further impede pedestrian access. The large mall is to be near the freeway, apartments and less expensive houses near the mall, and the big, expensive houses up on the hills above. Just as in so many other old-style suburban sprawl developments, all the streets will feed into a main road, and everybody will have to travel by car to get to this mall, because there won't be a single store within walking distance of any of the 3,400 houses that are going to be part of the entire project. And this is in the 1990s that we are planning something like this!

> *... it could have been a much better plan. The community was viewed as an afterthought and a hurdle to overcome.*

So this model of public-private partnership was not too successful, if one of the criteria for success is the relative satisfaction of the public. There was a large constituency of very unhappy residents, and this project became the main issue in the local election.

My personal view of Porter Ranch was that it could have been a much better plan. The community was viewed as an afterthought and a hurdle to overcome. They weren't viewed as if they had anything constructive to offer. I believe that much of the opposition that ensued there could have been eliminated by a very different approach. Why were the people saying that they wanted nothing out there? What were they really saying? What aspects of the western San Fernando Valley did they want to preserve? What types of development would have worked on this land? None of these questions was meaningfully explored throughout this entire process. The result was a plan that resembles development plans characteristic of the 1950s and 1960s.

PLAYA VISTA

Now I will turn to Playa Vista, because there are so many striking similarities with respect to size and location, and the controversial nature of the issues surrounding the two projects. Yet they were done and approached in vastly different ways. Playa Vista is a 1,000-acre site located in Westchester and, like Porter Ranch, controversial because of its location in a community that has historically opposed plans for development on this land. The issues also are similar: traffic, growth, too much commercial development. Yet the approach being taken by these developers is completely different than what happened at Porter Ranch.

> *. . . the developers spent almost a year holding day long workshops and evening meetings with the community.*

With Playa Vista, after purchasing the property from the Summa Corporation, the developers spent almost a year holding day-long workshops and evening meetings with all segments of the community. They made hundreds of phone calls, and spent hours of time with residents all over Westchester, Venice and Marina del Rey to elicit their thoughts on the area, find out what issues were important to the residents, find out what characterized the way of life in this part of town, what people wanted to preserve. Although Maguire Thomas undoubtedly had ideas for the development of this land before they started this process, they did not even begin putting pen to paper until they had spent a number of months talking to people throughout the community, and unlike the developers of Porter Ranch, they had no preconceived plan. They viewed the input of the community as an integral part of the development of the plan itself.

The ideas of Playa Vista's planners always appeared to be fluid and subject to change, evolution and improvement. There has been a sense of cooperation and respect for other people's ideas throughout the development of the plan. Another striking difference that has resulted from this approach to the project is the types of consultants that were chosen. By listening to issues and concerns raised by the community, and by trying to create a project that actually becomes an asset to this existing community, these developers didn't select engineers to design the project, as they did in Porter Ranch. They had urban designers, site planners, town planners (Andres Duany was one of the consultants), and landscape architects planning the development. This kind of expertise created an entirely different set of alternatives from what we found in Porter Ranch. Here, uses are being mixed throughout the project. All different types and costs of housing are being integrated. Open spaces are being designed so that people will use them. Small commercial uses that people need to access on a daily basis are within walking distance of everybody, mitigating the need for massive numbers of cars forced onto a single street for every conceivable errand. The whole plan reflects a completely different approach to planning.

Without prejudging the results of the plan that will ultimately emerge, I can say that I have seen the community move in large part from a stance of very vocal opposition before Maguire Thomas became involved, to one of participation and cooperation. This is not to say that everybody thinks this is a perfect plan, but from a process point of view, there are substantially better benefits to both the community and to the developer than in the Porter Ranch project.

CENTRAL CITY WEST

Central City West is a 465-acre site in downtown Los Angeles, just to the west of the Harbor Freeway.

This plan was designed to integrate land use, transportation and housing, and ultimately to allow for 25 million square feet of development in Central City West. Here, the property was owned by a number of property owners who got together and approached the City with a proposal to engage in a public-private partnership to prepare a plan for their land, not unlike the initial approach of the Porter Ranch developer. However, the structure for this partnership was a very different model. At the outset, before anything was done at all, a rigidly structured steering committee was set up, composed of five members: the Departments of Planning, Transportation, the two City Council Offices, and one representative of the Central City West property owners.

This committee was responsible for all the policy decisions concerning the plan: what it should contain, its direction, and the urban design. Everything was decided jointly, with all parties having an equal voice. Central City West property owners never controlled this project. The steering committee selected the consultants, not the developer, as in Porter Ranch. The steering committee approved every work task before a check was written to a consultant. The developers did not control the money. The decision-making was not done by the developers and the planning staff, as in Porter Ranch, but entirely by the steering committee. During the development of this plan, many workshops were held with the community. The Temple-Beaudry Neighbors, which was the organized neighborhood group representing the most significant intact neighborhood in that area, articulated their views to the consultants, to Councilwoman Molina and to the Planning Department. They were seen as a part of the existing community, and as a part of the new community that would ultimately be built as part of this plan.

> *Consensus building in this plan involved not only the community, but also a myriad of City and State departments ...*

Consensus building in this plan involved not only the community, but also a myriad of City and State departments and agencies that would ultimately be required to approve this plan. The steering committee structure kept everybody on an equal footing. It assured that all the information being developed by consultants was shared, and that all parties agreed to each step in developing the plan. Nothing went forward without consensus about the previous issues and work tasks.

The structure and process of the Central City West Plan also proved to be extremely successful. The residents of Temple-Beaudry, who were vocally opposed to this plan at the outset and had hired a Legal Aid attorney to help them prepare a legal challenge, ended up coming to the hearings to support the plan. In fact, by the conclusion of the process, there was very little opposition at all to the plan. All the City Departments ended up supporting the plan (which doesn't happen all the time either), and the City Council Office supported the plan. The developers and the property owners in Central City West spent a lot of money on consultants in the planning process, and obligated themselves to pay for expensive infrastructure improvements in the future, including $530 million for transportation improvements, all to be paid by the property owners. Some of the transportation improvements will include extending the Harbor Transit Way being constructed south of downtown, major street widenings, and new freeway on-ramps onto the Harbor Freeway. Additionally, they obligated themselves to build an incredible amount of housing: about 18,000 units, of which a large portion will be for very low-income families.

So, essentially, the owners of property in Central City West traded this cost for a degree of certainty about what they could do in the future. This became a win-win experience for everyone: the City, the community and the property owners.

THE FARMER'S MARKET

The final model, a completely different approach, is the charette process created to look at the Beverly Fairfax community and the Farmer's Market project. This is a proposed project to be built on the parking lot and the other land adjacent to and surrounding the existing Farmer's Market. Here, the owner of the land who is an heir of the Gilmore family — the original owners of the Market — wanted to build a two-million-square-foot mall, a hotel and office complex, all around the Market. At the time, there were several other very large projects being proposed within walking distance of the Farmer's Market, including 2,200 new housing units at Park La Brea, the May Company's proposal to replace its store with two office buildings and a 500-room hotel, the Cedars Sinai proposal of 700,000 square feet of new office space, and the Craft and Folk Art Museum's proposal of a mixed-use project to include a new museum, office space and 66 condos in a 20-story or more building.

All of this was being proposed for one of the densest areas of the City, and an area where over 30% of the population are seniors.

The question here was: how can you evaluate a plan for the Farmer's Market without looking at it together with all these other projects? How will they all work together, or will they? What will all of them together do to this very fragile neighborhood?

Well, the City has no real process for looking at multiple projects in this manner. We have an EIR process, which identifies "related projects" and lists the proposed transportation improvements of each. And we have hearings that are held separately for each individual project. But we have no process for looking at them together.

So the Mayor and the AIA put together an intensive, four-day workshop with a team of highly-qualified professionals to tackle this issue. We worked with the staffs of Councilmen Ferraro, Holden and Yaroslavsky, and others in identifying the issues and all the key people that needed to be involved. We put together an eleven-member team of experts in the fields of planning, architecture, urban design, transportation, gerontology, housing and development. We also had a support team with more specialized expertise in geology, landscape architecture, historic preservation, the Jewish community, and retail development. Nobody on the team had any vested interest in this community, and all of them worked for four days and nights for free.

> *Nobody on the team had any vested interest in this community, and all of them worked for four days and nights for free.*

The team interviewed over 200 people who have some interest in the community, including residents, community groups, social service providers, merchants, property owners, elected officials, school principals, and representatives from the social, cultural and religious organizations throughout the area. There was a great deal of publicity, and an intensive effort to contact a wide range of people interested in this community from all different perspectives.

By the end of the workshop, the team had developed a number of recommendations about the community, and some of the specific projects. A document was produced at the end of the workshop, and made available to the public within a few days.

The Farmer's Market project was going through the city hearings at the same time that the workshop team recommended that in the context of the community, the site was more appropriate as a dense housing location, rather than as a mall. Although a commercial project was ultimately approved, the type of commercial project and the scale changed drastically, and no legal challenge was filed. Some of the logic of the workshop was reflected in the final proposal — a series of retail stores open to the sky, reflecting the character of the historic Farmer's Market.

While the workshop team's recommendations did not result in a residential project, some positives did come out of this experience. The level of involvement of everybody in the community made people feel that they were more a part of the process. They were truly listened to, and they could see their input in the results of the workshop, and in the thinking behind the workshop team's recommendations. This is a step in the right direction, although there is still room for improved communication and interaction. If the shopping plaza had been redesigned with a mixed-use overlay which included some of the higher-density housing reflected in the results of the workshop, this would have been an even more satisfactory resolution to the dialog. But the fact that the interaction took place at all is something that all parties involved can be proud of.

Now we need to seek the next level of interaction, in which developers can enter into an even greater level of partnership with the communities where their projects are planned. Certainly one of the cornerstones to such a relationship is consulting with all parties involved, at an early enough point in the project so that reshaping does not mean undoing a large amount of completed work. If developers can come to the table without feeling they may lose a lot of money, time and energy already invested in drawing up a given set of plans, it will be easier for them to approach the process with a more flexible frame of mind.

We are still in the early stages of a learning curve that will result in developers, government and citizens being able to follow a well-mapped path toward a more consensual process. What is clear from the examples I have cited, is that spending the time at the front-end of the planning cycle to incorporate the input of all parties concerned, is a lot more positive and fruitful than having a project slowed and even permanently stopped by legal action at the tail-end.

CHANGING THE RULES OF THE GAME

THE PEDESTRIAN BILL OF RIGHTS

Michael Woo

Michael Woo is one of only two trained urban planners to serve on the Los Angeles City Council. Since his 1985 first election to the Council, his environmentally conscious agenda has included preventing hillside overdevelopment, preserving scenic Fryman Canyon, reforming urban forest policy, crusading on behalf of pedestrian rights, and an ongoing effort to redevelop Hollywood's blighted areas on a more sustainable basis.

*Councilman Michael Woo
City Hall, Room 23
200 North Spring Street
Los Angeles, CA 90012
(213) 485-3353*

Following is a summary of ten motions known as the Pedestrian Bill of Rights. Sponsored by Los Angeles City Councilman Michael Woo, these rights are in various stages of planning and implementation by appropriate City Departments. The full text of the motions can be obtained from Councilman Woo's Office, City Hall, Room 239, 200 North Spring St., Los Angeles, CA 90012, (213) 485-3353.

1 - Statement of Rights. The people of Los Angeles have the right to:
- Safe roads and safe places to cross streets.
- Pedestrian-oriented building facades.
- Pedestrian amenities located on streets, such as trees, flower stands, trash cans, awnings, etc.
- Safe and comfortable bus stops and public transit stations.
- Appealing use of landscaping and available open space.
- Full notification of all street widening that impinges on public open space and sidewalks.
- Access to streets and buildings for disabled people.
- Clean surroundings, including removal of graffiti and advertisements from public property.
- As much consideration of the needs of pedestrians as drivers currently receive.
- Public works of art.

2 - Save the Crosswalks. Throughout the city, neighborhood residents are outraged when a crosswalk is painted out or paved over by the Department of Transportation (DOT). DOT policy is based on reports that suggest crosswalks give pedestrians a "false sense of security." This motion requires that in all future cases, when the DOT plans not to repaint a crosswalk after it has been paved or painted over, City Council approval is needed. DOT shall submit to the Council, on a case-by-case analysis, facts explaining why a crosswalk is unsafe or unneeded. This motion also calls for the length of crossing lights, diagonal crosswalks, and crosswalks near freeway entrances, to be carefully evaluated.

3 - Increase the Number of Street Vendors and Sidewalk Cafes in the City. Tough Health and Building and Safety regulations currently make it nearly impossible for street vendors and owners of sidewalk cafes to get operation permits. This motion requires the City of L.A. to recommend ways the City can relax regulations, thereby encouraging street vendors and sidewalk cafes.

4 - Promote New Development That Encourages People to Live Near Their Work Places. Direct the Planning Department to develop incentives for pedestrian-oriented residential/mixed-use development that discourages the use of automobiles. Other City departments, including the Department of Transportation, Building and Safety, and Public Works, will be asked to carefully analyze current procedures, with the view toward recommending ways to encourage pedestrian centers of activity.

5 - Double the Fines for Littering on Sidewalks.

6 - Create the Position of Advocate for Pedestrians. Because pedestrian needs should be an integral part of the approval process for any new development project, the City needs a "pedestrian advocate." This staff person within the Planning Department would be required to monitor community reaction as to how a development project will impact a community. The advocate will pay special attention to issues such as street widening, which results in narrower sidewalks.

7 - Expand Auto-Free Zones Around the City. The auto-free area in Westwood on weekend nights is a popular and effective way for the City to make an area more pedestrian-friendly. Other areas of the City may benefit from a similar arrangement. The DOT and Planning Department should prepare a feasibility study for the City Council on how auto-free zones might be expanded to other parts of the City.

9 - Educate the Public About Pedestrians' Rights. Drivers and pedestrians alike show a general disregard for the "rules of the road." Jaywalking by pedestrians and illegal left turns by drivers are common occurrences. The Los Angeles Police Department and DOT shall develop a public information plan to help educate drivers and pedestrians.

10 - Create More Open Space. The Planning Department shall prepare a report, with recommendations on how to encourage builders to incorporate open space areas into development projects.

This set of motions is offered here, inviting suggestions for your City to adopt, if the pedestrian is becoming an endangered species in a car-oriented domain.

ENVIRONMENTAL REGULATIONS

Dick Russell

*Dick Russell is an environmental writer whose work has appeared in numerous national magazines, including **Amicus Journal**, **The Nation**, "E" **The Environmental Magazine** and **In These Times**. He has also been the Environmental Coordinator for Fort Hill Construction Company, a major remodeling firm in the Los Angeles area.*

Fort Hill Construction
8118 Hollywood Boulevard
Los Angeles, CA 90069
(213) 656-7425

Dick Russell
(617) 445-4426

I started working with the Fort Hill Construction Co. in L.A. as environmental coordinator in September 1990. Besides Fort Hill's own concern about the environment, another reason why I started doing research into more sustainable building products was the strong concern expressed by several of our clients. Little by little we've started incorporating new products like Air-Crete insulation. Air-Crete contains no fiberglass or other toxins, but unfortunately, at the moment, Air-Crete is a good deal more expensive than conventional fiberglass insulation, and so it's mainly used by high-end clients, because the great majority of us haven't begun looking past the price tag, to all the environmentally-sound reasons for using it. This is true of many other new products and, of course, it's going to take greater demand to start bringing the costs down. Besides heightened public awareness, part of this demand will be created by tighter regulations.

WASTE MANAGEMENT

Let's consider the situation surrounding job-site waste in Los Angeles. With all the talk about our landfills reaching capacity and the need for recycling, there has been very little consideration given here so far to what is known as C&D, construction and demolition debris. A sizable part of the waste stream is taken up by C&D. There has been no study done in the L.A. area that I know of, but a 1986 report done for the EPA by Franklin Associates estimated that construction and demolition waste comprised almost one-quarter of the municipal solid-waste stream in the United States. A task force in New Jersey estimated it at 32%, and I would imagine that figure might be similar for L.A. Now the fact is, a tremendous amount of C&D waste is recyclable. We're talking about bricks, concrete, wood, drywall, plaster, roofing shingles, etc.

When I started looking into ways that we could better deal with our job-waste situation, I was surprised to find so few options available. There were a few places that our hauler would take clean loads of old wood to be used in co-generation. The organization Tree People was anxious for used lumber, and one of our employees took other materials down to Mexico, where they could be put to good use. But there were no provisions by private companies or incentives from the City to do more than that. Now a big reason for this, I was told, was the incredibly low tipping fee charged at Los Angeles landfills, which is about $17 a ton. Compare that to $100 a ton, say, in New York City. The fact is, it just isn't yet cost-effective to separate out recyclables in places where people don't have a clear economic reason for doing so. In Seattle, by contrast, the City offers haulers a 22% discount off a $62-per-ton disposal fee, and so promotes source separation of things like clean, nonpainted, nontreated wood.

We did successfully encourage our hauler to open up a whole new transfer station just for construction and demolition waste, and he is in the process of acquiring the land for it. Another encouraging sign is recent legislation by the State of California, which requires the Department of Transportation to review and modify its bid specifications for road-base materials, to include the use of recycled materials. What needs to happen is a major increase in the landfill tipping fees. This would then force haulers to promote job-site recycling by convincing contractors to use separate dumpsters for wood waste. Also, if old buildings are dismantled instead of being bulldozed, the amount of recyclable lumber will increase dramatically.

There is also another opportunity here. As you probably know, a number of companies are already involved in making and selling various recycling containers. Most of them, in my opinion, are little more than overpriced plastic boxes. An excellent entrepreneurial opportunity exists here for someone to develop a good and space-effective system of divided dumpsters for job sites. Maybe the city could embark on an informational and educational program of some kind for builders and developers. Construction and demolition debris is an overlooked nationwide problem. When the EPA started its new recycling data base a few years back and typed in the words C&D, it came up with only one citation from among 6,000 entries. This has got to change, and it's one way that the building industry could make a difference.

CFCs are a very different and dangerous kind of waste. At one point in our work, at a huge project in Bel Air, we ran into a massive number of old refrigeration units that had to be removed. If we had just torn them out, we would have released a substantial quantity of CFCs into the atmosphere and contributed to still more destruction of the ozone layer. So I started calling around, looking for a company that could come out and reclaim and recycle the Freon. Finding someone with this capability was almost impossible. Finally, I hooked up

> *. . . the city could embark on an informational and educational program of some kind for builders and developers.*

with a fellow named C. J. from the Kimmel-Motz Refrigeration Corporation in Los Angeles, and he said they were the only company they knew of in Southern California that could do this. They came out to the job site, and for $100 an hour with a 3-hour minimum recaptured the Freon.

At the time, I wasn't even aware that there is a new regulation on the books from the Air Quality Management District that, starting the second quarter of 1991, "requires recovery or recycling equipment during industrial or commercial refrigerator or air-conditioner servicing or dismantling to reduce CFC emissions". That's all well and good, but what I'd like to know is, who's going to do it? I also mention this because there is a tremendous entrepreneurial opportunity here for somebody, and because there is little communication about such a vitally important regulation.

When it comes to the residential sector, with all the remodeling going on in Los Angeles, why isn't there a push to open an appliance recycling center, like those now operating in Minneapolis, Minnesota, Milwaukee, Wisconsin and Jacksonville, Florida? Right now used household appliances are simply being discarded. Older models are full of PCBs, and they're venting all the CFCs into the atmosphere. It's crazy, but this is still the case. It seems to me that practical ways of dealing with such problems today are often overlooked, while everybody talks about phasing out CFCs and coming up with substitutes by the end of the century. The fact is, CFCs aren't going to just go away, so we've got to do something about the CFCs already in our homes, automobile refrigeration and air-conditioning systems.

AIR QUALITY

I would like to discuss a little more about the regulations of the Air Quality Management District (AQMD). I should preface my criticisms by saying that I believe AQMD is far ahead of most of the country when it comes to trying to do something about air quality. I spent a lot of time with the director, Jim Lentz, a couple of years ago while doing a story, and I came away very impressed with his visionary approach. But I'm afraid there's a big gap between goals and practical realities, at least when it comes to the building trades. The other day I was talking with our wood finisher about the problems he faces. Here's a man who is very concerned about the environment, but whose work requires that he handle sprays and coatings and so on. Unfortunately, most of the new less-toxic materials that he has tested so far just aren't sufficiently durable. He certainly doesn't want to add to the air-pollution problem of our City. But he has ended up very confused by the conflicting opinions of various inspectors and by the regulations themselves.

The AQMD needs to vastly simplify the definitions of their rulings, to make them comprehensible to the people who have to work with these materials every day. Clarity is certainly lacking in interpretations of the regulations. Here are a few examples of the dilemmas I'm talking about: The currently approved spray gun gives off far more overspray, according to our finisher, than another gun in his shop that is not approved. He can't help thinking that

> *The AQMD needs to simplify the definitions of their rulings, to make them comprehensible to the people who have to work with these materials every day.*

politics are involved in what's legal and what isn't. Or consider this: The fire department will walk into a shop and say you can't spray outside, because you need a booth. But the AQMD inspector comes along and says it's okay to spray outside, as long as it's not more than one gallon a day.

Such mixed messages can go to absurd lengths. The AQMD a while back came to our shop foreman, and said that all the rags should be placed in a closed container. The trouble with this is it causes spontaneous combustion! So when the foreman informed the next inspector that complying with this regulation might burn down the shop, he was told to "talk to the fire department". In order to comply with new regulations on volatile organic compounds, or VOCs, paint companies in California are now making their paints thicker, and because they're more concentrated, charging you more for them. But then you must use some kind of thinner, which in turn raises the VOC content back up again. What the AQMD recommends is trichlorethylene (TCE), which is low in VOC content but is also very high in other toxics, which may not adversely affect air quality, but certainly is bad for workers' long-term health. Besides, TCE doesn't work. It won't mix properly with the lacquer. An answer to this particular problem may be provided by Glidden Paint which is starting to produce a water-based paint that is VOC-free.

Clearly, somebody ought to be thinking about these problems in more concrete ways. The technical department at AQMD ought to be working closely with the alternative products companies that are already based here in California, in order to come up with improvements in their product lines that will really do a first-class job. Here's a suggestion. You've got all these new domestic and European paints, varnishes, adhesives, sealers, and so on. But there has been little official testing done on these products. No data base developed. A painter or a wood finisher wants to know how these products are going to hold up, how long they'll last. The resource guide that's being developed by the American Institute of Architects is terrific, but it's going to take a long time to be completed. So why couldn't an agency like AQMD, or some other public agency, or a consortium of agencies, come up with funds that can be used by the people working with these materials regularly, in order to collect some field data on the performance of these new materials? There seems to be a real communication problem here. The word is not getting out in a cohesive fashion to the people who need to hear it, and the various regulatory agencies are not really talking to one another.

I was stunned to hear Arthur Jokela, whose specialty for many years has been water resource management, describe to me how attempts to clean up our air by a narrow, single-purpose approach can end up damaging our water quality, and vice versa. He said, consider long-term global warming and the drought. If you don't water the landscape, you will have less moisture in the atmosphere, and you create a net urban-warming effect. According to the Lawrence Berkeley lab, reducing evapotranspiration is responsible for about 30% of our air pollution because of the reaction rate of chemicals. Arthur's point is that if you regulate water to the point where you can't recycle it, which the health department has been doing, you end up with a constraint where graywater can't get back into the atmosphere, and you have a negative closed-loop of irreducible problems that impact each other indefinitely. In short, we should ease up on restrictive regulations on water recycling, so we can get more water into the atmosphere. Although graywater codes are starting to become more prevalent, this does point up a key problem: We have become so specialized that often one discipline does not consult with another area of specialization, because they don't realize both are working on different facets of the same problem. Until the air quality regulators start really communicating with the water quality and the health regulators, we're going to continue to see increasingly serious problems evolve out of all these well-meaning efforts.

These issues need to be discussed both in technological terms, and in terms of the consciousness adjustments that people have to make. Along with all this we need to discuss the critical need for greater communication among various environmental organizations, researchers, developers, builders, city planners, and government agencies. If we don't work on this as if we're all in it together, which we are, nothing on the scale that's needed is going to get accomplished.

A CONSOLIDATED APPROACH TO AIR QUALITY IMPROVEMENT

Cindy Simovich Greenwald

Cindy Simovich Greenwald is Director of Air Quality, L.A. Environmental Affairs Department. She is a committed spokesperson for mixed use, pedestrian-oriented development as a critical element in our clean air strategy. Cindy received her J.D. from USC, and worked in the legal division of South Coast Air Quality Management District before joining the E.A.D.

Environmental Affairs Dept.
200 North Main Street
MS 177
Los Angeles, CA 90012
(213) 485-9961

T he air quality challenges of today require wide-ranging regional solutions, as well as multiple "low-tech" program applications. Gone are the days of expensive source-specific controls that would remedy all the ills of past practice. It is time to recognize that it is not just our past failings which are responsible for our current problems, but our present practices, which must change, if we are ever to achieve clean air in an area such as Southern California.

The Draft South Coast Air Quality Management Plan (AQMP) illustrates how extensive and multi-dimensional the problem is. Attainment of the ambient air quality standards will require 80% to 90% reduction from the current allowable emissions. But that current baseline already represents a 90% reduction from the uncontrolled emission level. So, what is required to attain these standards amounts to a 90% reduction in the remaining 10% of emissions. The smaller the increment of remaining emissions, the more costly the control becomes.

Gone are the days of the quick-fix where you could slap on a piece of high technology equipment to control emissions from the large factory or stationary source. Simply controlling the "large stationary sources" is no longer the answer. Stationary sources are estimated to contribute roughly 40% of total current emissions, with the remaining 60% coming from mobile sources. In other words, we could close down every refinery, manufacturing plant, painting operation, dry cleaner or other stationary source in the Basin, whether large or small, and we would still not come close to attaining the ambient standard.

Similarly, we could ban the use of mobile sources, never use a car or truck again in the South Coast Basin, and still be in violation of the State and Federal air quality standards. The answer is clear; control must come from all sources: mobile, stationary, commercial and residential alike. Integrated control of all source types is essential if we are ever to have clean, healthy air in this Basin.

We are moving into a new era, where personal transportation choices are no longer sacrosanct. Changing air quality requires changing behavior at the individual level. Change does not necessarily mean sacrifice. We currently view these changes as a sacrifice only because we try to undertake them in an environment working against their use, not for them. If we are going to ask individuals to alter behaviors which negatively affect the environment, then we must make it easy, practical and inexpensive to do so. The solution lies within the problem. We must change patterns and behaviors from the ground up.

The guiding force in air quality improvement and regulation in the South Coast Air Basin is the Air Quality Management Plan (AQMP) developed by the South Coast Air Quality Management District (SCAQMD) and the Southern California Association of Governments (SCAG). The present plan, and the proposed modifications to it, place a great deal of responsibility on local governments to improve air quality.

Local governments are required by the AQMP to adopt Air Quality Elements (AQE) as part of their General Plans. These AQEs must identify how the City will address the issues of parking management, auto use restrictions, and truck rerouting and rescheduling. The related issue of growth management must also be addressed as a General Plan amendment, though, not as part of the Air Quality Element. Other air quality responsibilities placed on local government will be achieved through the adoption of ordinances or other regulatory schemes, and are not specifically required for inclusion in a General Plan Element.

In addition to the City of Los Angeles Air Quality Element, the City is in the process of developing a Growth Management Element and a Mixed Use Incentive Ordinance. It is the first local government to have developed a truck management ordinance that will regulate the operation of heavy duty trucks on city streets during the peak commute hours. The truck ordinance has been approved by the Board of Transportation Commissioners, and will move on for City Council consideration. Add to all of those the City's involvement with the Congestion Management Plan and Deficiency Plans, and you can get a feel for the range and complexity of the City's air quality activities. It becomes apparent that coordination of these actions is necessary to assure that these efforts work together, and are in fact employed and not lost in the morass of plans and promises.

> *Integrated control of all source types is essential if we are ever to have clean, healthy air.*

The City of Los Angeles has recognized the multi-faceted approach that is called for, and has therefore instituted an interdepartmental working group which brings together all City departments and operations that affect air quality. This working group is chaired and coordinated through the Environmental Affairs Department. The primary purpose is to develop a Clean Air Program (CAP) for the City. The Clean Air Program will provide a single consolidated resource in which all City policies, programs and projects affecting air quality can be integrated. Such consolidation allows departments to develop and revise programs and operations that will work together synergistically.

Without this level of communication and exchange, we could see the programs of one department developing in such a manner as to hinder the efforts of another. In addition to the City departmental representation, the CAP will include the development of a community, environmental and business group coalition. The final, but perhaps most essential, component of the program, will be an educational element.

By instituting the CAP, the City of Los Angeles is committing itself to taking a leadership role in air quality improvement. The cornerstone of the Clean Air Program, at least in respect to mobile and indirect source control, is a "back to basics" attitude. If we in the South Coast want to reduce congestion and get people out of their single occupant vehicles, we must provide them with a community that does not require the automobile. It is not enough to make alternative transportation available — we must go beyond that, making it convenient, practical, safe, effective and economical.

The challenges that we in Los Angeles face in that regard are two-fold: those of existing development and those of new development. While it may be desirable to start from scratch and create a perfectly planned, mixed-use, balanced growth utopia, we cannot in a practical sense achieve that. We can, however, stop making it worse, and in fact make it better, if we just step back and look at the big picture.

The impacts of existing developments must be mitigated by providing accessible transportation and commercial services, thereby reducing the need for individual auto use, and encouraging the use of alternative modes of conveyance, such as bicycling and walking. That is where the Mixed Use Ordinance and Balanced Growth Element can come into play. Where there is a heavy concentration of jobs but little housing, attempts will be made to in-fill with housing of the appropriate price range. Balance in the true sense is not achieved by providing equal numbers of jobs to housing units. We must address the economic balance as part of the formula, and provide affordable and attractive housing to those who would fill the nearby jobs. The next step requires the development of support services appropriate to that particular community. The addition of either housing or support services may require zoning changes. If those changes are in fact required, then having the planners at the discussion table from the start will make the process that much smoother. In-filling can, however, take time and be very expensive.

The development of mass transit systems may have the powerful impact we all hope for, but the development of the comprehensive network needed will take years. We cannot afford to, nor should we have to, wait years for a healthy environment. We must move forward now, and the "low-tech", relatively low cost solutions for reducing vehicle miles traveled (VMT) can help us to make that transition. Something as simple as changing the format of information delivery so that it is possible to determine what services and options are available in the nearby area, could result in a decrease in residents driving to secure services to which they could walk or take mass transit. Part of the handicap of the present system is not knowing what is available in the current mix. Every trip that we eliminate not only reduces congestion and its attendant emission, but more importantly it eliminates the vehicle's "cold-start", the major source of mobile emissions.

> *The best intentions and most insightful plans mean nothing if they do not serve the needs and desires of the community.*

Simultaneously, the Balanced Growth Element should assure that new projects and developments begin with a balance of jobs to housing. They must be designed to encourage pedestrian and bicycle traffic, with accessible and attractive veloways and pedestrian paths. The creation of pedestrian and bicycle paths and pockets that are inaccessible except by vehicle, defeats the purpose, and does nothing to eliminate the "cold-start" problem.

New developments must support energy-efficient lifestyles, including solar energy and landscaping plans, which enhance natural cooling and warming patterns. The provision of telecommunication capability and electric vehicle facilitation should be as integral to the building process as the standard utility supply. If the new development includes a community access telecommunications center, even those not lucky enough to work and live in the newly "balanced" development can take advantage of the service to bring their work closer to home. A balance of mixed uses and effective mass transit can help to make tomorrow's developments the solution, not the problem.

The Clean Air Program hopes to facilitate the achievement of all of these goals by bringing City departments, whose operations can help to correct or mitigate the existing problems, together with those whose planning and development programs can provide a more environmentally conscientious and responsible direction for tomorrow.

The best intentions and most insightful plans will, however, mean nothing if they do not serve the needs and desires of the community. Public input is, therefore, an essential feature of the CAP, as is education. These efforts will include educating and informing the general public on issues of air quality, and the role we all can play in its improvement, through the choices we make each day regarding the purchase of goods and services. More importantly, the educational element will seek to implement an environmental education unit requirement in the Los Angeles public school system. It is at the level of behavioral development that a concern and respect for the environment must be cultivated. If we can teach our children now the importance of protecting and preserving the environment, they will not be faced with our burden of correcting the errors of the past, but rather will be able to concentrate on improving the future.

WORKS IN PROGRESS

PLAYA VISTA:
THE PLANNING PROCESS

Douglas Gardner

Douglas Gardner is Project Manager for Maguire Thomas Partners' Playa Vista Project, a planned community in Los Angeles proposed for a site of 1,000 acres bordering the ocean. His specific responsibilities include supervision of all master planning work, coordination of the project approval process and on-going interface with the neighboring communities.

*Maguire Thomas Partners
13250 Jefferson Boulevard
Los Angeles, CA 90094
(310) 822-0074*

Playa Vista is a proposed mixed-use community located on approximately 957 acres adjacent to the airport and the communities of Westchester, Playa del Rey, Venice, Marina del Rey and Mar Vista. The land was acquired by Howard Hughes in the early 1940s to serve as the site for certain of his aircraft testing and manufacturing facilities. Since the mid-1970s, a variety of master plans have been proposed for the property and ultimately one became the basis of a General and Specific Plan approved by the City of Los Angeles for the property. Increasing community concern with the potential development impacts of this site in particular, and growth in general in the Los Angeles basin, culminated in the 1987 election of Councilwoman Ruth Galanter, who strongly opposed the then proposed development plan for Playa Vista. Galanter's upset defeat of City Council President Pat Russell underscored the critical importance of growth issues, and made apparent the deep concern, and latent power, of local communities.

Maguire Thomas Partners became Managing General Partner for the Playa Vista Project in February 1989. Early discussions with Councilwoman Galanter made clear that the project would have no support unless the Master Plan was dramatically altered in a manner directly responsive to community concerns, and that any replanning effort would involve significant public participation. Therefore, as a first step in the process, Maguire Thomas Partners met directly with the wide variety of community groups and individuals who had expressed opposition to the existing zoning and proposed plan. The concerns raised in the course of these discussions were numerous, and often contradictory between varying community groups, but three fundamental issues emerged as common:

- Restoration and expansion of the Ballona Wetlands, a degraded natural habitat occupying the western portion of the site.

- Establishment of building height guidelines consistent with the scale of the surrounding communities.

- Incorporation of transportation planning initiatives which would reduce traffic impacts associated with conventional development strategies.

The Council Office also insisted that the project address the impact of the proposed development on existing infrastructure with particular emphasis on issues of water, waste water and solid waste management. To respond to this challenge, Maguire Thomas Partners-Playa Vista (MTP-PV) assembled a master planning team consisting of architects, landscape architects, urban planners, engineers, and other specialists. Criteria for the selection of this team included demonstration of new and creative thinking regarding urban planning, and a willingness to work with the community.

The Playa Vista development is one of enormous complexity, involving overlapping city, county, state, and federal jurisdictions, and subject to the changing dynamics of environmental regulation. A development of this size and scope must also inevitably confront the crucial issues of growth in the Los Angeles Basin, and the public policy issues which accompany growth. With these complexities in mind, a planning strategy was established based on a multi-disciplinary workshop approach. These workshops were intended to bring together in one place, over a concentrated period of time, the wide array of interests which had a stake in the project. In addition to Maguire Thomas Partners-Playa Vista and their planning team, representatives from the community, local government, engineering and technical disciplines, and environmental groups met during an initial ten-day workshop which brought into sharp focus the crucial issues requiring attention, and established preliminary strategies for addressing them. By the end of this workshop, new planning concepts had emerged and were presented to the public for review, comment, and questions. A series of subsequent workshops conducted over a six-month period resulted in revisions and refinements to the plan which better addressed the basic community concerns, and credited the developer with a forthright and open approach to the planning process.

A separate but parallel series of workshops explored in depth critical ecological issues which face the region. Representatives from technical professions, utility companies, city and county agencies and Maguire Thomas Partners reviewed issues related to transportation, energy, water management, waste management and resource preservation. As a result, a comprehensive strategy for dealing with the ecology of the project emerged very early in the planning process. This program included solid waste and waste water treatment facilities, natural systems for storm water purification, the restoration and expansion of the Ballona Wetlands, and a comprehensive approach to alternative transportation and land use planning.

With regard to three specific proposed systems — waste water recycling, organic waste recycling, and solid waste recycling — MTP-PV has investigated available technology and concluded that systems could be installed which would be compatible with the proposed development plan. However, before these systems can be deployed, they must be determined to be community compatible, approvable by a variety of regulatory agencies, and financeable for the life of the development. MTP-PV is committed to work toward solving these problems and is optimistic about the outcome.

Existing zoning permitted development within a portion of the Ballona Wetlands considered by an environmentally-sensitive community group to be critical habitat. A lawsuit challenging the legitimacy of the certified Local Coastal Plan,

filed by the Friends of Ballona, was inherited by MTP-PV. An exhaustive and intensive series of meetings, negotiations, technical studies and design sessions ultimately resulted in a settlement to the lawsuit and a feasible proposal for the full restoration of the largest remaining wetland in Los Angeles County. A rare collaboration of development and environmental interests has resulted in a beneficial outcome for both.

Similarly, an extended series of negotiations with neighbors led to a carefully modulated series of building height envelopes, responsive to concerns of view corridors and scale. Happily, the vision for the project — a low-rise but compact urban framework intended to maximize the efficiency of infrastructure while fostering a strong sense of community — was compatible with the neighbors' desire for reasonably scaled buildings.

Finally, a key objective of the Revised Playa Vista Plan was to reduce the traffic congestion and air pollution impacts which would result from conventional development applied to the existing zoning. Measures which were identified to achieve this goal were as follows:

1. Linkage of Jobs and Housing — The opportunity should exist for those who work in offices, stores, and hotels at Playa Vista to be able to live within the development. Housing will be provided in proximity to offices so that employees will have the option to walk, bicycle, or ride an internal transit system to work. The proximity of jobs to housing alone is not sufficient to ensure a degree of linkage; housing must also be available in a range of product types and pricing structures. Fifteen percent of Playa Vista's housing, almost 2,000 units, will be "affordable" as defined by City of Los Angeles criteria. Virtually all residential units will be multi-family with a mixture of rental and for-sale products offering a wide range of pricing.

2. Mix of Land Uses — The extent to which daily needs can be met within close proximity of any resident or employee can dramatically reduce vehicle miles traveled. The plan as proposed is comprised of a series of neighborhoods within which an array of uses — office, residential, retail, community services, recreational — can be made available within a short driving distance, or better yet, within walking distance.

> *It is increasingly evident that community participation is not merely an option to the developer, but a mandatory part of the planning process.*

3. Establishment of a Viable Pedestrian Environment — A critical and often neglected aspect of any alternative transportation strategy is the provision of a workable and vibrant pedestrian realm. The master plan proposes street, sidewalk, landscape, lighting, setbacks, curb and frontage standards intended to reconcile the needs of both vehicles and pedestrians.

4. Internal Transit System — The entire project will be served by a low-emission internal transit system intended to move employees and residents throughout the site, and provide linkages to other transit systems. Compressed natural gas and electric vehicle prototypes are under study.

5. Transportation Demand Management (TDM) — An aggressive, progressive series of TDM programs — car pooling, ride sharing, public transit incentives, etc. — will be actively pursued in a setting which through design and function diminishes dependency on the single occupancy vehicle. Parking disincentives, guaranteed rides home, and provision of adjacent shopping and service facilities greatly enhance the effectiveness of TDM programs.

> *We anticipate that the interest of both the developers and the community can be accommodated as the project moves forward.*

The strategy of engaging surrounding communities in major land planning projects is perceived by many developers as a risky course of action. Risks do, in fact, exist; for example, it is impossible to control what is said at public meetings, and the concessions sought by members of the community may be physically or economically unfeasible. Community groups often have conflicting goals and aspirations, frustrating attempts at consensus. Even a high level of community support ensures neither an expedited approval process, nor project approval on any basis.

Despite these legitimate concerns, it is increasingly evident that community participation is not merely an option to the developer, but a mandatory part of the planning process. A well organized community may exhibit far more staying power than the developer, and the developer who insists on fighting this fact may not long remain in business. Therefore, the public process should be accepted, and perhaps considered as beneficial, for very real benefits are attainable. For example, concerns expressed early in the planning process can often be accommodated by the developer at little or no cost. The flexibility to incorporate such changes may be lost as designs become finalized.

Public comment can also result in changes which represent genuine improvements; a variety of such refinements occurred during the course of planning Playa Vista, such as the incorporation of neighborhood Little League fields. Discussions can also educate the community in regard to the development process itself, and contribute to an understanding of constraints, thereby encouraging realistic compromise. The simple act of dialogue may begin to establish a sense of trust; and while the tension and wariness between community and developer may always exist, the possibility of workable solutions is increased dramatically if a level of mutual credibility can be achieved. Finally, the developer may as well be candid about the project proposal up front, since full disclosure of the project and its impact underlie the entire environmental review process. Inadequate or misleading

Environmental Impact Reporsts are easy targets for lawsuits, and since the best deterrent to a successful lawsuit is a complete statement of facts, it makes sense that the developer put them forward early in the process.

At Playa Vista, we discovered that community participation need not be terrifying, nor confrontational. Arguably, the approvals process itself may induce far more anxiety than the most outspoken community group. Even relatively simple projects face a vast array of agency approvals prior to construction; complex projects may be hopelessly bogged down amidst lengthy and complicated regulatory processes. Many developers might readily alter proposed projects in direct response to community concern if such compromise resulted in a speedier approvals process.

Unfortunately, this approvals process, not activism per se, has become the more effective deterrent to growth. While some may see benefit in this result, it is clearly not the intended function of regulating agencies. Furthermore, as we sensed at Playa Vista, most citizens recognize that growth is both necessary and important, but must be managed with care. The community also understands that government is hard pressed to perform ongoing maintenance of, not to mention improvements to, the infrastructure of the city, and that great pressure is therefore put upon the development community to assist in this role. Viewed in this light, development is not necessarily considered by the community as evil, and should, in fact, enhance existing conditions.

Playa Vista as it is now proposed, consists of approximately 5.0 million square feet of office space, 2.0 million of which now exists on the site; over 13,000 residential units, 600,000 square feet of community-serving retail; 1,050 hotel rooms; a 700 slip marina; and an array of civic and cultural uses. The plan calls for these elements to be combined in a mixed-use configuration which draws upon traditional building prototypes in the context of a more urban model than has typically characterized post-war development in southern California. Additionally, over 260 acres of land will be preserved and restored as a wetland which both provides habitat for a wide variety of plant and animal life, and helps address the significant water quality issues now confronting the Los Angeles Basin.

The Playa Vista development still faces a challenging approval process. We anticipate that the community will continue to remain active in the project, and that the interest of both the developers and the community can be accommodated as the project moves forward.

LANDLAB: THE INSTITUTE FOR REGENERATIVE STUDIES

John Lyle

Many of the practices that establish the physical and biological support for modern civilization, that provide food and shelter, and dispose of wastes developed during a time when supplies of energy and materials seemed unlimited. The result is a technological base that requires continuing infusions of immense quantities of energy, water, nutrients, and a range of other materials. Over the past three decades, enough shortages have occurred to make it clear that these resources are finite, that we are depleting our non-renewable resources, and that we are using renewable resources faster than they can be regenerated. Our essential sources of support — food, air, energy, water — are in danger.

This points out the need for research and development to find ways of supporting the human population with predictably available supplies of energy and materials, in harmony with our environment. In recent years, various means for using solar energy, recycling water, maintaining the fertility of soils, and other basic functions have been developed. Collectively, such techniques and devices might be called regenerative technologies, regenerative in the sense of being self-renewing. A great deal more work is needed in the development and testing of such technologies. In order to make this possible, the Institute for Regenerative Studies is under construction at Cal Poly in Pomona.

*John Lyle is the Director of the Institute for Regenerative Studies and an award winning professor of Landscape Architecture at Cal Poly, Pomona. He has been a visiting professor at universities in Italy, Brazil, Yugoslavia and Japan, has participated in many ecological planning and design projects for local and federal agencies, and is the author of the book **Design for Human Ecosystems**.*

Department of Landscape Architecture
Cal Poly University at Pomona
Pomona, CA 91768
(714) 869-2684

PURPOSE

The Institute for Regenerative Studies will provide a unique university-based setting for education, demonstration and research in regenerative technologies. On a 16-acre site on the Cal Poly campus, it will incorporate facilities for a broad range of practices dealing with food production, shelter, waste disposal, and other essential functions. It will become a community of about 90 students working with regenerative technologies as integral parts of their daily lives, thus providing means for studying these practices as part of the ongoing routines. For effective and benign application, the relationships between regenerative practices and human attitudes and behavior are probably as important as the functioning of the technologies themselves. The Institute's mission includes education, demonstration and research.

EDUCATION — In the polytechnic tradition, graduate and undergraduate students will learn by doing in laboratory courses conducted on the site. Students will grow food using various regenerative agricultural and aquaculture techniques. They will also design, build and operate devices for generating energy, disposing of wastes, and carrying out other basic tasks.

DEMONSTRATION — As the facilities develop and become operational, they will be open for visitors and will provide tours and demonstrations for educational groups, including school children. The Institute will also offer guidance and consultation services to those interested in applications of practices within its areas of expertise. Such public education is an important part of the Institute's mission. Public knowledge of regenerative technologies is presently very limited and is crucial to widespread acceptance and application.

RESEARCH — Ultimately, the Institute's development will depend on research because both educational and demonstration programs can best grow from research. Communication has already been established between the Institute and other facilities carrying on similar research.

ORGANIZATION

The Institute is a part of the University's LandLab development, a 339-acre parcel of land on the southern part of the campus. According to its Master Plan, LandLab will be devoted to education and research in the sustainable use of resources. The Institute for Regenerative Studies will be LandLab's integrative force because it will explore and exemplify the full range of activities included within the whole laboratory. It is anticipated that some practices initiated within the Institute will be expanded to other LandLab sites for more extensive research and demonstration.

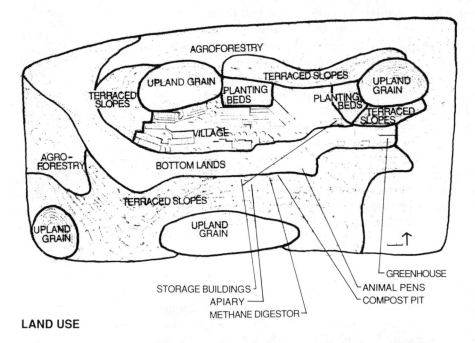

LAND USE

Both LandLab and the Institute for Regenerative Studies will be integral parts of the educational and research programs of the University. In all facets of education, demonstration, and research, integrating the activities that traditionally belong to various disciplines is a basic premise of the Institute. A major difficulty of industrial era technologies is their division into sectors of activity, the boundaries of which are rarely crossed. For example, agriculture is separate from housing, and both are separate from waste disposal. In contrast, regenerative technologies offer opportunities for integrating certain aspects of activities conventionally considered quite different, with considerable potentially synergistic benefit.

The integration of agriculture and aquaculture, for example, offers opportunities for using agricultural wastes to feed fish and for using enriched water drained from ponds to irrigate crops. Treated sewage effluent can, under certain conditions, be used for crop irrigation. Solaria and other sunspaces can be used as heat collectors for climate control in buildings and can also provide controlled environments for propagating and growing plants. Aquaculture tanks placed within solaria have been used for thermal storage in stabilizing internal climates. These are only a few examples of integration that become possible when the boundaries between sectors are removed.

Such integration often allows one process to provide the services of two, or turns a problem or pollutant or waste into a resource. But perhaps the most fundamental integration is that of regenerative technologies within daily life and social organization. Successful application of these practices and technologies will ultimately depend upon their being more integrally related to other aspects of life than industrial technologies have been. In fact, there may be considerable social and psychic benefits in such integration. Thus, the Institute is conceived as a microcosm, incorporating the full range of life-support functions for a small society in a manageable space.

> **LandLab will be devoted to education and research in the sustainable use of resources.**

Exploring the possibilities of interaction, both among disparate techniques and between these and the people who work with them, requires the focused efforts of students and investigators in various disciplines. The University, with its broad range of disciplines and diverse expertise, is uniquely equipped to provide a setting in which such interaction can take place. The work of the design team for the Institute provides an example of the kind of concerted interdisciplinary efforts that are needed. The team includes specialists in agronomy, anthropology, aquaculture, architecture, landscape architecture, solar energy, international agriculture, business management, sewage treatment, and hydrology. This cooperative effort provides a model for ongoing interdisciplinary activity within the Institute.

THE SITE AND ITS USE

The Institute's 16 acres include a narrow valley that runs through its length in the east-west direction and slopes up to rounded knolls on its north and south sides. The site is particularly suitable for the Institute's purposes because it includes a diverse array of physiographic conditions. Slopes range from virtually flat to over fifty percent, though most areas are between five and thirty percent. Slope aspects face every point on the compass, though most are approximately north or south facing.

The diverse situations in the site represent on a small scale many of the topographic conditions found in most of the food producing areas of the world. Thus, we can view the site as a microcosm of the global agricultural landscape. With careful selection of specific locations within the site, it will be possible to replicate a great diversity of food growing situations.

> **The most fundamental integration is that of regenerative technologies within daily life and social organization.**

Approximately five acres of the site will be devoted to growing crops and animals, using only hand tools. This manual technology, or hand-tech area, will simulate the conditions that exist on over one hundred million small farms of ten acres or less in food-deficit, non-industrialized countries. The University's International Agriculture Program and the new inter-disciplinary graduate program in International Development will concentrate much of their activity in this area. In the hand-tech area, as well as in other areas of the site where there will be no limits on levels of technology, a few basic principles will govern activity. Important among these are:

1. To make optimum use of energy and materials available on the site, at the same time minimizing the use of energy and materials imported from offsite.

2. To provide maximum recycling of water, nutrients and all other materials, including those normally considered as wastes.

3. To avoid any material collecting in any area in amounts that might be damaging.

FOOD PRODUCTION

Educational and research efforts in this area will work toward a common goal: food production systems that function in the self-renewing ways of natural ecosystems. Particular attention will be given to practices that protect and enhance the soil; reduce energy consumption and the use of fossil fuel-derived fertilizers and other chemicals; maximize multiple use potentials; and reduce water consumption.

A regenerative agriculture seeks to enhance the physical and biological environment and, at the same time, to bring greater dignity and welfare to the producer and the community. With these purposes in mind, the food production areas will search for ways to manage biological means of production on a sustainable basis.

Though the site is small in contrast with the scale of most conventional agricultural production, its range of topographic and microclimatic conditions makes it possible to include demonstrations of a wide variety of agricultural practices and techniques. Practices that conserve resources will be emphasized, even though they may require higher levels of management and labor than conventional practices. Educational and research efforts in this area will be integrated toward a common goal: food production systems that function in the self-renewing ways of natural ecosystems. Particular attention will be given to practices that protect and enhance the soil, reduce energy consumption and the

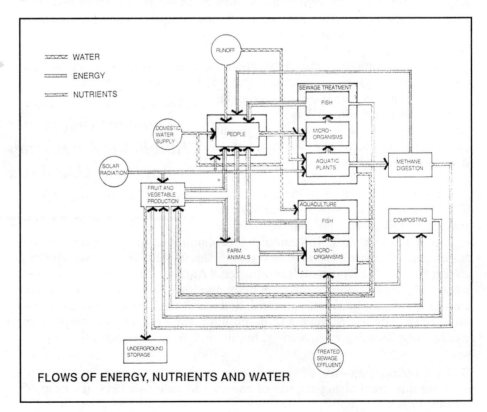

FLOWS OF ENERGY, NUTRIENTS AND WATER

use of fossil fuel-derived fertilizers and other chemicals, maximize multiple use potential and recycling, and reduce water use. To the greatest extent possible, all materials, including those normally considered as wastes, will be recycled within the system.

As these goals suggest, the Institute's food production areas are designed and managed according to principles quite different from those of conventional agriculture. Most importantly, biological diversity will be optimized rather than reduced, following the ecological principle that stability is best developed through a diverse range of interactions among heterogeneous species selected for specific site conditions. Particular efforts will be made to work with plants adapted to the climatic and topographic conditions of the site as a whole and to specific locations within it.

> *There will be an emphasis on growing the food consumed by the resident population.*

Included will be an array of agricultural systems and practices, with potential applications in both industrialized and non-industrialized countries. Given the location in an urbanizing area, there will be some emphasis on practices suitable for food production under urban conditions and at the urban/rural interface. Since integration with the community is also an important goal of the Institute, there will be an emphasis on growing the food consumed by the resident population. While projections indicate that at times more food will be grown on the site than can be consumed by the community, students' dietary habits suggest that some food items will probably have to be brought in and quantities of others will have to be exported.

OVERVIEW OF PRODUCTION AREAS

Topography and other local conditions determine relationships between biotic productivity and landscape. Within the six types of production areas — bottom lands, planting beds, terraced slopes, forested slopes, upland grain production areas and human use areas — specific practices will include the following:

A. Bottom Lands: 2.4 acres
- Integrated agriculture/aquaculture/livestock production as a fundamental means of recycling nutrients in animal wastes
- Paddy rice
- Productive aquatic plants

B. Planting Beds: 7.4 acres
- Diversified vegetable production

C. Terraced Slopes: 3.5 acres
- Polycultures, including various combinations of species intermixed and occupying different vertical layers
- Forage crops and green manures

D. Agroforestry: 5.1 acres
- Trees for fuel wood as well as for fruits and nuts will be interplanted in different patterns and densities with various perennial and annual crop species

E. Upland Grain: 2.4 acres
- Diverse grain crops, especially barley, wheat, maize and oats

F. The Village: 2.2 acres
  • Plants with high esthetic quality that also serve other purposes such as food production and environmental control
  • Productive trees useful in urban situations
  • Rooftop plantings, including herbs, various shallow-rooted vegetables, container plants and seedlings to be replanted in other locations

G. All Areas
  • Pest control systems for small-scale integrated pest management
  • Composting and use of composted material
  • Propagation and growing of seedlings

ANIMALS

A small number of animals will be kept for milk and meat as well as for research and demonstration of the roles of animals in agroecosystems. Recycling of nutrients in animal wastes is of particular interest, as is the feeding of animals with various crops and crop residues.

In the hand-tech area, pens will be provided for cows, swine, and goats. At least one platform house for swine will be built over a fish pond in order to experiment with the recycling of manure through the pond ecosystem. Cows, swine, and goats will also be maintained in the multi-tech area in close proximity to composting and methane digestion facilities. Platforms for ducks and swine will be built over two of the fish ponds.

WATER MANAGEMENT

Water management is among the major issues to be addressed by the Institute. Infrastructure will provide for a wide range of water uses. Efficient use and recycling of water and the interrelationships between water and other resources will be important subjects of education and research.

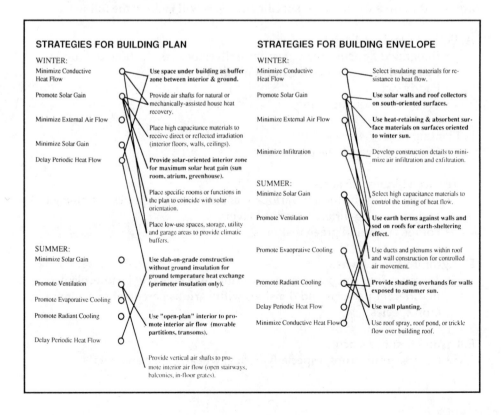

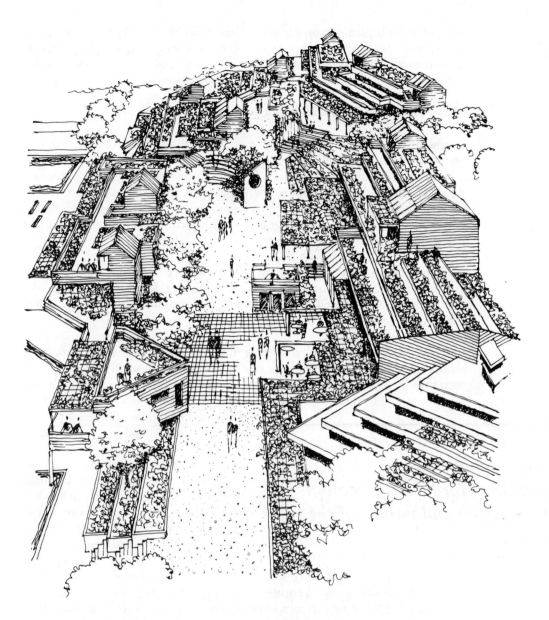

Aquaculture plays a key and pivotal role in the Institute's activities. The initial aquaculture facilities will be devoted primarily to demonstrations. However, the plan calls for rapid development and expansion of both the facilities and the program to engage in appropriate research as soon as possible. This will meet a growing need for improvement in aquaculture technologies. This need is currently most obvious in the non-industrial world, but it is likely to increase in developed nations as well.

The waste processing and recycling role of aquaculture in this context is even more important than productivity. Both animal wastes and feed plants will be introduced into ponds. Some plants will be introduced into some of the ponds to provide nutrients for the growth of organisms at the base of the food chain, which eventually produces the organisms eaten by the fish. On the output side, pond water enriched with fish wastes provides nutrient-laden irrigation water.

SEWAGE TREATMENT — The biological treatment system designed for the Institute will require careful control. This system is a proven technology that carries the approval of the U.S. Environmental Protection Agency, and there are several built plants in operation in California. Nevertheless, it is not yet in widespread use, and many questions remain concerning the details of its performance. After the treatment, water will be used for irrigation in those situations where such use is permitted by health codes.

OPERATION AND COMMUNITY

Regenerative practices and technologies, as they are defined here, function best in close concert with the people working with them. Interactions are complex and continuous, requiring frequent decisions. This suggests that users should have detailed understanding, even a sense of emotional involvement, with these technologies. Thus, regenerative practices might avoid the pervasive alienation of people from their supporting technologies that is a serious malady of the industrial era.

Exploring these interactions, finding the best ways of working with regenerative techniques, and defining the relationships that emerge between people and environment, as well as those among the people themselves are major purposes of the Institute.

However, it is important to recognize that the Institute community is in no sense an ideal or model community or an isolated, independent, or self-sufficient group. As an integral part of the University, the community is dependent upon it for legitimacy and survival and will follow University regulations, maintain good relations, and partake of University intellectual and social life.

> *The architecture and landscape of the community village will give visible form to the ecological approach and values of the Institute.*

THE VILLAGE — Will include housing for 90 students, as well as common rooms, seminar and meeting rooms, a kitchen and common dinning room, a classroom, a laboratory, office space, and faculty apartments. The architecture and landscape of the community village will give visible form to the ecological approach and values of the Institute for Regenerative Studies. In addition to sheltering the Institute's residents, three basic purposes combine in shaping the building forms: a harmonious relationship with the land, optimal use of available energy, and reinforcement of social interactions.

In the interests of both demonstration and research, three basic building types will be represented at the Institute: the raised form, the earth-sheltered form, and the sun-space. All are solar buildings designed to function without use of fossil fuels or any imported energy sources. To reflect their close relationship with the earth, the buildings step up the knoll in a series of terraces in the same manner as most of the agricultural lands.

BUDGET — Development costs for the Institute facilities, including grading and preparation of all agricultural lands, roads and fencing, building construction, aquaculture ponds and all fees, are estimated at $5.5 million.

THE LOS ANGELES ECO VILLAGE: A SUSTAINABLE URBAN COMMUNITY

Lois Arkin

SUSTAINABLE DEVELOPMENT: THE BASIS FOR THE THE ECO VILLAGE CONCEPT

S ustainable development utilizes a whole systems approach to design. Physical, social and economic systems are integrated into the whole project design. In sustainable communities, people can be close to where much of their food is grown and to their livelihoods. The physical and economic environment is arranged so that quality time with family, friends, and community is possible. Leisure, recreational, and civic activities, too, along with work and family life are within walking or short non-polluting commute distance. In short, sustainable development allows us to meet our own needs without diminishing the ability of future generations to meet their needs. We have taken all of these factors into consideration in establishing major goals of the project.

*Lois Arkin is the Founder and Executive Director of the 11-year old non-profit Cooperative Resources and Services Project (CRSP), a coordinating co-sponsor of the **First Los Angeles Ecological Cities Conference**. She is also the coordinator of L.A. EcoVillage and has stewarded its vision during the past six years.*

CRSP
3551 White House Place
Los Angeles, CA 90004
(213) 738-1254.

Sustainable development provides the framework for the eco village concept. Robert Gilman of the Context Institute defines an eco village as a place that:

- is a human-scale community
- is a full-featured settlement
- harmlessly integrates human activities into the natural world
- supports healthy human development
- can be successfully continued into the indefinite future

Gilman elaborates on each phrase of this definition in the Summer 1991 issue of *In Context*, and I urge people interested in the Eco Village movement to get a copy (see Resources).

It is not our intent to be isolationist within the city. A high level of self-reliance within the context of a dynamic urban fabric adds quality of life elements to the whole city by reducing air pollution, garbage, crime and crime breeding conditions, and increasing energy conservation, community participation and non-monetized social and ecological services. Eco villages also demonstrate to other urban dwellers both here and throughout the world, that the growing eco village movement can design and build sustainably within the urban setting.

THE PURPOSES OF AN ECO VILLAGE

In the late 20th century, the primary purposes of urban eco villages in the industrialized world are to:

- model low-impact high-quality life styles appropriate for achieving sustainable neighborhoods
- reduce the burden of government

- reverse negative environmental impacts on the city and the planet
- model sustainable patterns of development for Third World communities and nations, thereby helping to stimulate development patterns which will bypass the currently unsustainable patterns of the industrialized world (Los Angeles has a particularly major responsibility on this count).

HISTORY OF LOS ANGELES ECO VILLAGE

The core of the Los Angeles EcoVillage is planned for an 11-acre landfill in the Montecito Heights area, about five miles northeast of downtown Los Angeles.

> *An urban eco village helps to stimulate development patterns which will by-pass the currently unsustainable patterns.*

About three to four acres are conventionally buildable. The property, owned by the Department of Water and Power (DWP), is an inert landfill consisting of DWP construction debris such as sand, rock, dirt, gravel, and concrete. The center of the fill area is up to 70 feet deep. Although asbestos was part of the debris permitted to be dumped in this site, we don't know that any was. If testing ultimately proves this site unworkable, we expect to develop a commitment from the City to work with us on alternative sites. And we could continue to be helpful to the existing neighborhoods surrounding the DWP site in retrofitting their communities for sustainability.

The landfill was closed in 1978 and scheduled to go to public auction in 1986. CRSP and the Eco-Home Network, working through the political process, were instrumental in having the property removed from the auction and reserved as a likely site for the Village. The Commerce, Energy and Natural Resources Committee of the L.A. City Council, which oversees the DDWP, has instructed the DWP to work with us and give the EcoVillage concept every consideration. We have asked the City Council Committee to give the EcoVillage planning group one full year after approval of ground water tests to provide a feasibility study and plan for the Village.

Recently completed State mandated ground water tests are expected to be approved by the California Water Quality Control Board in the coming year. After that time, EcoVillage planners expect to begin community composting and gardening activities on the site, with the initial construction phase scheduled for Spring, 1994. Basic completion of the 11-acre site is scheduled by 2000; however, the EcoVillage is expected to continue evolving within the surrounding neighborhoods, and in other neighborhoods throughout the L.A. area.

THE PROCESS AND PROGRESS

It's been important to build constituency for EcoVillage at every level of our city, so that when it's time to begin the actual development process, we will be in partnership with all of those needed to make it happen without a big hassle. To facilitate this process, we have:

- met annually with the City Council Committee which oversees the Department of Water and Power to keep the vision of the EcoVillage politically viable
- kept Councilman Alatorre's office informed of our activities — the site is in his 14th District

- continued to go door to door within the existing neighborhoods to invite residents to sign a petition in favor of the concept of the Village and to become associated with the project
- met with management in the DWP to begin to seek out a partnership relationship with that agency
- met with a group of planners within the City Planning Department to bring them onboard and keep them all regularly updated on our progress
- continued to inform our grass roots constituencies about the Village and its progress and recruit future residents and other participants onto our open all-volunteer Planning Committee

In addition, we have recently worked with the Community Project Area Committee (CPAC), a 20-person City Council-appointed group, which is coordinated by the City Planning Department. We are making recommendations to the CPAC to include the EcoVillage concept in the community plan for their district. On another edge, we have been successful at incorporating the EcoVillage as a proposed project for implementing the City's housing policies in the draft of the City's new Housing Element expected to be approved by the City Council in Spring, 1992. We are also working with the Planning Department on developing appropriate language for the City's General Plan to include the Eco Village concept as a strategy for creating sustainable neighborhoods throughout the City for both new developments and older neighborhoods. A pamphlet has been completed, which sets forth an extensive list of commonly asked questions and answers about the L.A. EcoVillage.

In our most recent meeting with the City Council Committee on Energy and Natural Resources, we formally invited the City and its Department of Water and Power to be partners in the EcoVillage project. This partnership relation is important because we view all of our work as within the public interest and part of the effort to reduce the burden of government. The City's up-front support now will greatly reduce its burdens down the road in such areas as energy savings, infrastructure, social costs, affordable housing, etc. We are asking the City to provide the land for the project and to allow EcoVillage the latitude it needs for Zoning, Building and Safety, Health Department and other agency approvals to permit full and efficient flowering of the EcoVillage potential.

> *It's been important to build constituency for EcoVillage at every level of our city, so we will be in partnership with all of those needed to make it happen.*

We have also begun discussions with the City's Housing Preservation and Production Department regarding their potential participation in the housing component of EcoVillage, the Department of Public Works regarding a neighborhood composting demonstration on the site, and the County Department of Parks and Recreation regarding an ecological center in Debbs Park, which is adjacent to the site. It is from this park location, eventually, that tours may be made of the Village with virtually no impact on the surrounding neighborhoods with respect to traffic, noise, etc.

The cities of Los Angeles and St. Petersburg, Russia are Sister Cities, and we are working with a grass roots group in St. Petersburg which plans to build an eco village just outside the city. The City of Los Angeles is planning to establish environmental committees for each of our Sister City programs. This will be especially useful for the exchange of EcoVillage information and other sustainable technologies with our Sister City.

Three exploratory design studies have been completed for L.A. EcoVillage, one by Berkeley-based architect Harry Jordan, and the others by UCLA student Jim Matsuo and USC student David Bell. Dick Schoen's UCLA graduate class in solar architecture is expected to use the EcoVillage site for a study in 1992, and a group of public policy students at USC have been using the L.A. Eco Village in "The L.A. Semester" series under the guidance of Elpidio Rocha. A group of graduate landscape architecture students at Cal Poly Pomona is planning to do an in-depth analysis and project plan beginning in January, 1993 under the guidance of Professor John Lyle. The City of Los Angeles Planning Department has indicated they will co-sponsor that study with CRSP.

> *We must keep defining our performance objectives. This keeps our work very understandable, grounded, and pragmatic.*

One very exciting outcome of all of this student work is a monthly informal intercollegiate gathering, where graduate and undergraduate students from different disciplines are sharing their ideas and progress on EcoVillage work. Students from architecture, planning, landscape architecture, public policy, business, the arts, environmental sciences and anthropology are involved so far, and the group is growing. These students are creating their own grass roots multi-disciplinary cooperative learning experience for creating a sustainable future.

PERFORMANCE OBJECTIVES

Wil Orr and John Wesley Miller remind us that in planning for sustainable communities, such as their 820-acre Tucson Solar Village (TSV), we must keep defining our performance objectives. This keeps our work very understandable, grounded, and pragmatic. People can visualize the translation of those goals and objectives to their own lives. When I met John Wesley Miller at a quarterly board meeting of the National Association of Home Builders a few years ago, he handed me a piece of paper outlining TSV's performance objectives. I knew immediately that this is the way we must begin describing the EcoVillage, and we began right away to translate our goals into this format.

Below is an overview of the EcoVillage Performance Objectives. Keep in mind, once again, that all systems must be integrated, so there's a constant interplay in the planning, design, development and living with, and ultimately in, the EcoVillage to insure that everything is related to everything else. Everyone involved must have a modicum of knowledge in all of the disciplines related to the project. Also keep in mind that the physical, social and economic boundaries of EcoVillage will be highly permeable to include diverse opportunities for residents in the surrounding neighborhoods and the broader society for participating in Village life. Ultimately, of course, we expect that many resident groups in adjacent areas and throughout the city will opt for converting their neighborhoods into eco villages.

ECOLOGICAL SYSTEMS

Organic Food Production — EcoVillage residents will produce up to 40% of their own food in community gardens and orchards. Other neighborhood residents will have the opportunity through membership in the Community Land Trust to have garden plots within the Village.

Water Conservation and Reclamation — Water conservation and reclamation systems will reduce water use by 90%.

Alternative Energy Systems — Passive solar design, conservation and efficiency, combined with new solar, wind and biomass technologies will reduce conventional energy needs by 75%.

Solid Waste — Landfill-destined solid wastes will be 90% lower than average for the Los Angeles area through changed purchasing patterns, community recycling and composting activities.

Non-toxic Building Materials — Non-toxic, local, regional, and recycled building materials will be used wherever possible and practical.

Transportation — Non-polluting fuels, minimal use of automobiles, human-scale walking and biking design patterns, neighborhood electric vans connecting with nearby light rail and low-cost auto/truck rental from community-owned multiple vehicle pools will provide a broad range of alternatives to conventional auto use. Indeed, we hope to provide leadership in transforming L.A.'s auto dependent culture.

SOCIAL DESIGN FEATURES

CoHousing Clusters — Self-contained attached housing units clustered around a common house extend community life for voluntary meal sharing, child care, the arts, home-based business centers and social life. Up to four cohousing clusters of 18 to 30 units each are projected for EcoVillage. These might house a total of 150 to 300 persons. All housing clusters will be pedestrian-oriented.

Collaborative Design and Building — Interactive design processes and options for self-building will help create good designs, trust and strong friendships with future neighbors in EcoVillage and the surrounding neighborhoods.

Shared Values — Shared ecological and cooperative values provide the common interests upon which residents can create a friendly neighborhood built on trust and mutual caring.

Consensus Decision Processes — On-going education and training in consensus seeking decision processes will help create broad-based support for community actions and mitigate the divisiveness that often results from "majority rule" decisions.

> *The physical, social and economic boundaries will be permeable to include residents in the surrounding neighborhoods and the broader society in Village life.*

On-Going Education and Training — There will be on-going education and training opportunities for EcoVillage residents and others in the surrounding neighborhoods on all aspects of sustainable urban living.

Intergenerational, Mixed Income and Multi-Cultural Population — Diversity in age, incomes and cultural backgrounds will represent the rich texture of our urban social fabric.

Community-Owned Center — Community-owned and controlled child development center, cafe, market and community center will provide basic community services and the foundation for expanding services.

ECONOMIC CONSIDERATIONS

Homeownership Opportunities — Residents will have the opportunity for non-speculative cooperative home ownership through membership in the non-profit Los Angeles Mutual Housing Association and Community Land Trust. Unit costs are expected to range from $75,000 to $200,000.

Socially Responsible Investment Opportunities — EcoVillage will provide a variety of opportunities for the socially responsible investor. The development of a waiting list of qualified future homeowners ensures that EcoVillage will be completely pre-sold and have a waiting list for future vacancies. We believe that one of the potential sources of investment in EcoVillage is from residents in the existing neighborhoods who will have the opportunity to participate in the planning process.

Mixed-Use Neighborhood Provides Sustainable Enterprise Opportunities — Home-based businesses, employment within walking and biking distance can account for up to 80% of employment and livelihood opportunities for residents at project completion. A small ecological business incubator is planned within walking distance of the Village site. Here, EcoVillage and other neighborhood residents will be able to get the technical assistance and other types of support needed for establishing producer and community-owned enterprises specializing in non-polluting products and services.

Local Exchange Trading System (LETS) — The LETSystem, an indirect barter system, can provide for up to 50% of services in EcoVillage and the surrounding neighborhoods.

Non-Monetized Social Services — Where people are in good neighborly relations with one another, there is social validation for mutual caring and aid, thus mitigating expensive social services.

THE ECO VILLAGE PLANNING GROUP

Members of our 50-member all-volunteer planning group meet regularly to hear from experts on a variety of related subjects, such as graywater systems, telecommuting, cohousing, organic gardening and composting, etc. People from all walks of life have joined the group — gardeners, teachers, students, food workers, engineers, artists, planners, secretaries, carpenters, computer experts, lawyers, architects, and doctors. We also meet for social gatherings and in working committees to forward the work of EcoVillage. About 20 members of the design team intend to live in EcoVillage. Regular informal orientations to EcoVillage are held Monday evenings at CRSP; (213) 738-1254.

> *One of the potential sources of investment in EcoVillage is from residents in the existing neighborhoods.*

THE OVERSIGHT CONSORTIUM

Seven prominent non-profit environmental organizations in Southern California make up an informal consortium intended to provide constituency for the EcoVillage as well as expertise and guidance. Besides CRSP they include the Eco-Home Network, TreePeople, the Community Environmental Council, the Permaculture Institute of Southern California, the Ecological Life Systems Institute, and the Institute for Natural Resources. These are all organizations whose leadership you have been hearing from at this conference.

THE LARGER ECO VILLAGE MOVEMENT

Of course, it's important to remember that the EcoVillage concept is by no means limited to Los Angeles. International eco-village and eco-cities networks are gathering momentum and doing a great deal of information sharing. A heartening spirit of cooperation is common in these networks because we all want to expedite our mutual learning curves in our urgency to heal the planet. The Summer, 1991 issue (No. 29) of the magazine *In Context: A Quarterly of Humane Sustainable Culture* devoted its whole issue to Eco Villages and held an international invitational seminar in September, 1991 in conjunction with Gaia Trust in Denmark to discuss advancing the eco village movement.

> *International eco-village and eco-cities networks are gathering momentum.*

We hope you'll stay tuned for further developments on building in our urban environments in balance with nature. We will be providing regular updates on EcoVillage in the CRSP *L.A. Co-ops Newsletter* and Eco-Home's *Ecolution* newsletter.

RESOURCES:

CRSP, *Draft for Eco Village Policy for City of Los Angeles General Plan*, 1992. Send $2 to CRSP, 3551 White House Place, L.A., CA 90004.

CRSP, *Commonly Asked Questions on the Los Angeles EcoVillage*, 1992. Send $2 to CRSP, 3551 White House Place, L.A., CA 90004.

CRSP, *L.A. Co-ops and the EcoVillage Networker Newsletter*, $10/6 issues ($20 foreign), CRSP, 3551 White House Place, L.A., CA 90004.

Context Institute, *Eco-Villages and Sustainable Communities, A Report for Gaia Trust*, 1991. P.O. Box 11470, Bainbridge Island, WA 98110, 213 pp., (206) 842-0216. Contact the Context Institute.

Center for Religion, Ethics and Social Policy (CRESP), *Eco Village at Ithaca Newsletter*. Anabel Taylor Hall, Cornell University, Ithaca, NY 14853, $20/yr.

Fellowship for Intentional Communities sponsors *A Celebration of Community*, August 26-31, 1993 at Evergreen State College, Olympia, Washington. For information, write FIC, c/o Center for Communal Studies, 8600 University Blvd., Evansville, IN 47712.

Fellowship for Intentional Communities and Communities Publications Cooperative, *Directory of Intentional Communities: A Guide to Cooperative Living,"* 1991. To receive this 328-page directory send $19 to Sandhill Farm, Route 1, Box 155, Rutledge, Missouri 63563, USA. Lists comprehensive information on more than 400 North American communities and 50 on other continents, plus 40 articles about community living and over 250 alternative resources and services.

In Context: A Quarterly of Humane Sustainable Culture, P.O. Box 11470, Bainbridge Island, WA 98110. Issue 29 is entirely on sustainable community development and eco villages and is available for $5.00. Subscriptions $18/yr. (Contact them for foreign subscription information.)

McCamant, Kathryn and Durrett, Charles, *CoHousing: A Contemporary Approach to Housing Ourselves*, Habitat Press/Ten Speed Press, 1988, 208 pp., $22 from CRSP ($25 foreign).

South Island Development Cooperative, *Bamberton News*, Suite 550, 2950 Douglas St., Victoria, BC V8T 4N4. They are planning a suburban sustainable new town 32 km north of Victoria for 12,000 people in contiguous eco villages.

University of Calgary, Faculty of Environmental Design, Affordable Sustainable Community Project (ASC), *ASC News*, 2500 University Dr. NW, Calgary, AL T2N 1N4. The ASC Project is working with the Community Redevelopment Agency to retrofit an existing central city neighborhood to an eco village.

CIVANO — TUCSON SOLAR VILLAGE

John Wesley Miller & Wil Orr

ivano or the *Tucson Solar Village* is a public-sector initiative responding to the increasing environmental and societal costs of urban growth. The project goal is to build an environmentally harmonious community using less energy, creating less waste and pollution with an affordable and pleasant lifestyle and an active business district. Public sector's role is to provide the leadership and incentives which encourage local builders and developers to build neighborhoods of this quality.

Civano is planned as a biking/pedestrian-oriented community with employment and shopping opportunities available internally. This mixed-use project is being planned for 820 acres of Arizona State Trust Land on Tucson's southeast side. Some 5,000 residents will live in 2,300 housing units ranging from single-family detached to high density multi-family. These neighborhood clusters will be planned around 60% open space.

The business district will provide jobs for 1200 persons with home/studio professional offices encouraged by zoning and building ordinances. Teleconferencing will be available to further cut down on automobile use. The high-density Village Center will provide complete business incubator and child/elder care services.

Although automobile access is planned, the internal circulation pattern will greatly favor walking/biking. "Human-scale transit" via the green-space and path system will be the most pleasant and refreshing mode of transport. Streets and auto-related services will be reduced or absent with safe-play and pleasant open spaces given predominance. Connection with mass transit and low-cost auto/truck rental will provide a viable alternative to multiple vehicle ownership. Electric vehicles will be a featured option for local use.

Design parameters include sufficient solar electric generating capacity to supply the village's total energy use of approximately five megawatts. The plan is to generate an excess of solar power during the day equivalent to the village's nighttime needs. In this manner, the amount of CO_2 created by the standard fuel burning power plants that will provide the village's nighttime electricity, can be offset by supplying an equal amount of clean solar power which the village will feed back into the grid during the day.

Assisted by the Arizona Energy Office, the Tucson-Pima County Metropolitan Energy Commission coordinated almost 50 different public/private organizations as well as strong citizen-participation during the planning and re-zoning phase completed in late 1991 when the City Council voted unanimously to approve the required zoning on the 820-acre parcel. They approved the Development Plan with performance targets for:

John Wesley Miller is the conceptualizer of the 820 acre Tucson Solar Village. He is a Board Member of the National Association of Home Builders; the National Research Center for Housing; the Smart House Joint Venture; and the Primavera Foundation for the Homeless. He chairs the Arizona Solar Energy Advisory Council and has served as consultant on Biosphere II.

Tucson Solar Village
4500 Santana
Tucson, AZ 85715
(602) 749-3366

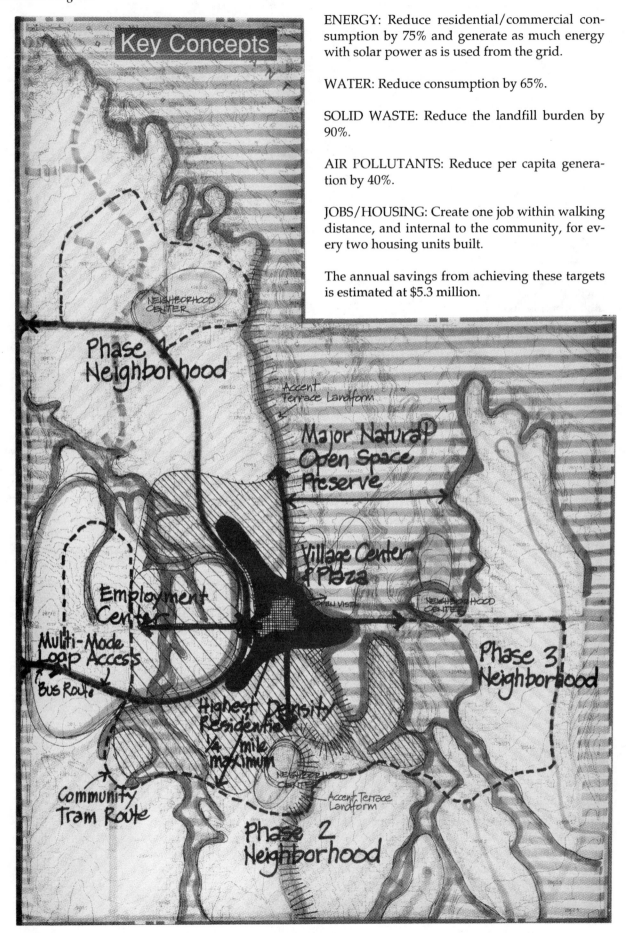

ENERGY: Reduce residential/commercial consumption by 75% and generate as much energy with solar power as is used from the grid.

WATER: Reduce consumption by 65%.

SOLID WASTE: Reduce the landfill burden by 90%.

AIR POLLUTANTS: Reduce per capita generation by 40%.

JOBS/HOUSING: Create one job within walking distance, and internal to the community, for every two housing units built.

The annual savings from achieving these targets is estimated at $5.3 million.

ORGANIZATION

A non-profit (501c-3) corporation will serve as the master developer for the project, providing financial, technical, and training assistance to builders over the 15-year buildout. A diverse Board of Directors will represent the increasing statewide public interest in building resource-efficient communities. This organization will raise the initial capital from foundations, corporations, and possibly some federal sources. As resales of property occur, this capital, originally used for land purchase and infrastructure, will be reinvested in other resource-conserving community development projects.

Some of the project's partners include: City of Tucson, Arizona Energy Office, Arizona State Land Department, Tucson Local Development Corporation, Greater Tucson Economic Council, National Association of Home Builders, Arizona Solar Energy Advisory Council, Southern Arizona Home Builders Association, Public Technology, Inc., Pima County, Tucson Electric Power, Environmental Research Lab, University of Arizona, National Research Center, P & D Technologies, Department of Energy, Urban Consortium and Sandia National Labs.

FINANCING

With commitments of $1.2 million to date, the Project is funded through the initial planning and re-zoning phase. Partnerships and funding totaling $10 million will be needed for a revolving fund to purchase the land from the State Land Department. The return of these funds as the Project is sold in smaller parcels to builders will permit the development corporation to provide financial and technical services to builders and developers throughout the state for similar advanced community development projects.

Civano is gaining national attention with construction expected to begin in 1993 and continue over a 15-year period at a cost of some $500 million. Its public/private partnership can serve as a model for other cities.

Sustainable community design is very complex. Normally isolated technological disciplines, public agencies, private-sector builders and citizens must all work together. And this should occur at the local level where responsibility for sustainability is laid at no single organization's feet. More sustainable communities are inevitable, both for new and infill development. Our option is not whether to build sustainably, but when. We may voluntarily move in this positive direction to our economic and environmental advantage, or delay and do so later under duress.

With *Civano* we are opting for sooner rather than later.

Wil Orr is responsible for the integration of Federal, State, County, City and private resources for the Tucson Solar Village. *He and his brother David founded the Meadowcreek Project, a 1,500 acre environmental education center in Arkansas. There he coordinated the funding, design and construction of passive solar facilities and built the largest solar space and potable water heating system in the State.*

City of Tucson
PO Box 27210
Tucson, AZ 85726-7210
(602) 791-5414

CERRO GORDO: ECO VILLAGE BUILDING & ECO-CITY NETWORKING

Christopher Canfield

*Chris Canfield is the founder and community development coordinator of **Cerro Gordo**, a prototype ecosystem community being built near Eugene, Oregon. He has over 20 years of experience in all phases of ecological community organizing, planning, financing and building, is the editor of the* International Ecocity Conference 1990 Report *and continues to be one of the principal organizers of the international Ecocity Network.*

Cerro Gordo
Dorena Lake
Box 569
Cottage Grove, OR 97424
(503) 942-7720

learly, our civilization isn't sustainable when we consume fossil sunlight at a million times the rate it was accumulated, and when our per capita production of "renewables" like fish, grain, fiber and wood has been decreasing for decades. Our civilization isn't sustainable because we've lost touch with how things are done on this planet. We've come to define wealth with ever increasing consumption, and so we're burning our house to keep warm.

Most "development" has been based upon extractive economics and a predatory or even a parasitic approach, which has been increasingly destructive to our real source of wealth: the biosphere. This four-billion-year-old miracle has brought the sun's energy to life here on earth. In defiance of entropy, the biosphere has kept growing and evolving, becoming more and more complex. Out of life has come more life and richer life. This is real development. The evolving, developing biosphere has been the source of all of our wealth from the air we breathe to our clever little brains. If we want to figure out how to do sustainable development, sustainable cities and a sustainable civilization, we need to look to the larger community of the biosphere, of which the human community is only a small and dependent part. Development will be sustainable only to the extent it works with the natural life-enhancing cycles of the biosphere.

CERRO GORDO PROTOTYPE SYMBIOTIC COMMUNITY

Cerro Gordo is a prototype symbiotic community now being built for up to 2,500 people on 1,200 acres on the north shore of Dorena Lake, near Eugene, Oregon. Our purpose is to explore ways to add the human community with as little disturbance as possible to the existing natural community, thereby developing a more complex symbiosis. We don't pretend to have all the answers, but we do have a living laboratory with a planned population sufficient to support all of the basic everyday activities and services.

We've adopted the strategy of building a new town because we believe fundamentally different land use patterns are needed. We spent over two years searching for the right site. Cerro Gordo includes an entire south-facing valley, surrounded on three sides by government forest and on the south by Dorena Lake. About half of the property has relatively unproductive soils, so it's a good place for people (Oregon has the most rigorous statewide land use requirements in the country, with the basic goals of preserving prime farm and forest lands).

Before we purchased the property, we conducted extensive ecological studies to determine the site's carrying capacity and intrinsic suitabilities for various land uses. Twenty-five different factors were mapped and combined in the manner advanced by Ian McHarg in *Design With Nature*. Different combinations of factors represented the perspectives of the builder, the economist and the ecologist. A hydrological study determined carrying capacity and tolerance to impervious cover acre-by-acre. These composites guided the intial planning efforts, but later we decided to be even more protective by mapping large wildlife corridors and all of the prime forest lands and prohibiting any construction in these areas. A comprehensive wildlife management plan and a perpetual-yield forestry program are the basis of our plan to preserve the natural ecosystem at Cerro Gordo. Over 1,000 acres of natural forest and meadow are permanently protected through the Cerro Gordo Community Trust.

From the beginning, Cerro Gordo has always been an intensively participatory process. The goal is to create a genuine community, so we're working together as an extended community of future residents and supporters, starting with formulating the vision and choosing a site and continuing with planning, financing, building, economic, and community development. The participatory planning process has been invaluable as a way to clarify community values and goals and putting them in a dialog with the opportunities and constraints of the natural ecosystem. This has been a tremendous educational experience for the community members, as they get to know one another, the site, and the implications of their personal dreams for living in harmony with nature.

In an initial questionnaire, two-thirds of the households said they wanted to live in detached homes on acreage homesites. Most of our members come from urban or suburban settings, so their initial images are often motivated by getting away from the pressures of urban life. Less than two years later, however, after taking part in the extensive community planning process, the group reversed

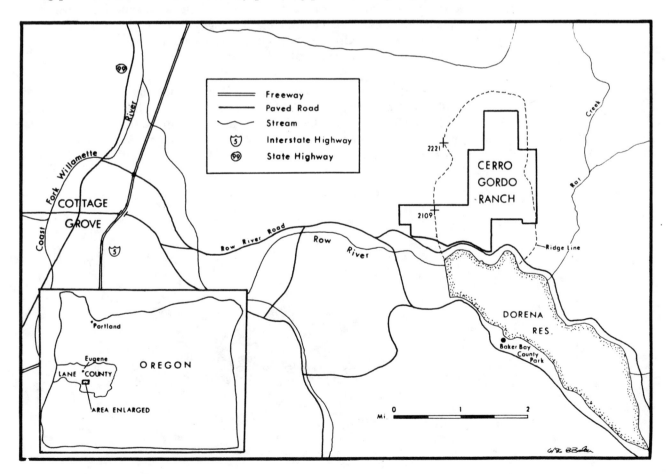

itself and over two-thirds said they wanted to live in attached homes in or near the village center. Part of this change was simply educational, as community members got to know the site and saw how scattering hundreds of homes across the Cerro Gordo valley would suburbanize the natural environment we want to preserve. But along with the learning process a more fundamental change occurred: the participants began to function as a community. As people got to know one another, their motivations changed from getting away from the city to moving toward the village; and along with choosing prospective neighbors there emerged a new image of living with nature. Instead of scattering homes across the landscape, they'll be clustered into a village, preserving over 90% of the site in its natural state.

As the heart of our community, we have long carried the image of the traditional pedestrian village with its shops and services, livelihood and community life. The image of the Medieval European village spoke to our yearnings for genuine human community. But most of these villages were walled towns, with the landscape paved over with buildings, streets and plazas. The wall

contained the village and preserved the surrounding fields and forests; but the homes had little contact with the natural environment. Cerro Gordo will have its mixed-use village center including most of the commercial and community buildings and some residences in townhouses and apartments above shops; but most of the homes will be clustered elsewhere so each home can have both village and nature. On one side of each home will be located some portion of the thousand-acre natural commons, permanently protected by the Cerro Gordo Trust. On the other side will be the village courtyard created by the neighboring homes, often including a cluster common building. Indeed, this clustering concept evolved out of the first cluster planning group who met weekly for most of 1975, and developed a plan much like the Danish *bofoellesskaber* as described by Kathryn McCamant and Charles Durrett in *Cohousing*.

The housing clusters and neighborhoods will be located within a quarter-mile radius of the village center, joined by paths to facilitate walking and bicycling and to eliminate the private automobile within the townsite. This has always been a fundamental tenet of the Cerro Gordo Plan: a community for people, not cars. How this will work is easy to envision when Cerro Gordo grows to its

VIEW FROM BARN OF VILLAGE CENTER, OFFICE & SHOPS
CHARLES HOWARD architect/planner 10 May '85

maximum population of 2,500, and employment and all the everyday activities can be found within the village. The challenge is building a no-car community one house at a time. The current reality is that our first dozen homes are dependent upon services in Cottage Grove, a town of 7,000 six miles west of us. Furthermore, county planning regulations usually require all homes have access via two-lane roads on 60-foot right-of-ways.

After some extensive planning and negotiating, we've come up with a system that meets practical and code requirements with one-lane, one-way loops through each cluster for emergency vehicles and large deliveries; and cluster parking areas that can be moved adjacent to the county road when we have a sufficient population to provide services on site. At that point many residents may eliminate the expense of a car of their own by forming a motor pool maintained by the Cerro Gordo Community Cooperative, our nonprofit residents' association. And most of the one-lane access loops will be incorporated into the bicycle and delivery path system or built as greenways with turf growing in concrete blocks.

The Oregon statewide planning laws provide the best protections in the country, but they also created horrendous delays for Cerro Gordo. When we started studying the property in 1973, Lane County planners warned us we wouldn't be able to proceed until the county completed and obtained state approval for its county comprehensive plan and zoning, which would take "a year or two." Each year after that the prognosis was the same: another "year or two." Eleven years later, on its third try, the county finally obtained approval for its rural comprehensive plan from the Oregon Land Conservation & Development Commission in 1984. The saga continued when the approval was appealed to the courts, and it wasn't until 1989 that Cerro Gordo's approvals became final. Sixteen years of planning delays created serious financial and organizational problems, but Cerro Gordo survived even though several well-financed commercial developments failed, and now we're building the ecological village we've always envisioned.

So far a dozen homes have been built with a variety of passive solar and energy conservation features. The first small manufacturing business has moved on site: Equinox Industries, producers of quality bicycle trailers which is an appropriate product for the no-car community of Cerro Gordo. It provides jobs to residents, who can commute to work by strolling down a forest path. The Cerro Gordo Forestry Cooperative is now in its sixth year of its perpetual-yield forestry program, producing enough lumber each year for 25 homes while permanenty protecting a diverse forest ecosystem. In the middle of clearcut country, the Forestry Co-op is demonstrating how we can have both the forest and the trees—a "real world," dollars-and-cents demonstration of the axiom of symbiotic community: the ecosystem is the larger economy.

ECOCITY NETWORKING

Currently we're planning construction of the Cerro Gordo Lodge and conference center, which will include a mini-village of clustered shops and offices and an outdoor amphitheater. This new mini-village will be the focus of our increasing networking, publishing and educational programs on Cerro Gordo and the growing global Ecocity Network. Last year Cerro Gordo was pleased to co-sponsor the *First International Ecocity Conference* organized by Urban Ecology in Berkeley, California. 150 speakers addressed the broad spectrum of how we can rebuild our civilization in balance with nature; and all 80 sessions are summarized in the 128-page book we co-published with Urban Ecology, Ecocity Conference 1990. Cerro Gordo is taking a key role in the growing Ecocity Network organized by the conference, and we look forward to networking with the Los Angeles Eco-Cities Council organized by the First Los Angeles Ecological Cities Conference. In April, 1992, the international ecocity discussion continued in Australia with Ecocity 2.

> *The first small manufacturing business provides jobs to residents, who can commute to work by strolling down a forest path.*

For more information about Cerro Gordo and the global Ecocity Network, write to the Cerro Gordo Town Forum, Dorena Lake, Box 569, Cottage Grove, Oregon 97424. Phone: (503) 942-7720; Econet: "cerrogordo". The newly updated Cerro Gordo Community Plan will be available soon for $5; *Ecocity Conference 1990* is available for $7; and the *Cerro Gordo Town Forum, Journal of Symbiotic Community* is available for $15 per year.

THE LONG VIEW

ECO-L.A.: A FUTURE SCENARIO

Sim Van der Ryn, AIA

L et's try and visualize what L.A. might be like 50 years from now.

Oil costs $300 a barrel in 1990 prices. It's too expensive to fuel cars or to heat and cool buildings. A substantial world-wide carbon extraction tax imposed on fossil fuel producers, and a carbon dioxide tax on fossil fuel burners are paying to purchase the remaining tropical rain forests and other biologically significant areas to be preserved as a planetary commons.

In Europe, Japan, and North America, fossil fuel use by consumers, both direct and indirect, is rationed and monitored. Each citizen is issued a quarterly ECO-Credit Card. Everyone has equal fixed entitlements to fossil fuel consumption, pollution, and virgin materials use. All commodities, from fuel, to food, and manufactured goods, are bar-coded as to their direct or indirect energy/pollution/extraction effects. More highly processed foods have a much higher energy content than local produce, and thus use up more energy credits. The direct use of raw fossil fuels such as gasoline is extremely limited, because even the use of a small amount, say a few gallons a day, would use up your entire energy budget for all other purchases that week. Products made with virgin materials use up more material credit, while goods that pollute, or whose manufacture cause pollution, use up more pollution credits.

All purchases and their energy/pollution/extraction values are magnetically encoded on the ECO-card whenever you buy anything. The card, when slid into a computer or TV slot, gives you an instant printout of how you are doing. When you've used up all your quarterly credits, the card is rejected, just like an ATM machine that spits out your card when you request more money than you have in your account. Each citizen receives electronic credits for 100,000 BTUs/day, about a tenth of 1990 per capita energy consumption. If your quarterly credits are used up, you can buy the unused portions of someone else's card, and there is a lively free market in personal energy/pollution/extraction entitlements. Bingers hang around transit stations looking for open cards to buy. Some people living a really low-energy life style, can live off the income from selling their unused ECO-credits.

People are free to spend their credits any way they wish. For his 70th birthday, my grandson goes on an energy binge, using up a week's worth of energy credits to take his grandkids out for a few hours drive in my antique 1987 Honda, the last car ever bought in my family, and well preserved. "Just think, kids, grandfather drove this petro-pig everyday by himself just to get to work. You know what it eats, dinosaur juice. They sure did funny things in the old fossil fuel folly days."

The freeways are still there. A light rail runs underneath the elevated roads, along a linear path of shops, offices, and apartments. On the old freeway, two center lanes are planted in fruit trees. There is one lane of auto traffic on each

*Sim Van der Ryn is an award winning architect and co-author of **Sustainable Communities**. His firm has designed a range of projects from new communities to public buildings to mixed-use facilities and custom homes. As California State Architect, he initiated a landmark program in energy efficient building. He teaches at U.C. Berkeley, and is President of the Farallones Institute, which has been a leading center for research in environmentally sustainable design.*

Sim Van der Ryn & Associates
55 Gate 5 Road
Sausilito, CA 94965
(415) 332-5806

side, and the two outer lanes are covered with photovoltaics that power the light rail and battery stations for the electric cars. The L.A. River, that used to run in a horrible concrete ditch through the city, the scene for many violent auto chases created by obsessed late twentieth century film makers, has been restored to its original state and is a lovely natural riparian habitat again. Drought, fires, and earthquakes have emptied the foothills of their foolhardy residents many years back, and the native chaparral-wildlife ecosystem is slowly recovering. Although it's a warm summer day with little wind, you can see the San Gabriel mountains clearly from the Santa Monica coast.

Downtown, the sealed glass buildings have been opened up. The air conditioning used up too many energy credits. Also, in the 1990s, occupants of these sealed buildings, from corporate presidents to computer clerks, were struck with a serious epidemic which after years was traced to spores of fungi, molds, and viruses growing in the filters of central air conditioning equipment and carried throughout the building.

A second transparent "bioskin" has been added to the high-rise buildings, creating a new space 10 to 20 feet wide, filled with growing food, plants of every variety: mangoes, bananas, dwarf citrus, vegetables. These hanging gardens provide food for the city, and exchange their oxygen with the CO_2 produced by building occupants. The plants are cared for by professional gardeners. There are many thousands of them in L.A., but if you want to, you can spend your lunch tending these high-rise farms and learn new techniques for your home garden, or you can run up and down the stairs for a noon workout. The elevators are reserved for moving essentials such as soil and produce.

> *Hanging gardens provide food for the city, and exchange their oxygen with the CO_2 produced by building occupants.*

The building's sewage is processed in clear plastic cylinders around the perimeter, and the resulting nutrient-rich soup flows to feed the plants. In the old days, it is said that a single sewage treatment plant in L.A. threw away a half-billion gallons of nutrient-rich waste water each day, polluting ocean life, and wasting enough nutrients to grow a pound of vegetables a day for every resident of the city. Each house and building in the city has an underground cistern to collect rainwater during the winter rains. This is also used to water gardens and landscape during the dry months.

In the neighborhoods, streets built to accommodate two lanes of traffic and two lanes of parking have been torn up and narrowed to pedestrian paths and bikeways; the asphalt recycled and turned into La Brea Tar building blocks with a dinosaur logo. What were streets have been turned into basketball courts, tot lots, shaded places for chess and reading. Every neighborhood has community food gardens connected to elementary schools. In the center of one garden, second graders are counting, weighing and measuring earthworms as a lesson in arithmetic and ecology. No one graduates high school without passing a test in eco-literacy.

In the early 1990s at UCLA, an L.A. Region EPIC or Environmental Planning Information Center was set up. EPIC was conceived as a regionally-based environmental situation room that through interactive computer graphics helps citizens, planners, politicians, students, and interested community groups, builders and developers, clearly understand their environment, how it is changing, and test the implications of proposed changes. EPIC is a major tool for redesigning communities towards sustainability.

Today, special interests control the planning process because only those few with a heavy stake in the process have access to the information, or time to understand what is going on. Sustainable design however, calls for honest information, clearly understood and easily accessible by whoever wants to know. Today's planning is done through a cumbersome framework of special interest agencies talking to special interests. No wonder NIMBY has become such a force. Most people give up, and only get involved when something threatens to affect them directly in their immediate environments.

Now, back to our future scenario: On a wall-size computer graphics image screen, during an environmental health planning session in 1995, researchers are overlaying a map generated from public health data of L.A. with a dot showing the home address of every 1990 cancer death. On top of this, they punch in another map showing air quality contours for the L.A. basin. On top of this, is layered census data showing tracts with more than 59% percent black, Hispanic, or white residents. A visual pattern emerges.

In the military and in the public and private sectors, new technologies and processes are rapidly emerging. These need to be employed to meet the critical challenges we face in our communities. In war situations, strategic and tactical decisions must be made on the basis of complex, dynamic and rapidly changing information. Out of this need, the military created Command Information Control Centers (CICC) which are a key tool for visually presenting all conditions affecting decisions using computer screens. CICC is an electronic war room. Maps and pins have been replaced by digitized databases which can be translated into computer-generated pictures and big rear-screen pictures.

Right now Geographic Information Systems (GIS) technology is developing very rapidly. All types of environmental and urban planning data, generated from maps, remote sensing data and other sources, can be digitized and presented in the form of computer maps. We have the technology available right now to create community-based environmental situation rooms using environmental and land-use data, singly or overlaid so you can begin to see real-time patterns of what's happening. Then we can stop arguing because there is no clear picture, and start seeing what is actually happening.

> We have the technology available to create community-based environmental situation rooms using environmental and land-use data.

The other necessary ingredient for a community-based center is team and group-oriented problem solving and design processes. In corporations, individualized decision making by compartmentalized specialties is being replaced by team problem identification and planning. The need for greater teamwork and integration of diverse specialties in order to respond to complexity and rapid change in today's organizations is being supported by the development of new team process technologies. These techniques can and should be used by citizen and local groups to improve communication, increase participation in the planning process, and to streamline the cumbersome, time consuming process that bogs down so much public planning today.

I visualize a network of regional EPICs around the planet linked electronically. Each one integrates visual group processes and electronic databases. Each EPIC is the center of a locally based decentralized neural network from which many different forms of sustainable community can be created and implemented.

By the time of our 2050 story, EPIC has grown into a global network. At a regional scale, a huge bank of GIS data exists, much of it collected at a very fine grain by junior high and high school students. The work of gathering information in their local environments is integrated into most of their formal areas of study. Now, by simply turning on the eco-channel on your cable and using the interactive command box, you can zoom in on your block and read every plant species there. Or you can overlay a map where fast food joints used to be, with that of the gardens and neighborhood centers that replaced them.

When a new project is proposed, instead of going to endless hearings with maps you can't see and people droning on with their particular opinions, you can insert your Voter Registration card in the TV slot, call up the development maps, use computer animation to show how the site will change, look at the site plan, study the impact on the local transit station, and when you've made up your mind, register your vote electronically.

Moving again back to the present, the beauty of creating fantasy futures is that it provides a forum to advance the discussion about how we are going to begin to behave. What is realistic, doable? What is possible, given the present state of social, economic and physical constraints? Or are there any constraints, really?

I say, let us get on with it!

WHERE DO WE GO FROM HERE?

Bob Walter & Lois Arkin

R ight now, our cities drain resources from the world around them and repay this gift of bounty with pollution and waste impossible to contain. Our challenge is to take less and give back something better, particularly since by accomplishing this rebalancing, we will provide improved quality of life for our current communities, and leave future generations a legacy to build on.

There is hardly a more archetypal place, ripe and ready for this rebalancing act, than the Los Angeles area. There are those who say there is no hope for L.A., that the city is lost, that the only sane course of action is to bail out for a destination not yet environmentally past hope. After all, our sewage system is overloading, sending pollutants into the Bay. Our air is shot. The last usable major source of groundwater has become polluted. Reports abound of cancer-risk. We are being buried in our own garbage. Crime rates are up. Housing has become unaffordable. . . .

But there is this other image which many of us keep sheltered in our mind. It is of the city seen on that rare day when winds have blown the air clean, when vistas are in focus and our city sparkles in the sun. It is a city of infinite promise. A city the world watches for trends and direction. A place of great cultural diversity, rich in all manner of exciting resources. This image is something we can cherish and focus on the same way we did on those first photographs of the Earth floating in space that so galvanized transformative thought about our whole planet.

> *There is this other image of the city seen on that rare day when winds have blown the air clean, when our vistas are in focus and our city sparkles in the sun.*

If each one of us begins to hold this kind of "infinite-promise" city-image in our mind, it can similarly transform our thinking and allow us to move forward with a basic level of agreement amongst ourselves, toward building a city that fulfills this vision every day of the year. But as our goals align, the question then arises: We know where we want to go, so how do we get there?

One answer is to make sure environmental guidelines are the foundation upon which any development is built.

CITIZEN-BASED VOLUNTEER ORGANIZATIONS

Another answer is for us to become more involved in helping shape the city. There is a growing awareness that the best city design is not accomplished in planning departments or in the drafting rooms of development companies or in response to politicians' perceived needs for their communities, but can only result when all these parties work in close relationship with the people whose lives will be affected. Many cities have already had citizen-based volunteer organizations spring up that enable citizens to express themselves as a coalition about development plans in their area. In many cases, these organizations also produce agendas that can serve as environmental guidelines for redrafting their cities' General Plans.

The energy these groups expend is not an idle exercise. Imbued with the necessary knowledge and possessing many original ideas, they have been able to enlist professional architects and planners to help shape their counter-proposals, and have gained the ear of those who would otherwise have proceeded without hearing what the community had to offer. In fact, where dialog and not confrontation was achieved, the creativity of these citizen-based organizations has been incorporated into the actual projects.

> *Where dialog and not confrontation was achieved, the creativity of citizen-based organizations has been incorporated into actual projects.*

Associations of this sort are sprouting up around the country and the world. The Sustainable City Project which links San Francisco, San Jose and Portland for sustainability planning is a good example. The Sustainable Seattle group is a voluntary association of individuals and representatives from business and government committed to making that city sustainable. The Eco-Justice Project and Network at Cornell University in Ithaca New York, recently organized a sustainable communities conference which grew out of a voluntary association of persons committed to creating an eco-village there.

The Global Cities Project sponsored by the Center for the Study of Law and Politics is an association of government, business and voluntary groups throughout the country, committed to ecological cities. Chattanooga Venture, based in that Tennessee city, is a non-profit organization which involves citizens, businesses and a diversity of other groups in public decision-making, especially through its training of volunteers as community facilitators.

Organizations of this type whose work is represented in this book include Urban Ecology in Berkeley, the Environmental Council of Sacramento (ECOS), the Citizen Planners of Ventura County and the EOS Institute.

THE LOS ANGELES ECO-CITIES COUNCIL

In the case of Los Angeles, one way citizens can play a more active role in the planning process is to take part in the Los Angeles Eco-Cities Council. This association was established by the planners of the *First Los Angeles Ecological Cities Conference* to continue the work begun at that event. Founded on the partnership approach initiated at the conference, the Eco-Cities Council is creating strategies to implement environmentally and economically-sound development policies for the greater Los Angeles area. We offer some of the Council's organizing elements as input for anyone seeking involvement or planning to start a similar organization in their city.

The four major goals of the Eco-Cities Council include:

1. Educating stakeholders.
2. Influencing public policy and private industry.
3. Promoting the implementation of ecological projects.
4. Serving as an information clearinghouse and network.

To promote efficiency and flexibility, the Los Angeles Eco-Cities Council seeks to minimize its formal structure in favor of a non-traditional organization based on project groups. The key organizing concept is that any work done on behalf of the Council must conform to a set of basic design principles that are a slightly modified arrangement of the eight *Ecological Planning Principles for Sustainable Living* which appear earlier in this book. This is a simple way of allowing someone to determine if they are interested in joining the Council and is also a means to evaluate any work done on the Council's behalf.

Although the core group of the Council is working on a wide variety of Council business, individuals or groups can join the Council in different ways and for a range of reasons: An individual can call for Council assistance on a specific problem of importance to their neighborhood. An architect or planner who may not have the time to involve themselves in on-going Council business can lend the clout of their name and make themselves available for consultation on key questions. If someone is putting their energy into a neighborhood-based group such as a homeowner's association, a church-based affordable housing developer or an interim single-issue organization, they can still affiliate their group with the Council in a loose coalition which can be to everyone's advantage.

> *It will be the citizens who decide which way our cities and the whole world will go.*

The range of projects the Council is undertaking is limited only by our collective imagination and the time we are willing to put in. Members are already working on making public comment on general plans and draft EIRs, and providing resources and support to those working in the direction of sustainable development. Helping actual projects which can bring sustainable cities into practical reality is also part of the Council agenda, as is presenting and collaborating on educational events which expand knowledge and promote interaction among all stakeholders in the future of our city.

The Los Angeles Eco-Cities Council will be happy to share any of its organizing information and help in any other ways that we can. You may also want to review the section of this book entitled: *The Human Component.*

AT THE CROSSROADS

These rapidly growing voluntary efforts are an important indication of peoples' commitment to healing the planet and a recognition of our longing to establish community, common purpose and personal empowerment. What is critical at this juncture is that large numbers of people from all walks of life begin to behave very quickly in radically different ways in order to secure survival of our species and improve our quality of life.

We are at a crossroads. It is a time that will decide whether we pass along a planet filled with the staggering natural beauty and promise which it still retains, or whether our legacy, our bequeathal, is a choked orb of collapsing systems leading to spacesuit safety measures, shortened lifespans, and a continual battle to keep afloat just above the poisonous debris of our day to day.

The vast disparity between these choices is heightened by another surprise. It will be the citizens who make the choice, who decide which way our cities and the whole world will go. Many decision makers may still wish to perpetuate existing systems to protect the status quo, so it will be we and our neighbors whose actions literally shape the destiny of this planet and lead our leaders toward a new way of life.

So many of the answers we need to save our cities, heal the planet and, in general, better our existence are contained in the magnificent flood of data and torrent of new technologies that threaten to sweep us off our feet. By taking this new information and leavening it with wisdom from our past about how to live in better balance on the planet, we can develop an ease with which to keep our footing. It is this sense of balance and the degree to which we let this synthesis shape our future that will mark the extent of our success.

Imagine strolling through tree-lined streets past a park to a picturesque commercial district where you can run some errands and stop at a sidewalk cafe that looks out on the town square alive with people and notable for an absence of car noise and fumes. Imagine actually having a neighborhood where people connect and storekeepers know your name. Imagine that the place where you live has a built-in set of telecommunication-ready office suites where you can "leave your house to go to work in the morning" and yet be only a few steps away from your home. Or picture taking a brief walk or bike ride to work.

If you can imagine being in a large city that provides all the amenities and high technology of urban living but combines these with the desirable small-town quality of life and sense of place that has been largely lost in our cities, then you are primed to play a part in making sustainable cities a reality.

We stand at the Gateway to Eden. The key to enter is within our reach. With an opportunity like this at hand, will we walk away?

It's our move.

RESOURCE GUIDE

This resource guide is a companion to the wealth of ideas and information presented in *Sustainable Cities*. The guide provides an introductory compendium to organizations, consultants and publications in the field of ecological building and community design. Resources listed are interrelated parts of the whole system of ecological city development. Between these and the individual bibliographies and resources at the end of some chapters, (see *Index* under "Bibliographies") you can probe more deeply into subjects of particular interest.

BUILDING A SUSTAINABLE FUTURE
ORGANIZATIONS AND CONSULTANTS

Paul Bierman-Lytle, AIA
P.O. Box 514
New Canaan, CT 06840
(203) 966-3541
President of The Masters Corporation and Environmental Outfitters and a member of the AIA Steering Committee on the Environment. One of the nation's leading advocates for non-toxic building.

Community Environmental Council, Gildea Resource Center
930 Miramonte Drive
Santa Barbara CA 93109
(805) 963-0583
A non-profit ecological resource center specializing in all aspects of recycling, waste water, sludge, composting, solar technology and ecological gardening. Research, training, publications, community outreach.

Cooperative Resources and Services Project (CRSP)
Lois Arkin, Director
3551 White House Pl.
Los Angeles CA 90004
(213) 738-1254
Lead organization for the Los Angeles Eco Village project. Non-profit education, training and development center for all kinds of cooperatives and communities. Community barter system, community loan fund, collaborative housing network, mutual housing association, community land trust, newsletter. Membership $25-$50

Eco-Home Network
Julia Russell, Director
Bob Walter, President
4344 Russell Avenue
Los Angeles CA 90027
(213) 662-5207
The Eco-Home Network is a non-profit, tax-exempt organization whose mission is to create a sustainable future for our cities through demonstration, education and building a constituency for ecological urban living. The Network's programs range from city-scale projects, such as the First Los Angeles Ecological Cities Conference, to bite-size, affordable solutions that can be implemented by individuals in their every day lives as demonstrated in the Eco-Home ecological demonstration home in Los Angeles. Tours twice weekly. Membership $25-$50.

Ecological Life Systems Institute
Jim Bell, Director
2923 East Spruce Street
San Diego CA 92104
(619) 281-1447
A non-profit organization that provides education materials for lectures, seminars, and published materials. Offers consulting and design services for home-owners, businesses and developers on ecologically integrated design.

Eco-Net
3228 Sacramento Street
San Francisco CA 94115
(415) 923-0900
Eco-Net is an inexpensive international telecommunications network linking environmental organizations and experts with E-mail, conferences, bulletin boards and gateways to other systems.

EOS Institute
1550 Bayside Drive
Corona Del Mar CA 92625
(714) 644-7111
Educational research and demonstration center on sustainable development; ongoing lectures, seminars and workshops; publishes quarterly journal, EARTHWORD. Primary sponsors of EOS are Architects, Designers and Planners for Social Responsibility and the Permaculture Institute of Southern California. A major goal of EOS is to create an ecologically integrated cooperative village in Orange County.

Global Cities Project
Center for the Study of Law and Politics
2962 Fillmore Street
San Francisco CA 94123
(415) 775-0791, Fax: (415) 775-4159
Deals with a full range of sustainable development issues. Publishes a series of handbooks aimed at city officials for building sustainable communities. Consulting with local governments and corporations. Handbook series includes water conservation, solid waste, toxics, transportation, energy , land use, air quality, greenhouse gases, urban forestry, open space, water quality, environmental management.

Institute for Regenerative Studies
California Polytechnical University
3801 West Temple Avenue
Pomona CA 91768
(714) 869-2684
Providing a university setting for education, demonstration and research in regenerative technologies. Plans include the 16 acre Landlab, a student community to explore new systems for energy, water, shelter, food production, and waste disposal.

Los Angeles Ecological Cities Council
Howard Cohen, Esq.
855 S. Shenandoah St., No. 1
Los Angeles CA 90035
(310) 854-5941
An association of diverse design and development professionals, environmentalists, educators and citizen activists committed to influencing public policy, promoting eco developments in the L.A. area, and providing education, networking and resources. Works through action task groups. Speakers bureau and media library on sustainable development.

Permaculture Institute of Southern California
Dr. Bill Roley, Director
1027 Summit Way
Laguna Beach CA 92651
(714) 494-5843
Demonstrates sustainable development principles of ecological house and gardens, Sprout Acres. Consultation and classes on water management systems, waste-cycling and composting, organic and edible landscaping, home design and energy management. Co-Sponsor of Eos Institute and EARTHWORD journal.

Planet Drum Foundation
Box 31251
San Francisco, CA 94131
(415) 285-6556
Grass roots ecological educational organization emphasizing sustainable community, self determination and regional self reliance. Developed concept of bioregions and actively pursues a green city project.

Richard Register
Ecocity Builders
5427 Telegraph Avenue W2
Oakland, CA 94609
(510) 649-1817
Richard, founder of Urban Ecology in Berkeley, and convenor of the First International Eco Cities Conference in 1990, is now focussing on creating ecologically built projects.

Rocky Mountain Institute
Amory and Hunter Lovins
1739 Snowmass Creek Road
Snowmass CO 81654
(303) 927-3851
Major center for energy conservation information, consulting.

Smart Legal Research
Esfandiar Abbassi
1205 N. Serrano Ave., No. 1
Los Angeles CA 90029
(213) 463-3797 Fax: (213) 463-1797
Provides information gathering and document retrieval for all aspects of eco city design and development.

Sustainable Urban Enterprise Explorations
Andrew Euston, FAIA, Director
HUD, Room 7244
Washington DC 20410
(202) 708-2504

Urban Ecology
P.O. Box 10144
Berkeley CA 94709
(415) 549-1724
Active in urban educational and environmental health action projects, ecological urban planning, citizen planners association, writing energy ordinances, and creek restoration projects. Organized the First International Ecological City Conference, 1990, at Berkeley, CA.

Worldwatch Institute
1776 Massachusetts Avenue, NW
Washington DC 20036
(202) 452-1999
Worldwatch Institute is an independent, nonprofit organization created to analyze and to focus attention on global environmental problems. Several publications are available on sustainable development.

BUILDING A SUSTAINABLE FUTURE
PUBLICATIONS

Bottom line: Restructuring for Sustainability
By Anthony Dominski, Jon Clark and Paul Relis
Community Environmental Council/Gildea Resource Center
930 Miramonte Drive
Santa Barbara, CA 93109
(805) 963-0583

Business Ethics: The Magazine of Socially Responsible Business
Mavis Publications, Inc.
1107 Hazeltine Blvd., #530
Chaska MN 55318
(612)448-8864
$49 annual subscription.

City Building Education: A Way to Learn
By Doreen Nelson
Center for City Building Educational Programs
2210 Wilshire Boulevard, 303
Santa Monica CA 90403

City of Man
By Leopold Kohr
University of Puerto Rico Press
Original thinking on functional urban scale, by the man who taught E.F. Schumacher about small being beautiful.

Death and Life of Great American Cities
By Jane Jacobs
New York: Vintage Books
The book that changed the planning profession, and still offers lessons we have not learned about how to build healthy and habitable citites.

Design with Nature
By Ian McHarg
Garden City, NY: American Museum of Natural History, Natural History Press, 1969.

Directory of Environmental Organizations 1991
Educational Communications
P.O. Box 35473
Los Angeles CA 90035

E: The Environmental Magazine
P.O. Box 6667
Syracuse, NY 13217
(303) 224-0083
A clearing house for information, news and comentary on environmental issues.

Earth in the Balance: Ecology and the Human Spirit
By Albert Gore
New York: Houghton Mifflin, 1992
In a brilliant and comprehensive plan for action, Gore addresses issues of the Earth's ecology, population trends, appropriate technology and environmental education.

Earth Island Institute Journal
300 Broadway
San Francisco CA 94133-3312
Critical news from the cutting edge of environmental technology, legislation and hot spots.

Earthword Magazine: The Journal of Environmental and Social Responsibility
EOS Institute
1550 Bayside Drive
Corona Del Mar CA 92625
(714) 644-711
Covers a variety of topics in depth of interest to the design and development community.

Ecocity Berkeley: Building Cities for a Healthy Future
By Richard Register
North Atlantic Books: Berkeley, 1987, $10.

Eco Expo Resources Directory
National Marketplace for the Environment
14260 Ventura Boulevard, Suite 201
Sherman Oaks CA 91423
(818) 906-2700
Extensive Listing of Eco Businesses and Non Profit Organizations

Ecotopia and Ecotopia Emerging
By Ernest Callenbach
Bantam Books
New York: 10103

First International Ecological Cities Conference 1990, a Conference Report
Edited by Christopher Canfield, 1990
Urban Ecology and Cerro Gordo Town Forum
$9. Order from Urban Ecology, P.O Box 10144, Berkeley, CA 94709 (510)549-1724

Garbage: The Practical Journal for the Environment
Old House Journal Corporation
435 9th Street
Brooklyn NY 11215
(800) 274-9909

Green City Program for San Francisco Bay Area Cities and Towns
By Peter Berg, Beryl Magilavy, and Seth Zuckerman
Planet Drum Books, 1989, $10.
P.O. Box 31251
San Francisco CA 94131
(415) 285-6556

Green Pages: The Local Handbook for Planet Maintenance
Green Media Group, 1990
P.O. Box 11314
Berkeley CA 94701
$20

In Business: The Magazine for Environmental Entrepreneuring
Box 323
Emmaus PA 18049
Bimonthly publication with regular supplements to Directory of Environmental Entrepreneurs and catalogues, including wide variety of building materials. $18/6 issues.

In Context: A Quarterly of Humane Sustainable Culture
P.O. Box 11470
Bainbridge Island WA 98110
Committed to finding practical steps and useful insights for creating a more sustainable planet. Cutting edge publication on sustainability issues. $24/yr.

Knowledge Systems
7777 West Morris Street
Indianapolis IN 46321
(800) 999-8517
Publication list on a sustainable future.

LandLab Newsletter
LandLab
3801 West Temple Ave., Bldg. 97
Pomona CA 91768
(714) 869-3341 Fax: (714) 869-3282
News from the Institute for Regenerative Studies at Cal Poly Pomona

Life in Jacksonville: Quality Indicators for Progress
Prepared by Jacksonville Chamber of Commerce
November 1990
This report notes positive trends while recognizing early warning signs so that problems can be addressed before they reach crisis proportions. Contact David Swain, 1001 Kings Ave., Suite 201, Jacksonville, FL 32207, 904/396-3052.

Los Angeles Follies: Design and Other Diversions in a Fractured Metropolis
By Sam Hall Kaplan
Cityscape Press, 1989
Santa Monica CA 90403
$5. Available from CRSP.

Los Angeles: History of the Future
By Paul Glover
Eco-Home Network
4344 Russell Ave.
Los Angeles CA 90027
(213) 662-5207. $5.

Mixed Use Developments
By Abbett and Glandstone
Washington, DC: Urban Land Institute, 1976

NAHB Library Bulletin
15th and M Streets, NW
Washinton DC 20006
(202) 822-0203
This National Association of Home Builders' bimonthly publication provides an extensive index on published articles on every aspect of the homebuilding industry, including topic areas on energy, conservation, environment, etc.

National Association of Home Builders Publications List
15 and M Streets, N.W.
Washington DC 20005
(800) 368-5242
Many books and publications on energy efficient buildings and all other aspects of the building industry.

New Paradigm Digest
1118 5th Street, #1
Santa Monica CA 90403
(800) 543-9316
A new quarterly overview of life enhancing social and business trends. $60/yr.

Our Common Future: Report from the World Commission on Environment and Development
Oxford University Press. Set up as an independent body in 1983 by the U.N. and Chaired by Prime Minister of Norway Gro Harlem Brundtland. This is considered by some to be the most important document of the decade on the future of the world. 1989. $10.95.

Paradigms in Progress: Life Beyond Economics
By Hazel Henderson
Knowledge Systems, Inc., 1991
7777 West Morris St.
Indianapolis IN 46231
(317)241-0749 Fax: (317)248-1503
New sets of personal, institutional and global standards pointing the way toward a more workable human ecology. Gives new directions, expanded context, and new scorecards for measuring a saner, more equitable, gender balanced, ecology conscious future. True cost pricing and growth/development indicators that can replace the GNP. $17. Available from CRSP (213)738-1254

Planners Network
1601 Connecticut Avenue, NW
Washington DC 20009
(202) 234-9382
An association of professionals, activists, academics, and students involved in physical, social, economic and environmental planning in urban and rural areas. Bi-monthly newsletter on who's doing what and where.

Policy Before Planning: Solving California's Growth Problems
By Dr. Judith Kunofsky
Sierra Club California, 1991
Sacramento CA
Green State of the State Report
$10

Race, Poverty and the Environment
c/o Earth Island Institute,
300 Broadway
San Francisco, CA 94133-3312
A newsletter expressing the environmental concerns of mainly urban people of color, who bear the brunt of toxic pollution as well as poverty.

Recycling Cities for People: The Urban Design Process
By Lawrence Stephen Culther and Sherrie Stephens
Boston: Cahners Book Int'l, Inc., 1976
Out of print but worth looking up.

Reinhabiting Cities and Towns: Designing for Sustainability
By John Todd with George Tukel
Planet Drum Foundation, 1981
P.O. Box 31251
San Francisco CA 94131
(415) 285-6556
Out of print, but worth looking up.

Resettling America: Energy, Ecology and Community: The Movement Toward Local Self-Reliance
By Gary Coates
Brick House Publishing Company, 1981
P.O. Box 134
Action MA 01720
(508) 635-9800

Save LA: An Environmental Resource Directory for the Greater Los Angeles Area
By Tricia R. Hoffman and Nan Kathryn Fuchs
Chronicle Books, 1991
275 Fifth Street
San Francisco CA 94103

Second International Ecological City Conference Proceedings
Paul Downton, Editor
Urban Ecology Australia, Inc., 1992
P.O. Box 3040 Grenfell St.
Adelaide, SA, Australia 5000
(08) 379-1984
Earthnet/Pegasus - peg.pdownton
Includes papers on a full range of international eco cities and sustainable development issues, including social and economic issues.

Seventh Generation
By Alan Newman
10 Farrell Street
South Burlington VT 05403
(802) 862-2999
Products for a healthy planet

State of the World [Annual]— A Worldwatch Institute Report on Progress Toward a Sustainable Society
Worldwatch Institute
1776 Massachusetts Ave. NW
Washington DC 20036
(202)452-1999
An annual report describing the currents and countercurrents of humanity's interaction with the global environment, with recommendations on how to shift the currents in sustainable directions. $10.95.
Available from W.W. Norton & Company, 500 Fifth Avenue, New York, NY 10111. Also at bookstores.

Sustainable Communities: A New Design Synthesis for Cities, Suburbs and Towns
By Sim Van der Ryn and Peter Calthrope
Sierra Club Books, 1986. $15.00.
730 Polk Street
San Francisco CA 94109
(415) 923-5600

Toward an Eco-City: Calming the Traffic
By David Engwicht
Envirobook, 1992
18 Argyle St.
Sidney, NSW Australia 2000
Defines the city as a concentration of exchange opportunities brought together to minimize the need for travel or movement. Provides extensive research that shows how economic and social exchange actually decrease as private auto travel increases. Makes extensive recommendations for making our cities more habitable. Includes guidelines for rebuilding existing cities, eco-rights section, glossary, and bibliography. 190 pp. Available from CRSP (213) 738-1254.

Toward Sustainable Communities: A Resource Book for Municipal and Local Governments.
By Mark Roseland (University of British Columbia)
National Roundtable on the Environment and Development, 1992.
1 Nicholas Street, Suite 520
Ottawa, Ontario K1N 7B7 Canada

Transnational Institute for Appropriate Technology (TRANET)
Box 567
Rangley ME
(207) 864-2252
Comprehensive quarterly newsletter and directory on who is doing what and where all over the world on sustainable technologies, especially at the grass roots level. $30-$150. Inquire P.O.Box 567, Rangeley, ME 04970, 207/864-2252.

ARCHITECTURE/ RESOURCE EFFICIENT DESIGN
ORGANIZATIONS AND CONSULTANTS

American Institute of Architects, Environmental Committee, Los Angeles Chapter Richard Schoen

6964 Shoup Avenue
Canoga Park CA 91307
(818) 702-9654

Architects, Designers and Planners for Social Responsibility (ADPSR)
Kermit Dorius, President
1550 Bayside Drive
Corona Del Mar CA 92625
(714) 644-7111
Part of a national organization providing a forum and outlet for architects, designers and planners to offer public education in matters which impact the welfare of citizens, communities, the nation and the earth as a whole. Offers ongoing lectures in Sustainable Development.

Blue Basin Development
Carol Houst, President
11212 Tujunga Canyon Blvd.
Los Angeles, CA 91402-1250
(818) 353-7459
Development/consulting firm specializing in site location, specification of healthy products, and enviromentally sound waste-water treatment and energy systems. Center for new Geographic Information Systems Technology (GIS) information.

Dennis Bottom, AIA
4627 Coldwater Canyon, #210
Studio City CA 91614
(818) 766-7315
Specializes in solar new design and retrofits of existing buildings.

Calthrope Associates
Peter Calthorpe
246 First Street, Suite 400
San Francisco CA 94105
(415) 777-0181
Architects and planners. Originator of Pedestrian Pockets, new strategies for ecologically sound suburban growth.

Brian Cearnal
523-1/2 State Street
Santa Barbara CA 93101
(805) 963-8077
Architect of Community Environmental Council Headquarters in Santa Barbara. Passive Solar orientation.

CoHousing Company
Kathryn McCamant and Charles Durrett
48 Shattuck Sq., Suite 15
Berkeley CA 94704
(415) 549-9980
Kathryn McCamant and Charles Durrett, architects
and planners and authors of the book *CoHousing, A
Contemporary Approach to Housing Ourselves.*
CoHousing is a new archtype in housing combining
individual dwellings with common facilities which
facilitate community life.

Jock de Swart
12533 Woodgreen Street
Los Angeles, CA 90066-2723
(310) 390-6793
An architect with a long background in environmentally sensitive construction. One of the original
planners of Cerro Gordo and a collaborator on the
innovative Rocky Mountain Institute headquarters,
he also brings a spiritual component into his architecture and planning.

Ecological Life Systems Institute
Jim Bell, Director
2923 East Spruce Street
San Diego CA 92104
(619) 281-1447
A non-profit organization that provides education
materials for lectures, seminars, and published
materials. Offers consulting and design services for
home-owners, businesses and developers on ecologically integrated design.

Ecology by Design
Audrey Hoodkiss
1341 Ocean Avenue, #73
Santa Monica CA 90401
(213) 394-4146
Environmental interior design.

Elizabeth Moule & Stefanos Polyzoides Architects
Stefanos Polyzoides, Architect
706 South Hill Street, 11th Floor
Los Angeles CA 90014
(213) 624-3381
Designer of major urban design projects such as
Playa Vista New Town in Los Angeles and Orange
Tree Plaza project in Riverside. They are also prepar-
ing a study for the future of downtown Los Angeles.

Energy Efficient Builders Association (EEBA)
Howard M. Faulkner, Executive Director
Technology Center, University of South Maine
Graham MN 04038
(207) 780-544
International organization dedicated to the design,
construction and operation of quality energy-efficient
buildings which are healthy, durable and affordable.

Energy Management Consultants, Inc.
Principal, Douglas Simms Stenhouse
20329 Roslin Avenue
Torrance CA 90503-2515
Provides energy conservation consulting services to
federal, state and local governments agencies, school
boards, architects, engineers, developers, building
contractors, owners and professional design associations.

Environmental Projects
2633 Laguna Canyon Road
Laguna Beach CA 92651
(714) 497-4401
Architects, general contractors and interior designers
involved in land planning and cooperatively designed buildings and projects.

Paul Glover
814 N. Cayuga St.
Ithaca NY 14850
(607) 272-2143
Urban Planner/ecological designer. Author of *Los
Angeles: A History of the Future*. Designer of Ithaca
Hours, a community based currency system.

Harry Jordan
P.O. Box 1066
Berkeley CA 94701
(415) 548-5652
Architect specializing in sustainable community
design, individual houses, whole neighborhoods and
intentional communities.

Sam Hall Kaplan, Consultant
823 20th Street
Santa Monica CA 90403
(213) 829-1942
Specializes in ecological urban design for neighborhood, community and cities.

Nader Khalili
P.O. Box 145
Claremont CA 91711
(714) 624-5251
Architect, author (*Racing Alone* and *Ceramic Houses)*
and founder of the Geltaftan Institute specializing in
the research and development of earth architecture
utilizing earth, water, air and fire. Professor of
architecture at SCI-ARC. Provides hands-on workshops for individuals and community groups. Books
available for $20.00 each plus $2.00 postage from
above address.

Managed Environments
Richard Crenshaw, AIA
940 Bay Ridge Avenue
Annapolis MD 21403
(301) 268-3592
Solar design and construction.

Mogavero Notestine Associates, Architects
David Mogavero, Principal
229 J. Street
Sacramento CA 95816
(916) 443-1033
Specializes in pedestrian and transit oriented mixed-
use development.

Ken Norwood, AIA
2375 Shattuck
Berkeley CA 94704
(415) 548-6608
Architect, founder of the Shared Living Resource
Center. Specializes in shared living community,
participatory design processes with residents, new
construction and rehabilitation.

Sim van der Ryn and Associates, Architects
55 Gate 5 Road
Sausalito CA 94965
(415) 332-5806
Specializes in environmentally sustainable design.

Glen Small, AIA
3021 Airport Avenue
Santa Monica CA 90405
(213) 391-1989
Architect, internationally known for his innovative
Green Machine, an ecologically integrated vertical
mobile home park and other ecological designs. Co-
founder and former professor at the Southern California Institute of Architecture, Santa Monica.

Joseph Smyth
509 Marin Street, #134
Thousand Oaks CA 91360
(805) 373-3712
Planned, designed and developed ecological communities on both the East and West coasts. Pioneer of a
participatory planning process to create a financially
and environmentally sound master plan for Ventura
County; pedestrian-oriented community planning.
Coordinating the development of an international
ecological planning and development consortium,
EcoCo.

Solar Survival Architecture
Michael E. Reynolds
High Mesa Foundation
P.O. Box 2267
Taos NM 87571
Architect for Dennis Weaver's new Colorado home
incorporating recycled tires and aluminum cans.
Authored two books: *A Coming of Wizards* ($12.95)
and *Earthship* ($24.95) available from A. Lewis
Bookseller, 1565 Altivo Way, L.A., CA 90026, 213/
668-0275. Discounts available.

Frank Villalobos
Barrio Planners
5271 East Beverly Boulevard
Los Angeles CA 90022
(213) 726-7734
Environmental planning, landscape architecture,
urban design, emphasizing citizen involvement.

Urban Ecology
P.O. Box 10144
Berkeley CA 94709
(415) 549-1724
Active in urban educational and environmental
health action projects, ecological urban planning,
citizen planners association, writing energy ordinances, and creek restoration projects. Organized the
First International Ecological City Conference, 1990,
at Berkeley, CA.

ARCHITECTURE/
RESOURCE EFFICIENT DESIGN
PUBLICATIONS

Autonomous House
By Brenda and Robert Vale
New York: Universe Books, 1977

Bioshelters, Ocean Arks, and City Farming
By Nancy and John Todd
Sierra Club Books, 1984.
A wide spectrum of innovative experiments integrating small, self-adapting systems with 21st century biotechnologies. Reports on individual projects as well as whole experimental environments from building interiors to whole deserts. Available from E. F. Schumacher Society also.

Breaking New Ground
By John N. Cole and Charles Wing
Little, Brown and Company, 1986.

Climactic Design
By Donald Watson, FAIA and Kenneth Labs
McGraw-Hill, 1983
Out of print. Copies available from author Donald Watson, FAIA, Dean, School of Architecture, Rensselaer Polytechnic Institute, Troy, NY

Cooling with Ventilation
By Subrato Chandra, Philip Fairey, and Michael Houston
U.S. Government Printing Office
Washington DC 20402-9325
(202) 783-3238
Publication #061-000-00688-5

Design Notes and Energy Notes
Florida Solar Energy Center, Public Information Office
300 State Road, #401
Cape Kennedy FL 32920
(407) 783-0300

Earthbuilders Encyclopedia
By Joseph Tibbets
Southwest Solaradobe School
P.O. Box 153
Bosque NM 87006

Ecological House
By Robert Brown Botter
New York: Morgan & Morgan Publishing Co., 1981

Gentle Architecture
By Malcolm Wells
McGraw-Hill, 1987

Green Architecture: Design for a Sustainable Future
By Brenda Vale
London: Thames and Hudson, 1991
Includes bibliographical references and index.
UCLA AAUPL/ARTS NA 2542.3 V35 1991b

Guide to Resource Efficient Building Elements
Center for Resourceful Building Technology, 1991
P.O. Box 3413
Missoula MT 59806
(406)549-7678

Integral Urban House: Self Reliant Living in the City
By Helga Olkowski, Bill Olkowski, Tom Javits, and Farallones Institute Staff
Random House, 1979
Authoritative work on creating ecologically integrated homes.
$19.06. Available from Eco-Home Network, 4344 Russell Ave., L.A., CA 90027, (213) 662-5207

Making Space: Design for Compact Living
By Rick Ball
Overlook Press, 1989

Man, Climate and Architecture, 2nd ed.
By B. Givoni
New York: Van Nostrand Reinhold, 1976

Modest Mansions: Designs for Luxurious Living in Less Space
By Donald Prowler
Rodale Press, 1985

More Homes and Other Garbage: For Self Reliant Living
By Jim Lecklie, Gil Masters, Larry Whitehead, and Lilly Young
Sierra Club Books, 1981
(415) 923-5600

Natural House Book
By David Pearson
Simon & Schuster, 1989
$21.86. Available from Eco-Home Network. 4344
Russell Ave., L.A., CA 90027, (213)662-5207.

Production of Houses
By Christopher Alexander
Oxford University Press, 1985

Progressive Architecture, Special Issue: Architects and the Environment
John Morris Dixon, FAIA, Editor
600 Summer Street, P.O. Box 1361
Stanford CT 06904
(213) 348-7531 Fax: (203) 348-4023
Subscription inquiries: (216) 696-7000, ext. 4150

Regional Guidelines for Building Passive Energy Conserving Homes
By AIA Research Corporation
Washington, DC: U.S. Government Printing Office, 1978

Resource-Efficient Housing Guide
Rocky Mountain Institute
1739 Snowmass Creek Road
Snowmass CO 81654
(303) 927-3851
A selected annotated bibliography and directory of helpful organizations.

Underground Buildings
By Malcom Wells
673 Satucket Road
Brewster MA 02631
Malcolm Wells, 1990, $14.95 postpaid

HEALTHY HOMES AND ECOLOGICAL BUILDING MATERIALS
ORGANIZATIONS AND CONSULTANTS

Air Control Technology Environmental (A.C.T.)
Lou Alonzo, Senior Consultant
22647 Ventura Boulevard, #239
Woodland Hills CA 91364
(818) 594-4143 or (213) 715-8225
Tests and remediates any type of indoor air quality problems.

Blue Basin Development, Carol Houst
11212 Tujunga Canyon Blvd.
Los Angeles, CA 91402-1250
(818) 353-7459
List of environmentally responsible building materials from insulation to plumbing. Available upon request for $15.

E² Environmental Enterprises Inc.
Attn: John Picard
12915 Greene Avenue
Los Angeles, CA 90066
(310) 827-1217

Clint Good
P.O. Box 143 ·
Lincoln VA 22078
(703) 478-1352
Architect specializing in non-toxic home design and construction.

Nader Khalili
P.O. Box 145
Claremont CA 91711
(714) 624-5251
Architect, author (*Racing Alone* and *Ceramic Houses*) and founder of the Geltaftan Institute specializing in the research and development of earth architecture utilizing earth, water, air and fire. Professor of architecture at the SCI-ARC. Provides hands-on workshops for individuals and community groups. Books available for $20.00 plus $2.00 postage each from above address.

Out On Bale (Un)Ltd.
Matts Myhrman
1037 East Linden St.
Tucson, AZ 85719
(602) 624-1673
Provides workshops, resources networking and technical assistance on straw bale construction.

HEALTHY HOMES AND ECOLOGICAL BUILDING MATERIALS
PUBLICATIONS

American Institute of Architects
Environmental Resource Guide
1735 New York Avenue, NW
Washington DC 20006
(800) 365-ARCH

Clean and Green
By Annie Berthold-Bond
Ceres Pres, 1990

Eco Source: Products for a Safer, Cleaner World
P.O. Box 1658 A
Sebastapol CA 95473
(800) 274-7040
Free 48-page catalog

Environ
Box 2204
Ft. Collins CO 80522
(303) 224-0083
Provides information on environmental illness and non-toxic building materials. $15/4 issues. Box 2204, Ft. Collins, CO 80522.

Healthy Home: An Attic to Basement Guide to Toxin-Free Living
By Linda Mason Hunter
Rodale Press, 1988

Healthful Houses
By Clint Good
Guaranty Press, 1989

Healthy House: How to Buy One, How to Build One, How to Cure a Sick One
By John Bower
Carol Communications, 1989
600 Madison Avenue
New York NY 10022

Indoor Air: Risks and Remedies
By Richard Crother, FAIA, 1989
Directions Publisher
P.O. Box 61135
Denver CO 80206
(303) 388-1875

Journal of Light Construction
440 Grand Avenue, # 300
Oakland CA 94610
(510) 465-4161
Monthly journal targeted to the small and medium size residential contractor. Covers building techniques, materials, tools, business etc. with an environmental orientation. $32.50/yr.

The Masters Corporation
Paul Bierman-Lytle, AIA
PO Box 514
New Canaan, CT 06840
(203) 966-3541
One of the nation's leading non-toxic building and design firms.

Nontoxic Home
By Debra Lynn Dadd
Jeremy Tarcher, 1986

Nontoxic, Natural & Earthwise
By Debra Lynn Dadd
Jeremy Tarcher, 1990

Pacific Northwest Eco Building Network Directory
Learned Integrated Habits
(206)850-7456

Safe Home Resource Guide
24 East Avenue #1300
New Canaan CT 06840
(203)966-2099
Also publishes *Safe Home Digest* bimonthly newsletter.

Why Your House is Hazardous to Your Health
By Alfred Zamm, MD
Prentice Hall, 1982

Your Home, Your Health, and Well Being
By David Rousseau
Ten Speed Press, 1988

WATER TREATMENT AND CONSERVATION
ORGANIZATIONS AND CONSULTANTS

Ecological Life Systems Institute
Jim Bell, Director
2923 East Spruce Street
San Diego CA 92104
(619) 281-1447
A non-profit organization that provides education materials for lectures, seminars, and published materials. Offers consulting and design services for home-owners, businesses and developers on ecologically integrated design.

Kodama Design Studio Waterforms
Joel Mueller
13820 Roscoe Boulevard
Van Nuys CA 91402
(818) 891-8331
Design and installation of flowing water environments capable of purifying water for commercial,
public and residential use.

**National Small Flows Clearinghouse, West Virgina
University**
P.O. Box 6064
Morgantown WV 26506-6064
(800) 624-8301

Office of Water Reclamation, City of Los Angeles
Dr. Bahman Sheikh, Director
City Hall Room 366
Los Angeles CA 90012
(213) 237-0887

Permaculture Institute of Southern California
Dr. Bill Roley, Director
1027 Summit Way
Laguna Beach CA 92651
(714) 494-5843
Demonstrates sustainable development principles of
ecological house and gardens, Sprout Acres. Consultation and classes on water management systems,
waste-cycling and composting, organic and edible
landscaping, home design and energy management.
Co-Sponsor of Eos Institute and EARTHWORD
journal.

Southern California Institute of Natural Resources
Arthur Jokela, Director
1 West California Blvd., Suite 123
Pasadena CA 91105
(818) 793-0877
Research and consultation on water conservation and
reuse, reforestation and repair, land design, urban
planning and institutional reform.

**Waters Task Force, A Subcommittee of the Sierra
Club Angeles Chapter Conservation Committee**
3550 West Sixth Street, Suite 321
Los Angeles CA 90020

WATER TREATMENT AND CONSERVATION
PUBLICATIONS

California Laws Related to Water Conservation
Department of Water Resources Central Records
Service
P.O. Box 942836
Sacramento CA 94236-0001
(916) 445-9371
Contains state and local laws pertaining to water
conservation along with brief descriptions of Depart-
ment of Water Resources's urban and agricultural
water conservation programs.

Earthword Magazine
EOS Institute
1550 Bayside Drive
Corona Del Mar CA 92625
(714) 644-7111
Fall, 1991 issue is devoted to urban water issues. $5.

Home Water Supply
By Sto Campbell
Vermont: Garden Way Publishing, 1983

In Business Magazine
J.G. Press, Inc.
419 State Avenue
Emmaus PA 18049
(215) 967-4135
Latest updates on ecological businesses and products.

Industrial Water Conservation Reference Papers
Contact: Charles Pike
Office of Water Conservation, Department of Water
Resources
P.O. Box 942836
Sacramento CA 94236-0001
(916) 323-5580

San Jose's Successful Residential Retrofit Program
Contact: Barbara Jordan
San Jose's Office of Environmental Management,
Water Resources and Conservation Programs
801 North First Street
San Jose CA 95110
(408) 277-5790

Save LA
Chronicle Books, 1990
275 Fifth Street
San Francisco CA 94103

Thirst for Growth: Water Agencies as Hidden Government in California
By Robert Gottlieb and Margaret Fitzsimmons
Focuses on six agencies in Southern California, overview of key issues of public accountability and water policy innovation, case studies, review of governance and public input process. $35 + $1.50 to University of Arizona Press, 1230 N.Park Ave., Tucson, AZ 85719, 1/800-426-3797.

Water 2020 : Sustainable Use for Water in the 21st Century
By Science Council of Canada
Ottawa : Minister of Supply and Services, 1988.
UCLA PAS Foreign WC 24, 1988

Water Conservation News
Office of Water Conservation, Department of Water Resources, Southern District
P.O. Box 6598
Los Angeles CA 90055
(213) 620-4107
Provides the latest information on urban and agricultural water conservation developments and activities.

SOLID WASTE MANAGEMENT AND RECYCLING
ORGANIZATIONS AND CONSULTANTS

Citizen's Clearinghouse for Hazardous Waste
P.O. Box 926
Arlington VA 22216
(703) 276-7070
Technical assistance and networking for grassroots organizations on a variety of waste issues. Publishes newsletter, "Everybody's Backyard" and "Action Bulletins."

Clements Engineering, Inc.
Chip Clements
6290 Sunset Boulevard, Suite 1223
Los Angeles CA 90028
(213) 469-4406
Environmental engineering and consulting to developers and public agencies, specializing in recycling, composting, and other waste management issues.

Community Environmental Council, Gildea Resource Center
930 Miramonte Drive
Santa Barbara CA 93109
(805) 963-0583
A non-profit ecological resource center specializing in all aspects of recycling, waste water, sludge, composting, solar technology and ecological gardening. Research, training, publications, community outreach.

Ecolo-Haul
Gary Peterson
P.O. Box 34819
Los Angeles CA 90034
(310) 838-5848
Comprehensive recycling planning and center.

Institute for Local Self Reliance
Neil Seldman
2425 18th Street, NW
Washington DC 20009
(202) 232-4108
A community resource organization for ecologically sound waste management systems.

Permaculture Institute of Southern California
Dr. Bill Roley, Director
1027 Summit Way
Laguna Beach CA 92651
(714) 494-5843
Demonstrates sustainable development principles of ecological house and gardens, Sprout Acres. Consultation and classes on water management systems, waste-cycling and composting, organic and edible landscaping, home design and energy management. Co-Sponsor of Eos Institute and "Earthword."

SOLID WASTE MANAGEMENT AND RECYCLING
PUBLICATIONS

Alternative Uses of Sewage Sludge
Oxford, England; New York: Pergamon Press
Proceedings of a conference organised by the Water Research Center (Great Britain) Medmenham and held at the University of York, UK on 5-7 September 1989/edited by J.E. Hall. Includes bibliographical references.
UCLA EMS TD 774 A38 1991

Backyard Composting: Your Complete Guide to Recycling Yard Clippings
By John Roulac
Harmonious Press
(800) 345-0096
$6.95

Bathrooms
By Alexander Kira
New York: Bantam Books, 1966

Municipal-Scale Composting in California: The Regulatory and Implementation Challenge Seminar Synopsis
Prepared by the Community Environmental Council, Gildea Resource Center
930 Miramonte Drive
Santa Barbara CA 93109
(805) 963-0583

Regeneration of Degraded Landscape Utilizing Composted Organic Waste
Cal Poly Pomona L.A. 606 Graduate Studies in Landscape Architecture, June 1988. Loan copies available at Eco-Home & CRSP.

Resource Recycling: North America's Recycling Journal
P.O. Box 10540
Portland OR 97209
(800) 227-1424

Toilet Papers
By Sim van der Ryn
Santa Barbara, CA: Capra Press, 1978

PERMACULTURE
ORGANIZATIONS AND CONSULTANTS

Dan Hemenway
2126 South Madison
Wichita KS 67211

Bill Mollison
P.O. Box 1
Tyalgum, NSW Australia 2484
(066)79-3442
Creator of permaculture concepts, designer, author, community consultant, workshops, founder of Permaculture Institute.

Dr. Bill Roley
1027 Summit Way
Laguna Beach CA 92651
(714) 494-5843
Sprout Acres demonstration center in Laguna Beach. Permaculture is the conscious design and maintenance of productive ecosystems which have the ability, stability and resilience of natural ecosystems.

PERMACULTURE
PUBLICATIONS

Best of Permaculture
By Max Lindegger and Robert Tap
The Permaculture Institute of Southern California
1027 Summit Way, Laguna Beach, CA 92651
(714) 494-5843

Introdution to Permaculture
By Bill Mollison, 1991, 198 pp., $25
A simple but complete introduction to the theory and practice of permaculture principles, especially geared for small landowner or backyard gardener.

Permaculture: A Designer's Manual and Permaculture One & Two
By Bill Mollison, 1988
The Permaculture Institute of Southern California
1027 Summit Way, Laguna Beach, CA 92651 (714) 494-5843

Permaculture: A Practical Guide for a Sustainable Future
by Bill Mollison, Island Press, 1990
1718 Connecticut Avenue, NW
Washington DC 20009

Sustainable Urban Renewal: Urban Permaculture in Bowden, Brompton and Ridleyton
By Colin Ball, et al
Armidale NSW, Australia: Social Impact Publications, 1985. Published in association with the Permaculture Association of South Australia. Includes bibliographical references. UCLA AAUPL/AUP HT 178 A82 H46 1985

XERSICAPING
ORGANIZATIONS AND CONSULTANTS

Cornell and Associates
2116 Arlington Avenue, #237
Los Angeles CA 90018
(818) 798-4763

Hummingbird Landscape Systems
13736 Goldenwest Street, Suite B
Westminister CA 92683-3192
(714) 841-7869
Specializing in herbs and edibles.

Verde: Custom Landscape and Design Installation
Ilene Adelman
(213) 470-2295
Licensed landscape contractor.

XERISCAPING
PUBLICATIONS

Plants for California Landscape: A Catalog of Drought Tolerant Plants
Bulletin 209, State of California
The Resources Agency, Dept. of Water Resources
P.O. Box 388
Sacramento CA 95802

Plants for Dry Climates: How to Select, Grow and Enjoy
By Mary Rose Duffield and Warner D. Jones
H.B. Books
(602) 889-2150

Sunset Water Wise Gardening
Sunset Publishing Corporation, Menlo Park CA

Taylor's Guide to Water-Saving Gardening
Houghton Mifflin
Two Park Street
Boston MA 02108

Trees and Shrubs for Dry California Landscapes: Plants for Water Conservation
By Bob Perry
Land Design Publishing
P.O. Box 857
San Dimas CA 91773

Water Conserving Plants and Landscapes for the Bay Area
East Bay Muncipal Utility District, San Francisco, 1990.

Xeriscape Information Packet
Eco Home Network
4344 Russell Avenue
Los Angeles CA 90027
(213) 662-5207
$4.00

URBAN AGRICULTURE
ORGANIZATIONS AND CONSULTANTS

American Community Gardening Association
c/o Philadelphia Green
325 Walnut Street
Philadelphia PA 19106

Common Ground Garden Program
Brenda Funches, Executive Director
2615 South Grand Avenue, #400
Los Angeles CA 90007
(213) 744-4341
Part of U.C. Extension Program. Provides full resources for low/moderate income community groups for creating community gardens. Working with more than a dozen organic food garden groups in public housing projects. Source of information on small farms, urban agriculture, community gardening and inner-city revitalization.

TreePeople
12601 Mulholland Drive
Beverly Hills CA 90210
(818) 753-4600
Urban forestry programs, including energy efficient siting of trees and food bearing trees.

URBAN AGRICULTURE
PUBLICATIONS

Gardener Supplies
128 Intervale Road
Burlington VT 05401-2804
(802) 863-1700
Aids for organic gardening and non-toxic pesticides and fertilizers.

Organic Gardening with Bountiful Gardens
Catalog, Ecology Action
5798 Ridgewood Rd.
Willits CA 95490
Over 230 untreated, open-pollinated seeds, green manure/cover crops, seed planning guides, best books, supplies for organic gardeners.

Simple Art of Planting a Tree: Healing Your Neighborhood, Your City and Your World
By TreePeople with Andy and Katie Lipkis
Jeremy P. Tarcher, Inc., 1990

ENERGY CONSERVATION
ORGANIZATIONS AND CONSULTANTS

Altman Construction
Jim Altman, President
1857 Lookout Drive
Agora Hills CA 91301
(818) 991-8955
Remodeling firm specializing in energy efficiency and built-in recycling systems.

American Solar Energy Society
2400 Central Avenue, Suite B-1
Boulder CO 80301
(303) 443-3130
A private, multi-disciplinary membership association dedicated to the development and utilization of reliable, renewable energy technologies. Publishes SOLAR TODAY magazine and ADVANCES IN ENERGY, hosts an annual roundtable in Washington, and distributes solar publications.

California Energy Commission
1516 9th Street MS 29
San Francisco CA 95814-5512
(916) 324-3298

Clearinghouse on Energy Financing Partnerships
2000 North 15th Street, No. 407
Arlington VA 22201
(703) 243-4900
Maintains an extensive collection of information and literature on alternative financing, with special emphasis on shared savings contracting and procurement issues pertinent to public-sector applications. Bibliographies, referrals, and other selected publications may be obtained free of charge.

Community Environmental Council, Gildea Resource Center
930 Miramonte Drive
Santa Barbara CA 93109
(805) 963-0583
A non-profit ecological resource center specializing in all aspects of recycling, waste water, sludge, composting, solar technology and ecological gardening. Research, training, publications, community outreach.

Conservation and Renewable Energy Inquiry and Referral Service (CARIERS)
Box 8900
Silver Springs MD 20907
(800) 523-2929
Renewable Energy Information.

Customer Technology Applications Center (CTAC)
6090 North Irwindale Avenue
Irwindale CA 91702
(800) 336-CTAC
Provides information about new electric technologies; industrial, commercial, residential; interactive video.

Department of Water and Power, City of Los Angeles
Planning and Conservation Department
111 North Hope Street
Los Angeles CA 90012
(213) 481-7700

Energy Management Consultants
Douglas Simms Stenhouse, Principal
20329 Roslin Avenue
Torrance CA 905035
(213) 370-6584
A multi-disciplinary firm providing energy conservation consulting services.

National Appropriate Technology Assistance Service (NATAS)
P.O. Box 2525
Butte MT 59702-2525
(800) 428-2525

National Center for Appropriate Technology
Barbara Miller
P.O. Box 3838
Butte MT 59702
(406) 494-4572
A national clearinghouse for appropriate technology information.

National Renewable Energy Laboratory
1617 Cole Boulevard
Golden CO 80401
(303) 231-7303
Conducts research and development on an array of advanced solar building technologies, including vacuum insulation, new heat-storing materials, solar cooling technology, indoor ventilation systems, solar water heating systems with lower costs and improved reliability, and advanced window technology.

Rocky Mountain Institute
Amory and Hunter Lovins
1739 Snowmass Creek Road
Snowmass CO 81654
(303) 927-3851
Major center for energy conservation information, consulting, publications.

Southern California Gas Company
810 South Flower Street
Los Angeles CA 90017
(213) 689-2336

Zond Systems, Inc.
P.O. Box 1910
Tehachapi CA 93581
(805) 822-6835
Designs, develops and operates wind facilities which generate over 15% of all wind power in California.

ENERGY CONSERVATION
PUBLICATIONS

111 Ways to Control Your Electric Bill
Booklet offers suggestions for energy conservation in areas of home heating, cooling, lighting, cooking, water heating, laundering, and refrigeration. It also gives tips on energy-efficient operation of numerous household appliances. 1991. Edison Electric Institute item No. 07-91-03. $65 per 200 copies. (20% discount for EEI members). Available from:
Edison Electric Institute
701 Pennsylvania Avenue NW
Washington, D.C. 20004-2696
Attn: Order and Billing
(202) 508-5424 or (202) 508-5425.

Builder's Guide to Energy Efficient Homes in Georgia
A State-of-the-art primer on energy-efficiency measures available to residential builders. Specific to the Georgia climate, but appropriate for other states. Includes comparative costs of different energy-saving packages. Covers heat and moisture flow, infiltration control techniques, insulation, windows and doors, HVAC, domestic hot water, appliances and lighting, passive solar design, and natural cooling. March 1990. 125 pp. Free. Available from:
The Governor's Office of Energy Resources
Suite 615
Trinity-Washington Building
Atlanta, GA 30334
(404) 656-5176.

Building Sustainable Communities: An Environmental Guide for Local Government
Includes extensive technical, legislative, policy, fincancial resources, case studies and a menu of projects, bibliography and organizational resources. Available from:
Global Cities Project,
2962 Fillmore Street
San Francisco, CA 94123
(415) 775-0791

Cooling our Cities: The Heat Island Reduction Guidebook
Hashem Akbari, Joe Huang, and Susan Davis, eds. Outlines research to date on effectiveness of landscape and design guidelines to reduce the urban heat island effect. Includes a chapter on model urban heat island ordinances. April 1991. 200 pp. $ 20. Copies available from:
Ron Ritschard
Lawrence Berkeley Laboratory
Mail Stop 90-3118
1 Cyclotron Road
Berkeley, CA 94720

Directory of Computer Software
Guide to machine-readable software compiled from more than 100 U.S. government agencies. It describes more than 1,600 programs from the National Energy Software Center. Available in Paperback or microfiche copies. Additional updated supplements are offered on a regular basis. Available from:
National Technical Information Service
5285 Port Royal
Springfield, VA 22161
(703) 487-4650.

Energy Casebook
By William Browning and L. Hunter Lovins.
Explores successful energy-related economic development projects from across the country. Provides an array of projects in energy efficiency, renewable energy, and economic development. Also includes sections on energy costs and the local economy, economic development and utilities, and a glossary of energy terms. October 1989. 64 pp. $20. Published by the Economic Renewal Program of Rocky Mountain Institute, 1739 Snowmass Creek Road, Snowmass, CO 81654, (303) 927-3851.

Energyware: The World Directory of Energy Conservation and Renewable Energy Software for the Microcomputer
A comprehensive list of developers and vendors of software systems used for residential energy audits. Available form Wind Books, P O Box 4008, St. Johnsbury, VT 05819, (802) 748-2425.

Environmental Auditing Skills Techniques Workbook
Discusses audit techniques used in the field. Provides the auditor with skills and techniques to conduct an effective audit, and includes specific principles, examples, and checklists. 1987. Edison Electric Institute item No. 06-87-25. $65 (20% discount for EEI members). Available from Edison Electric Institue, 701 Pennsylvania Avenue NW, Washington, D.C. 20004-2696, Attn: Order and Billing, (202) 508-5424 or (202) 508-5425.

Getting America Back on the Energy Efficiency Track
By Howard Geller, et al.
Study discusses and analyzes energy-efficiency improvements during the past 17 years. Identifies promising policy initiatives. 1991. 38 pp. $6. Available from the American Council for an Energy-efficient Economy (ACEEE), 2140 Shattuck Avenue, Berkeley, CA 94704, (415) 549-9914.

Global Ecology Handbook
By Global Tomorrow Coalition
Boston, MA: Beacon Press, 1990

Heating, Cooling, Lighting: Design Methods for Architects
By Norbert Lechner
John Wiley & Sons, Inc.
605 3rd Avenue
New York NY 10158-0012

Improving Street Climate Through Urban Design
1983, 34 pp. $16. This report examines three climatic factors that are influenced by the built environment and in turn influence street comfort: urban wind, urban heat islands, and urban precipitation. Shows how planners can ameliorate street climate. Available from Planners Bookstroe, 1313 E. 60th St., Chicago IL 60637, (312) 955-9100.

Innovative and Incentive Package to Reduce Municipal Energy Consumption, 1984.
72 pp. $15. Pub. No. 83-307. Analyzes potential creative financing methods for capital improvements related to energy management of public buildings. Discusses shared savings, bonding, and lease-purchase arrangements. Available from Public Technology, Inc. Urban Consortium Energy Task Force, Publications and Distribution, 1301 Pennsylvania Avenue, NW, Washington, DC, 20004, (202) 626-2400.

Landscaping for Energy Conservation
By Magdy Girgis
Discusses the value of using trees to cut household energy consumption, particularly for air conditioning. Offers helpful advice for determinig what to plant where, particularly for the Florida climate. Available from the Florida Solar Energy Center, 300 State Road 401, Cape Canaveral, FL 32920-4099, (407) 783-0300.

Landscaping: Energy Conservation in the Air-Conditioned House
By John Parker
1986. 46pp. $ 5.95. One in a series of booklets on building, landscaping, and living more comfortably and efficiently in warm humid climates. Accompanying video. Available form Miami-Dade Community College, Product Development & Distribution, 11011 SW 104 Street, Miami, FL 33176. (305) 347-2158.

Publications Catalog of the American Council for an Energy-Efficient Economy: Exploring the Frontiers of Energy Policy and Energy Conservation
American Council for an Energy Efficient Economy
1001 Connecticut Avenue NW, Suite 535
Washington DC 20036, (202) 429-8873
A resource guide to energy efficient appliances.

Real Goods: Alternative Energy Sourcebook
By John Schaeffer
966 Mazzoni Street
Ukiah CA 95482
(800) 762-7325
Alternative energy products for a cleaner and saner world. Free catalog available.

Sun, Rhythm, Form
By Ralph L. Knowles
Cambridge, MA: MIT Press, 1981

Sustainable City Project
HUD, Sustainable Enterprise Explorations
Rm. 7244
Washington DC 20410
(202)708-2504
1991. The report features innovative energy policy that lays groundwork for building a city's sustainable energy future, a planning process that links energy with community issues and enables a local jurisdiction to pursue sustainable energy programs. Includes bibliography.

Technology Assessment: Thermal Cool Storage in Commercial Buildings
By M.A. Piette, et al.
Investigates the current and potential use of thermal storage systems for cooling commercial buildings. January 1988. 53pp. $17. Order Document No. DE-88014043 from the National Technical Information Service, U.S. Department of Commerce, 5285 Port Royal Road, Springfield, VA 22161, (703) 487-4600.

SOLAR DESIGN
ORGANIZATIONS AND CONSULTANTS

American Solar Energy Society
2400 Central Avenue, Suite B-1
Boulder CO 80301
(303) 443-3130
A private, multi-disciplinary membership association dedicated to the development and utilization of reliable, renewable energy technologies. Publishes "Solar Today" magazine and "Advances in Energy," hosts an annual roundtable in Washington, and distributes solar publications.

California Solar Energy Industries Association
Delores Evarts, Executive Director
889 Riverside Avenue, Suite C
Roseville CA 95678
(916) 7822-4809
Founded in 1977 to promote the growth and advancement of solar energy and the solar industry in California. Referrals, newsletter, lobbying.

Gary Flo, Mechanical Engineer
1570 Jonive Rd.
Sebastopol CA 95742
(707) 874-1207
Solar system designs and installation, electric vehicle conversions

Earth Mind
Michael Hackleman
P.O. Box 743
Mariposa, CA 95338

National Renewable Energy Laboratory
1617 Cole Boulevard
Golden, CO 80401
(303) 231-7303
Conducts research and development on an array of advanced solar building technologies, including vacuum insulation, new heat-storing materials, solar cooling technology, indoor ventilation systems, solar water heating systems with lower costs and improved reliability, and advanced window technology.

Passive Solar Industries Council
Helen English, Executive Director
1090 Vermont Avenue, NW, Suite 1200
Washington DC 20005
(202) 371-0357
A council of building industry organizations and professionals founded to provide the industry with practical passive solar technology and energy-efficient building.

Richard Palmer & Associates, Inc.
Richard Palmer, Mechanical Engineer
1910 East Warner Avenue, #A
Santa Ana CA 92705
(714) 261-5704
Solar passive design for residential, multi-family and commercial.

Solar Electrical Engineering (SEE)
116 4th Street
Santa Rosa CA 95401
(800) 832-1986
SEE is a publicly held corporation committed to providing environmentally helpful products ranging from recycled paper and solar electric cells through electric cars. Largest manufacturer of electric vehicles in the U.S., and has been building the pollution free vehicle for over 10 years.

SOLAR DESIGN
PUBLICATIONS

Commercial Building Design: Integrating Climate, Comfort and Cost
Burt Hill Kosan Rittelmann Associates and Min Katrowitz Associates
New York: Van Nostrand Reinhold Co., 1987

Passive Solar Energy Book, Expanded Professional Edition
By Edward Mazria
Rodale Press, 1979

Real Goods: Alternative Energy Sourcebook
By John Schaeffer
966 Mazzoni Street
Ukiah CA 95482
(800) 762-7325
Alternative energy products for a cleaner and saner world. Free catalog available.

Solar Home Book: Heating, Cooling and Designing with the Sun
By Bruce Anderson and Michael Riordan
Harrisville, NH: Brick House Publishing Co., 1976

Solar Today
2400 Central Avenue, Suite B-1
Boulder CO 80301
(303) 443-3130 Fax: (303) 443-3212
Subscriptions $25/yr. $32 Outside USA

Village Homes' Solar House Designs: A Collection of 13 Energy-Conscious House Designs
By David Bainbridge, Judy Corbett and John Hofarce
Emmaus, PA: Rodale Press, 1979

TRANSPORTATION
PUBLICATIONS

Alternative Transportation News
Earthmind
P.O. Box 743
Mariposa, CA 95338
Bimonthly magazine on all the latest innovations.
$20/yr.

Alternatives to the Automobile: Transport for Livable Cities
By M.D. Lowe
Washington, D.C.: Worldwatch Insitute
1776 Massachusetts Ave. NW
Washington DC 20036
(202)452-1999

Cities and Automobile Dependence: An International Sourcebook, Transport Energy
By Peter Newman and Jeff Kenworthy
Institute for Science & Technology Policy (ISTP) at Murdoch University
Perth, WA, Australia
(09)332-2902 Fax: (09)310-5537
Seminal research substantiating the negative impacts of private automobiles on cities with respect to social, economic and ecological factors. Write for details.

Pedestrian Pocket Book
By Peter Calthrope and Mark Mack
246 1st Street, #400
San Francisco CA 94105

Rethinking the Role of the Automobile
by Michael Renner, Worldwatch Institute, 1988
(202) 452-1999

Toward an Eco-City: Calming the Traffic
By David Engwicht
Envirobook, 1992
18 Argyle St.
Sidney, NSW Australia 2000
Defines the city as a concentration of exchange opportunities brought together to minimize the need for travel. Provides extensive research that shows how economic and social exchange actually decrease as private auto travel increases. Makes extensive recommendations for making our cities more habitable. Includes guidelines for rebuilding existing cities, eco-rights section, glossary, and bibliography. 190 pp. Available from CRSP.

Transport Energy Conservation Policies for Australian Cities: Strategies for Reducing Automobile Dependence
Newman, Kennedy and Lyons
Murdock University, 1990
Western Australia
Eco Home Library.

TRANSIT SYSTEMS AND DESIGN
ORGANIZATIONS AND CONSULTANTS

Alliance for a Paving Moratorium, A Project of Fossil Fuels Policy Action Institute
John Lundberg, President
P.O. Box 8558
Fredericksburg VA 22404
(703) 371-0222

California Transit
1348 Sierra Avenue
San Jose CA 95126
(408) 985-1848

Campaign for New Transportation Priorities
c/o 236 Massachusetts Avenue, #603
Washington DC 20002
(202) 546-1550

Institute for Transportation Development and Policy (ITDP)
P.O. Box 56538
Washington DC 20011
(301) 589-1810

Los Angeles County Transportation Commission (LACTC)
403 West 8th Street, #500
Los Angeles CA 90014
(213) 623-1194

Los Angeles Transit League
P.O. Box 41198
Los Angeles CA 90041

Modern Transit Society
P.O. Box 5582
San Jose CA 95150

Southern California Rapid Transit District (RTD)
425 South Main Street
Los Angeles CA
(213) 972-6000

Transit Advocates for L.A.'s Environment
(213) 254-9041

TRANSIT SYSTEMS AND DESIGN
PUBLICATIONS

Cities and Automobile Dependencies: An International Sourcebook
By Peter Newman and Jeffrey Kenworthy
Gower Technical, 1989

City: Rediscovering the Center
By William H. Whyte
Doubleday, 1988
386 pages. $24.95.

Managing Urban Density in the San Francisco Bay Region
Department of Public Transportation, California State University, Hayward, (415) 881-3507.
May be ordered from the Hayward Bookstore.

Motorization of American Cities
By David J. St. Clair
Praeger, 1986

Steering a New Course: Transportation, Energy, and the Environment
By Deborah Gordon
Cambridge, MA: Union of Concerned Scientists, 1991
228 pages.

Traditional Neighborhood Developments: Will the Traffic Work?
By Walter Kulash
Bellevue, Washington, 1990
Paper presented at the 11th Annual Pedestrian Conference, (408) 626-9080.

BICYCLES
ORGANIZATIONS AND CONSULTANTS

Association to Advance Bicycling
John Gracie, Executive Director
7013 Pomelo Drive
West Hills CA 91307
(818) 883-1307

Bicycle Federation of America
1818 R Street NW
Washington DC 20009
(202) 332-6986
National clearinghouse for bicycle planning and advocacy. Publishes "Pro Bike News."

California Association of Bicycling
Organization Headquarters
P.O. Box 2684
Dublin CA 94568
(415) 967-5580
(213) 639-9348, Ruth Barnes
Publishes Proposals for Legislation to Benefit Bicyclists.

Human Powered Transit Association, Inc.
Nancy Wedeen
11219 Califa
North Hollywood CA 91601
(818) 985-8415

L.A. City Bicycle Advisory Committee
Alex Baum, Chair
5437 Corteen Place, #201
North Hollywood CA 91607
(818) 761-5576

Pasadena Bicycle Task Force
Tim Brick
(818) 792-2442

Ryan Snyder Associates, Inc.
Transportation Planning
1015 Gayley Avenue, #124
Los Angeles CA 90024
(310) 824-9931 Fax: (310) 824-1342
Publishes Strategies for Planning of Bicycle Friendly Communities and Citizens for the West L.A. Veloway Committee.

BICYCLES
PUBLICATIONS

Alternatives to the Automobile: Transport for Livable Cities
By M.D. Lowe
Washington, D.C.: Worldwatch Insitute
1776 Massachusetts Ave. NW
Washington DC 20036
(202)452-1999

The Bicycle: Vehicle for a Small Planet
by Marcia Lowe, Worldwatch Institute, 1989,
(202) 452-1999.

DEVELOPMENT OF COMMUNITY:
THE COLLABORATIVE APPROACH
ORGANIZATIONS AND CONSULTANTS

Lottie Cohen, Attorney
9841 Airport Blvd. Suite 900
Los Angeles CA 90045
(310) 215-9244
Attorney specializing in co-ops of all kinds.

Michael Corbett
(916) 756-5941
Designer of Village Homes, an ecologically integrated community in Davis, California.

Center for Cooperatives at UC Davis
Davis CA 95616
(916) 752-1336
Education, research, outreach, publications list. Co-op Directory for State of California.

Cerro Gordo/Town Forum
Chris Canfield, Coordinator
Dorena Lake
Box 569
Cottage Grove OR 97424
(503) 942-7720
An ecological community on 1200 acres of land developing sustainable technologies and design. Publishes the "Cerro Gordo Town Forum: Journal of Symbiotic Community," a quarterly newsletter, $15, and the Cerro Gordo Community Plan $5. Co-sponsors of the First International Ecological City Conference 1990. Publications List.

Co-op America
2100 M Street, NW, Suite 310
Washington DC 20063
(800) 424-2667
National market place for ecological co-op products and services, quarterly magazine "Building Economic Alternatives," co-op health insurance. Reduced membership through CRSP.

Co-op Resource Center
1442A Walnut Street, Suite 415
Berkeley CA 94709
(415) 538-0454
Extensive publications list, organizes annual summer Co-op Camp Sierra for all who are involved with or who want to learn about co-ops. Sponsors the Twin Pines Housing Co-op Institute, co-op conferences on various topics.

Community Service Books
P.O. Box 243
Yellow Spring OH 45387
(513) 767-2161
Specializing in publications on small communities and the social process of community building. Annual conference.

Cooperative Resources and Services Project (CRSP)
Lois Arkin, Director
3551 White House Pl.
Los Angeles CA
(213 738-1254
Lead organization for the Los Angeles Eco Village project. Non-profit education, training and development center for all kinds of cooperatives and communities. Community barter system, community loan fund, collaborative housing network, mutual housing association, community land trust, newsletter, publications list. Membership $25-$50.

Institute for Cultural Affairs (ICA)
4220 North 25th Street
Phoenix AZ 85016
(602) 955-4811
Shared responsibility is replacing hierarchical authority in governments, corporations and organizations. ICA catalyzes that responsibility in communities and organizations by demonstrating participatory approaches to leadership, planning and action. Workshops and seminars on developing a variety of facilitation and participatory skills. Extensive work with multi-cultural leadership development. Offices in 53 cities worldwide. Non-profit.

Los Angeles Eco Village Project
Lois Arkin
3551 White House Place
Los Angeles CA 90004
(213) 738-1254
EcoVillage is planned as a sustainable neighborhood integrating cooperative economics, social and physical systems, including co-housing, a community land trust, community transportation system, community center, business incubator, mutual housing association and more. Updates are provided in the "L.A. EcoVillage and Co-op Networker" newsletter from CRSP (subscriptions: $10/yr.).

National Association of Housing Cooperatives
1614 King Street
Alexandria VA 22314
(703) 549-5201
Newsletters, publications, conferences, co-op training workshops.

National Cooperative Business Association
1401 New York Avenue, NW, Suite 1100
Washington DC 20005
(202) 638-6222
An all co-ops federation for the U.S., monthly newspaper, publications list.

North American Students of Cooperation
Box 7715
Ann Arbor MI 48107
(313) 663-0889
Newsletter, publications, annual conference, assists students to develop and manage co-ops of all kinds, with special emphasis on student housing co-ops, co-op internship program.

Southern California Association of Non-Profit Housing (SCANPH)
4032 Wilshire Blvd., Suite 301
Los Angeles CA 90010
(213) 480-1249 Fax: (213) 480-1788
Membership association of non-profit housing developers, resource organizations, consultants. Provides many workshops and annual conference on all aspects of affordable housing. Member Directory $15.

Twin Pines Cooperative Housing Institute
Co-op Camp Sierra
1442A Walnut Street, Suite 415
Berkeley CA 94709
(510) 538-1454
A week long summer program held annually at Co-op Camp Sierra. The Institute brings together residents, activists and technical assistance providers to share their skills and visions to build stronger housing cooperatives and to encourage their expansion.

DEVELOPMENT OF COMMUNITY: THE COLLABORATIVE APPROACH
PUBLICATIONS

ArtHouse Live/Work Development Seminar 1992
California Lawyers for the Arts, 1992
315 W. 9th St., Suite 1101
Los Angeles CA 90015
(213)623-8311
Targeted for artists and others who want to have live/work spaces in same building. Includes codes, dealing with toxics, development process, financing and insurance, resources and appendix. Includes draft of home-based business ordinance for City of Los Angeles and summary of controversy. Inquire for price.

Bank Notes
National Cooperative Bank
1401 Eye Street, NW
Washington DC 20005
(800) 955-9NCB
Quarterly newsletter from the NCB.
Free

Builders of the Dawn: Community Lifestyles in a Changing World
By Corinne McLaughlin and Gordon Davidson
Book Publishing Co., 1986
Insightful overview of community lifestyles based on interviews with many community founders. Includes workable guidelines for starting communities, resource and address section of communities. 372 pp. $20.00. Avaiable from CRSP 3551 White House Place, Los Angeles, CA 90004

Building United Judgment: A Handbook for Consensus Decision Making
By the Center for Conflict Resolution
New Society Publishers
P.O. Box 582
Santa Cruz CA 95061-0582
(800) 333-9093
Guidelines for reaching group unity and creating decision-making structures that work for a particular group. Shows how to maximize cooperation and fully use the creativity of all members of a group. Shows how to recognize conflict as a source of growth, $9.96.

California Cooperative Directory and Resource Guide
Center for Cooperatives, 1991
University of California, Davis
Davis CA 95616
(916) 752-24
A 41 page guide to co-ops and co-op resources throughout California, including arts and crafts, childcare, credit unions, food co-ops, housing co-ops, memorial and funeral societies, student co-ops, worker co-ops and collectives; utility, cable TV, retail and insurance co-ops and other resources. $6.

Celebration of Community
Fellowship for Intentional Communities
8600 University Blvd.
Evansville IN 47712
(812) 464-1727
Communitarians share informationon a variety of topics in this quarterly publication.

City Building Education: A Way to Learn
By Doreen Nelson, 1982
(800) 333-9093

Co-op America Catalog
2100 M Street, NW, #310
Washington DC 20063
(800) 424-2667
Products from socially responsible businesses and organizations around the world. Includes quarterly publication"Co-op America Quarterly." $20/yr.

CoHousing: A Contemporary Approach to Housing Ourselves
By Kathrine McCamant and Charles Durrett
Habitat Press/Ten Speed Press, 1988
Redefining the concept of neighborhood to fit contemporary lifestyles, co-housing combines the autonomy of private dwellings with the advantages of shared facilities and communal living. Many photos, case studies, outline of development process, U.S. applications. 208 Pages. $22. Available from CRSP, 3551 White House Place, Los Angeles, CA 90004.

CoHousing Newsletter
c/o Innovative Housing
2169 East Francisco Blvd. Suite E
San Rafael, CA 94901
(415) 457-4593
Comprehensive tracking of the growing co-housing movement across America. $20/year (three issues)

Collaborative Communities: CoHousing, Central Living and Other New Forms of Housing with Shared Facilities
By Dorit Fromm
Van Nostrand Reinhold, 1991
115 Fifth Avenue
New York NY 10003
$45.

Communities Magazine
c/o FIC
8600 University Blvd.
Evansville IN 47712
(812) 464-1727
Comprehensive and in-depth articles on all aspects of cooperative living arrangements.

Community Design Primer
By Randolph T. Hester, Jr.
Ridge Times Press, 1990
Demonstrates how to collaboratively create places
that are loved and love us back, that provide for
private and collective action, that are just, meaningful
and sustainable. Hester is Chair of Dept. of Land-
scape Architecture at UC Berkeley. $15 + 2 P&H.
Available from CRSP, 3551 White House Place, Los
Angeles, CA 90004 (213) 738-1254

Community Land Trust Handbook
Institute for Community Economics
Rodale Press, 1982

Community Land Trust: A Community-Based
Alternative to Private Property Ownership
By Linda Ashman
CRSP
3551 White House Pl.
Los Angeles CA 90004
(213)738-1254
$5.

Comprehensive Housing Affordability Strategy
(CHAS)
City of Los Angeles, Hsg. Preservation and Produc-
tion Department, 1991
215 W. Sixth St.
Los Angeles CA 90013
The City of Los Angeles' Five Year Housing Plan.

Cooperative Housing Compendium
By Lottie Cohen and Lois Arkin
Center for Cooperatives, UC Davis
Davis CA 95616
(916) 752-2408
A concise cross referenced guide to all types of
collaborative housing, including legal, social, eco-
nomic and design descriptions and resouces.
Available Fall, 1992.

Creating Alternative Futures: Solutions to Economics
and Environmental Issues Bureaucracies Aren't
Solving
By Hazel Henderson
Knowledge Systems
7777 West Morris Street
Indianapolis IN 46321
(800) 999-8517
$ 12.95.

Directory of Intentional Communities
Edited by Geoph Kozeny, et al
Communities Magazine and the Fellowship for
Intentional Communities
Over 400 descriptions of intentional communities,
many articles and resources on community living and
development strategies. $18. Available from CRSP,
3551 White House Place, Los Angeles, CA 90004
(213) 738-1254.

Live/Work L.A.
California Lawyers for the Arts, 1990
315 W. 9th St., Suite 1101
Los Angeles CA 90015
(213)623-8311
Targeted for artists and others who want to have
live/work spaces in same building. Includes codes,
dealing with toxics, development process, financing
and insurance, resources and appendix. $15.

Manual for Group Facilitators
By Brian Auvine, Betsy Densmore, Mary Extrom,
Scott Poole and Michel Shanklin
New Society Publishers
P.O. Box 582
Santa Cruz CA 95061-0582
(800) 333-9093
A working manual for learning to communicate well,
doing effective planning, solving problems creatively,
dealing with conflict, and moving groups toward
fulfillment of their own goals.

Neighborhood Works
2125 West North Avenue
Chicago IL 60647
(312) 278-4800
Bi-monthly publication from the Center for Neighborhood Technology providing practical tools for
neighborhoods regarding energy use, job creation,
housing development, food production and waste
management. $25/yr.

New Households, New Housing
Edited by Karen A. Franck and Sherry Ahrentzen
Van Nostrand Reinhold, 1989
115 5th Ave.
New York NY 10003
Comprehensive research and case studies on non
traditional households and housing, including
collective and shared housing, cohousing, intentional
communities, single room occupancy housing, single
parent households, historical overviews and contemporary issues.

No Contest: The Case Against Competition; Why We Lose in Our Race to Win
By Alfie Kohn
Houghton Mifflin Co., 1986
2 Park St.
Boston MA 02108
This is the first book to argue that competition is inherently destructive in the classroom, in families, in athletic contests, and in business rivalries. Well researched and carefully reasoned study. Includes index and bibliography. $9+$1.50 p&h. Available from CRSP (213)738-1254

Shared Housing News
National Shared Housing Resource Center
136-1/2 Main St.
Montpelier VT 05602
(802)223-2627
Membership includes subscribtion to newsletter. Inquire for rates.

Transformations, Process and Theory: A Curriculum Guide to Creative Development
By Doreen Nelson, 1984
(800) 333-9093

We Build the Road as We Travel, Mondragon: A Cooperative Solution
By Roy Morrison
New Society Publishers
P.O. Box 582
Santa Cruz CA 950612
(800) 333-9093
Amazing story of the world's most innovative cooperative system, employing 22,000 people in more than 170 highly successful businesses in the Basque region of Spain. Many states in the U.S. now have cooperative laws based on the Mondrgon model, $20.

Winning Through Participation: Meeting the Challenge of Corporate Change with the Technology of Participation
By Laura Spencer with Foreword by Rosabeth Moss Kanter
ICA West
1504 25th Avenue
Seattle WA 98122
(206) 323-2100

Workbook
Southwest Research and Information Center
P.O. Box 4524
Albuqueque NW 87106
A fully-indexed bi-monthly catalog of sources of information about environmental, social and consumer problems. Helps people gain access to vital information for asserting control over their lives. Center believes that war, racism, sexism, poverty, crime and environmental destruction are all parts of the same problem. Solutions require action on many fronts. $25.

FINANCING, INCENTIVES, LENDING POLICIES
ORGANIZATIONS AND CONSULTANTS

California Futures
William Shireman, Founder
8498 Sunblaze Way
Sacramento CA 95823
(916) 929-9207
An organization working with forward-looking developers to design environmentally optimal communities.

Clearinghouse on Energy Financing Partnerships
2000 North 15th Street, No. 407
Arlington VA 22201
(703) 243-4900
Maintains an extensive collection of information and literature on alternative financing, with special emphasis on shared savings contracting and procurement issues pertinent to public-sector applications. Bibliographies, referrals, and other selected publications may be obtained free of charge.

E.F. Schumacher Society
Box 76 RD3
Great Barrington MA 01230
(413) 528-1737
Non-profit educational organization on sustainable economics. Publications list.

Institute for Community Economics
Greg Ramm, Executive Director
57 School Street
Springfield MA 01105
(413) 774-7956
22 year old non profit organization which provides technical assistance, development loans, research and education to community groups developing community land trusts.

National Cooperative Bank and NBC Development Corporation
1401 Eye St. NW, Suite 700
Washington DC 20005
(800) 955-9NCB Fax: (202) 336-7800
Makes loans exclusively to cooperatives of all kinds,
Provides technical assistance, newsletters.

Nippon Mortgage Company
Carol Houst, President
11212 Tujunga Canyon Blvd.
Los Angeles, CA 91402-1250
(818) 353-7459
Debt and Equity financing of ecological developments.

Urban Lending Associates
Carl Hanson, Founder
1509 Continental Street
San Diego, CA 92173-1737
(619) 661-5547

FINANCING, INCENTIVES, LENDING POLICIES
PUBLICATIONS

Building Sustainable Communities: Tools and Concepts for Self Reliant Economic Change
Edited by Ward Morehouse; contributors: C. George Benello, Robert Swann, Shann Turnbull; Bootstrap Press, NYC, A TOES Book, 1989; $11.70.
Based on the Schumacher Society Seminars on Community Economic Transformation, this book presents the underlying ideas and essential institutions for building sustainable communities. Three major sections deal with community land trusts, worker managed enterprises and community currency and banking.

Innovative and Incentive Package to Reduce Municipal Energy Consumption
1984. 72 pp. $15. Pub. No. 83-307. Analyzes potential creative financing methods for capital improvements related to energy management of public buildings. Discusses shared savings, bonding, and lease-purchase arrangements. Available from Public Technology, Inc. Urban Consortium Energy Task Force, Publications and Distribution, 1301 Pennsylvania Avenue, NW, Washington, DC, 20004, (202) 626-2400.

Politics of the Solar Age
By Hazel Henderson
Knowledge Systems
7777 West Morris Street
Indianapolis IN 46321
(800) 999-8517
New edition of the classic *How Economics (Politics in Disguise) Really Works*. $14.95

Redefining Wealth and Progress: The Caracas Report on Alternative Development Indicators
By Hazel Henderson
Knowledge Systems
7777 West Morris Street
Indianapolis IN 46321
(802) 223-2627
How we count determines what we get; counting only dollars, as in the GNP, has led to much human and environmental damage. Key contributors to the debate discuss alternative models on how to measure the quality of life. $15.

Saving Cities, Saving Money: Environmental Strategies that Work

By John Hart
Resource Renewal Institute, 1992
Sausalito CA
Available from AgAccess, P.O. Box 2008, Davis CA 95617, (916) 756-7177
Report based on 1991 workshop on New Environmental Strategies for Urban Prosperity. Includes case studies of cities around the world which are finding ways to profit from new environmental priorities.

Small is Beautiful

By E.F. Schumacher
New York: Harper & Row, 1973
A classic on sustainable economics. Available from the E.F. Schumacher Society, Box 76, RD 3, Great Barrington, MA 01230, $11.

AFFORDABLE HOUSING
ORGANIZATIONS AND CONSULTANTS

Note: See **Development of Community: The Collaborative Approach** *for resources on housing.*

Southern California Association of Non Profit Housing (SCANPH)
4032 Wilshire Blvd., Suite 301
Los Angeles CA 90010
(213) 480-1249 Fax: (213) 480-1788
Membership association of non-profit housing developers, resource organizations, consultants. Provides many workshops and annual conference on all aspects of affordable housing. Membership Directory of over 400 non profit housing developers, consultants, and resource organizations.

LIVELIHOOD
ORGANIZATIONS AND CONSULTANTS

Appalachian Center for Economic Networks
94 North Columbus Road
Athens, OH 45701
(614) 592-3854
ACEnet works to revitalize the economy of Appalachian Ohio. Committed to a sustainable regional economy based on economic justice, self determination and respect for diversity. Newsletter, technical assistance, network.

Ecological Entrepreneurs Network
Carol A. Houst, Director
11212 Tujunga Canyon Blvd.
Los Angeles, CA 91402-1250
(818) 353-7459
A non-profit forum and referral service with bi-monthly meetings. The EEN purpose is to empower and connect individuals to create services and products that sustain the environment, that are ethical, ecologically and economically sound.

Industrial Cooperative Association
20 Park Plaza, Suite 1127
Boston MA 02116
(617) 338-0010, Fax: (617) 338-2788
Major technical assistance provider for worker co-op businesses, both start ups and conversions. Research, conferences, revolving loan fund, publications list, newsletter.

Local Exchange Trading System (LETS) CRSP
3551 White House Place
Los Angeles CA 90004
(213) 464-3570
Community owned, third party computerized barter system

LIVELIHOOD
PUBLICATIONS

Business Opportunities Casebook
Business Opportunities Workbook
Small Business Association
(303) 844-2607
Created by the Rocky Mountain Institute, these books emphasize sustainable, decentralized economies for small towns. Highly adaptable for inner city areas.

Jobs in a Sustainable Economy
By Michael Renner
Washington, D.C. : Worldwatch Institute, 1991
1776 Massachusetts Ave. NW
Washington DC 20036
(202)452-1999

Prospects for Alternative Fuel Vehicle Use and Production in Southern California: Environmental Quality and Economic Development.
Lewis Center for Regional Policy Studies, UCLA, May, 1991.
$15 from UCLA-LCRP, 405 Hilgard, Los Angeles CA 90024-1467. (310) 206-4417.

Re-Inventing Corporations
By Shann Turnbull
MAI Services Pty Ltd.
GPO Box 4359
Sidney, NSW 2001, Australia
Description of the Ownership Transfer Corporation (OTC) which can be used as a method to promote economic efficiency, justice, self governance, social accountability, and environmental sustainability. $10.

LEGISLATION, POLICY AND REGULATION
ORGANIZATIONS AND CONSULTANTS

Association of Environmental Professionals
Rich Masters, President
c/o Montgomery Engineering
(818) 796-9141

Environmental Affairs Department
Lillian Kawasaki, General Manager
200 North Main Street, MS 177
Los Angeles CA 90012
(213) 237-0462
Makes policy recommendations to City Council on air quality, water and materials recycling, and other environmental issues that affect the City.

Environmental Council of Sacramento
909 12th Street
Sacramento CA 95814
(415) 443-1033

Foundation for Traditional Neighborhoods
R. Geoffery Ferrell and Duany Plater-Zyberk, Architects
10232 S.W. 25th Avenue
Miami FL 33135
(305) 644-1023
Will provide models, TND ordinances

Local Government Commission
Judy Corbett, Director
909 12th Street, Suite 205
Sacramento CA 95814
(916) 448-1198
The Commission researches and develops model programs on a wide variety of sustainable issues. It also publishes guidebooks on numerous topics, including energy conservation. LGC is a California-based membership organizaion of more than 450 city and county officials.

Planning and Conservation League
909 12th Street, Suite 203
Sacramento CA 95814
(916) 444-8726
This is a state-wide environmental advocay organization.

City of Los Angeles Planning Department
200 North Spring Street, 5th Floor
Los Angeles CA 90012
(213) 617-3698
Mixed use commercial/residential, home based businesses, residential planned development districts are examples of zoning ordinances established or being created by the city which can achieve more compact neighborhoods with adequate open space.

Southern California Association of Governments (SCAG) Environmental Department
818 West 7th Street, 12th Floor
Los Angeles CA 90017
(213) 236-1861

South Coast Air Quality Management District
21865 Copley Drive
Diamond Bar, CA 91765
(714) 396-2000
Sets air quality standards and recommends policies for meeting Federal and State air quality standards.

LEGISLATION, POLICY AND REGULATIONS
PUBLICATIONS

Building Sustainable Communities: An Environmental Guide for Local Government
Global Cities Project, Center for the Study of Law and Politics
2962 Fillmore St.
San Francisco, CA 94123
(415) 775-0791
A sampling of regulations is a component of each book in the series of 12 dealing with all aspects of the urban physical environment.

California Planning and Developers Report
c/o Fulton Associates
1257 Sunny Crest Avenue
Ventura CA 93003-1212
(805) 642-7838

Cooling our Cities: The Heat Island Reduction Guidebook
By Hashem Akbari, Joe Huang, and Susan Davis, eds. Outlines research to date on effectiveness of landscape and design guidelines to reduce the urban heat island effect. Includes a chapter on model urban heat island ordinances. April 1991. 200 pp. $ 20. Copies available from Ron Ritschard, Lawrance Berkeley Laboratory, Mail Stop 90-3118, 1 Cyclotron Road, Berkeley, CA 94720.

Live/Work L.A.
California Lawyers for the Arts, 1990
315 W. 9th St., Suite 1101
Los Angeles CA 90015
(213)623-8311
Targeted for artists and others who want to have live/work spaces in same building. Includes codes, dealing with toxics, development process, financing and insurance, resources and appendix. $15.

Model Ordinances for Environmental Protection, 1990.
Available from the Local Government Commission, 909 12th Street, Suite 205, Sacramento, CA 96814, (916) 448-1198

Toward Sustainable Communities: A Resource Book for Muncipal and Local Governments
By Mark Roseland (University of British Columbia)
National Roundtable on the Environment and Development, 1992.
1 Nicholas Street, Suite 520
Ottawa, Ontario K1N 7B7 Canada

ON-GOING EVENTS AND CONFERENCES

Celebration of Community
Fellowship for Intentional Communities
8600 University Blvd.
Evansville IN 47712
(812) 464-1727
Communitarians, technical assistance providers and seekers' gathering for a week long conference on all aspects of intentional communities, cohousing, eco-villages. Will provide extensive training on social, economic and physical systems for building a sustainable future. Aug. 26-31, 1993. Olympia, Washington

Facilitation Methods
Institute for Cultural Affairs (ICA)
3551 White House Place
Los Angeles CA 90004
(213) 738-1254
4420 N. 25th St.
Phoenix, AZ 85016
(602) 955-4811
Two day introductory and advanced workshops on facilitation methods techniques, including meeting facilitation, strategic planning, consensus decision making, discussion groups, etc.
Special group rates available.

International Ecological Cities Conference
Urban Ecology
P.O. Box 10144
Berkeley CA 94709
(510) 549-1724
Bi-annual event which brings together people and resources on the cutting edge of eco-city design and development.

International Making Cities Livable Conference
Suzanne H. Crowhurst Lennard, Ph.D., Director
P.O. Box 7586
Carmel CA 93921
(408) 626-9080
Annual conference. They also have slide sets illustrating essential features of livable cities and papers from previous conferences.

International Pedestrian Conference
City of Boulder, Patricia Archibald
P.O. Box 791
Boulder CO 80306
(303) 441-4260

National Association of Housing Cooperatives Annual Conference
1614 King Street
Alexandria VA 22314
(703) 549-5201
Brings together co-op housing residents, technical assistance providers, and others to learn about all aspects of cooperative housing.

Non Profit Board Training and Leadership Development Programs
United Way/Kellogg Regional Training Center
621 S. Virgil
Los Angeles CA 90020
(213) 736-1304
Training in board development, planning, fundraising, problem solving, volunteer development, etc. Special Afro-American and Hispanic leadership development programs.

Southern California Association of Non Profit Housing, Annual Conference
SCANPH
4032 Wilshire Blvd., Suite 301
Los Angeles CA 90010
(213) 480-1249
Fall conference covering a broad range of technical and financial aspects of affordable housing development. Also holds day-long workshops throughout the year on a variety of related topics.

Westside Urban Forum
James McCormick, Executive Director
2550 Beverly Blvd.
Los Angeles, CA 90057
(213) 389-6490
Association of concerned citizens including: real estate, development and land-use professionals, public officials, community and environmental activists. Sponsors monthly debates and forums on a wide variety of issues that affect urban environmental quality.

FIRST LOS ANGELES ECO-CITIES CONFERENCE

CREDITS

CONFERENCE PLANNING AND COORDINATING ORGANIZATIONS AND STAFF

Eco-Home Network:
Julia Russell, Executive Director; Bob Walter, President

Cooperative Resources & Services Project (CRSP):
Lois Arkin, Executive Director

UCLA Graduate School of Architecture and Urban Planning:
Richard Schoen, Architecture Faculty;
Stephanie Pincetl, Planning Faculty

CO-SPONSORS

The Los Angeles Westside Urban Forum's 1991 Westside Prize for Excellence in Land Use Planning and Urban Design was awarded to the First Los Angeles Ecological Cities Conference.

Special Thanks to the UCLA Graduate School of Architecture and Urban Planning, especially:

Erlyne Alvarez
Sue Ni
Stephanie Pincetl
Richard Schoen
Dean Richard Weinstein

AIA, Los Angeles Chapter, Environmental Resources Committee.
American Planning Association, L.A. Section. American Society of Landscape Architects (ASLA), L.A. Section
Architectects, Designers and Planners for Social Responsibility (ADPSR)
Association for Women in Architecture (AWA)
Association of Environmental Professionals (AEP), L.A. Section
Blue Basin Development
California Energy Commission
California Redevelopment Agencies Association
Cerro Gordo Town Forum
City of Los Angeles, Housing Preservation and Production Department (HPPD)
City of Santa Monica
City of West Hollywood, Environmental Department
Community Environmental Council/ Gildea Resource Center
Cooperative Resources and Services Project (CRSP) (A coordinating sponsor)
Co-opportunity Consumers Co-op
Councilman Michael Woo, City of Los Angeles
David Geffen Foundation
Department of Water and Power, City of Los Angeles
Eco-Home Network (A coordinating sponsor)

E-The Environmental Magazine
EOS Institute
Graduate School of Architecture and Urban Planning (A coordinating sponsor)
The Greens
Lincoln Place Tenant's Association
Maguire-Thomas Partners
Mayor Tom Bradley's Office
Michael K. Harris — Environmental Development Group
Natural Resources Defence Council (NRDC)
Passive Solar Industry Council (PSIC)
Permaculture Institute of Southern California
Planning and Conservation League
Program in Social Ecology (UC Irvine)
RAND Corporation, Domestic Research
Real Goods Trading Company
Recycle America
Solar Electric Engineering
South Coast Air Quality Management District
Southern California Association of Governments (SCAG)
Southern California Association of Non-Profit Housing
Southern California Edison
Southern California Gas Company
Southern California Institute of Architecture
Urban Ecology, Inc.
Venice Ocean Park Food Co-op
David Zucker, Film Writer/Director

VOLUNTEER COORDINATION

Shiva Bailey and James Bailey, Conference Package Research
Jackie Hedlund, Co-Sponsor and Info. Tables Coordinator
Mazie de Beaulieu, Co-sponsor Outreach
Sharon Dvora, Graphic Design
Sally Hanley, Planing Committee & Hospitality Coordinator
Dessa Kaye, Site and Catering Planning
Marlowe McAnnear, Childcare Coordinator
Patria McGuire, Co-sponsor Outreach

Sharin Pollak, Bookstore, Registration &Volunteer Coordination
Mary Proteau, Planning Committee and Site Coordination
Mary Renz, Bulletin Board
Lynda Reiche, Childcare Coordinator
Susan Sherod, Flyer Distribution
David Spellman, Conference Package Layout and Formatting
Don Strauss, Planning
Patrisha Thomson, Logo Design
Genny Tubridy, Volunteer Coordinator
Scott Wlaschin, Computer Consulting

OTHER GENERAL SUPPORT VOLUNTEERS

Grant Barnes
Lynne Bayless
Darlene Boord
Rey Castillo
Pearl Chen
Valerie Cooley
Jim Cornell
Jeff Coudayre
Karin Davolos
Maria Davalos
Mark DeKay
Steve Eidiger
Sue Erhlich
Anne Ferguson
Hermine Garcia
Bob Gaylord
Betty Gordon
Cal Hamilton

Mitchell Higa
Trish Hoffman
Torgen Johnson
Arthur Jokela
Harry Jordan
Rosalyn Kalmar
Lucy Kazakis
Lillian Laskin
Dave Little
Joel Lorimer
Rosanna Louie
James McCormick
Ian McIllvaine
Sherry Modell
Carol Moss
Brad Mowers
Violet Moyer
Anne Murphy

Doreen Nelson
Tom Penhale
Erik Peterson
Glen Ray
Jack Reed
Laurie Richardson
Sandy Roggero
Bill Roley
Marlena Ross
Jan Rucquoi
Beverly Rudolph
Dick Russell
Keith Sauter
David Sensiper
Sharon Seto
Thomas Slagel
Sarah Smiley
Harriet Smith

Diane Smithe
Penny Starr
Achva Stein
John Stevens
Sigfried Stokes
Trish Strouse
Ben Swets
Shyama Tampoe
Taylor Trowbridge
Jeff Tucker
Nancy Van Praag
Michael Weinberg
Steven Weissman
Dorothy White
J. Craig Williams
Barbara Wolfe
Calvin Yee

OUR THANKS TO THE FOLLOWING:

Jan Brown Public Relations
Co-opportunity Consumers Cooperative
Venice Ocean Park Food Cooperative
Santa Cruz Organic Juices
Cornell & Associates
EOS Institute
Fred Fyten, Printer
Al Jacobson, Garden of Eatin'

Sam Hall Kaplan
Pamela Patridge, The Imperial Group, Catering
Pick Up Artists, Recycling
Smart Kids
Southern California Gas Company
William Warren & Associates, Photographer

CONFERENCE ADVISORS

Paul Bierman-Lytle, *Author/Architect*
Jan Brown, *Public Relations*
Ernest Callenbach, *Author Ecotopia*
Leroy Graymer, *UCLA Extension*
Hazel Henderson, *Futurist Economist*
John Javna, *Publisher EarthWorks Press*
Sam Hall Kaplan, *Author / Design Critic*
John Lyle, *Faculty, Institute for Regenerative Studies, Cal Poly Pomona*
Andy & Katie Lipkis, *TreePeople*
Marvin Malecha, *Dean, College of Environmental Sciences Cal Poly Pomona.*
Pete Nelson, *Director, Community Development Dept., City of Chino*
Michael O'Brien, *Landscape Architect, City of LA Planning Dept.*
Richard Palmer, *Chair of Energy Committee, Calif. Building Industry Association*
Nancy Pearlman, *Executive Director, Ecology Center of Southern California*
Rose Marie Rabin, *Special Projects Coordinator, SCI-ARC*
Dr. Chester Rapkin, *Professor Emeritus, Princeton School of Urban Planning*
Richard Register, *Executive Director, Urban Ecology, Berkeley*
Richard Schoen, *Faculty, UCLA Grad. School of Architecture/Urban Planning*
April Smith, *Environmental Consultant*

FIRST LOS ANGELES
ECO-CITIES CONFERENCE
PARTICIPANT LIST

Note: Although we have tried to update addresses and phone numbers of all who came to the conference, there may be several listed here which are still out of date. We apologize for any inconvenience.

Calvin Abe
Calvin Abe & Associates, Inc.
8800 Venice Blvd., Suite L
Los Angeles, CA 90034
(213) 838-0448

Jeffrey Acker
Mobil Land Development
3401 Centrelake Dr., Suite 480
Ontario, CA 91764
(714)983-4680

Adolfo Aguirre
1186 S. Rochester Ave. #6
Los Angeles, CA 90025
(213) 575-3483

Robert Albano
PO Box 66189
Los Angeles, CA 90066
(213) 390-1895

Lou Alonso
Air Control Technologies
22647 Ventura Blvd., #239
Woodland Hills, CA 91364
(818) 893-8584

Jim & Mary Altmann
Altmann Construction
1857 Lookout Dr.
Agoura Hills, CA 91301
(818)991-8955

Karen Anderson
Mountain CARE
PO Box 96
Forest Falls, CA 92339
(714)794-5657

Thomas Andrusky
Economic Development-Huntngtn Bch.
2000 Main Street
Huntington Beach, CA 92648
(714) 840-6325

Jay April
Environmental Television
(213) 871-0076

Arnold Arch
A.A. Construction
2155 Verdugo Blvd.
Montrose, CA 91020
(213) 871-1219

Lois Arkin
CRSP
3551 White House Place
Los Angeles, CA 90004
(213) 738-1254

David Ashley
PO Box 85152 MB 344
San Diego, CA 92183
(619) 694-2178

Linda Ashman
8923 W. 25th St.
Los Angeles, CA 90034
(213) 930-0823

Mary Jane Ashton
Planning Consultant
33 Whistling Swan
Irvine, CA 92714
(714) 551-6120

David J. Baab
Baab & Associates
4199 Campus Dr., Suite 550
Irvine, CA 92715
(714) 552-3440

Diamara Bach
City of Ventura
5275 Colt Street, #3
Ventura, CA 93003
(805) 650-0884

Russ Baggerly
County of Ventura
119 South Poli Ave.
Ojai, CA 93023
(805) 646-0767

Shiva & James Bailey
1336 Ocean Park Blvd. #C
Santa Monica, CA 90405
(310)837-7710

Penrose Baldwin
Design Form
20032 State Rd.
Cerritos, CA 90701
(213) 865-5149

Tim Bamrick
L.A. County Transportation Commission
818 West Seventh Street, #1100
Los Angeles, CA 90017

Marjorie Bard
423 S. Crescent Dr.
Beverly Hills, CA 90212
(213)277-5976

Susan Barnett
City of Lancaster
4217 W Ave. L-2
Quartz Hll, CA 93536
(805) 943-7030

Lynn Bayless
EOS Institute
PO Box 1490
Wildomar, CA 92595
(714) 678-3081

Michael Bean
Michael Bean & Associates
PO Box 91733
Santa Barbara, CA 93190-1733
(805) 963-2972

Jim Bell
Ecological Life Systems Institute
2923 E. Spruce St.
San Diego, CA 92104
(619) 281-1447

Brock Bernstein
EcoAnalysis, Inc.
221 East Matilija Street, Suite A
Ojai, CA 93023
(805) 646-1461

Paul Bettenhauser

Paul Bierman-Lytle
The Masters Corporation
PO Box 514
New Canaan, CT 06840
(203) 966-9622

Robin Blair
SCRTD
425 South Main Street
Los Angeles, CA 90013
(213) 972-4806

Maury Blitz
Maguire Thomas Partners
25933 Sundalia Dr
Valencia, CA 91355
(805)253-2629

Jane Blumenfeld
City of Los Angeles
Office of the Mayor
200 North Spring Street - Room M1
Los Angeles, CA 90012
(213) 485-6301

Greg Bohne
Browning Ferris Industries
14905 South San Pedro Street
Gardena, CA 90247
(213)804-6011

Darlene Boord
Vegan
PO Box 2124
Orange, CA 92669
(714) 639-3791

Richard Alan Borkovetz
512 West Granada Court
Ontario, CA 91762
(714) 840-9885

Steven Boswell
UCLA Grad School Urban Planning
465 Jones St
Ventura, CA 93003
(805) 643-4929

Kegan Boyer

Don Brackenbush
Ahmanson Land Company
25343 W Mureau Rd
Calabasas, CA 91302
(818) 880-4325

Elaine Branding
Global Cities Project
2962 Fillmore Street
San Francisco, CA 94123
(415) 775-1931

Jan Brown
Jan Brown Public Relations
7822 Broadleaf Ave.
Panarama City, CA 91402
(818) 785-5624

Phil Brown
Phillip Jon Brown & Assoc.
5699 Holly Oak Ave.
Los Angeles, CA 90068
(213) 466-9160

Robert Brytan
Eric Equities
775 Havana Ave.
Long Beach, CA 90864
(213) 597-8075

Jim Bumstead
Owner-Developer
40710 Gibbel Rd.
Hemet, CA 92343
(714) 929-7205

Cindy Burgess
Torrance Planning Department
3031 Torrance Blvd
Torrance, CA 90503
(310) 618-5990

Kelly Ann Butts
Foresight Institute
10108 Hemlock Dr.
Overland Park, KS 66212
(913) 221-5274

Fred Cagle
3046 Fenelon Street
San Diego, CA 92106
(619) 224-1456

Raison J. Cain
1011 Sycamore Lane
Davis, CA 95616
(916) 758-2548

Lynn Call
7717 Hollywood Blvd #2
Los Angeles, CA 90046
(213) 876-0430

Larry Callahan
The Cousteau Society

Ernest Callenbach
1963 El Dorado Av.
Berkeley, CA 94707
(510) 524-2690

Peter Calthorpe
Calthorpe & Associates
246 First Street, #400
San Francisco, CA 94105
(415) 777-0181

Chris Canfield
Cerro Gordo Town Forum
Dorena Lake, Box 569
Cottage Grove, OR 97424
(503) 942-7720

Scott R. Carlson
Wilmore Develpment Corp.
3080 Bristol Street, Suite 250
Costa Mesa, CA 92626
(714)720-0478

Janet Carpenter
Artistic Environments
2518-1/2 Main Street
Santa Monica, CA 90405
(213) 392-3314

Christine Carr
Sasso Design Group
1351 North Crescent Heights, #303
West Hollywood, CA 90046
(213)656-5338

Steve Carr
Carr, Lynch, Hack & Sandell
1385 Cambridge Street
Cambridge, MA 02139
(617) 661-6566

Harden A. Carter
Horizon Information Network
750 E Green Street, #301
Pasadena, CA 91101
(818) 791-7995

Reydante T. Castillo
2795 Baltic Ave.
Long Beach, CA 90810
(213) 427-1482

Winston Chappell

Greg Chasen
Planning Consultants Research
2352 Ocean Ave.
Venice, CA 90291
(213)306-9865

Pearl Chen
24951 Hon Ave.
Laguna Hills, CA 92653
(714)837-1067

John Cicchetti
John Cicchetti Co.

Jim Clapp
KPBS Radio "Metropolitan Journal"
(619)265-6431

Claudia Cleaver
Morse & Cleaver
47 Sixth Street
Petaluma, CA 94952
(707) 763-4642

Chip Clements
Clements Engineering
6290 Sunset Blvd. Ste.1223
Los Angeles, CA 90028
(213) 664-7218

Wayne Clerk
Pacific Gas & Electric Co.
123 Mission Street, H2613
San Francisco, CA 94106
(415)973-3864

Chip Clitheroe
The Program in Social Ecology
UC Irvine
Irvine, CA

Lottie Cohen
Attorney
9840 Airport
Suite 900
Los Angeles, CA 90045
(310) 215-9244

Lory Cole
Troll Construction
282 Long Branch Circle
Brea, CA 92621

Terry Collins
Joseph Smyth Company

Annabel Cook
So. Coast Air Qual. Management
Dist.
9150 Flair Dr.
El Monte, CA 91731
(818) 572-6409

Kent Cooper
InterCommunications Inc
317 Fernado
Balboa, CA 92661
(714) 644-7520

Jeff Coudayre
16329 N Pacific Ave
Sunset Beach, CA 90742-1653

Christopher Covault
Architect
1921 Modjeska St
Los Angeles, CA 90039
(213)663-7927

Elinor Covault
Industrial Hygenist/Env. Eng.
1921 Modjeska St
Los Angeles, CA 90039
(213)663-7927

Larry A. Cowles
Usonian Design
13286 Tiverton Rd.
San Diego, CA 92130
(619) 793-0350

Jane Crawford
The Open School
6085 Airdrome Street
Los Angeles, CA 90035
(213) 385-2375

Richard Crenshaw
Architect
940 Bay Ridge Ave.
Annapolis, MD 21403
(301) 268-3592

David & Jennifer Cundiff
319 Grand Ave.
Long Beach, CA 90814
(310) 433-4809

Denise Cunningham
William Warren & Associates
5359 W 8th St
Los Angeles, CA 90036
(213) 935-6077

Mary Cutchin
Outerspace Landscape
Furnishings
7445 Girard Ave., Suite 3
La Jolla, CA 92037
(619) 459-8074

Michael Cutchin
Outerspace Landscape
Furnishings
7445 Girard Ave., Suite 3
La Jolla, CA 92037
(619) 459-8074

Jack Daniels
Real Goods Publications
285-0093

Maria Davalos
1211 S. New Hampshire
Los Angeles, CA 90006
(213)388-2473

Karin Davalos
3008 Finch St
Los Angeles, CA 90039
213-578-7747

W. Scott Davis
25742 Demeter Way
Mission Viejo, CA 92691
(714) 586-2122

Mazie de Beaulieu
100 S. Doheny #203
Los Angeles, CA 90048
(213)274-3264

Carlos de la Parra
Coles
416 W San Ysidro Blvd #L-437
San Diego, CA 92173

Francis H. Dean
Faculty - Cal Poly Pomona
31591 Mar Vista Ave.
Laguna Beach, CA 92677
(714) 499-1790

Charles DeDeurwaerder
DeDeurwaerder Associates
425 Lomita Street
El Segundo, CA 90245
(213) 640-0891

Mark DeKay
Department of Architecture
University of Oregon
Eugene, OR 97405
(503) 343-5023

Twyla Dell
Foresight Institute
10108 Hemlock Dr.
Overland Park, KS 66212
(913) 383-2454

Toni DeMarco
1165 Tunnel Rd
Santa Barbara, CA 93105
(805) 687-7871

Tamara Lynn Diamond
City of Palm Springs
3200 Taquitz Canyon
Palm Springs, CA
(619) 320-6944

Don Docray
Southern California Gas Co.

Paulette Dolin
Tree People
15740 Sherman Way #206
Van Nuys, CA 91406
(818) 994-1607

Tony Dominski
Community Environmentl Council
930 Miramonte Dr.
Santa Barbara, CA 93109
(805) 963-0583

Paul Doose
Southern California Edison
2244 Walnut Grove Ave., Room
405
Rosemead, CA 91770
(818) 302-4096

Kermit Dorius
ADPSR
1550 Bayside Dr.
Corona Del Mar, CA 92625
(714) 642-3213

Lisa Dorward
Concord Development
1888 Century Park East, #1777
Los Angeles, CA 90067
(805) 821-2515

Jill L. Dovre
Progressive Benefits
309 Santa Monica Blvd., #221
Santa Monica, CA 90401
(213) 399-7065

Nathan Downey
CEED Institute
1807 Second Street Studios, #2
Santa Fe, NM 87501
(505) 984-8761

Ena Dubnoff
Architect AIA
2506 Fourth Street
Santa Monica, CA 90405
(213) 396-8627

Jan Ducker
City of Lancaster
3531 W Ave. J-3
Lancaster, CA 93534
(805) 948-2248

Sharon Dvora
Graphic Arts
17263 Ave. de la Herradura
Pacific Palisades, CA 90272
(310) 454-0557

Raymond Dykeman
2751 Barry Ave.
Los Angeles, CA 90064

Virginia Elderkin-Thompson
The Program in Social Ecology
UC Irvine
Irvine, CA

Scott Ellinwood
Scott Ellinwood & Associates
196 South Fir Street Suite 200
Ventura, CA 93001
(805) 684-5930

Judith Von Euer
1401 1/2 Fifth Street
Glendale, CA 91201
(818) 246-3663

Andrew Euston, A.I.A.
HUD
Rm. 7244
Washington, DC 20410
(202) 708-2504

Abraham Falick
1706 S Roxbury Dr
Los Angeles, CA 90035
(213) 558-3738

Marilyn Farmer
3074 Bahia Court
San Luis Obispo, CA 93401
(805) 544-2494

Dan Fauchier
Consultant, General Contractor
985 Via Serana
Upland, CA 91786
(714) 949-4489

Jacob Feldman
CAL POLY
Architectural Engineering
711 Murray Ave
San Luis Obispo, CA 93401
(805) 544-9193

Sharron Fennell
Environmental Officer
City of Torrance
3031 Torrance Blvd
Torrance, CA 90503
(213) 618-593

Anne Ferguson
5000 Centinela Ave #216
Los Angeles, CA 90066
(213) 391-2563

Eugene L. Fisher
So. Coast Air Qual. Mgmt. Dist.
9150 Flair Dr.
El Monte, CA 91731
(818) 572-6409

Carol Fisher
102 Ocean Way
Santa Monica, CA 90402
(310) 459-4229

Mario Fonda-Bonardi
Fonda-Bernardi & Assoc Architects
1450 23rd Street
Santa Monica, CA 90404
(213) 453-1134

Gay Forbes
City of West Hollywood
8611 Santa Monica Blvd.
West Hollywood, CA 90069
(213) 854-7400

Dale Foster
Aerovironment Inc.
PO Box 5031
Monrovia, CA 91017
(818)358-3247

Rosemary Frazho
1648 Berwick
Westlake Village, CA 91361
(805) 496-7494

Kay Freyling
13617 Philadelphia Street Apt E
Whittier, CA 90601

Thomas Fulham
4513 Bidwell Street
Simi Valley, CA 93063
(805) 584-679

Bruce Fullerton
Angelil/Graham
6105 Melrose Ave.
Los Angeles, CA 90038
(213) 450-9274

Brenda Funches
Common Ground Co-Op
2615 S Grand Ave. #400
Los Angeles, CA 90007
(213) 669-8670

Marilyn Gabbard
City of Lancaster
42842 Sachs Dr.
Lancaster, CA 93536
(805) 943-9460

Bob Galbreath
Garden Technology
6118 West 77th Street
Los Angeles, CA 90045
(213) 216-0410

Alta Gale
Consultant
1775 Hill Dr.
Eagle Rock, CA 90041
(213) 256-6372

Judi Garber
795 N Beverly Glen
W Los Angeles, CA 90077
(213) 474-7722

Doug Gardner
Maguire Thomas Partners
13250 Jefferson Blvd.
Los Angeles, CA 90024
(310) 822-0074

Catriona Gay A.I.C.P.
Planning Consultant
32 West Anapamu Street, Suite
332
Santa Barbara, CA 93101
(805) 962-7031

Robert Gaylord
12524 Culver Blvd., #20
Los Angeles, CA 90066
(213) 821-6996

Michael Gelfand
De Anza Group, Inc.
9171 Wilshire Blvd., #627
Beverly Hills, CA 90210
(213) 459-8345

Ken Genser, Mayor
City of Santa Monica
1685 Main Street
Santa Monica, CA 90401-3295

Guy Giniadek
Ahmanson Land co.
25343 W Mureau Rd
Calabasas, CA 91302
(818) 595-1115

Mike Givel
KUCR-FM
1811 Keith St - E
Riverside, CA 92507
(714)684-9614

Carlin Glucksman
American Women in Architecture
4929 Calvin Ave.
Tarzana, CA 91356
(818) 345-6372

Richard Gollis
Robert Charles Lesser & Company
359 San Miguel Dr #300
Newport Beach, CA 92660
714-644-7457

Bob & Betty Gordon
130 S Flores St., Apt 101
Los Angeles, CA 90048
(213) 653-1329

Jeff Goudayre

Shelli Graff
The Pick Up Artists
(213) 559-9334

Jean Graham
Diversified Services
18021J Skypark Circle #136
Irvine, CA 92714
(714) 733-1422

Sal Grammatico
A Coalition of Concerned
Communities
5510 South Sepulveda
Culver City, CA 90230
(213) 390-1673

John T. Graves
The Irvine Company
550 Newport Center Dr.
Newport Beach, CA 92660
(714) 720-3441

Carolyn Green
So. Coast Air Quality Management
Dist.
9150 Flair Ave.
El Monte, CA 91731
(818) 572-6200

Allen Green
UC Davis
2722 Carlson Blvd.
Richmond, CA 74804
(415) 524-7245

Cindy Greenwald
City of Los Angeles
Environmental Affairs Department
200 North Main Street, MS 177
Los Angeles, CA 90012
(213) 485-9961

David Grider
3810 8th Ave
San Diego, CA 92103
(619)297-9309

Hugh Gumbiner
4121 Benedict Cyn Dr
Sherman Oaks, CA 91423
(818) 986-5864

James Guthrie
771 Mission Oaks Ln
Santa Barbara, CA 93105
(805) 687-6747

Michael Hackleman
Earth Mind
P.O. Box 743
Mariposa, CA 95338

Wendell Hahm
EcoAnalysis, Inc.
221 East Matilija Street, Sutie A
Ojai, CA 93023
(805) 646-1461

Karen Hamburger
8212 W 4th St
Los Angeles, CA 90048
(213) 938-2111

Cal Hamilton
6298 Warner Dr.
Los Angeles, CA 90048
(213) 981-5851

Kreigh Hampel
TreePeople
1104 North Lima
Burbank, CA 91505
(818) 846-2878

Sally Hanley
City of L.A.
Planning Department
844 Grant St. D
Santa Monica, CA 90405
(213) 396-8295

Carl & Marilyn Hanson
Urban Lending Associates
1509 Continental Street
San Diego, CA 92173-1737
(619) 661-2510

David J. Harris
Transformation 2000 Network
PO Box 1122
Del Mar, CA 92014
(619) 455-5438

Terry Hartig
Program in Social Ecology
UC Irvine
Irvine, CA

Lynne Hartley
224 9th Place
Manhattan Beach, CA 90266
(310) 318-0522

Gary Hasell, A.I.A.
Walt Disney Imagineering
1401 Flower Street
Glendale, CA 91221
(714) 538-8774

Daniel Hathaway
Urban Forest Institute, Director
PO Box 415
Honaunau, HI 96726
(808)328-8043

Ted Hayes
Homeless Advocate
1921 Modjeska St
Los Angeles, CA 90039
(213) 663-7927

Gary Headrick
Architectural Illustration
2837 Penasco
San Clemente, CA 992672
(714) 492-5020

Laurie Headrick
Architectural Illustration
2837 Penasco
San Clemente, CA 92672
(714) 492-5020

Jackie Hedlund
Environmental Federation
of California
225 Santa Monica Blvd. Suite 1102
Santa Monica, CA 90401
(310) 394-0446

Maggi Heinrich
Citizens Planning Association
411 West Sola Street
Santa Barbara, CA 93101
(805) 962-0713

Kevin Hendrick
City of West Hollywood
8611 Santa Monica Blvd.
West Hollywood, CA 90069
(213) 854-7400

Paul Herzog
Joseph Smyth Company

Phil Heymann
150 Haight Street, #206
San Francisco, CA 94102
(415) 554-0189

Mitchell Higa
Calif. Dept. of Transportation
120 South Spring Street
Los Angeles, CA 90012
(213) 478-5776

Robert Higgins
2064 Watsonia Terrace
Hollywood, CA 90068
(213) 851-6036

Kate Higgins
Fine Arts Federation of Burbank
1011 E Olive
Burbank, CA 91501
(818)566-7660

Mitja Hinderks
CAP company
1015 Gayley Ave #1228
Los Angeles, CA 90024
(213) 208-3335

Jim Hirsch
The Austin Hansen Group
10035 Barnes Canyon Rd.
San Diego, CA 92121
(619) 436-3972

Eiji Hishikari
DeDeurwaerder Associates
425 Lomita Street
El Segundo, CA 90245
(213) 640-0891

Mary Hito
13400 Cumpston St
Van Nuys, CA 91401
(818) 786-7602

Terry Hodell
KPFK
4033 Sunset Blvd., #3
Los Angeles, CA 90029
(213) 660-1240

Bill Hoffman
The Program in Social Ecology
UC Irvine
Irvine, CA

Patricia Hoffman
Board of Education:
Santa Monica/Malibu Schools
1651 16th St
Santa Monica, CA 90404
(310) 829-9472

Gretchen Holmblad
1124 E Lexington Dr #D
Glendale, CA 91206

Audrey Hoodkiss
Ecology by Design
801 Second Street, Suite 402
Santa Monica, CA 90403
(310) 394-4146

J. Michael Hook
J. Michael Hook Design Inc.
2305 30th Street
Santa Monica, CA 90405
(213) 450-3803

Frank Hotchkiss
24032 Caravel Place
Laguna Niguel, CA 92677
(714) 661-1798

Carol Houst
Nippon Mortgage
Eco Entrepreneurs Network
11212 Tujunga Canyon Blvd.
Los Angeles, CA 91402-1250
(818) 353-7459

Robert Hunter
7078 Thornhill Dr.
Oakland, CA 94611
(510) 339-3536

Jeff Hunter
New Paradigm Digest
Santa Monica, CA
(310) 393-2670

Claude Hurwicz
920-C Sealane Dr
Encinitas, CA 92024-5058

Colin F.W. Isaacs
Contemporary Information Analysis
2 Lakeview Dr.
Stoney Creek, Ontario L8E 5A5
(416) 643-1094

John Jakupcak
City of West Hollywood
8611 Santa Monica Blvd.
West Hollywood, CA 90069
(213) 854-7400

John Johnson
Moore Ruble Yudell
11911 Beatrice Street
Culver City, CA 90231
(213)578-1761

Janith Johnson
Southern California Edison Co.
2244 Walnut Grove Ave.
Rosemead, CA 91770
(&14) 338-5431

Torgen Johnson

Mark Johnson
Developer
714 Kettner Blvd.
San Diego, CA 92101
(619) 238-8188

Arthur Jokela
So. Calif. Institute
of Natural Resources
1 West California St., #123
Pasadena, CA 91105
(818) 577-7402

Paul Jones
Consultant
PO Box 56
Flagstaff, AZ 86002
(602) 779-2279

Rosalyn R. Kalmar
1524 S. Ogden Dr.
Los Angeles, CA 90019
(213) 559-5970

Sam Hall Kaplan
Ehrenkrantz, Eckstut & Whitlaw
823 20th Street
Santa Monica, CA 90403
(213) 829-1942

Dessa Kaye
P.O. Box 1397
Studio City, CA 91614
(818) 766-7318

Lucy Kazakes
1535 Harvard St. #A
Santa Monica, CA 90404
(310) 453-1776

Joan P. Kelly
Michael Brandman Associates
606 South Olive Street, Suite 600
Los Angeles, CA 90014
(213) 622-4443

Paula Kelly
1825 Walworth Ave.
Pasadena, CA 91104
(818) 797-6304

Stanley Keniston
Keniston & Mosher Architects
1430 Union St
San Diego, CA 92101
(619)235-6691

Mitch Kerman
McZand Herbal, Inc
PO Box 5312
Santa Monica, CA 90403
213-392-4561

Ralph Knowles
USC School of Architecture
2334 Kenilworth Ave.
Los Angeles, CA 90039
(213) 661-9126

Mary Knowles
(213)661-9126

Philip Koebel
Southern California Edison
2244 Walnut Grove Ave., Room 391
Rosemead, CA 91770
(818) 302-4718

Connie Koenenn
Los Angeles Times View Section
Times Miror Square
Los Angeles, CA 90053
(213) 237-5932

John Kopatsis
Tecton Enterprises
2828 3rd St #1
Santa Monica, CA 90405

Helene Kornblatt
Consultant
1358 Rubenstein Ave.
Cardiff-by-the-Sea, CA 92007
(619) 753-1426

Sonia Kosak
47 Nassington Rd
London, ENGLAND NW3 2TY

Leslie Kwartin
3848 Clayton Ave.
Los Angeles, CA 90027
(213) 662-3977

Lauren Labov
ERAS Center
4151-1/2 La Salle Ave.
Culver City, CA 91711
(213) 837-5026

Cherie LaGrange
Pulte Home Corporation

Robert B. Lamishaw
JPL Zoning Services
14423 Sylvan Street
Van Nuys, CA 91401
(818) 992-8291

Laurie Langford
De Anza Group, Inc.
9171 Wilshire Blvd.
Beverly Hills, CA 90210
(213) 550-1111

Michael Langs
1000 Wilshire Blvd #1800
Los Angeles, CA 90017
(213) 688-3610

Xavier Lanier
Earthly Goods
12120 Rochester Ave
Los Angeles, CA 90025
(213) 207-6038

Ray Laub
PO Box 945
Ojai, CA 93024
(805) 646-8748

Alan Lawson
City of Brea - Assoc. Planner
PO BOX 9475
Brea, CA 92622
(714) 671-6804

Chris Lazarus
Environmental Directions Radio
14631 Beach Ave
Irvine, CA 92714
(714) 857-6714

Michael S. Lehmberg
The Blurock Partnership
2300 Newport Blvd.
Newport Beach, CA 92663
(714)831-1347

Marina Lenney
5 Westminster Ave.
Venice, CA 90291
(213)396-4893

Stephen Liddington
University of Washington
211 Summit Ave. East #305
Seattle, WA 98102
(206) 325-4086

Karl Lisovski
Santa Monica College
1068 Elkgrove Ave #4
Venice, CA 90291
(310) 452-2825

Dave Little
234 S. Figueroa #831
Los Angeles, CA 90012
(213) 617-2984

Angela Liu
TreePeople
27 Ozone Ave #A
Venice, CA 90291
(818) 846-2878

Steven Lober
3636 Calle Quebracho
Thousand Oaks, CA 91360
(805) 492-6769

Kristina Loguist
City of LA Board of Public Works
1641 Granville Ave. #6
Los Angeles, CA 90025

Tim Lopez
Claremont McKenna College
Story House
Claremont, CA 91711
(714) 621-8712

Joel Lorimer
1014-1/2 Laguna Ave.
Los Angeles, CA 90026
(213) 250-2136

Jon Loring
Kinville Loring Architects
516 Pennsfield Place, Suite 103
Thousand Oaks, CA 91360
(805) 371-4424

Rosanna Louie
803 E. Broadway Suite A
Glendale, CA 91205
(818)500-0207

Judy Lubick
Sound Life Patterns
6250 Belmar Ave.
Reseda, CA 91336
(818) 343-0949

Ed Lubieniecki
Halcyon Ltd.
11444 West Olympic Blvd., 10th
floor
Los Angeles, CA 90064
(213) 312-9514

Clifford Lucas
575 West 19th Street #B211
Costa Mesa, CA 92627
(714) 722-8402

Art Ludwig
Oasis Biocompatible Products
1020 Veronica Springs Rd.
Santa Barbara, CA 93105-4532
(805) 682-3449

Jan Lundberg
Fossil Fuels Policy Action Inst.
P.O. Box 8558
Fredericksburg, VA 22404
(703) 371-0222

Kim Lutz
Clean Water Program
401 "B" Street #750
San Diego, CA 92101-4230
(619) 298-9138

John Lyle
Cal Poly Pomona
Dept of Landscape Architecture
Pomona, CA 91768
(818) 355-6786

Steve Lyon
UC Irvine Program in Social
Ecology
2822 Verano Place
Irvine, CA 92715
(714) 856-0636

Jeff Lyon, A.I.A
Jeff Lyon & Associates
2849 Reche Rd.
Fallbrook, CA 92028
(619)723-7575

Daniel G. Maloney
Ventura Group Architects, Inc.
2207 Ventura Blvd.
Camarillo, CA 93010
(805) 525-4315

Gil Mangaoang
Loyola Marymount University
1323 Micheltorena St #20
Los Angeles, CA 90026
(213) 660-6109

Bill Mangasang
(213)660-6109

Lourdes Martinez
So. Coast Air Quality Mgmt. Dist.

Cathy Martini
Environmental Consultant
15950 Skytop Rd.
Encino, CA 91436
(818) 788-4227

Mary Marvin Porter
Santa Barbara Greens
PO Box 91626
Santa Barbara, CA 93190
(213) 456-1664

Donald Mauritz
Southern California Edison Co.
2244 Walnut Grove Ave.
Rosemead, CA 91770
(818) 957-3674

Richard W. Mayer
Troller % Mayer Associates
1403 Kenneth Rd. Suite B
Glendale, CA 91201
(818) 509-1947

George Mazurik
811 Garnet
Redondo Bch., CA 90277
(310) 316-3397

Marlowe McAnear
3326 Sawtelle Blvd. #31
Los Angeles, CA 90066
(213) 397-0391

James McCormick, President
West Side Urban Forum
P.O. Box 157
Pacific Palisades, CA 90272
(310) 459-8516

Kevin McCourt
City of West Hollywood
8611 Santa Monica Blvd.
West Hollywood, CA 90069
(213) 854-7400

Jill Ann McDonald
2400 E. Lincoln Ave. #229
Anaheim, CA 92806
(714) 758-9905

Joseph H. McDougall
Michael Brandman Associates
606 S. Olive, Suite 600
Los Angeles, CA 90014
(213) 622-4443

Patrick McGaugh
KUCR-FM
(714)684-9614

Patria McGuire
(213) 882-4176

Ian McIlvaine
1636 S Barrington Ave #101
W Los Angeles, CA 90025
(310) 820-5694

James W. McIntyre
City of Bell Gardens
7100 Garfield Ave.
Bell Gardens, CA 90201
(310) 806-4500

Pat McMahon
13901 Wyandotte St. #98
Van Nuys, CA 91405
(818) 787-3169

Jean O. Melious
Nossaman, Gunthur, Knox & Elliot
650 Town Center Dr. Suite 1250
Costa Mesa, CA 92626-1981
(714) 885-9000

Carolyn Meredith
City of Glendora Planning Dept.
116 East Foothill Blvd.
Glendora, CA 91740
(818) 914-8217

Karen Merickel
Cypress College
775 Havana Ave
Long Beach, CA 90804
(310) 597-8075

Jim Merlino
Lincoln Place Apartments
2607 - 6th Street
Santa Monica, CA 90405
(213) 392-7551

Jerry Miller
EOS Institute
2633 Laguna Cyn. Rd.
Laguna Bch., CA 92651
*714) 497j-4401

Marcy Miller
1930 Preuss Rd
Los Angeles, CA 90034
(213) 841-0672

John Wesley Miller
Tucson Solar Village
4500 Santana
Tucson, AZ 85715
(602) 749-3366

Margaret Mills
2216 Fourth Street #1
Santa Monica, CA 90405
(213) 399-0326

Villa Mills
Affordable Housing Consultant
12272 Spruce Grove Place
San Diego, CA 92131
(619) 695-8638

Paul Mills, M.D.
Scripps Clinic
12272 Spruce Grove Place
San Diego, CA 92131
(619) 487-1800

Maria L. Miralles
Miralles Associates, Inc.
729 West Woodbury Rd.
Altadena, CA 91001
(818) 791-7691

David Mogavero
Mogavero, Notestine Associates
2229 J Street
Sacramento, CA 95816
(916) 443-1033

Alex Moisa
Manatt, Phelps & Phillips
11355 W Olympic Blvd
Los Angeles, CA 90064
(213) 312-4000

Ann Moore
L.A. Architect
380-4595

Max & Mellisa Moritz
2175 Maine Ave
Long Beach, CA 90806
(213) 591-0494

Jan Wilson Morris
Sun West Consultants, Inc.
PO Box 2383
Redondo Beach, CA 90278
(310) 370-6214

Ross Moster
Venice Ocean Park Food Co-op
40 Rose Ave #6
Venice, CA 90291
(213) 399-8758

Amer Moustafa
USC/ S CA Association of
Government
PO Box 3402
Santa Monica, CA 90403
(310) 829-4765

L. Kendall Mower Jr.
Daniel, Mann, Johnson &
Mendenhall
3250 Wilshire
Los Angeles, CA 90010
(213)545-8624

Brad Mowers
1935 1/2 Barry Ave.
Los Angeles, CA 90025
(213)444-0022

Violet Moyer
City of Los Angeles
Planning Department
6200 Oak Crest Way
Los Angeles, CA 90042
(213) 666-1709

Susan Munves
City of Santa Monica
1685 Main Street
Santa Monica, CA 90401
(213) 458-8221

Gordon Murley
Fed. of Hillside & Canyon Assoc.
4128 Morro Dr.
Woodland Hills, CA 91364
(818) 346-5842

Anne Murphy
So. Calif. Assoc. of Non-
Profit Housing
4032 Wilshire Blvd., Suite 301
Los Angeles, CA 90010
(213) 480-1249

Roger Neal
CRSP
9468 Cedar Street
Bellflower, CA 90706-6513
(213) 439-0870

Eric Nee
New York Times
54 Winfield Rd.
San Francisco, CA 94110
(415) 282-7493

John Neel
John Neel Architect
18002 Skypark Cir
Irvine, CA 92714
(714) 526-2095

Pete Nelson
City of Chino
PO Box 667
Chino, CA 91708-0667
(714) 591-9816

William Newland
Green Field Equipment Co.
PO Box 1448
Greenfield, CA 93927
(800) 244-1940

Robert Nicolais
Architect
5225 Wilshire Blvd Suite 618
Los Angeles, CA 90036
(213) 294-0892

Wanda & Rich Noble
2132 Royal Oaks Dr.
Duarte, CA 91010
(818)358-6345

Anne & Michael Nolan

Michael O'Brien
City of L.A. Planning Department
2551 Siver Ridge Ave.
Los Angeles, CA 90039
(213) 485-3402

Sean O'Malley
21711 Wesley Dr - B
Laguna Beach, CA 92651

Wil Orr
City of Tucson
PO Box 27210
Tucson, AZ 85726-7210
(602) 791-5414

Peter Orzechowski
224 9th Place
Manhattan Beach, CA 90266
(310) 318-0522

Karen Palley
Karen Palley & Assciates
Santa Monica, CA

Richard Palmer
Richard A. Palmer & Associates
Fullerton, CA

Pam Parkin
Torrance Planning Department
3031 Torrance Blvd
Torrance, CA 90503

Kathryn D. Parks
L.A. Reader
2069 Stanley Hills Dr
Los Angeles, CA 90046
(213) 654-8971

Mary Jane Parks
Pasadena Water & Power
150 South Los Robles Ave. Sutie
200
Pasadena, CA 91101
(818) 568-0798

Tom Penhale
6343 Morse Ave. #204
No. Hollywood, CA 91606
(818) 508-9752

Craig Perkins
City of Santa Monica
1685 Main Street
Santa Monica, CA 90401
(213) 393-4425

Erik Peterson
CRSP
2364 W 230th St
Torrance, CA 90501
213) 326-4293

Suzanne Pfister
Dames & Moore

John Picard
12915 Greene Ave.
Los Angeles, CA 90066
(310) 827-1217

Byron Pinckert
Hill Pinckert Architects, Inc.
16969 Von Karman
Irvine, CA 92714
(714) 863-1770

John Polk

Mark Poll
West L.A. Cluster Group
1032 East Santa Anita
Burbank, CA 91501
(818) 845-5149

Sharin Pollak
9188 W. Pico Blvd. #120
Los Angeles, CA 90035
(213) 204-5607

Stefanos Polyzoides
Moule & Polyzoides Architects
706 South Hill Street 11th Floor
Los Angeles, CA 90014
(213) 624-3381

James Poole, A.I.A.
Walt Disney Imagineering
PO Box 1654
Topanga, CA 90290
(213) 455-2688

Flavia Potenza
Business Ethics Magazine
KPFK/NPR
455-1182

Bob Pressman
The L.A. Group Inc.
23621 Park Sorrento, #101
Calabasas, CA 91302
(818) 593-5333

Helen & Jesse Proctor
5330 W 127th St
Hawthorne, CA 90250
(213)643-5770

Mary Proteau
Eco-Home Network
147-1/2 South Sycamore Ave.
Los Angeles, CA 90036
(213) 934-7058

Bill Quinn
Southern California Gas Co.

John Raatz
Business Ethics Magazine
(310) 395-4416

Rose Marie Rabin
SCI-ARC
1800 Berkeley Street
Santa Monica, CA
(213) 393-3848

Rarefinds International, LTD
14631 Beach Ave
Irvine, CA 92714
(714) 552-7273

Glen Ray, Jr.
Terra Power & Vegetable
Rt. 3200-C West Ocean
Lompoc, CA 93436
(805)736-5470

Jack Reed
3500 W. Adams
Los Angeles, CA 90018
(213) 735-4344

Suzanne Reed
Fairbank Bregman & Maullin Inc.
2401 Colorado Ave. #180
Santa Monica, CA 90404
(213) 828-1183

Robert Reed
Robert's Development Co.
890 La Mirada Street
Laguna Beach, CA 92651
(714) 494-3164

Richard Register
Ecocity Builders & Urban Ecology
2633 Benvenue #7
Berkeley, CA
(510) 644-9704

Thea-Mai Reinap
TR Resources & Environmental
Design
4848 C San Gordiano
Santa Barbara, CA 93111
(805) 965-3355

Adam H. Relin
Nossaman, Gunthur, Knox & Elliot
650 Town Center Dr., Suite 1250
Costa Mesa, CA 92626-1981
(714) 885-9000

Mary Renaker
Cottonwood Creek Conservancy
PO Box 232422
Leucadia, CA 92007
(619) 942-1194

Mary Renz
3246 Cahuenga Blvd.
Los Angeles, CA 90068
(213)876-4363

Lynda Rescia
832 N. Lafayette Park Place
Los Angeles, CA 90026
(213)483-0110

Jeffrey Rhoads, A.I.A.
The Newhall Land & Farming Co.
23823 Valencia Blvd.
Valencia, CA 91355
(805) 255-4053

Lori Richardson
2917 Tioga Way
Sacramento, CA 95821
(916) 971-1183

Robert Ringstrom
City of Long Beach
333 West Ocean Blvd.
Long Beach, CA 90802
(213) 590-6193

Bill Roalman
City of San Luis Obispo
PO Box 8100
San Luis Obispo, CA 93403-8100
(805) 549-7113

Joseph Robinson
Architect, Artist, Film Maker
717 - 11th Street
Santa Monica, CA 90402
(310) 475-3304

Richard W. Roether
Planning Consultant
PO Box 5905
Pasadena, CA 91117-0905
(818) 577-8073

Cheryl Rogers
Los Angeles City Planning
1050 Seco Street
Pasadena, CA 91103
(213) 485-3443

Sandra Roggero
10919 Wellworth Ave., #110
Los Angeles, CA 90024
(310) 479-7025

Bill Roley
Permaculture Institute of So. Calif.
1027 Summit Way
Laguna Beach, CA 92651
(714) 494-5843

Andrea Rolston
22763 Cavalier St.
Woodland Hills, CA 91364
(818) 716-9241

Allen M. Rosenthal
306 Bora Bora Way #308
Marina Del Rey, CA 90292
(213) 821-9453

Marlena Ross
10784 Northgate ST
Cuvlver City, CA 90230
(310) 838-0797

Stuart Rowley
Stuart Rowley Design
11465 Venice Blvd #5
Los Angeles, CA 90066
(213) 397-4570

David Rubenson
RAND
1700 Main St
Santa Monica, CA 90406
(310) 398-1730

Jerry Rubin
Alliance for Survival
(310) 399-1000

Jann Rucquoi
7100 Trask Ave.
Playa del Rey, CA 90293
(310) 823-6640

Beverly Rudolph
PO Box 2516
Sebastopol, CA 95473
(707) 829-8831

Jerry Russell
15230 Calle Juanita
San Diego, CA 92127
(619) 485-8551

Julia Russell
Eco-Home Network
4344 Russell Ave.
Los Angeles, CA 90027
(213) 662-5207

Dick Russell
Fort Hill Construction
8118 Hollywood Blvd.
Los Angeles, CA 90069
(213) 656-7425

David Rutherford
So. Coast Air Quality
Management Dist.

John Stitt Sanyika
Drew University of Medicine &
Science
1621 E 120th St
Los Angeles, CA 90059
(213) 563-5823

Joseph Schilling
City of San Diego
1010 2nd Ave. Suite 300
San Diego, CA 92101
(619) 533-3155

Martin Schmitt
21051 Saddle Peak Rd
Topanga, CA 90290
(310) 455-2081

Richard Schoen
RSA Architects
UCLA - GSAUP
6964 Shoup Ave.
Canoga Park, CA 91307
(818) 883-7808

Joanne & Rocky Schumann
5345 Hersholt Ave.
Lakewood, CA 90712
(213) 920-2920

Allan Schurr
Pacific Gas & Electric Co.
123 Mission Street, H2662
San Francisco, CA 94106
(415)973-5903

Sandy Sdeckling
Catholic Community Service
344 North 102nd Street
Seattle, WA 98102
(206) 781-1327

Merry Seabold
Southern California Edison Co.
6090 North Irwindale Ave.
Irwindale, CA 91702
(818) 812-7563

William Seavey
Relocation Research Newsletter
PO Box 1122
Sierra Madre, CA 91025
(818) 568-8484

Marianne Seifert
The Program in Social Ecology
UC Irvine
Irvine, CA

Helen Selph
13725 Erwood Ave
Norwalk, CA 90650
(213) 868-8841

David Sensiper
PO Box 63
Harbor City, CA 90710
(213) 823-3816

Sharon Seto
1113 Marco Pl.
Venice, CA 90291
(310) 399-3154

Michael Shames
6975 Camino Amero
San Diego, CA 92111-7633
(619) 268-8328

Danny Shapiro
KPBS Radio "Metropolitan Journal"
(619)265-6431

Joel Shapiro
439 Sherman Canal
Venice, CA 90291
(310) 301-8174

Neal Shapiro
The Cousteau Society
8440 Santa Monica Blvd.
Los Angeles, CA 90069
(213) 656-4422

Helen Shaw
Southern California Gas Co.

Bahman Sheikh
Office of Water Reclamation
City of Los Angeles
City Hall Room 366
Los Angeles, CA 90012
(213) 237-0887

Susan Sherod
202 S. Kingsley
Los Angeles, CA 90004
(213) 388-4334

William Shireman
California Futures
8498 Sunblaze Way
Sacramento, CA 95823
(916) 929-9207

James Siebert
James Siebert & Associates
1510 St. Francis Dr.
Santa Fe, NM 87501
(505) 988-4634

Wally Siembab
Strategic Telecommunications
Planning Consultant
5944 Chariton Ave.
Los Angeles, CA 90056
(310) 649-6326

Jacob Singer
Esalen Institute
Big Sur, CA 93920
(408) 667-3000

Diane Sionko
11919 Idaho Ave #4
W Los Angeles, CA 90025

Jon Sirugo
Southern California Edison Co.
6020 North Irwindale Ave.
Irwindale, CSA 91702
(818) 303-3284

Thomas Slagle
2742 Coolidge Ave
Los Angeles, CA 90064
(213) 479-5326

William Slater
Life Chiropractic Center
500 South Sepulveda Blvd #106
Manhattan Beach, CA 90266
(310) 374-4013

April Smith
1600 Oak St.
Santa Monica, CA 90405
(310) 450-4507

Sue Smith
Department of Water & Power
111 North Hope Street
Los Angeles, CA 90012
(213) 481-7700

Larry E. Smith
Daniel Mann Johnson Mendenhall
3250 Wilshire Blvd.
Los Angeles, CA 90010-1599
(213) 381-3663

Joseph Smyth
Joseph Smyth Company
509 Marin St #134
Thousand Oaks, CA 91360
(805) 373-3712

Jody Smyth

Lyn Snow
Ecological Life Systems Institute
2923 East Spruce
San Diego, CA 92104
(619) 281-1447

Tim Spears
3120 East Lester
Tucson, AZ 85716
(602) 323-6289

David Spellman
616 North Kenwood Street #19
Glendale, CA 91206-2382
(818) 247-0866

Sally Spencer & Layne Dicker
830 Haverford Ave. #1
Pacific Palisades, CA 90272
(213) 396-6340

Charles R. Stapleton
Cal Poly Pomona
469 Bougainvillea Lane
Glendora, CA 91740
(714) 869-2688

Penny Starr
647-1/2 Crestmoore Place
Venice, CA 90291

Achva Stein, Landscape
Architect, Faculty, USC
School of Architecture
1116 Diamond Ave
S Pasadena, CA 91030

Kari Steinberg
The Pick Up Artists
(213)559-9334

Douglas Stenhouse
Energy Management Consultants
20329 Roslin Ave.
Torrance, CA 90503-2515
(213) 370-0076

Joel Stensby
Maguire Thomas Partners

Jon Stevens
Public Electronic Network
1825 -C Euclid St
Santa Monica, CA 90404
(310) 450-1680

Melanie Stevens
LA Community Design Center
315 West 9th Street Suite 410
Los Angeles, CA 90015
(213) 629-2702

Carol B. Stevens
Santa Monica Mountains
Conservancy
3700 Solstice Canyon Rd.
Malibu, CA 90265
(213) 456-5046

John Stodder
PS Enterprises
309 Santa Monica Blvd. #322
Santa Monica, CA 90401
(310) 393-3703

Sigfried Stokes
735 Iliff St.
Pacific Palisades, CA 90272
(310) 454-0434

Donald Strauss
1124 12th Street
Santa Monica, CA 90403
(310)208-3274

Trish Strouse
912 9th St #9
Santa Monica, CA 90403
(310) 393-9144

Kent Strumpell
6483 Nancy St.
Los Angeles, CA 90045
(213) 215-0114

Gregory Sullivan
21731 Saticoy St #42
Canoga Park, CA 91304
(818) 883-3878

Coral Suter
11465 Venice Blvd. #7
Los Angeles, CA 90066
(213) 391-2723

Dirk Sutro
Architecture Magazine
960 Nolby St
Cardiff, CA 92007

Eric Swanson
Community Environmental Council
930 Miramark Dr
Santa Barbara, CA 93109
(805) 963-0583

Maroon Taboll
(310) 821-7377

Joyce Tapper
CKT Associates
6514 Langdon Ave.
Van Nuys, CA 91406
(818) 785-3965

Eric Taylor
VTN West, Inc.
8540 Balboa Blvd #200
Northridge, CA 91335
805-641-0801

Patrisha Thomson
Patrisha Thomson Designs
1118 9th St. #3
Santa Monica, CA 90403
(213)393-6004

Elizabeth Thurston
806 1/2 N Alvarado
Los Angeles, CA 90026
(213) 483-6692

Jay Trevino
City of Brea - Senior Planner
#1 Civic Center Circle
Brea, CA 92621
(714) 990-7574

William Trexel
6460 El Roble Street
Long Beach, CA 90815
(213) 431-7644

Jeff Trexel
433 2nd Street
Encinitas, CA 92024
(619) 632-1701

Marian Trotter
8187 Via Mallorca
La Jolla, CA 92037
(619) 458-0012

Taylor Trowbridge
13202 Zanja St
Los Angeles, CA 90066
(213) 301-6648

Judy Trumbo
LA County Regional Planning Dept
320 West Temple Street Room
1187
Los Angeles, CA 90012
(213) 974-9481

Shirley Tseng

Genny Tubridy
4144 Woodman
Sherman Oaks, CA
(818) 986-5736

Ike Ubaka
SCRTD

Sim Van der Ryn
Sim Van der Ryn & Associates
55 Gate 5 Rd.
Sausilito, CA 94965
(415) 332-5806

Paul Van Dyke
P.S. Enterprises
309 Santa Monica Blvd., Suite 322
Santa Monica, CA 90401
(213) 393-3703

Carolyn Van Horn
Councilmember Malibu
28843 Selfridge
Malibu, CA 90265
(310) 457-7397

Nancy Van Praag
1235 Sunset Plaza DR
Los Angeles, CA 90069
(213) 659-8831

Maria Vanderkolk
County of Ventura Supervisor
199 W. Hillcrest Dr. Suite 201
Thousand Oaks, CA 91360
(805) 656-1500 x8312

Dr. Karen Varcoe
Urban & Environmental Outreach
UC Riverside
Riverside, CA 92521
(714) 787-5421

Lupe Vela
City of LA Board of Public Works
5081 College View Ave.
Eagle Rock, CA 90041
(213) 231-1445

Michael & Sacha Vignieri
M Vignieri Associates
337 S Clark Dr
Beverly Hills, CA 90211
(213) 289-9490

Mary-Jane Wagle
10794 Weyburn Ave.
Los Angeles, CA 90024
(213) 474-5106

Deborah Ruth Wallen
3363 Gregory
San Diego, CA 92104
(619) 280-1839

Bob Walter
Eco-Home Network
4344 Russell Ave.
Los Angeles, CA 90027
(213) 664-7706

William Warren
William Warren & Associates
509 S. Grammercy Pl. #1
Los Angeles, CA 90020
(213) 383-0500

Kashi Way
City of Los Angeles
Board of Public Works

Tara Teilmann & Greg Way
Architect
163 North A Street
Tustin, CA 92680
(714) 544-5237
(714)573-0580

Susan Webster
Space Changers
1309 Poppy Street
Long Beach, CA 90805
(213) 396-6735

Steven Weissman
Local Government Commission
180 Brookside Dr
Berkeley, CA 94705
(510) 654-3316

Eric Werbalowsky
City of Ventura
Recycling Office
5275 Colt Street
Ventura, CA 93003
(805) 650-0884

Wendy Wert
AeroVironment, Inc.
PO Box 5031
Monrovia, CA 91017
(818) 357-9983

Howard & Dorothy Westley
525 Gretna Green Way
Los Angeles, CA 90049
(213) 472-9965

Dorothy White
City of Malibu
Environmental Task Force
6797 S Shearwater Ln
Malibu, CA 90265
(310) 457-3904

Susan Willcox
2751 Barry Ave.
Los Angeles, CA 90064
(213) 479-6839

Jane Willeboordse, AIA
NAHB Research Center
400 Prince Georges Blvd.
Upper Marlboro, MD 20772
(301) 249-4000

Steve Wilson
County of San Bernadino
825 East 3rd Street
San Bernadino, CA 92415-0802
(714) 387-2858

Mark Winogrond
Culver City Planning Director
4095 Overland Avenue
Culver City, CA 90232
(310) 837-5211

Stephen Winterhalter
DMC Energy
385 Laurie Meadows Dr. #223
San Mateo, C A 94403
(415)548-7247

Tony Witt
City Planner, City of Claremont
443 West Tenth Street
Claremont, CA 91711
(714) 399-5470

Barbara Wolfe

Joshua Wolfe
Save Montreal
3597 Jeanne-Mance #4
Montreal, Quebec H2X 2K2
(619) 365-3327

Krista Wong
Coalition Action Network
200 North Cordova Street
Alhambra, CA 91801
(818) 282-3254

Joel & Joan Woodhull
Southern California RTD
163 S. Wilton Dr.
Los Angeles, CA 90004
(213) 972-4850

Howard Wright

Dwayne Wyatt
Los Angeles City Planning
2233 South Hobart Street
Los Angeles, CA 90018
(213) 485-3443

Robert Yates
SCRTD

Calvin Yee
1208 South Marago Ave. #E
Alhambra, CA 91805
(818) 576-5049

Ines Yettra
Mid City Neighbors
612 Colorado Ave #106
Santa Monica, CA 90401
(310) 828-2784

John S. Zinner
Independent Consultant
916 15th Street #10
Santa Monica, CA 90403
(213) 395-5720

Jirayr, Dabney & Alan Zorthian
Zorthian & Company
3990 North Fair Oaks Ave.
Altadena, CA 91001
(818) 797-3359

INDEX

X

Y

Z

ORDER FORM

If your local retailer or mail-order company is out of *Sustainable Cities*,
you can order copies by phone or by mail from:

Eco-Home Media
4344 Russell Avenue
Los Angeles, CA 90027
(213) 662-5207

Total books_____ x $20.00 cost per book = $_____

California residents please add:
8.25% ($1.65) sales tax for each book ordered = $_____

Shipping: $3.50 for 1st copy, $2.00 for each additional copy = $_____

Total = $_____

_____
Print Name

_____
Address

_____
City   State   Zip Code
(_____) _____
Telephone

Please make check or money order payable to: **Eco-Home.**

Please include the correct shipping and sales tax
for us to be able to process your order.

If your organization would like to sell this book,
please contact Eco-Home Media for details.